THE
DULUTH, SOUTH SHORE & ATLANTIC
RAILWAY

RAILROADS PAST & PRESENT

George M. Smerk, editor

A list of books in the series appears at the end of this volume.

THE DULUTH, SOUTH SHORE & ATLANTIC RAILWAY

D.S.S.&A.

A HISTORY OF THE LAKE SUPERIOR DISTRICT'S PIONEER IRON ORE HAULER

JOHN GAERTNER

Indiana University Press ◉ Bloomington & Indianapolis

This book is a publication of

Indiana University Press
601 North Morton Street
Bloomington, IN 47404-3797 USA

http://iupress.indiana.edu

Telephone orders   800-842-6796
Fax orders   812-855-7931
Orders by e-mail   iuporder@indiana.edu

The paper used in this publication meets the minimum requirements of American National Standard for Information Sciences—Permanence of Paper for Printed Library Materials, ANSI Z39.48-1984.

Manufactured in the United States of America

Library of Congress Cataloging-in-Publication Data

Gaertner, John T., date
    The Duluth, South Shore & Atlantic Railway : a history of the Lake Superior District's Pioneer Iron Ore Hauler / John Gaertner.
        p. cm.
    Includes bibliographical references and index.
    ISBN 978-0-253-35192-0 (cloth : alk. paper)   1. Duluth, South Shore, and Atlantic Railroad Company—History—20th century.   2. Railroads—Minnesota—Duluth—History—20th century.   3. Railroads—Minnesota—Duluth—History—19th century.   I. Title.
    TF25.D857G37 2009
    385.0973—dc22
                                                                                                2008019743

1 2 3 4 5 14 13 12 11 10 09

This book is dedicated to the memory of Roy Paananen, who worked tirelessly to foster interest in the South Shore and who contributed greatly to this work.

CONTENTS

ACKNOWLEDGMENTS

The following former DSS&A employees provided countless hours of invaluable assistance in bringing the South Shore story to life: Leo Anderson, John Becker, Glenn Engman, Ed Hermanson, Tom Oliver, and especially the late Don Hart.

Thanks also to the Soo Line Historical Society Archives Committee for giving me the opportunity to go through the DSS&A AFEs in their collection. Railroad historian Stuart Nelson was good enough to let me go through his almost complete collection of DSS&A annual reports. Andrew Roth provided correspondence and newspaper items, while Jim Welton shared insights from his research on the Western Division. Thanks to Leroy Barnett for helping with matters at the Michigan State Library at Lansing. The late Roy Paananen in his final years generously mailed me practically his entire collection, which brought to light countless items I would never have uncovered on my own.

The locomotive rosters in the appendix were aided by the earlier efforts of John Campbell, Aurele Durocher, Wesley Perron, and Leon Shaddelee. Jim Mattson helped with the creation of the maps, which drew upon previous renderings by the Copper Range Railroad, DSS&A Railway, Great Northern Railway, *Narrow Gauge & Short Line Gazette,* Northern Pacific Railway, Sanborn Insurance Company, Soo Line Historical Society, and USGS. Thanks also to Kerstin Hodne for her help in preparing the photographs. Appreciation is also due to Jeffrey Koehler for carefully reading the manuscript and offering suggestions

DSS&A System Map, June 13, 1926

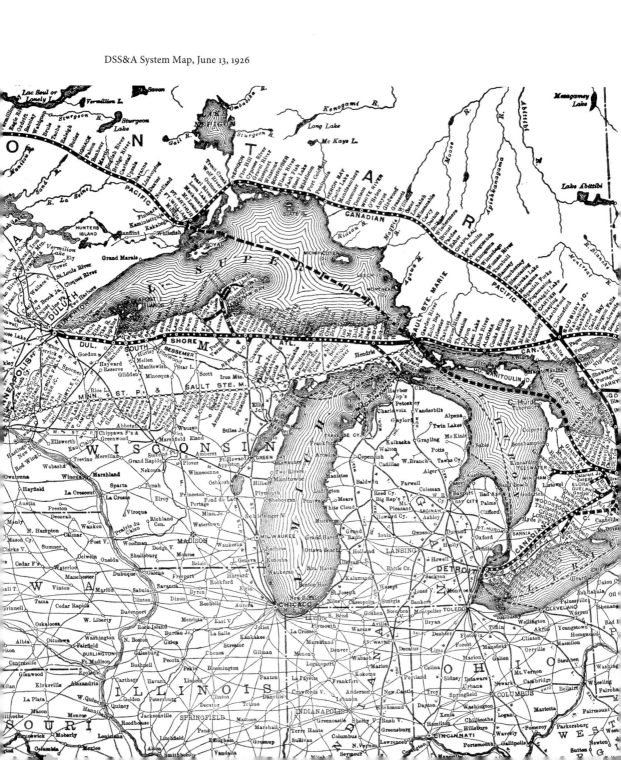

INTRODUCTION

The 1880s represented the zenith of railroad construction in the United States, with some 70,330 miles of new lines being built during the decade, or an increase of 43 percent nationwide. Some of this trackage was built to serve an existing need, while other roads were built on speculation, through unproven territory, in hopes that prosperity in the form of agricultural, manufacturing, and commercial activity would take hold upon completion of the new line. Even communities already served by rail actively sought new construction as a means of expanding their spheres of influence. New rail connections were also looked to as a means of giving competitive leverage, in this pre-regulatory age, in regards to service and rates. In the Northwest, another major factor in railroad projections was the desire to connect with the new transcontinental, the Northern Pacific (NP). Practically every Midwest carrier was building toward or had designs of reaching Duluth, Minnesota, the NP's eastern terminus. In addition to receiving a share of traffic off the new transcontinental, Duluth was felt to be a burgeoning metropolis in its own right.

The formation of the Duluth, South Shore and Atlantic Railway (DSS&A) in 1887 was a product of all these factors. Two of its predecessors, the Marquette, Houghton & Ontonagon (MH&O) and the Mineral Range (MR), were started on the Upper Peninsula (UP) of Michigan to provide iron ore and copper rock deposits access to Lake Superior. From the ports of Marquette, in the case of iron, and Hancock, in the case of copper, these resources were transported by boat via the Great Lakes to eastern markets. Another DSS&A predecessor, the Detroit, Mackinac and Marquette (DM&M), which built from the Straits of Mackinac to Marquette, was much more speculative in nature, seeking to tie the two peninsulas of Michigan together with year-round rail service, to develop the barren tracts of the eastern UP, and to give Detroit jobbers an opportunity to reassert their dominance in a region that was being increasingly lost to Chicago and Milwaukee interests. This loss had come about as the result of the penetration into the UP by the Chicago and Northwestern (C&NW, or North Western) from the south.

Although the MH&O and MR were quite successful financially, as their services were required from the onset to transport readily available resources, the same could not be said for the DM&M. Its promoters sought to rectify the situation by launching the Duluth, South Shore & Atlantic. This road, also speculative in nature, sought to develop the resources of the western UP and act as a short cut between the Northern Pacific to the west and the Lower Peninsula of Michigan and New England to the east. Its potential strategic importance led to the road being acquired by the Canadian Pacific Railway (CPR) shortly after completion. Unfortunately this move was more to protect the CPR's flanks than to exercise the South Shore's potential. Although the CPR made up the almost yearly deficits, it gave the road an excessive capitalization and furnished the road with little in the way of traffic. The CPR further hurt the DSS&A by merging many of its functions with the CPR's other U.S. property, the Soo Line—the DSS&A's principal competitor. This resulting loss of independence badly hurt the South Shore's ability to solicit bridge traffic between its connections at Superior and eastern destinations, and forced it to rely almost exclusively on local business in a territory whose natural resources were being diminished after years of exploitation.

The Great Depression saw the South Shore's financial house of cards collapse, but the resulting reorganization relieved the DSS&A of its excessive debt as well as giving it independence from the Soo Line and a new ability to solicit traffic. This resulted in the road's first profitability in almost half a century. Unfortunately, as costs mounted in the late fifties, the CPR pressed for economies in its American properties, economies which were felt to be best accommodated through assimilation. This resulted in a merger of the Soo Line and DSS&A in 1961, a siphoning off of the South Shore's traffic and a gradual dismembering of its route structure.

From a purely economic standpoint, it is questionable whether the speculative DM&M and DSS&A extensions should have been built, as for many years traffic continued to be overwhelmingly confined to earlier MH&O and MR construction. The new extensions, however, did open up vast areas of "howling wilderness" and provided employment for many on the UP. When independence finally arrived for the DSS&A in shedding the yoke of the Soo Line, the line's strategic importance as an alternative to using the crowded Chicago gateway was ably and profitably demonstrated in the last decade before merger.

THE
DULUTH, SOUTH SHORE & ATLANTIC
RAILWAY

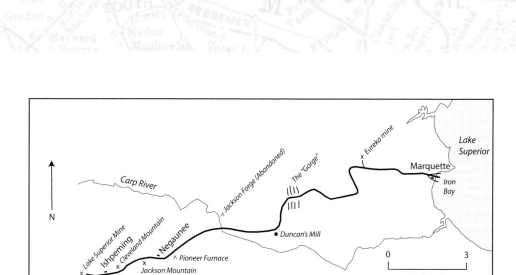

Iron Mountain Railroad, October 1857

1

STRAP AND T RAILS TO THE IRON MOUNTAINS

The state of Michigan, newly formed in 1837, gained its Upper Peninsula in the settlement of a boundary dispute with Ohio that had nearly resulted in the "Toledo War." The compromise generated sentiments similar to those inspired by "Seward's Folly" in later years. Many shared the views of the explorer Lahontan, who described the UP as the "fag end of creation." These sentiments could not have been more mistaken as the UP would develop into one of the richest mining regions in the country. The area's copper deposits, long used by native people, had been discovered by the Europeans as early as 1672 during the explorations of the Jesuit missionary Jacques Marquette. The massive iron deposits went unnoticed until receiving scant mention in an 1841 report by Michigan state geologist Dr. Douglas Houghton, who even then questioned their potential value.[1]

Such misconceptions were put to rest on September 19, 1844, when William A. Burt, United States Deputy Surveyor, and his crew were running lines near what became the city of Negaunee and noticed their compass behaving erratically due to magnetism. A little exploration led to the discovery of an outcrop that became the Jackson mine. The following year, Philo Everett, on his way to the UP to explore for copper, learned of the discoveries at Sault Ste. Marie, and was able to locate them through the help of Chippewa chief Marji Gesick. Everett returned to his home in Jackson, Michigan, and organized the Jackson Mining Company, which laid claims to the area.

Upon returning to the UP in 1846, Everett and his party started to work the 150-foot-high mound of rich iron ore known as Jackson Mountain. This was the pioneer activity in the great Lake Superior Iron District, which would go on to furnish the majority of the nation's iron ore needs for more than a century. A forge, to melt the iron into blooms, was built on the Carp River about 3 miles east of Jackson Mountain, and went into operation on February 10, 1848. Unfortunately for the Jackson company, the lack of adequate transportation remained a stumbling block.

Iron ore from the mine was hauled to the forge by teams and wagons, or sleighs in the winter. The same method of transport brought the forge's usual 3-ton daily production of blooms down the steep and winding road through mosquito-infested swamps to Iron Bay on Lake Superior, near present-day Marquette. After a boat took the blooms to Sault Ste. Marie, they were portaged around the St. Mary's rapids and placed on another boat for movement to eastern furnaces. The inefficient transportation resulted in the

Jackson blooms going for $200 a ton at Pittsburgh, while local iron ore was only $80 a ton.

Another concern, the Cleveland Iron Mining Company, got its start in 1850 mining a nearby mound known as Cleveland Mountain, later Ishpeming. Although briefly operating a forge near what became downtown Marquette, the Cleveland company decided to await transportation improvements before making active shipments. William Burt noted in 1846 that no matter how rich were the resources of Upper Michigan, they were valueless unless the federal government provided incentives for building roads or railroads in the area. Burt thought the best route would be from some point on Lake Michigan, passing through the iron region and then up to the Copper Country of the Keweenaw Peninsula. Loading ore or ingots on Lake Michigan would do away with the bottleneck at the Sault, as there were no rapids through the Straits of Mackinac between Lake Huron and Lake Michigan.

The first real action to improve the transportation picture saw the incorporation of the Iron Bay and Carp River Plank Road Company on March 20, 1850, by men largely associated with the Jackson mine. The charter proposed "to lay out, establish, and construct a plank road and all necessary buildings from Iron Bay, on the South Side of Lake Superior, in the county of Marquette, to or near the village of Carp River [site of the Jackson forge] in said county."[2] Before the plank road had a chance to get off the ground, Heman B. Ely came on the scene with the promise of a railroad. Ely, from a Rochester milling family, dabbled in law, telegraph, and canals before becoming actively involved in the Cleveland, Painesville and Ashtabula Rail Road. After a visit to Marquette, Ely became engrossed with the idea of connecting the mines to the lake by rail.

After successfully negotiating exclusive 15-year hauling contracts with the Jackson and Cleveland companies, Ely filed articles of association for the Green Bay and Lake Superior Rail Road Company (GB&LS) on November 25, 1851. The road, using Burt's rationale of avoiding the bottleneck at the Sault, would run from the Iron Mountains to Marquette and then on to Lake Michigan, eventually terminating in Green Bay. The route selected would necessitate hauling the heavy iron ore down into Marquette and then up over the ridge separating Lake Superior and Lake Michigan.[3]

At a meeting of the GB&LS board of directors a month later, arrangements were made to place surveyors in the field and to build between the Iron Mountains and Marquette before the next season of navigation. The most difficult segment would be the climb out of Iron Bay with its steep grades and numerous gullies. Construction, the first of any railroad in the UP, commenced upon completion of the survey work, and, by the fall of 1852, the line had been largely cleared and some grubbing and grading had taken place. The lack of capital then brought the process to a halt, with the financial community not yet sold on the isolated iron resources of Lake Superior.

The lack of progress alienated the mine owners, who were anxious to see a return on their investment. Tower Jackson, agent of the Cleveland Iron Mining Company, seemingly unaware of the tremendous tonnages underfoot, wrote his principals in Cleveland on December 5, 1852: "We want a plank road to the Cleveland Mountain. It would be better than a railroad, for if we had a plank road we could haul the year round and the farmers can haul you all the coal [charcoal] you want which you cannot transport on a railroad. A plank road would build you up a nice town and a railroad would not. One hundred teams, which would run daily on a plank road, would occupy a good many men and teams and the people would settle here and clear up farms, make coal and haul their products to market, and that would have the country prosperous; but a railroad will fill the pockets of a few Eastern men and that would be an end to your business. The only prospect of a railroad in my opinion is that it never will be built."[4]

Ely did not soothe feelings by demanding, in the spring of 1853, that the Cleveland and Jackson companies give him $50,000 in cash before he would proceed with further construction. By this time the original Jackson company owners had tired of the project and sold their interest to the Sharon Iron Company of Pennsylvania. The Cleveland and Sharon companies refused to make any advances to Ely, and that summer they contracted with David Himrod, Jackson Iron Company agent, to proceed with the plank road scheme. As they intended for the plank road to use approximately the same route to Marquette as the GB&LS, Ely obtained an injunction to stop them from building on his right of way. This was followed by countersuits of the Cleveland and Jackson mining companies against Ely. Plank road construction proceeded in other locations, with every mile of road from Iron Bay to the Jackson mine under contract by February 1854. Half of the grading was completed by the end of spring, including the most difficult stretch out of Iron Bay.

In spite of the early sentiments of Tower Jackson, the Jackson and Cleveland companies came to realize in the summer of 1854 that a plank road would be incapable of handling the potential iron ore tonnage, and the idea of a strap railroad was substituted. This poor man's railroad consisted of two parallel timbers, protected by $1'' \times 2''$ angle iron, laid about 3 feet apart, and mounted perpendicular to cross ties. The mining companies' new tack took the form of the Iron Mountain Railway Company, which was incorporated under the laws of Michigan on March 14, 1855, with a capitalization of $140,000. The company purchased the assets of the Iron Bay & Carp River Plank Road two days later.[5]

The bitter legal dispute between the mining companies' strap railroad and Ely's steam railroad remained a major stumbling block. Finally on September 13, 1855, the parties agreed to submit their dispute to Charles Harvey, the initial engineer and general agent of the Sault Ste. Marie canal project, to act as arbitrator. Harvey made quick work of the dispute and on October 2 announced an agreement had been reached which carefully spelled out where the two roads would cross and how they would be constructed in the contested areas.

At that point, the Iron Mountain Railway had completed its plank road nearly the entire length to the Jackson mine and strap rails were laid 4 miles out of Marquette. With the settlement, gaps on the disputed right of way were quickly filled, and the strap railway was pronounced ready for operation on November 1, 1855. The strap road cost $120,000 to build, with one of the costlier items being a long cut in Marquette which allowed the railroad to go under Front Street and out on a trestle into the bay. The trestle descended until it was 8 feet above the 800-foot-long Jackson dock, which in turn was 4.5 feet off the water. The Cleveland company built its dock at the foot of Superior Street, later Baraga Avenue, in 1855. This dock, reached by a spur off the strap railway, differed from the Jackson dock in that the flat cars were driven right onto the dock itself, rather than onto an overhead trestle.

Iron ore was brought down from the Jackson and Cleveland mines by mule and flat car combinations. The flat cars were 4-wheeled affairs with a capacity of 4 tons. With 15

The old Main Street cut in Marquette, originally used by the Iron Mountain Railroad to reach the Ely Dock, is pictured in 1911. The trackage was used at this time to access the Spear coal dock and other industry along the bayfront. The semaphores at the far end of the cut protect the LS&I and DSS&A diamonds at Lake Street. The South Shore passenger depot is visible to the right of the cut.
Roy Paananen Collection

sets in operation, making one round trip a day, 60 tons could be handled, about the capacity of one later railroad ore car. Accidents were not uncommon. The track would get out of gauge, resulting in derailments. The steep grade down to the dock caused the flat cars to get out of control and run over the expensive mules.

Upon reaching Marquette, the ore had to be shoveled out of the cars onto the dock, where it was again loaded into wheelbarrows and dumped into the hold of what was usually a sailing vessel. Steamboat companies, usually engaged in carrying passengers, did not want to wait at the dock for the long loading period. It would take a crew of twenty to thirty men three to six days to load a boat with 200 to 300 tons of ore, the usual cargo at that time. After having been loaded with ore, the boat would usually be listing heavily and a crew of trimmers would go down into the hold to level out the cargo. The Marquette Range mines did manage to ship out 6,790 tons of ore in 1856, which, considering the equipment at hand, was quite remarkable. Completion of the strap railway also resulted in freight rates dropping from $3.00 per ton in 1855 to $1.27 in 1856.

This iron ore movement would still not have been possible without a parallel development at Sault Ste. Marie. In 1852, the U.S. Congress authorized a land grant of 750,000 acres in Michigan to any company that would construct a canal through the St. Mary's rapids, joining Lake Superior with Lake Huron. The grant required that two 70′×350′ locks be constructed to overcome the 18-foot difference in elevation. Charles T. Harvey, agent for the Fairbanks Morse Scale Company at the Sault, persuaded his company and other eastern capitalists to bid on the job. After they secured the contract, the St. Mary's Ship Canal Company was formed and construction started on June 4, 1853. Harvey, only 23 years of age, was given supervision of 1,600 men working year-round to build the canal. Harvey's youth and inexperience began to show as the project dragged on for several years, and, in 1855, a more professional engineer was hired to see the project to completion. The steamer *Illinois* made the first transit on June 18, 1855, and on August 17 the brig *Columbia* locked through with a deck load of 132 tons of iron ore from the Cleveland Mining Company, the first of many millions of tons from the Lake Superior District.[6]

Still another early mining concern on the Marquette Range was Lake Superior Iron Company. Organized by Heman Ely and others on February 5, 1853, Lake Superior Iron came to possess mineral lands west of Cleveland Mountain. The company also became the financing vehicle for the Green Bay & Lake Superior Rail Road, issuing $50,000 in bonds. Ely was contracted to build the 17 miles of railroad from the mine property to Iron Bay at a cost not over $2,000 per mile. The GB&LS purchased property in Marquette for docks, warehouses, and yards, and, in the spring of 1853, put down its first rails. This trackage, the first in the UP, was laid to a gauge of 4′10″, no doubt based on Ely's familiarity with the Cleveland, Painesville & Ashtabula and other Ohio roads, which were of similar construction. The GB&LS soon encountered rough terrain out of Marquette, and estimates for completing the road exploded to $12,586 per mile. More financing was arranged at the Lake Superior Iron board of directors meeting on June 13, when the amount of bonds was raised to $100,000.[7]

With the impending completion of the Sault Locks, it was no longer necessary for the railroad to go to Lake Michigan, and the Ely interests organized a new concern on February 15, 1855, called the Iron Mountain Rail Road Company. Its charter called for a 25-mile line from Marquette to a terminus in Township 47 north, Range 27 west, thought to be the western limit of the Marquette Iron Range.[8]

Helping to speed work on the Iron Mountain was the arrival of the locomotive *Sebastopol* on August 7, 1855. The little 25-ton 4-4-0, named for the Russian Black Sea port recently made famous in the Crimean War, was the first locomotive to appear in the UP. Continued acrimony with the Sharon Iron Company was evident, as it was questionable for a time whether the brig *Columbia* would be allowed to unload *Sebastopol* at their dock. The mule drivers of the strap railroad were also on hand and unimpressed with the new sign of progress. Heman Ely brought along his pistol to ensure the unloading went smoothly.

After the steamer *Delaware* brought 26 tons of T rail to Marquette the last week of August, the *Sebastopol* was soon engaged in work train service, advancing the track toward the Iron Mountains. The rail was one of the first cargoes to be landed on the new Ely dock, under construction off the end of Main Street. Another rock cut, similar to that of the Iron Mountain Railway, was put in under Front Street in Marquette to reach the new dock. By September 24, 1855, the track gang passed the Eureka mine, 2½ miles out, and a ¼-mile spur was laid into that location.[9]

Inclement weather put an end to construction, but building resumed again as the snows receded in the spring of 1856. Progress remained painfully slow, although grading was under contract for the entire 17-mile distance to the Lake Superior Iron holdings. Most of the grading was completed that year, except for a difficult 3-mile stretch

In this early view of Marquette, taken about 1862, a number of 4-wheel ore cars are seen on the Cleveland dock in the foreground. Several sailing ships are tied up along the Lake Superior dock, taking ore from the trend-setting chutes incorporated into that dock. Behind the Lake Superior dock was the location of the third ore dock in use at that time, the Jackson. *Wesley Perron Collection, Peter White Public Library, Marquette, Mich.*

between the Cleveland and Lake Superior mines. One bright spot saw the Ely dock handle its first revenue ore shipments from the Eureka mine, marking the first Lake Superior District iron ore handled by rail to a Lake Superior port. Although there were signs of the bank Panic of 1857 taking hold as early as April, the Iron Mountain continued to push its way to the mines. One trouble spot, a sinkhole west of the "gorge," was finally conquered on the fourth attempt, when a locomotive and cars passed over on July 10, 1857. After crossing the Carp River Marsh, track laying was held up for almost two weeks by an uncompleted rock cut.[10]

The steam railroad opened for business in early August, and by the end of the month, *C. Donkersley,* a second locomotive which had arrived in early June and was named for the road's master mechanic, was bringing down two ore trains a day. With the track over the Carp Marsh still unsettled, Cleveland mine ore was picked up at Duncan's Mill, where it was transloaded off the strap railway. Ore from the Jackson mine was loaded three-quarters of a mile to the east. By mid-September, the track had stabilized enough to allow the steam railroad to spot empties directly at the Cleveland mine. This brought an end to the reload at Duncan's Mill and the remaining usefulness of the strap railway. Almost immediately facilities proved insufficient, as the Iron Mountain faced what would be a perennial problem for Lake Superior District iron ore carriers, a shortage of ore cars. By August 15, there were twelve sailing vessels and one steamboat waiting their turn at the dock, with ore being loaded immediately upon arrival. Successful trials were even made running the old horse cars on the T rail. The *Lake Superior Journal* reported it was always "darkest just before the dawn; so now our companies are having the greatest difficulty in supplying their vessels, just before the time when ore can be brought down like an avalanche at the rate of 1200 tons per diem."[11]

The Iron Mountain was also busy preparing facilities at Marquette. A car and machine shop was completed during the summer of 1857 between Front and Third streets. To handle ore from the affiliated Lake Superior mine, which made its first shipments on October 10, the old Ely dock was rebuilt at the foot of Main Street. This dock was a trendsetter as it saw the first use of chutes and pockets for the handling of iron ore on the lakes. Railroad cars dumped their loads into pockets located below the trestlework, dispensing with time-consuming manual shoveling. Ore was then let down into the vessel holds by chutes. The idea met resistance from some vessel captains, as they feared that iron ore crashing into their boats from such great heights would surely send them to the bottom. These fears proved unfounded and the efficiency of the transloading process was greatly improved. The tracks on the Lake Superior dock were 25 feet above the water and initially made use of 27 pockets along the dock's south side, giving a capacity of around 2,000 tons. Later modified to provide 75 pockets, the 558-foot dock was a combination ore and merchandise dock, with a warehouse located at the far end.

With the completion of the railroad, Marquette Range iron ore shipments mushroomed to 25,646 tons in 1857, or almost four times the level of the year before. This was in spite of the fact that the railroad only operated a short time before navigation ended. Operations were not maintained over the winter months as navigation ceased with the freezing of portions of the Great Lakes, leaving little if any business between the isolated outposts of Marquette and the Iron Mountains. After the success of the Lake Superior dock, the Cleveland dock was modified into a pocket dock that winter, with the addition of a 30-foot-high trestle, three tracks wide. The new configuration had 29 vessel pockets and 6 for use of steamboats, with a total capacity of 2,300 tons.

The coming of an efficient mode of transportation did not signal an end to the practice of smelting iron ore on the Marquette Range. In the summer of 1857, the Pioneer Iron Company began construction of the UP's first charcoal blast furnace at Negaunee. Some of the Iron Mountain's first revenue shipments were 5 cars of brick for the plant. The first pig iron was produced on April 26, 1858, furnishing the Iron Mountain with additional eastbound tonnage for transloading at Marquette. In addition to Negaunee, another boom town on the range was Ishpeming, located 3 miles to the west. This village, near the Cleveland mine, was incorporated in 1859 and for some years had a larger population than Marquette. As the elevation of Ishpeming was higher than that of Negaunee, the Chippewa word for "high ground" was used in naming the village. Negaunee was Chippewa for "pioneer."[12]

Samuel Ely went on to take a leading role in the affairs of the Iron Mountain Rail Road and its successors, the Bay de Noquet & Marquette, Marquette & Ontonagon, and Marquette, Houghton & Ontonagon, following the death of his brother Heman in 1856. *Peter White Public Library, Marquette, Mich.*

The main force behind the Iron Mountain Rail Road, Heman B. Ely, did not live to see his road completed, passing away on October 13, 1856. The remainder of the project was left to his brothers, Samuel, then 30 years old, and George. By 1856 the Elys, who had invested over $300,000, saw that another $75,000 would be required to complete the road. Rather than put their Rochester flour milling interests at risk, they decided to sell a one-third share in the road and Lake Superior Iron to outside investors, including Joseph Greenough, of Rochester; Joseph Fay, of Boston; and Edwin Parsons, of New York.

BAY DE NOQUET & MARQUETTE

Although a railroad now existed between the mines and Marquette, it did nothing to remove the isolation that afflicted the region during the winter months when portions of Lake Superior froze over and navigation ceased. Communication with the outside world was possible only by snowshoe. There was hope this isolation had been addressed when the U.S. government, on June 3, 1856, granted the state of Michigan alternate sections of land, six sections wide, to be used in aiding the construction of railroads along three routes out of Marquette. One ran to Little Bay de Noquet on Lake Michigan, near present day Escanaba, a second to the Wisconsin boundary along the Menominee River, near Menominee, and a third to the Montreal River, which formed the UP's western boundary with Wisconsin. Connecting grants in Wisconsin provided for lines between the Montreal River and Fond du Lac, Minnesota (13 miles west of Duluth up the St. Louis River), and south of the Menominee River towards Chicago.[13]

In order to gain the Michigan grant and make the UP a part of their commercial sphere, Chicago and Wisconsin interests backing the Chicago, St. Paul and Fond du Lac Rail Road (CStP&FdL), then building north out of Chicago, formed the Ontonagon and State Line Railroad Company on June 21, 1856. Ely interests countered by filing articles for a new road, the Iron Mountain and Wisconsin Rail Road Company, on July 3, 1856. The Iron Mountain & Wisconsin would build off of the west end of the Iron Mountain Rail Road, head southwest to the Michigammi River, follow that stream to near what later became Iron Mountain, Michigan, and then run along the Menominee River to Green Bay, where connections would be made for the south.[14]

While the Iron Mountain & Wisconsin covered the land grant running directly to the Wisconsin border, the Ely interests formed another company, the Bay de Noquet and Marquette Rail Road (BdN&M), on October 24, 1856, to build a 70-mile-long line between those two points. This line, basically the south half of the old Green Bay & Lake

Superior, was capitalized at $150,000 with backing from the Ely brothers—George H., Samuel P., and John F.—along with John Burt.[15]

Still another line south out of Marquette, one in which the Ely-Burt syndicate had a half-interest, was the Marquette and State Line Rail Road, incorporated on January 14, 1857. This road, some 75 miles in length, would run directly south from Marquette to the Wisconsin state line, near Menominee. Capitalization was set at $2,000,000, with the remaining stock owned by the Cleveland, Jackson, and Eureka mining companies.[16]

The Ontonagon & State Line, Bay de Noquet & Marquette, Marquette & State Line, and still another road known as the Marquette and Ontonagon Railway (M&O Ry), which hoped to take in the western Michigan grant to the Montreal River, were all authorized by the state on February 14, 1857, to receive land grants for construction of their respective lines. As the Bay de Noquet & Marquette and Marquette & State Line would parallel one another out of Marquette until the former branched off to Bay de Noquet, a potential conflict over lands was in the making right from the start. As only one railroad could be justified to handle the business between the UP and Chicago, instead of the four existing on paper, consolidation seemed to be the best alternative and for a while things moved in that direction.[17]

Merger negotiations included the Chicago, St. Paul & Fond du Lac Railroad Company, which had reached the last named point in 1854. Under a plan agreed to by the board of directors of the Marquette & State Line and CStP&FdL on March 21, 1857, the two roads would consolidate, and the Marquette & State Line would purchase the Iron Mountain Rail Road, the Iron Mountain Railway, and 2 miles of track owned by the Cleveland Iron Company beyond the Jackson mine. On May 16, Iron Mountain Rail Road stockholders ratified the agreement under which the Iron Mountain would complete its railroad at the expense of the Fond du Lac road. A deed for $315,000 was passed to the CStP&FdL on June 11, 1857.[18]

The bank Panic of 1857 soon doomed these consolidation efforts. In early August, CStP&FdL president William Butler Ogden, a popular Chicago real estate promoter and its first mayor, admitted to the Elys that he would be unable to fulfill any of the drafts covering construction of the Iron Mountain Rail Road. Under an agreement signed September 26, 1857, the trustees of the Chicago, St. Paul & Fond du Lac gave up any claims to the Iron Mountain, and the Elys returned $210,000 received from the CStP&FdL. The Ely syndicate continued to press for a merger after the economic recovery, but for unknown reasons Ogden decided to go it alone despite the monopoly this would have given the Chicago interests on the Marquette Range.

Continuing to seek a southern outlet, the Ely and Burt interests revived the Bay de Noquet & Marquette, making arrangements for a survey in July 1857. Starting at the Ely dock in Marquette, surveyors headed south and east along Lake Superior, unsuccessfully trying to find an opening in the ridge that separated Lake Superior from Lake Michigan. The syndicate then came to the conclusion that the best grades could be attained by extending south off the west end of Iron Mountain Rail Road. As the west end of the Iron Mountain was already on top of the ridge, it would be a simple matter to head south 8 miles to the head of the Escabauby (later Escanaba) River, and follow that stream to Little Bay de Noquet. This would also shorten the route 17 miles. Incorporating the existing Iron Mountain trackage into the mix would also be expeditious, as 20 miles of completed road were necessary to obtain the land grant. The trouble was that the charter of the BdN&M called for a line running directly south of Marquette to Bay de Noquet, and a change to its route would need the approval of the General Land Office in Washington, D.C.

John Burt, president of the Bay de Noquet & Marquette, went to visit state and federal officials and, although winning their concurrence for the line change, failed to obtain a formal agreement. It seemed the culprit in withholding the official decrees was the Chicago, St. Paul & Fond du Lac, which, in a short time, had turned from ally to adversary and was lobbying in both Lansing and Washington against the change. The newly shifted Bay de Noquet & Marquette would come into direct conflict with a route contemplated by the CStP&FdL to reach the Iron Mountains. The owners of the Fond du Lac road also did not want the BdN&M to have a head start towards obtaining a land grant in the congested area around Marquette. The Chicago, St. Paul & Fond du Lac, in desperate financial straits, managed to reach Oshkosh before an August 1, 1858, deadline to earn its land grant, but there construction ceased. The BdN&M became complacent as a result and lost its best opportunity to take part in the Lake Michigan trade.

In what amounted to a paper transfer, the Iron Mountain Rail Road was sold to the Bay de Noquet & Marquette on December 31, 1858. Even a simple merger such as this was not without its problems. The transaction had to be approved by the Michigan legislature, and opposition was met from Detroit iron interests who felt it would direct ore business to Chicago. The merger authorization bill passed on February 12, 1859, but in a last bit of satire an amendment was offered to rename the legislation "A Bill Selling the Iron Interests of the Upper Peninsula of Michigan to the City of Chicago." The BdN&M also officially picked up 2 additional miles of road on March 21, 1860, when the Cleveland Iron Company agreed to sell its trackage between Jackson Mountain and the Cleveland mine for $20,000. This left but 3 additional miles to meet the 20-mile land grant requirement.[19]

The 1859 season opened on a bright note, when word was received on April 12 that the General Land Office would allow the Bay de Noquet & Marquette to build to Lake Michigan off the end of the old Iron Mountain Rail Road. The BdN&M dallied for several more years and did not commence grading the final 3 miles of line needed to obtain a land grant until 1861. This segment, completed in September 1862, resulted in a main line of 20.03 miles. The new trackage headed south towards Bay de Noquet, and in later years formed the Winthrop branch. In order that the BdN&M could gain the 120 sections of land, "a committee of honorable and impartial men" examined the line and reported it had been completed to proper standard. Governor Austin Blair went on to issue a certification of completion on November 20, 1862. Before obtaining possession of the land grant, however, the BdN&M needed General Land Office certification, but met with the usual delay.[20]

Certification was important as the Bay de Noquet road once again faced a challenge from the south. The old Chicago, St. Paul & Fond du Lac, resurrected as the Chicago & North Western Railway on June 6, 1859, had resumed construction northward. The BdN&M placed surveyors in the field for a southern extension, with work expected to start in the spring of 1863. More inaction followed, and along with it passed the final opportunity for the Bay de Noquet road to take part in the predominantly north-south traffic pattern of the region, or at least to make itself a more appealing takeover target for the C&NW.[21]

The North Western–backed Peninsula Railroad, formed on April 22, 1862, secured government approval to alter the Marquette & State Line charter for a line to Ontonagon via Bay de Noquet and the Marquette Range, with branches to Marquette and Houghton (on the Keweenaw Peninsula). As journeying to the UP required traversing almost 200 miles of mostly "unbroken wilderness," defense considerations played a part in the approval of the line change. With the Civil War on, and British sympathies closely allied with the Confederacy, the building of such a railroad was thought to be of great benefit in defending the region against a potentially hostile neighbor to the north. Ogden asked for help from the Chicago merchants, saying the road would help bring the UP's iron and copper resources into Chicago's sphere and break the monopoly of the Bay de Noquet & Marquette railroad. The *Chicago Tribune* commented, "This will bring Chicago, within 22 hours of Lake Superior, and the bulk of its trade will soon be ours." Some $100,000 in Peninsula stock was subscribed by Chicago interests.[22]

Construction of the Peninsula Railroad started on July 4, 1863, at the new settlement of Escanaba on Little Bay de Noquet. The Peninsula, officially consolidated into the C&NW on October 21, 1864, completed its 62-mile-long line to Negaunee on December 22, ending the Elys' domination of the Marquette Range in the process. The first iron ore shipments were made to the newly completed Escanaba ore dock on May 12, 1865. Unlike the BdN&M, the C&NW operated passenger and merchandise service over the winter months, in spite of the high costs of snow removal. To ensure traffic for the Peninsula road, Ogden and other C&NW investors created the Iron Cliffs Mining Company in the spring of 1864. Besides purchasing 34,000 acres of mineral land, Iron Cliffs took over the Jackson mine.

To alleviate impending conflicts, Congress, on March 3, 1865, passed legislation specifying a line to the north and west of which the BdN&M and Marquette & Ontonagon Railway would make land grant selections, while the C&NW made its selections to the south and east. The secretary of the interior was also authorized to award 200 sections to the BdN&M as soon as the completion of 20 miles of line was verified by the State of Michigan. The boost to 200 sections resulted from the act's increase in compensation from 6 to 10 sections per mile of completed trackage.[23]

Further agreements saw the North Western give up on its Marquette branch, in exchange for which the BdN&M abandoned its extension to Bay de Noquet. The BdN&M, with its 4′10″ gauge, was initially unable to interchange equipment with the C&NW on account of the latter's use of the standard gauge of 4′8½″. The North Western later equipped some of its boxcars with wider wheels, allowing them to journey into Marquette over the BdN&M. These cars, known as "compromise cars," followed the precedent of the Red Ball freight lines, whose cars traveled over a similar mix of gauges between New York and Chicago.[24]

Railroading in the UP at this early stage was rather primitive by later standards. With no water tanks along the BdN&M, each engine was equipped with a dozen pails which were used to scoop water from nearby streams. This task was performed two or three times daily. Lacking air brakes, each train had an engineer, a fireman, a conductor, and six brakemen, who rode out on the train setting brakes by hand. Twelve to fifteen 4-wheeled cars, capable of handling 5 to 6 tons of ore, made a typical train. This gave the Bay de Noquet a capacity of handling 600 to 800 tons daily from the mines. In

This view of the Jackson mine at Negaunee shows the labor-intensive methods used in early days to extract iron ore and load it into ore cars.
Paananen Collection

spite of the loss of locomotive *C. Donkersley* early in the season due to a derailment, the BdN&M was able to handle some 83,078 tons of ore and 4,683 tons of pig iron in 1859.

Traffic nearly doubled in 1860, growing to 150,903 tons as steelmakers found that only low-phosphorous iron ore, such as was found on the Marquette Range, would work in the newly introduced Bessemer process. The Bay de Noquet scheduled five rounds trips a day between Marquette and the Lake Superior mine, with running time figured at about 1 hour and 45 minutes for the 18-mile run. Trains grew in length to 20–25 cars, and the road's lone passenger car occupied the tail end on every other round trip. Passengers were taken at the new 26′×36′ Marquette passenger depot, which had been built that spring at the intersection of Baraga and Front streets.

The BdN&M daily capacity rose to 2,000 tons of ore per day in 1862, following the addition of two New Jersey 4-4-0 locomotives, *Samuel P. Ely* and *Marquette*. Shipping continued to be confined to the three old companies on the range, the Jackson, the Cleveland, and the Lake Superior, which sent out 140,453 tons that year. Ed Anthony, an early BdN&M trainman, recalled a conversation with Harry Merry, captain of the Jackson, who remarked, "Ed, what in the world are they going to do with all the iron ore we are shipping them?" Vessel size was also increasing, and it seemed to take forever to fill one of the new 500-ton schooners by hand. Prosperity was finally delivered into the hands of the mine owners, with dividends being declared for the first time. Some of the early investors had already left, having lost most of their investment before profitability set in.[25]

To keep up with the escalating tonnages, the Jackson dock was converted over to chutes during the winter of 1862–1863. In spite of high freight charges and labor shortages, all the mines reported tonnage gains during 1863 due to the continued prosecution of the Civil War. The Lake Superior mine experienced remarkable growth, with tonnages rising from 25,200 in 1861 to 74,057 in 1863, while the entire range shipped out 217,656 tons that season. The Civil War also generated a boom for UP pig iron, with prices since the start of the war rising from $23 to $45 a ton. BdN&M backers formed the Morgan Iron Company, whose plant at the top of the hill went into blast on November 27, 1863.

It was fortunate that the C&NW arrived during these boom times, as both roads were able to remain profitable even with the division of tonnage. With the purchase of the Jackson mine by Iron Cliffs, all its ore started to move to Escanaba, and Jackson's Marquette dock saw no use after the 1864 season. The rate on ore to Marquette remained around $1.10 per ton in spite of the new competition. Even with the new competition, the BdN&M found it necessary to construct a 600-foot-long, 35-foot-high combination ore and merchandise dock just to the south of the Lake Superior dock in 1864. New tonnage that year came from the Lake Angeline mine near Ishpeming. The following year the New England mine made its first shipments by hauling ore out by wagon to a transload site north of Winthrop.

MARQUETTE & ONTONAGON RAILROAD

Formed to take early advantage of the western component of Upper Michigan's 1856 land grant was the Marquette and Ontonagon Railway. Filing articles of association for a 100-mile line between Marquette and Houghton on February 6, 1857, the M&O Ry, organized largely by Detroit businessmen, came to be awarded the western land grant by the Michigan legislature just eight days later. Although its directive later proved impractical, the grant specified that the line had to pass through Ontonagon on its way to the state's western border. Ontonagon was the site of a flourishing, but isolated, copper mining region.[26]

An M&O Ry survey called for a low-grade line originating 3 miles north of Marquette, opposite Partridge Island. The line then headed southwest, crossing the Iron Mountain Rail Road 2 miles east of the "Gorge," and followed the Carp River to Teal Lake and Cleveland Mountain. This grade was far superior to that of the Iron Mountain Rail Road, and it was felt that that road would eventually dry up as an inefficient competitor. After passing Lake Michigammi, the M&O Ry would drop down into

L'Anse, the "best harbor on the entire lake [Superior]," and then turn northwest, crossing the Keweenaw Peninsula divide near the Toltec mine. From there the plank road would be followed to Ontonagon. In spite of the planned line's superior grade, no action was taken beyond surveying and the line lapsed into a long period of slumber.[27]

With the battle to build south lost to the C&NW, the BdN&M decided to head west—an option still available due to inactivity on the part of the Marquette & Ontonagon Ry. On January 2, 1863, articles of association were filed for the Marquette and Ontonagon *Railroad* (M&O RR) to build a 125-mile line between Marquette and Ontonagon via the Iron Mountains and L'Anse Bay. The Michigan legislature was petitioned to confer the expired M&O Ry grant upon the new M&O RR, maintaining that the Copper Country had waited long enough for a railroad connection and that L'Anse Bay needed rail service to develop its nearby iron and timber resources. The M&O Ry countered that large sums had been expended for survey, and only the Panic of 1857 followed by the Civil War had delayed the road's construction. The M&O Ry also believed that competition was needed to stifle the heavy tariffs being charged by the Bay de Noquet & Marquette.[28]

James Pendill, who carried the M&O Railroad bill in the Michigan legislature, argued there was no need for another line between the Iron Mountains and Marquette and that the Bay de Noquet & Marquette had yet to reach its carrying capacity. Another line would result in "ruinous competition," which would result in "common disaster" to both lines. Pendill also argued that there was no real traffic to be handled between Marquette and Ontonagon and that this traffic would route via the C&NW to the south. Pendill believed the M&O Ry would never build west of the iron mining region.[29]

Pendill's arguments proved convincing, and on March 17, 1863, the Michigan legislature passed an act forfeiting the M&O Ry's land grant due to non-compliance, awarding it to the Marquette & Ontonagon Railroad. As consolation, the M&O RR was required to pay the M&O Ry for its survey work. The M&O RR was required to have its first 20 miles of line completed by July 1, 1865, and to build an additional 20 miles each year thereafter. Initial construction was to start at a point on the Bay de Noquet & Marquette near the Lake Superior mine.[30]

An M&O RR party did not stick to the old M&O Ry survey, but tried to gain a more level route via St. Clair Mountain and the south shore of Lake Michigammi. Upon completion of the survey, a contract was let to T. T. Hurley for the first 10 miles, connecting with the BdN&M 2 miles north of Winthrop at a point known as Ontonagon Jct. Grading began on August 25, 1863, and, by the fall, 1,000 men were employed. Although still a long way off, even Ontonagon became excited, and its newspaper urged the citizenry to buy M&O RR stock. After a winter's reprieve, the opening of the 1864 construction season saw matters continuing to be pushed on the first 10-mile segment. By mid-June 3 miles of trackage had been laid out of Ontonagon Jct., and Hurley hoped to reach St. Clair Mountain by late summer. Several iron mining firms engaged on the south side of Lake Michigammi motivated the M&O RR to head in that direction rather than taking the more direct route along the north shore.

After another winter layoff, work resumed in the spring of 1865, and the last rail on the 20-mile extension was put down a few days before the July 1 deadline. A picnic excursion train was run out of Marquette on the Fourth of July to celebrate the opening of the new line. Some 700 people took part in the event, riding the M&O RR's few pieces of passenger equipment and platform cars (as flat cars were called in those days), fitted with seats, to the end of the track along the south shore of Lake Michigammi.

After completion of its first 20-mile segment, the M&O RR went about the never easy task of obtaining its land grant land from the state. Governor Henry Crapo appointed Alex Campbell to inspect the line, and, upon receiving his report, certified completion to the secretary of the interior on November 17, 1865. Rumors then became current that the M&O RR had no intention of operating beyond Champion, and that the last 5½ miles had been built only to gain the land grant. It was also determined that 3½ miles of rail had already been pulled up west of the Washington mine. When informed of this Governor Crapo replied to Campbell, "I could hardly think that any honorable business men would commit such a gross outrage with the public confidence." Samuel Ely responded that while it was true that the rails had been removed, the purpose was to swap them with the lighter 50-pound rail east of the Washington mine. As the season was getting late and no trains were running west of the mine, it was decided to wait until spring to relay the secondhand rail on the western segment. Ely promised the governor that there was no intention of "abandoning any portion of their track." It was expected that the M&O RR would receive "a large freighting business" from iron mines on that side of the lake in which the company was "directly or indirectly" interested.[31]

In spite of the end of the Civil War, the country's need for steel rails continued the strong demand for iron ore of Bessemer grade, providing an active traffic base for the new extension. The previously mentioned Washington mine, opened by Edward Breitung and M&O RR officials in 1865, was located some 10 miles west of Ontonagon Jct. A few miles to the west of the Washington was the Edwards mine, which made its first shipments in 1866. Also opened by the M&O RR owners in 1868 was the Champion mine, located on a hill just south of the village, and reached by a 1.9-mile spur which branched from the main line east of town.

Along the original BdN&M segment, the New England mine received a new spur in 1868, while the nearby Winthrop mine, at the end of the ill-fated southern extension, received a 2,000-foot spur in 1870. In the spring of 1871 a new spur was laid south of Negaunee to the McComber mine. Another mine along this branch, the Rolling Mill, made its first shipments the same year. The Saginaw mine was reached by a spur out of Ontonagon Jct. in 1872.

Additional work begun by the M&O RR in 1871 included a branch line from near the Washington mine to the promising finds at Smith Mountain being operated by the Republic Iron Company. Work on the 9-mile branch, under contractor Robert Nelson, commenced in October 1871, with some trackage being laid before the snow fell. Work continued through the winter, especially on the rock cuts, and was resumed at full force in the spring of 1872. A labor shortage delayed work that summer, and, on August 5, the Republic mine shut down its operations to allow its laborers to assist the contractors in finishing the branch. Republic was not reached until September, with the first cars of iron ore being shipped on October 2. The Republic went on to become one of the major traffic sources of the M&O RR and its successors. Passenger service on the Republic branch was provided by stub runs, which connected with the main line trains at Humboldt.

1868. **1868.**

Bay de N. & M. and M. & O.R.R.

TIME TABLE No. 2
PASSENGER TRAIN TIME

To take effect at 7 o'clock A.M., Friday, May 1st, 1868.

For the Information of Employees only. The Company reserve the right to vary the same as circumstances may require.

	A.M. TRAIN.		P.M. TRAIN.	
Marquette, ...	7 00	1 35	5 30	8 25
Bancroft, ...	7 20	1 20	5 45	8 10
Franklin, ...	7 30	1 10	5 52	8 02
Gorge, ...	7 40	1 00	6 00	7 52
Morgan, ...	7 45	12 52	6 05	7 47
Eagle Mill, ...	7 55	12 45	6 12	7 40
Negaunee, ...	8 15	12 25	6 30	7 25
Cleveland, ...	8 27	12 10	6 40	7 15
Ishpeming, ...	8 35	12 05	6 45	7 10
Lake Angeline, ...	8 40	12 00		
Ont. Junction, ...	8 45	11 55		
Greenwood, ...	9 10	11 30		
Clarksburg, ...	9 35	11 10		
Washington, ...	9 45	11 00		
Champion, ...	10 15	10 35		

(A.M. TRAIN: GOING WEST / GOING EAST; P.M. TRAIN: GOING WEST / GOING EAST)

C. DONKERSLEY, Supt.

In addition to their mining activity, the M&O RR owners were involved in the erection of several charcoal furnaces along the line. The Greenwood, 5 miles west of Ontonagon Jct., made its first blast in June 1865 and resulted in iron ore moving both ways on the M&O RR, east to the docks and west to the furnace. At nearby Clarksburg, Cornelius Donkersley built a sawmill in 1865, and Michigan Iron Company erected a charcoal furnace which went into blast in February 1867. Most of the ore feeding this furnace came from the nearby Washington and Lake Superior mines. Michigan Iron later took over the Clarksburg sawmill and expanded it into one of the largest in the UP.

Morgan Iron built still another furnace along the M&O RR at Champion, and this went into blast on December 4, 1867. Something different was tried at Marquette, where the M&O owners organized the Marquette and Pacific Rolling Mill Company. Instead of being a charcoal furnace, this one was fueled by bituminous coal. This operation, "one of the largest in the country," was located on M&O RR land along Lake Street south of town and made its first cast on July 14, 1871. A spur was laid to the site in the spring of 1870 from the Jackson cut.[32]

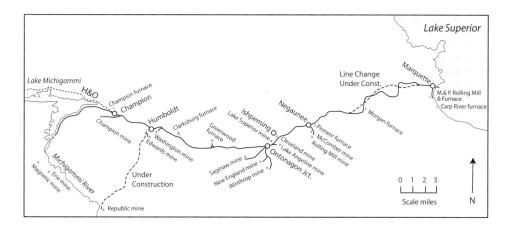

Marquette & Ontonagon Railroad, Spring 1872

Handling ore and pig traffic on the heavy grade into Marquette was always a thorn in the railroad's side, and in the fall of 1870, Chief Engineer Charles Cavis surveyed a new line between Marquette and Bruce. As well as reducing the ruling grade to 142 feet to the mile, the new line was 3 miles shorter. Work on the line change started in the summer of 1871 but was hampered by poor weather. The project then languished as resources were put into other projects, and it was not until May 15, 1873, that the morning passenger train made the first scheduled run over the long-awaited segment.

The railroad scene at Marquette was forever changed as the result of a horrific fire on June 11, 1868. The M&O RR enjoyed a fairly complete shop facility at Front and Main streets at that time, but a little before midnight a fire started in the machine shops and quickly spread, destroying the blacksmith shop, carpenter shop, pattern room, gas house, tank house, and office, along with records and expensive machinery. The fire then leapt across Front Street to the center of town, largely destroying the business district. The blaze then worked its way east to the docks along the bay. The M&O RR dock, the Lake Superior dock, and the Jackson dock were soon on fire. Except for the last 200 feet of the M&O dock, all were entirely destroyed. The only dock left completely standing when the conflagration ended was the Cleveland at the foot of Superior Street. The M&O RR suffered an estimated $200,000 loss from the fire.

The Lake Superior Iron Co., the M&O RR, and the Cleveland Company arranged to operate the latter's dock 24 hours a day, with each company having 8 hours' access. Work was soon under way rebuilding the M&O and Lake Superior docks. In the process the Lake Superior dock became a merchandise dock and the M&O an exclusive 9,000-ton ore dock, capable of loading 6 sailing vessels simultaneously and from 12 to 14 vessels per day. The schooner *Anna Grover* took the first load of ore off the new M&O dock on August 31, 1868. Nighttime operation became possible when the dock was lit for the first time on June 14, 1870. The merchandise dock received supplies and was also a place to transload pig iron shipments.

Cleveland Iron Company tore down its dock in the fall of 1870 in order to construct a new facility that would keep up with larger vessel sizes. The new dock, with a capacity of 2,200 tons, stood 7 feet higher, or 36½ feet above the water, and was ready for the opening of the 1871 navigation season. Two tracks ran along the 770-foot dock, serving 29 vessel pockets, with a separate spur for the 6 steamboat pockets on the end.

The Marquette shops were relocated to Fifth Street and rebuilt in permanent fashion out of local red sandstone with iron roofs. The new shop buildings included a 9-stall roundhouse, a 52′ × 113′ machine shop, a foundry, and a forge. All these buildings were under one roof. Rolling stock was handled in a detached carpenter shop made of white brick. A new brick storehouse was added in 1870. Given their isolation, the M&O RR shops were capable of making practically everything needed to keep the rolling stock in operation. The only things bought from the outside were chains, springs, and copper for making brass fittings. The M&O RR built all its ore cars as well as the baggage car and two coaches used on the passenger runs.

Traffic generated by new furnaces and mines along the M&O RR had a very favorable effect on the total system revenue. Iron ore movements in 1866 totaled 197,381 tons, along with 15,020 tons of pig iron. This figure climbed in 1867 to 283,417 tons of ore and 23,313 tons of pig iron. The large increase was due in part to the shipping of soft hematite ores, which had previously been considered of little value. The moisture in the soft ore posed quite a problem late in the season when temperatures started to fall and caused the loads to freeze in the cars and in the pockets on the docks. The higher traffic levels in 1867 allowed the Bay de Noquet & Marquette, the name still used in official reports, to issue its first dividends, which totaled 7 percent during the year.

The 1867 season saw the M&O RR operate eleven scheduled ore trains a day in addition to two passenger runs. The ore runs included three each to the Cleveland, Lake Superior, and Lake Angeline mines, and two to the Washington mine. Train lengths grew, and, in early September, engineer Thomas Steele brought down 59 loads of ore with the *Joseph Fay*. Although the ore cars only averaged 9 tons, this was the largest train ever handled over the road. The separate passenger runs were quite an improvement over the rough ride experienced heretofore on the tail end of one of the mine runs. The speed was still nothing to brag about, though, as it took 3 hours and 15 minutes to make the 32-mile run between Marquette and Champion.

In spite of the fire trouble, 1868 still turned out to be a successful year, with the M&O RR handling 275,564 tons of ore and 24,502 tons of pig iron. The road even managed a 3 percent dividend. By this time the ore business had come to be largely split with the C&NW, that road carrying 257,150 tons of ore and 9,200 tons of pig during 1868. The newcomer served the Jackson, New York, Cleveland, Barnum, Lake Angeline, and Iron Mountain mines, while the M&O RR had exclusive trackage into the Lake Superior, New England, Edwards, Washington, and Champion mines. Traffic from the Cleveland and Lake Angeline mines was shared, and the M&O RR received some Jackson ore for local furnaces.

The M&O RR's 1869 timetable saw a large increase in the number of scheduled movements per day (36), reflecting the new mines that were coming on line. The M&O RR came to handle 341,554 tons of ore that year, but the C&NW pulled ahead for the first time, carrying 367,883 tons to Escanaba. Although the M&O RR had lower freight rates to the docks, given its shorter distance, vessel rates from Escanaba were much less. Combining the rail and vessel rates resulted in total transportation charges to mills in Cleveland, Ohio, that were only slightly more expensive via Escanaba. The C&NW also enjoyed a clear advantage in handling ore to furnaces on Lake Michigan. The M&O RR still enjoyed a sizable lead in pig iron shipments, handling 21,231 tons versus 11,000 via the North Western in 1869.

The M&O RR operated on a reduced schedule for the first time over the winter of 1870–1871. Up to this time, the limited passenger and merchandise business received off the C&NW connection at Negaunee during the winter months had been handled to Marquette by wagons and sleighs. With the start of the 1871 ore season, the M&O RR's schedule ballooned to 46 regular trains. This resulted in the M&O RR carrying an impressive 451,255 tons of ore, 27,612 tons of pig iron, 28,244 tons of other freight (most of which was vegetables and forest products), and 85,329 passengers. The Lake Superior Iron Company, with 177,011 tons of ore, by far generated the largest tonnage. Ore from the Lake Angeline and New England mines, as well as some from the Winthrop, was handled in "compromise" cars and turned over to the North Western at Lake Angeline Jct. for movement to Escanaba.

THE M&O RR FLEET

As the iron ore business showed no letup with the end of the Civil War, the M&O RR considerably expanded its locomotive fleet in 1866. Two 4-4-0s (*Joseph S. Fay*, later renamed *J. F. Greenough*, and *John Carter Brown*) were added as well as the road's first Mogul (*Heman B. Ely*), a powerful 2-6-0 ideally suited for hauling iron ore. About this time, all new power came to bear the Marquette & Ontonagon Railroad name, although M&O RR and BdN&M power and equipment had come to be used interchangeably. The new additions brought the locomotive fleet up to eight. Over 400 freight cars were in service, most of which were ore cars. The ore car fleet expanded to over 800 by 1870, after some 250 drop-bottom cars were constructed in the M&O RR shops the previous winter. The road picked up another new Mogul (*Joseph Fay*) shortly before the start of the 1870 ore season, and a little 0-4-0 switcher (*Birch Rod*). At Marquette, inbound ore trains usually terminated in the yard up on the hill near the roundhouse, with the loads then being let down to the docks as needed by switchmen, without a locomotive. It would then be the job of a small engine like the *Birch Rod* to spot the cars over the dock pockets for dumping.

The winter of 1870–1871 saw a major transition in the M&O RR fleet with the arrival of a large Taunton 4-6-0 (*Edwin Parsons*). The new locomotive was a coal-burner, and similar conversions were made to the entire fleet that winter. Company coal was received from lake vessels at the M&O RR merchandise dock at the foot of Main Street. Another major change saw the M&O RR convert its rolling stock during the winter of 1871–1872 from 4′10″ to the standard gauge of 4′8½″. Trackage was changed over in the spring, allowing free interchange of all equipment with the C&NW and ending the use of "compromise" cars. During that same winter's slowdown, the M&O RR shops completed construction of a 22-ton 0-4-0, which demonstrated the capabilities of the isolated facility. As the M&O RR had started numbering its locomotives, the new addition received the number 12 as well as the name *Champion*. Another new Taunton 4-6-0 (13—*Michigammi*) was received by the M&O RR later in the year.

The *Birch Rod,* a tiny 12-ton 0-4-0, is seen at the Porter, Bell & Company locomotive works before being sent on its way to the Marquette & Ontonagon Railroad. The engine was used in spotting cars on the docks and at ore loading stockpiles.
Collection of Harold K. Vollrath

Although the entire road had been referred to as the Marquette & Ontonagon Railroad for many years, the Bay de Noquet & Marquette Rail Road Company still technically operated the trackage east of Ontonagon Jct. In early 1871, the board of directors effected a consolidation, retaining the Marquette & Ontonagon Railroad Company name, and exchanging M&O RR shares one for one for those of the BdN&M, giving a total capital stock of $3,500,000. The merger became effective on August 24, with Joseph Fay continuing on as president and S. P. Ely, vice president.[33]

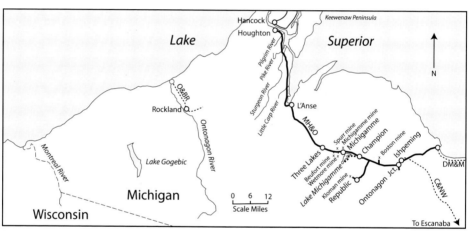

Marquette, Houghton & Ontonagon Railroad, November 14, 1883

2

IRRESOLVABLE CONFLICTS CREATE THE MH&O

The Marquette & Ontonagon Railroad felt no rush to build into Ontonagon, as the copper industry had been in the doldrums for some time. The copper that was produced went to eastern markets by boat and there was little likelihood this pattern would change, even with advent of a more expensive rail option. An extension to Ontonagon would also use up resources needed to develop the M&O RR and the mining properties. The only way a western extension could be made viable was as part of a through connection with the Northern Pacific or an international transcontinental Canadian railroad, both of which were under discussion at this time.

John Gregory Smith, who held down dual presidencies of the NP and the Vermont Central, and Jay Cooke, the very successful Civil War financier from Philadelphia and principal fundraiser of the NP, expressed an interest in the early 1870s of building eastward from Duluth along the south shore of Lake Superior to the Sault, where connections would be made with railroads building west out of Ontario. They in turn would funnel traffic back and forth to Smith's Vermont Central. A very compatible plan was under consideration by Sir Hugh Allan, head of the Intercolonial Railroad, to link the existing Confederation in Eastern Canada with British Columbia and the newly opened lands of the Hudson Bay Company. Allan felt a route along the south shore of Lake Superior would be much more pragmatic than trying to pierce the foreboding Laurentian Shield on the north side of the lake.

Both of these designs were doomed to failure. Allan could not overcome the deep suspicion of the Dominion government, especially Prime Minister John Macdonald, of any American involvement which might lead to the U.S. annexation of Western Canada. Cooke's vision dissipated with the bank Panic of 1873, which saw his banking house collapse, and his loss of control of the NP.

HOUGHTON & ONTONAGON RAILROAD

The continued inactivity of the M&O RR did not sit well with the folks around Ontonagon, and, on January 17, 1870, the Houghton and Ontonagon Railroad Company (H&O) was formed. In addition to local backers, the H&O was aided by Lower Peninsula men, including Henry Walker, shareholder in four UP copper mining companies, and James F. Joy, who had substantial stakes in the Michigan Central (MC) and Chicago, Burlington and Quincy railroads. This would be the first of several efforts on the part of Detroit interests to reestablish their claim to the UP over Chicago interests. The H&O proposed to build a 70-mile line from the end of the M&O RR at Lake Michigammi to Ontonagon. Capitalization was set at $560,000, with Joy being the largest shareholder.[1]

The following week, H&O applied to the state for a transfer of the M&O RR land grant to their company. Michigan officials were anxious to have work begun on the line, as they were concerned the lands would have to be returned to the federal government if no action was taken soon. The Michigan Board of Control, which oversaw land and swampland grants to the railroads, convened on April 19, 1870, concluded that the M&O RR had forfeited its grant, and conferred the grant upon the Houghton & Ontonagon. The Michigan legislature then handed the H&O another victory by giving the road until December 31, 1871, to construct the first 10 miles of road, and until the end of the 1872 to complete an additional 20. This was important, as it would have been impossible to fulfill the time requirements of the original M&O RR grant.[2]

The U.S. Congress also proved helpful, passing a bill on April 20, 1871, which authorized a resurvey of the line to do away with the jog around the south end of Lake Michigammi. This change was felt desirable as new mining discoveries along the north shore of the lake were believed to be more promising than those along the south shore. The Houghton & Ontonagon then launched a further attack upon the M&O RR, claiming that its 20 miles of trackage west of Ontonagon Jct. had not be completed by the July 1, 1865 deadline, and that it had not fulfilled its obligation to construct 20 additional miles of trackage in subsequent years. Consequently, the H&O argued, the M&O RR land grant should be forfeited.[3]

Rumors were circulated in Lansing that the M&O RR had been abandoned, in spite of the fact that the line had generated 90,000 tons of ore and 5,000 tons of pig iron in 1869. The trackage beyond Champion did remain inactive; as Samuel Ely wrote Governor H. P. Baldwin, "There is not even a single human habitation on the other six miles of the line." To counter moves of the H&O, Ely invited Baldwin to personally inspect the Marquette & Ontonagon Railroad. This offer was accepted, and, with one of the homebuilt coaches and a locomotive, the party went out to the end of the track on July 27, 1871. This action at least put to rest the claim that the 5.5 miles beyond Champion had been abandoned.[4]

The M&O RR's inability to secure patents for its land grant even threatened the road's valuable mineral and furnace properties, as they had been included in an April 24, 1871, list of lands available to the H&O. The H&O selected some 40,000 of the 76,800 acres of the original M&O RR claim, including the Champion mine in which the M&O RR had invested over $300,000. Joseph Fay wrote Governor Baldwin, "we have been surprised at the proceedings of this Company and are taking vigorous steps to maintain our rights. Having built 20 miles of railroad we believe . . . that we have earned the land grant for that distance, and . . . that neither Congress nor the state can legislate away our 'vested rights.' While, it is not pleasant to be involved in litigation, nor can I see why the H&O Co. persists in making us their enemies by trying to get away our property, by any means, legal or illegal."[5]

H&O chief engineer Jacob Houghton received instructions in the spring of 1871 to begin survey work. The new line went off the M&O RR at Champion, along the north side of Lake Michigammi, and then on to L'Anse. Part of the survey work entailed looking for mineral deposits, which would aid in making selections under the land grant. As part of its potential role as a transcontinental link, the H&O even sent a party west of Ontonagon in the fall of 1871 to explore an extension to the Montreal River, supposed eastern terminus of the NP. The H&O received a bit of a shock when James Joy announced he was pulling out of the company in the spring of 1871, but by that time the road's credibility allowed a $2,000,000 loan to be negotiated with eastern capitalists. Among the major investors in the H&O bonds were New York investors John Jacob Astor, John Stewart, Moses Taylor, and the Farmer's Loan and Trust Company. Astor had inherited his family's New York real estate fortune, while Stewart and Taylor were associated with the Delaware, Lackawanna & Western railroad.

With surveys completed, D. L. Wells of Milwaukee was awarded a contract calling for completion of 10 miles by December 31, 1871, and the remaining 22 miles on or before August 1, 1872. Construction started at L'Anse on July 26, 1871. Wells advertised for 1,000 men and 300 teams, with at least one year's work guaranteed at $2.00 a day. Men with teams received $4.50 a day with board being provided at $4.50 a week. Construction work was started all along the line in order to accomplish as much as possible before the ground froze. Other men were engaged in the woods getting out ties. A boat brought in 500 tons of iron, or enough to lay 6 miles of trackage, on September 23, 1871, and the first rail was laid four days later. Two locomotives, *Groton* and *Keweenaw*, and some flat cars were received for work train service.

At L'Anse, surveys were undertaken for an expanded town site which hopefully would mushroom into a thriving community. A merchandise dock and 30′ × 160′ warehouse were constructed to land materials for the new road. Contractors Muloch and Shields were awarded the L'Anse ore dock, with work to begin the following spring. The new dock, 546 feet long, 36 feet wide, and 38 feet high, would have 80 vessel pockets of 75-ton capacity. At the end would be four additional pockets for steamboat loading. While vessel pockets loaded directly into the holds of the boats through spouts, the steamboat pockets loaded into vehicles, which were then wheeled onto the boats and dumped. The dock was laid out with three tracks, with the center track handling empties transferred from the outer two tracks by means of a transfer table. It was hoped that the new dock would serve the Spurr and Michigammi mines under exploration at the west end of Lake Michigammi, as well as other mines along the H&O.

Although construction work progressed at a fairly good rate throughout the summer, by fall things had slowed considerably due to rainy weather and several construction camp fires, making it unlikely the H&O could meet the 10-mile requirement before the end of the year. H&O president Walker pleaded at a November 17 meeting of the Michigan Board of Control that the railroad had entered into a contract to have the road finished by the time required, but bad weather and increased costs had set back the project. The H&O was granted an extension until May 15, 1872, to complete the first segment, and the contractor continued to press the work over the winter months despite sub-zero temperatures and heavy snowfall.

That winter, the H&O was reported to be surveying a line from Champion east to a connection with the C&NW, and the articles of association were changed on January 25, 1872, to provide for an eastern terminus at Marquette. The Marquette *Mining Journal*, an M&O RR ally, commented, "Without wishing to appear officious, we venture to suggest that it would be more in keeping with the public interest for the company [H&O] to expend the same effort in building that many miles from L'Anse westward, towards Houghton or Ontonagon."[6]

Walker tried to enlist Marquette to the H&O cause, writing: "Our present policy is to show the old Co. [M&O RR] that it is in their interests to consolidate the two companies and make one interest of it. This of course would make Marquette a much more important outlet than it is now. If the fact is established that they did not finish their road, then they forfeited their land grant, and they will be glad to unite with us. If they drive us away from Marquette we shall inevitably fall into the hands of the Chicago & N. W. and all the business of our line will be diverted to Chicago & N. W." This argument would prove to have little real merit as most of the commercial business would always gravitate toward Chicago, and the iron mines on the Western Marquette Range, being of poor quality, would generate little tonnage for Marquette.[7]

Discussions were held in Detroit between M&O RR and H&O representatives seeking to unite the two interests and thus put an end to "all entanglements."[8] Walker laid out the H&O's terms and said the only alternative was the courts. Negotiations did not progress smoothly as the H&O felt the M&O RR was asking too much for its property, and that it would be cheaper for the company to build an independent line into Marquette. The H&O's New York backers foolishly favored an independent line, directing the company's chief engineer to have surveys completed "with a view to construct such a line."[9] The M&O RR officials continued to try to escape their difficulties through a merger with the C&NW but were "repulsed or met with an illiberal spirit."[10]

The H&O faced problems of its own east of L'Anse. The May 15 deadline for completion of the first 10 miles of trackage was rapidly approaching and by early April only 7 or 8 miles of track had been laid. Fewer than 400 men were available to the contractors due to a labor shortage. Although the required 10 miles of track were completed by early May, frost in the ground hampered ballasting, and the road's work trains were tied up with the contractor who was grading additional mileage. Walker wrote Governor Baldwin promising that if the H&O was given an extension to September 1, the entire 32 miles of line from L'Anse to Champion would be operational. At a May 10 meeting of the Board of Control, an extension was granted to August 1.

The legal entanglements continued, with the M&O RR filing suit against the Farmer's Loan and Trust Company and the H&O, claiming the $2,000,000 loan granted in June 1871 created a lien upon M&O RR properties, which could not now be sold. The H&O in turn filed a brief with the General Land Office on May 3, 1872, supporting Michigan's claim that the M&O RR's grant should be forfeited. Several days later, however, the H&O requested that the brief be returned, as the merger negotiations being held in New York finally came to a successful conclusion.

MH&O RAILROAD

The land grant conflict and future disputes over handling through traffic were alleviated when the M&O RR and H&O boards of directors decided to merge on May 25, 1872, creating a new road known as the Marquette, Houghton & Ontonagon Railroad (MH&O). With a capitalization of $2,040,000, the MH&O filed articles of incorporation in the state of Michigan on September 2, 1872, inheriting all the rights, property, and franchises of the H&O and the M&O RR. Although Henry N. Walker was elected president and Samuel Ely, vice president, control of the new road rested largely with the eastern capitalists who had provided loans to fuel the expansion on the range. Among the directors were John Jacob Astor, Quincy A. Shaw, and Alexander Agassiz. Agassiz and Shaw, actively involved with Calumet and Hecla (C&H), rich copper mining interests on the Keweenaw Peninsula, would ensure that the MH&O did not dawdle in reaching the Copper Country.[11]

At the time of its forming, the MH&O was heavily involved in railroad construction. Although Walker had promised that the entire 32.78 miles from Champion to L'Anse would be completed by September 1872, the line was still 10 miles short in October. On the L'Anse end, 16 miles had been laid, but work on a large cut required several more months to complete. Construction also began off the east end junction with the old M&O RR just west of Champion, heading for Michigammi City. Upon completion of the big cut, track laying continued unabated and the last rail was laid on December 15, 1872. Chief Engineer Jacob Houghton, Assistant Engineer Chas. H. Palmer, and W. D. Williams, the road's attorney, brought an engine from the previously isolated H&O trackage all the way into Marquette, marking the first through movement. The new trackage was certified by Michigan governor John Bagley on January 6, 1873, and the MH&O received 178,121 acres of land for its effort. The grant for the remainder of the route to Ontonagon did not expire until January 1, 1878, but it was hoped the two mineral ranges would be joined by rail long before then.

An even more important advancement in passenger and freight travel on the UP came about with the opening of the C&NW's 65-mile line between Menominee and Escanaba on December 2, 1872. This resulted in the previously isolated MH&O and the C&NW Peninsula division being tied into the entire U.S. rail network for the first time. While putting an end to the isolation of the Upper Peninsula, the new line furthered the trend of driving the territory into the sphere of Chicago interests. The journey was not a swift one, with a 2½-hour stop at Menominee and an overnight at Escanaba. This caused the Marquette paper to comment, "Passengers from Chicago have no reason to complain of being tired on their arrival here. Of the forty-one hours time used, sixteen and a half are devoted to 'rest' waiting for trains."[12]

The new MH&O L'Anse extension allowed the Michigammi mine to make its first shipment in late November 1872. As result of Michigammi Mining Company's association with Iron Cliffs Iron Co., early ore shipments were interchanged with the C&NW for movement to Escanaba. Additional traffic was provided by the company sawmill at nearby Michigammi village which was capable of cutting 40,000 feet of lumber per day. The Spurr Mountain mine, a little over a mile west of Michigammi, received a double-ended siding in 1872. H&O President H. N. Walker had bought an interest in the Spurr Mountain property in the summer of 1872, becoming president of the firm. As a Chicago correspondent wrote of the MH&O management, "None of the officers are poor men, neither are they dependent upon their salaries. They are too deeply interested in the largest mines to quibble about compensation."[13]

The forlorn 5.5 miles of track along the south shore of Lake Michigammi fell into disrepair as mining activity failed to develop. Finally, in 1872, the always controversial trackage was listed as abandoned by the Michigan Railroad Commission. The MH&O directors were interested in serving the territory south of Champion, but felt it was better to do so by building west out of Republic. Surveys were started in late winter 1872, and a

This view shows the Marquette & Ontonagon grade along the south shore of Lake Michigamme slowly returning to nature. The Houghton & Ontonagon built along the north side of the lake on its way to Houghton, resulting in the abandonment of this much-disputed stub. *Courtesy of Roy Paananen*

1.77-mile spur was completed to the Kloman mine in 1874. Extending the branch north-westerly to the main line west of Champion would give Republic-area mines an outlet to reach the L'Anse ore dock.

Iron ore shipments for the MH&O's first year of operation in 1872 were stymied by the lack of vessel and rail capacity. Some mines were even unable to deliver the entire amount of their contracts. The MH&O haul reached 454,312 tons of iron ore, 28,991 tons of pig iron, and 38,570 tons of other freight that year. The Lake Superior Iron Company dominated all shippers, sending out 191,459 tons of ore to the docks and furnaces.

To improve ore handling, a new 350-foot extension, with 54 pockets, was added to the Cleveland dock in Marquette during the winter of 1872–1873. The L'Anse ore dock also came on line, with the bark *Cambridge* taking out the first load on May 30, 1873. Vessel captains and owners praised the prompt loading they received at L'Anse as well as the "ease [with which] they can sail out of the harbor on any wind." Shipments came primarily from the Spurr Mountain and the Michigammi mines. In addition to the depot, merchandise dock, and warehouse, railroad facilities at L'Anse included a 7-stall roundhouse and machine shops, used to service engines based on the west end of the line.[14]

New equipment was also purchased to ease the burden of moving the heavy ore traffic. To complement the sixteen engines inherited from the M&O RR and H&O, Su-

Engine 25 was one of three 4-6-0s ordered for freight service from Taunton in September 1872. Equipped with 54-inch drivers, these engines were the first new freight power purchased for the Marquette, Houghton & Ontonagon. *Collection of Harold K. Vollrath*

perintendent D. H. Merritt went east in September 1872 and ordered three passenger 4-4-0s (20–22) and three 4-6-0s (23–25) for freight service from Taunton Locomotive Works; they were to be delivered before the start of the next ore season. Townsend Engineering Company also constructed a small 0-4-0 (19) for ore dock service which was received in February 1873. Some questioned whether even this would be enough power, and the board of directors, at their November 13 meeting, decided to order five more 4-4-0s from Dickson. The Dickson engines (26–30) had 54-inch drivers, which allowed them to be used in passenger as well as freight service. The MH&O shops also completed work on a small switching locomotive (14). This massive program more than doubled the MH&O locomotive fleet and required the Marquette roundhouse to undergo a similar expansion.

With MH&O forecasting 1873's business at 800,000 tons, 700 ore cars were constructed in the Marquette shops over the winter of 1872–1873, with an order for an additional 300 going to a Chicago manufacturer. The Marquette shops were capable of turning out 3 ore cars a day, and the new construction more than doubled the fleet of 900 ore cars then in service. A new baggage-smoker and two new passenger coaches were also part of the winter program. In addition the MH&O shops somehow also found time to construct machinery for local mines.

The new locomotives and rolling stock allowed the MH&O to put 83 scheduled trains, mostly in ore service, on its 1873 summer time card. Two passenger trains provided daily service between Marquette and L'Anse. The morning mail and passenger from Marquette got into L'Anse at 11:55 AM, making connections for the Copper Country via the steamer *Ivanhoe*, which would leave Hancock at 7:30 in the morning, and, after a stop at Houghton, would arrive at L'Anse at 11:00 AM. Passengers for Marquette and points south would depart on the afternoon passenger around 2:20 PM, with the *Ivanhoe* departing at 2:00 PM for the Copper Country.

During the winter months, after navigation ceased, L'Anse developed into quite a transshipment point, with horse-drawn sleighs and wagons bringing down copper ingots from the Lake Superior Smelting company (just east of Hancock) and returning with supplies. Because of the smelter's location on Portage Lake (a body of water that split the Keweenaw Peninsula and fed on both ends into Lake Superior), most of its production went out by boat, except when the lake froze over. Passengers to and from the Copper Country were handled by sleighs of the L'Anse and Houghton Transit Company after the *Ivanhoe* tied up for the season.

The expanded equipment and facilities helped the Marquette Range ore production reach new heights in 1873, with over a million tons being sent out. The MH&O handled 659,084 tons of ore, compared with 503,922 on the C&NW. Ninety percent of all tonnage was still being handled by sailing ships, and the *Pelican* took out a record 1,250 tons of ore that season. People wondered how such a large boat could ever be profitable in the ore trade. People also worried that flooding the market with so much ore in one season would seriously hamper future mining operations. As it turned out, this figure would not be repeated for some time, due to the repercussions from the Panic which started with the failure of the Jay Cooke's banking house on September 18.

The price of pig iron fell as the result of the Panic, causing the short-lived Grace furnace in Marquette, which had gone into blast at the end of 1872 on the old Jackson dock site, to blow out on March 24, 1874, never to resume production. Another ill-timed Marquette furnace was the Carp, located at the mouth of the river of the same name. After receiving a 2.08-mile MH&O spur for inbound ore shipments, the Carp made its first cast on April 24, 1874, only to go out of production that December due to a poor iron market. The works were revived periodically for short periods until 1907. The remaining Marquette-area furnace, the Marquette and Pacific, closed in August 1881. Further west, Michigan Iron Company continued to work the Greenwood and Clarksburg furnaces, but they too succumbed to the inevitable as the firm filed for bankruptcy on January 4, 1875. Fire struck Morgan Iron's Champion Furnace on April 11, 1874, and with insufficient insurance, the works were not rebuilt. The Morgan Furnace at the top of the hill shut down for good in December 1876.

As the effects of the Panic were felt for some time after 1873, the MH&O made little effort to advance toward the Copper Country, causing Ontonagon to look for encouragement wherever it could. When the Wisconsin Central Railroad (WC), building south out of the new Lake Superior port of Ashland, Wisconsin, began survey work to connect with the NP at Northern Pacific Jct. (later Carlton), Minnesota, the *Miner* reported it would only be a matter of time before the MH&O was building into Ontonagon on its way to a transcontinental connection at Ashland. In reality, the MH&O had little money available for extensions. Earnings underwent a steep decline from $1,070,653 in 1873 to $552,671 in 1878, reflecting the erosion in demand for Marquette Range iron ore, a commodity which accounted for over 90 percent of the MH&O's traffic.

Although the Panic of 1873 put an end to any new expansions, the MH&O had developed impressive credentials. Thirty locomotives operated over 63.1 miles of main line and 45.7 miles of branches. Passenger service was provided by five coaches and four head-end cars. In keeping with the railroad's primary purpose, 1,696 4-wheeled ore cars dominated the freight equipment, with 28 boxcars and 73 flats rounding out the roster. As the MH&O was Marquette's largest employer, its 550 employees were the lifeblood of the community, whose very existence depended upon the road's shops, general offices, and transloading facilities for ore, pig iron, coal, and general merchandise. Aside from a

A large number of diminutive MH&O 4-wheel ore cars are seen at Lake Superior No. 4 shaft on June 3, 1879. The Lake Superior was the second-leading shipper on the MH&O that year after the Republic mine.   *Paananen Collection*

few train and enginemen who manned outlying jobs on the Marquette Range and at L'Anse, the turnaround nature of the MH&O runs allowed most of these employees to make Marquette their home.

Management of the MH&O in 1873 came increasingly under the control of New York men associated with the Delaware, Lackawanna and Western. Samuel Sloan, president of the Lackawanna, assumed the same position on the MH&O, replacing Walker. Samuel Schoch, formerly of the Morris & Essex, a Lackawanna acquisition, took over as general manager. Samuel P. Ely also retired from the vice presidency of the MH&O and related mine holdings at this time. Ely had watched over the Iron Mountain and Marquette and Ontonagon railroads during their formative years and managed to obtain the necessary financial backing from the East to allow their survival. He went on to invest in the Minnesota Iron Company, which operated on the new Vermillion Range. Ely, Minnesota, one of the principal communities on that range, is named in his honor. Ely died in Paris in 1900.

The MH&O's operations were always very seasonal, given the cessation of ore hauling during the winter months. Only sixteen of the MH&O's thirty locomotives were needed to keep the traffic moving during the winter of 1874–1875, as train mileage was cut in half from its summertime peak. With the start of the 1875 ore season, twelve additional trains were added. Five of these went out as far as Ishpeming, four to Republic, and one to Champion. Two additional trains made a round trip from Michigamme to the L'Anse docks. These movements resulted in 463,939 tons of ore being handled through Marquette and an additional 70,003 tons through L'Anse for the 1875 season. Ore shipments for 1878 finally edged over a million tons as the economy awakened from its lethargy following the Panic of five years before. Movements from the MH&O-served docks at L'Anse and

A gang of ore punchers is depicted on the Marquette ore dock. Their long rods were used to poke loose stubborn iron ore from the cars into the dock pockets and also out of the pockets into the chutes. *Paananen Collection*

Marquette totaled 566,245 tons, with the remainder moving via Escanaba and the C&NW. The largest shipper that year was the Republic mine, which sent out 176,223 tons.

A number of mines reopened in 1879, and MH&O received over 50,000 tons of ore that year from the Republic, Lake Superior, Champion, Cleveland, and Michigamme. The Michigamme shipped their product via both the L'Anse and Marquette docks, as well as about a third to Escanaba, via the C&NW. Traffic from the furnaces never did seem to recover from the Panic, due to higher costs for diminishing charcoal supplies, coupled with lower pig iron prices. Only the Carp and Pioneer furnaces shipped over the MH&O in 1879. The pig iron continued to be transloaded to lake boats at the MH&O merchandise dock at Marquette.

The continuing recovery in iron ore (prices at Lake Erie mills were above $9 a ton) saw the MH&O construct a number of spurs into new mining developments on the western Marquette Range in the early 1880s. The principal of these were a spur to the Boston mine, a mile east of Clarksburg, built in 1880, and the Wetmore and Beaufort mine spurs, built in 1882, 1 mile and 2.7 miles west of Michigamme respectively. The largely hematite mines on the western Marquette Range, never capable of producing the same quality of ore as their counterparts on the eastern range, were generally operated only in times of high ore prices. The recession of 1884 quickly put a stop to most of the western production.

Vessel owners came to feel that the increased ore business was being poorly handled by the MH&O. At times up to fifty ships lay at anchor behind Marquette breakwater waiting their turn at the ore dock. Over the winter of 1881–1882, the MH&O attempted to address this problem by adding a 450-foot extension to its dock. This provided sixty additional pockets or 5,000 tons capacity to the original 6,000-ton dock. The new extension, 2.5 feet higher than the old dock, had 80-ton pockets which were spaced so they would line up with a string of ore cars. This was not the case on the older part of the dock, a circumstance that necessitated much additional switching. The old dock was raised 2.5 feet to match the new construction.

REAWAKENING THE "SOUTH SHORE" RAILROAD

There were new stirrings in early 1880 about the "South Shore" railroad. Duluth, having shaken its nearly deadly bout with the Panic of 1873, was now a growing metropolis of 30,000 seeking a railroad outlet along the south shore of Lake Superior to provide year-round links with Eastern Canada, New England, and Detroit. This impetus became stronger with the June 1879 takeover of the St. Paul and Duluth by James J. Hill's St. Paul, Minneapolis and Manitoba and various Chicago roads. The building of the south shore road was thought to be an ideal way to shake the "Chicago anaconda." Col. J. B. Culver of Duluth led the organizing efforts and seemingly won support in many quarters.[15]

Encouragement from Minneapolis and St. Paul came from W. D. Washburn, president of the Minneapolis and St. Louis, who envisioned extending his road to a port on Lake Superior while another branch headed to the Montreal River. Traffic would utilize the Lake Superior port during navigation season, while the Montreal branch would handle the winter traffic. How a line east of the Montreal River was to survive with only four to five months' worth of traffic was not made apparent.

In the East, control of the MH&O had recently changed from a New York–based directorate to one composed largely of Bostonians. Reflecting this change, J. L. Stackpole was elected president in place of Samuel Sloan, and the head offices were moved to Boston. Samuel Schoch retained the post of general manager, with headquarters in Marquette. The new management saw the south shore route as a positive development not only for the MH&O, but for Boston, and agreed to build off their line at Three Lakes to the Ontonagon River, the west end of their land grant. MH&O surveyors were put into the field that spring for the nearly 40-mile route, which would bypass Ontonagon. The line was said to be an easy one, and it was hoped the board of directors would view the report favorably so construction could commence.

NP President Frederick Billings, under pressure from the states of Wisconsin and Michigan to fulfill the railroad's charter, promised to have a line from Duluth to the Montreal River—the east end of their grant—"built in time to connect with the eastern links." The NP also put surveyors in the field, and after a meeting of the NP board of directors that fall, President Charles Colby of the Wisconsin Central said everything was ready to commence active work the following year. The *Duluth Tribune* quoted Colonel Gray, an NP attorney, as saying that the road would no longer "pay tribute" to the Chicago and Milwaukee roads and would build all the way to L'Anse if necessary.[16]

Culver and other Duluth men, as well as General Manager Schoch, formed a new company, the Ontonagon and Montreal River Railroad Company, to build the 50 miles between the NP and MH&O land grants, and raised a subscription for surveys. Another party to sign on to the south shore plan was the Detroit, Mackinac & Marquette Railroad, currently constructing a line in the eastern UP between Marquette and the Straits of Mackinac. They agreed to build a short branch into Sault Ste. Marie to complete the link with prospective Canadian roads. A committee of these various factions and the Wisconsin Central met in Boston on September 18, 1880, to consider the proposals. Even the financial markets became enthusiastic about the MH&O, given its potential as part of a through route between the East and West. The land grant was also thought to be valuable, with property selling at good prices to local mining companies.

The south shore route's viability took a turn for the worse with the formation of the Canadian Pacific Railroad in 1880. Its charter for an all-Canada line to the Pacific Coast largely brought an end to any hope for an international transcontinental route along the south shore of Lake Superior. The NP, with Henry Villard assuming the presidency, also seemed to cool on the eastern extension, having more than enough commitments in hand to complete the road to Puget Sound. The St. Paul *Pioneer Press* quoted NP Vice President Thomas Oakes as saying that his road was compelled to build to the Montreal River by its charter, and that the remainder of the road would be built by the Marquette roads, but that "all these things are things of the future, about which there is nothing definite to be said."[17]

By 1882 the MH&O had no intention of ever going to Ontonagon, and a bill was introduced in the Michigan legislature to allow the road to build directly west from the Three Lakes area to the Montreal River. At the Montreal River it was hoped the Northern Pacific would be waiting or at least on its way. A time extension was also asked by the MH&O, who said construction could not begin towards the Montreal until the NP's intentions were known. At that time the southern part of Ontonagon County was nothing more than a "howling wilderness, with no human habitation south or west of Rockland." L'Anse and Ontonagon interests were opposed to the line change, not wanting to be left off the transcontinental map. The horrendous grade coming east out of L'Anse, worse than anything the NP would encounter crossing the Rockies or the Cascades, made their stand difficult to defend. The area between Three Lakes and the Montreal River was rich in timber, and as early as 1881 large timber interests were buying up the best pinelands.[18]

Ontonagon residents, tired of waiting for rail connections, formed their own company, the Ontonagon and Brule River Railroad Company (O&BR) on September 10, 1880. The line would build south from Ontonagon to a connection with the Milwaukee and Northern (M&N), then building north out of Green Bay. After obtaining a transfer of the old Ontonagon & State Line land grant from the Michigan legislature in 1881, the O&BR began construction on July 11, 1881, and completed its first 20-mile segment, to a short distance beyond Rockland, on February 11, 1882. The O&BR interests then petitioned the Michigan Board of Control to disallow the MH&O land grant between Rockland and Ontonagon as unnecessary duplication. Detroit business interests, no doubt afraid the O&BR would further pull the UP into Chicago's sphere of influence, objected and sought to force the MH&O to extend to Ontonagon in 1882 so they could fairly compete. The Board of Control took no action after the MH&O promised to connect with the O&BR that season.[19]

THE HOUGHTON EXTENSION

The residents of Houghton and the Copper Country did not view the expensive and cumbersome transloading operation at L'Anse favorably. Through the efforts of Jay A. Hubbell, a director of the Mineral Range railroad, Edwin J. Hulbert, discoverer of the Calumet and Hecla copper lode, and others, the Michigan legislature awarded, on April 27, 1875, a state swamp land grant of five sections to the mile to any party who would construct a line from L'Anse to Houghton. Nothing came of the incentive given the tough economic times, and the Houghton paper commented, "The Legislature by its niggardly taxable bestowal shows how little sympathy the enterprise has in that quarter." Hubbell and others sought to revive the project with the formation of the Houghton and L'Anse Railroad Company on June 4, 1881. This company, with a capitalization of $1,000,000, was to build a 33-mile line between those points, but took little action aside from some surveying.[20]

The MH&O finally agreed to launch its Houghton extension in the fall of 1882. A contract to construct the first 10 miles towards Houghton was awarded to Thomas McKeown, whose workers began clearing and tackling some of the heavier cuts on December 15, 1882. At L'Anse, the line curved off the main line one-half mile west and some 80 feet above the merchandise dock. This also became the site of the new L'Anse depot. On February 1, 1883, the MH&O purchased a controlling interest in the Houghton & L'Anse, thereby acquiring its franchise and the 70,000-acre land grant.[21]

By April 1883 some 10 miles had been graded out of L'Anse when the Little Carp flooded and washed out part of the line. It was decided to span the 75-foot-high Little Carp gorge with a 180-foot-long iron lattice girder bridge, which took Rust and Coolidge of Chicago two months to construct. McKeown was awarded the contract for the remainder of the line into Houghton, which would be comparatively easy, aside from a 195-foot bridge over the Sturgeon River and a 2,200-foot span over the Pike River.

By June 1883 the MH&O had graded some 16 miles north of L'Anse. Soon after, difficulties arose in obtaining a right of way west of the Pilgrim River between the bluffs and Portage Lake. At the condemnation hearing, the commissioners gave the property such a high valuation that the MH&O announced it was calling in its contractor and would make its terminus at the Pilgrim River. This no doubt caught the eye of Houghton residents, who had had enough long sleigh rides to catch the train, and the outcome of a new valuation proceeding proved more satisfactory to the MH&O. Terminal facilities at Houghton were laid out at a site east of town, where some 30,000 cubic yards were removed from a nearby hill to make a level site for the depot, freight house, turntable, and water tank along Portage Lake. Rails had been laid some 20 miles out of L'Anse by the first of September, with grading largely completed except for the disputed territory.

The line formally opened on November 14, 1883, when some 140 Copper Country guests braved cold weather and a snow storm to ride an excursion from Houghton to Marquette and back. The excursion engine was gaily decorated with U.S. flags, and draped around the headlight was a chain made up of six alternating links of copper and iron, symbolizing the tying together of the iron and copper ranges. After an inspection the following day by Governor Josiah W. Begole, Michigan Railroad Commissioner Innes, President Stackpole, and General Manager Schoch, the new line was pronounced as qualifying the MH&O to obtain some 82,450 acres of land from the State of Michigan.

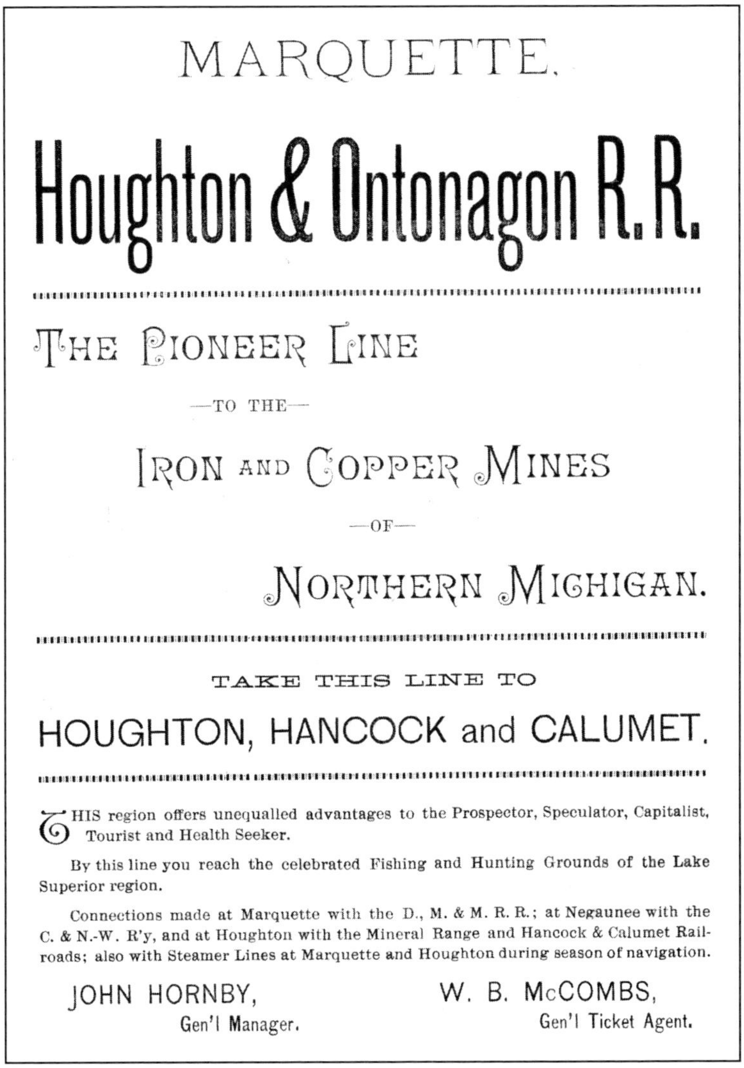

MARQUETTE,
Houghton & Ontonagon R.R.
THE PIONEER LINE
—TO THE—
IRON AND COPPER MINES
—OF—
NORTHERN MICHIGAN.
TAKE THIS LINE TO
HOUGHTON, HANCOCK and CALUMET.
THIS region offers unequalled advantages to the Prospector, Speculator, Capitalist, Tourist and Health Seeker.
By this line you reach the celebrated Fishing and Hunting Grounds of the Lake Superior region.
Connections made at Marquette with the D., M. & M. R. R.; at Negaunee with the C. & N.-W. R'y, and at Houghton with the Mineral Range and Hancock & Calumet Railroads; also with Steamer Lines at Marquette and Houghton during season of navigation.
JOHN HORNBY,
Gen'l Manager.
W. B. McCOMBS,
Gen'l Ticket Agent.

An MH&O advertisement found in the 1885 *Marquette City Directory*. *Perron Collection*

The MH&O extended daily passenger service into Houghton on November 19, 1883, with the Railway Post Office following suit on December 1. Additional MH&O passenger service covered the mining district with two daily round trips out of Michigamme to Marquette, the "Chicago Special" between Marquette and Ishpeming (making connections with the C&NW), and the stub runs between Humboldt and Republic.[22]

Although L'Anse had benefited greatly over the summer, serving as the supply base for the new construction, the community suffered from the loss of transloading operations over the winter months. This trade had employed over one hundred men and teams in past seasons. Another casualty of change was the steamer *Ivanhoe,* which for a dozen years had carried Copper Country residents between Houghton and the MH&O dock at L'Anse. As she steamed out of Houghton for the last time on November 18, 1883, for new duties in Detroit, salutes were exchanged with the whistles of the stamp mills, mines, and locomotives along Portage Lake, as many residents waved a last farewell.

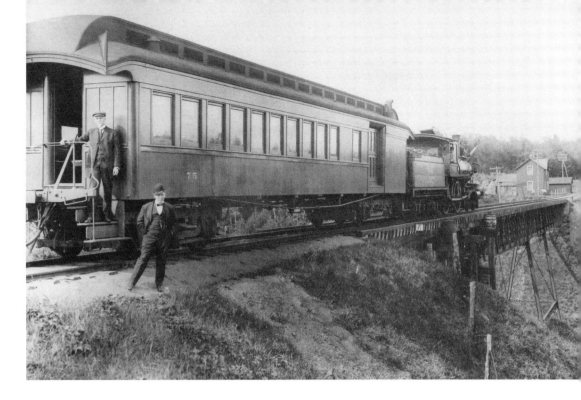

Iron Bridge, MP 26 on the Houghton line, was considered quite an engineering feat in its day. Two 70- and one 40-foot lattice deck girders and a 58½-foot trestle approach were used to cross the 80-foot-deep ravine of the Little Carp River.
Paananen Collection

As the MH&O finally came out of the doldrums associated with the Panic of 1873, it addressed the need to serve the new west end mines coming on line by ordering two road locomotives and three switch engines from Rogers during the winter of 1881–1882. The two road engines (31, 32), of the Mogul type, were the largest locomotives ever received by the MH&O. The two new 40-ton 0-6-0s (33, 34) dwarfed the little 0-4-0s then in yard service, while the remaining switch engine (35), although an 0-4-0, was 5 tons heavier than those already on the roster. In addition 200 new ore cars were purchased and 50 constructed in the MH&O shops. The homemade cars served as replacements for a like number retired, giving a net of 200 over the previous season.

Over the winter of 1882–1883, Samuel Schoch put in another large equipment order in anticipation of new traffic off the Houghton extension as well as bright iron mining prospects. Seven new locomotives were ordered from Hinkley, four of which were road engines and three switch engines. The road power consisted of two Moguls (36, 37) of the same general dimensions as the two received from Rogers in 1882, and two 37-ton Americans (38, 39) with 60-inch drivers. The three switchers (40–42) were 30-ton 0-4-0s. Another 200 ore cars were also ordered.

The Houghton extension was partly financed with bonds, but as the MH&O was felt to have a high capitalization per mile of road, this was alleviated by retiring $2,500,000 of land grant bonds through the sale of its remaining property to Michigan Land and Iron Company. The original construction bonds still outstanding were also

The MH&O passenger train schedule as it appeared in the Marquette *Mining Journal* on April 23, 1885.   *Perron Collection*

MARQUETTE,
Houghton & Ontonagon
RAILROAD.

TIME TABLE—IN EFFECT DEC. 7TH., 1884.

GOING WEST.

STATIONS.	PASS. NO. 3.	SUNDY NO. 7.	MAIL No. 1.	PASS NO. 5
	A. M.	P. M.	P. M.	P. M.
Marquette.........	8.40	12.30	12.45	5.26
Negaunee.........	9.10	1.00	1.35	5.50
Ishpeming.........	9.20	1 10	1.56	6.00
Clarksburgh.......	9.42	.....	2.14	6.24
Humboldt.........	9.46	.....	2.19	6.28
(Republic)	10.15	.....	2.45	7.00
Champion.........	9.55	.....	2.28	6.37
Michigamme	10.20	.....	2.50	7.00
L'Anse............	.....	.....	3.50	.....
Baraga............	.....	.....	4.05	.....
Houghton.........	.....	.....	5.10	.....
Hancock..........	.....	.....	5.40	.....
	A. M.	P. M.	P. M.	P. M.

GOING EAST.

STATIONS.	PASS. NO. 4.	MAIL NO. 2.	SUNDY NO. 8.	PASS. NO. 6.
	A. M.	A. M.	P. M.	P. M.
Hancock	.....	9.00	.....	....
Houghton	.....	9.30	.....	.....
Baraga............	.....	10.35	....	.....
L'Anse	.....	10.50	....	....
Michigamme	7.40	11.50	.....	3.00
Champion.........	8.05	12.20	.....	3.25
(Republic)........	7.45	12.00	.....	3.05
Humboldt.........	8.15	12.30	.....	3.35
Clarksburgh.......	8.18	12.34	.....	3.39
Ishpeming.........	8.40	1.00	1.25	4.00
Negaunee	8.50	1.35	1.35	.10
Marquette.........	9.20	2.05	2.05	.40
	A. M.	P. M.	P.	

Train No. 1 connects at Negaunee with C. & N W. R'y train to and from Chicago, and for Houghton and the copper district.

Train No. 2 connects at Negaunee with C. & N. W. R'y to and from Chicago, and at Marquette with D., M. & M. B. R. for Detroit.

Trains Nos. 1, 2, 3, 4, 5 and 6 run daily except Sundays.

Trains Nos. 7 and 8 run Sundays only, and connect at Negaunee with C. & N. W R'y. to and from Chicago.

JOHN HORNBY,   W. B. McCOMBS,
Gen'l Manager.   Gen'l Ticket Agt

General Offices; MARQUETTE MICH.

9 '84

converted into preferred stock. Although well on the way to new prosperity by the summer of 1884, the MH&O then came upon a major challenge. A new competitor started cutting into the monopoly the road had enjoyed between Marquette and the iron range for almost 30 years.

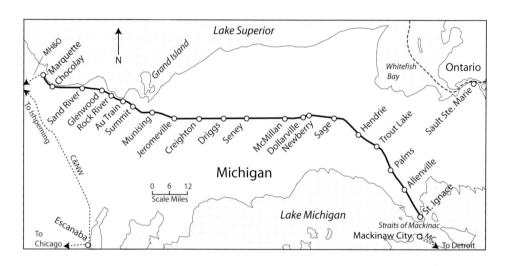

Detroit, Mackinac & Marquette Railroad, 1882

3

THE MACKINAC ROAD

Although the two peninsulas of Michigan were one in name, geographically they were quite isolated, especially for four to five months each winter when there was no navigation on the Great Lakes. A railroad tying the two halves together through the Straits of Mackinac had long been desired for both political and business purposes. The only available option for traveling or shipping goods by rail from Detroit to Marquette necessitated going through the "foreign soil" of Indiana, Illinois, and Wisconsin, adding some 300 miles in the process.[1]

Beginning in 1856, a number of appeals were sent off to Washington by the Michigan legislature asking for a grant of lands to be used in the construction of a railroad out of Detroit to Lake Superior. The gap in federal land grants between the Straits of Mackinac and Marquette was said to be a horrible omission and would drastically impede the region's development. The *Detroit Free Press* said "it is certain that the general government will not sell the lands along this line in the next quarter of a century unless a road is built." Unfortunately, due to perceived abuses on the part of the Union Pacific and Northern Pacific, the desire to issue new grants had cooled considerably by 1872. Congress also realistically felt that important areas of Michigan's Upper Peninsula were more naturally served by existing rail lines in Wisconsin and Minnesota, and that the eastern UP was little more than a wasteland.[2]

There was no doubt that the UP was turning increasingly towards Chicago and Milwaukee with its trade, especially since the opening of the Peninsula Railroad in 1864. Marquette was reputed to have bought more goods from Detroit in 1857 than it did in 1873, despite the tremendous growth in the area. Since the completion of the C&NW, about 75 percent of the business once enjoyed by Detroit jobbers had been diverted to Chicago suppliers. Even a railroad across the eastern UP, however, would not erase the greater distances Detroit would face in competing with Milwaukee and Chicago jobbers for the business of the iron and copper ranges.

About the only enticement the state of Michigan could offer a prospective railroad builder across the eastern UP was its swamplands, some 1,789,613 acres of which in the UP had been given by the federal government to aid in development projects. This acreage had been judged by federal surveyors to be "overflowed" and "unfit" for farming. If more than half a 40-acre subdivision was swamp it was given to the state in which it was located. Seeking to take advantage of a swampland grant, William L. Wetmore and others of Marquette filed articles for the Marquette, Sault Ste. Marie and Mackinaw Railroad (MSSM&M) on December 23, 1872. They proposed to build from Marquette to the Sault and a branch to the Straits of Mackinac, with a capitalization of $6,000,000. An unusual 3.5-foot gauge was specified, which seems illogical given the road was talked of as a possible link in a transcontinental system connecting the NP with Eastern Canada and the Lower Peninsula.[3]

Details of the swampland grant were finalized in a bill passed by the Michigan legislature in 1873, which gave ten sections of swamplands for each mile of standard gauge railroad constructed between the Straits of Mackinac and Marquette. Parties were to express an interest by July 1, post a $10,000 bond, and complete all construction by December 31, 1875. After the MSSM&M's bid was accepted, a survey party went out into the field in June 1873. The 150-mile line, as located, followed the south shore of Lake Superior from Marquette to Au Train, where it began to climb out of the Lake Superior basin on a ruling grade of 63 feet to the mile. Upon reaching the summit, at a point opposite Grand Island, the rest of the route proved comparatively easy due to the much more gradual descent to Lake Michigan. At Point La Barbe, a car ferry connection would be made across the Straits of Mackinac to old Mackinaw, said to be the destination of two roads under construction in Lower Michigan.

Unfortunately for the MSSM&M, completion of its survey work coincided with the beginning of the Panic of 1873. This put a stop to the great majority of railroad projects in the country, especially speculative ones such as MSSM&M. The state felt that the reasons for the original grant were still valid, and Governor John Bagley, addressing the legislature on January 7, 1875, said, "I do not know that any action can be taken by you that will hasten the work; but if any responsible and proper addition to the grant would do it, I most earnestly recommend it. . . . When it is remembered that we have in the Upper Peninsula a population of 61,800 persons, who export everything they produce, and import everything they consume, it would seem that this great commerce of our citizens ought not be to be diverted from us to other states, as it is now."[4]

The legislature improved the terms of the swampland grant in early 1875, and also extended its completion date to December 31, 1877. The new bill made the lands exempt from taxation for 16 years or until sold. Under the original act, lands became subject to taxation as soon as they were awarded to the railroad. The idea was to help local governments, but the local populace said that no taxes were currently generated under state ownership and that only with a railroad would development be assured. Some of the counties along the route were even losing population. The number of sections awarded for each mile of line was also increased from ten to sixteen.[5]

No matter how much land was given out, many doubted its worth. Much of the land was tamarack and cedar swamps. Many viewed with skepticism reports that lands traversed by the proposed railroad would prove as valuable as prairie for wheat growing, with shorter distances to the market. The C&NW, seeking to maintain its monopoly on the UP, was also quick to "advise" prospective builders on the short comings of the eastern UP. How much of the region's business Detroit would gain was also questionable, given the shorter distance to Chicago. Perhaps some NP business would filter down into Detroit, but the closest NP trackage was still many miles to the west, and the new road as yet lacked Lower Peninsula connections at Mackinaw City or Canadian connections at the Sault. For whatever reason, even with the new provisions, the MSSM&M was unable to secure financing.[6]

For lack of a viable alternative, the Board of Control had no choice but to award the expanded swampland grant to the old MSSM&M backers on May 8, 1876. Further ex-

James McMillan, as President of the Detroit, Mackinac & Marquette, was one of the main backers of the scheme to reestablish Detroit's dominance in the Upper Peninsula of Michigan. *Courtesy Archives of Michigan*

tensions were gained from the legislature to December 31, 1879, and then to December 31, 1881. This in turn caused grumbling in the UP about the 1,326,965 acres of land seemingly tied up without purpose. The MSSM&M agreed on January 9, 1879, to transfer the grant to any group willing to complete the project.[7]

DETROIT, MACKINAC & MARQUETTE RAILROAD

James McMillan and a group of other prominent Detroit businessmen provided the first real hope of taking back the UP from the Chicago interests with the formation of the Detroit, Mackinac and Marquette Railroad on August 20, 1879. Like the ill-fated MSSM&M, the DM&M would be 150 miles in length, and would run from the Straits of Mackinac to Marquette. Capitalization was set at $1,200,000, with the rest of the money to be raised by bonds. McMillan was elected president and George Hendrie, secretary-treasury.[8]

McMillan, born in Hamilton, Ontario, in 1838, was the son of one of the founders of the Great Western Railroad. After receiving a public school education, McMillan came to Detroit at 17 years of age and took a job as a purchasing agent for the Detroit and Milwaukee Railroad. Later work as a supply agent for a railroad contractor allowed him to acquire enough means to become a founder of the Michigan Car Works in 1864. Subsequent investments in Detroit real estate and the Detroit and Cleveland Navigation Co. made McMillan a millionaire.

The McMillan syndicate wasted little time, reaching agreement on September 4, 1879, with the Board of Control to complete 20 miles of the DM&M by July 1, 1880, and the entire road by December 31, 1881. Survey work on the first 40 miles east out of Marquette—the most difficult portion of the route until the divide between Lake Superior and Lake Michigan was reached—began on October 14, 1879. After the first 20 miles of road had been located, Donald McDermid and John S. Hendrie were given a contract to make the segment ready for steel. They moved their outfits into position near Chocolay on January 19, 1880, and began work on rock cuts and filling bridge approaches.

Survey work continued over the winter on the east end, with one crew starting out of Point St. Ignace and another going east from Munising to meet them. Besides connections with the Michigan Central (MC) and Grand Rapids and Indiana (GR&I) railroads at Mackinaw, the DM&M envisioned a line into Sault Ste. Marie to connect with the new Canadian Pacific. The desire for a short branch into the Sault kept the main line running to the north before cutting sharply to the southeast to reach the Straits. The Sault branch was to be built by the Sault Ste. Marie and Marquette Railroad Company, formed by the DM&M syndicate on February 6, 1880. The idea of using a separate company to build the branch was short-lived, and the DM&M franchise was altered on July 20, 1881, to provide for a 48-mile branch from a point "about 50 miles from Pt. St. Ignace to village of Sault Ste. Marie." Although the line into the Sault was located in early 1881, the DM&M had its hands full with existing construction and the Canadian Pacific had only advanced to French River, Ontario, still some ways off.[9]

McDermid and Hendrie were able to make good progress over the winter of 1879–1880, and by May 1, the first 20-mile segment was nearly graded. As a result of this fine showing, the DM&M awarded the contractors an additional 22 miles. Some 400 men and 50 teams were at work by mid-May between Glenwood and Munising. The first rail was landed at Marquette in late May 1880, and a steel gang put to work. To expedite track laying and ballasting, 20 flat cars were sent to Marquette, followed on June 12 by a 32-ton locomotive off the Michigan Central. The platform cars were right out of McMillan's Michigan Car Company shops and proudly carried "Detroit, Mackinac & Marquette Railroad" on their sides.

The tracklayers reached the end of the first 20-mile segment on July 23, 1880. Over 16 miles of line had been ballasted, and citizens who went out to watch a spike-driving ceremony were treated to a 40-mile-per-hour ride. The DM&M put on an accommodation train each way daily between Glenwood and Marquette to take care of hauling supplies and what commercial business could be found. On August 24, 1880, Governor Charles M. Croswell and members of the Michigan Board of Control examined the first 20-mile section between Marquette and Glenwood, and, finding it met all requirements, transferred 128,000 acres of state swampland to the DM&M.

Matters progressed slowly on the second 20-mile section due to labor shortages. Track laying commenced east out of Glenwood in early September and proceeded to mile 25, where it was stymied by incomplete trestlework. By Christmas, the tracklayers had reached Rock River, where a turntable was installed so that the DM&M could extend service to that point. Although track laying continued to the east, Rock River remained the temporary terminus due to the lack of business—an unfortunate omen of things to come.

Another Canadian contractor, John D. McDonald, was given a contract for the first 60 miles west of the new port terminal of St. Ignace. Work did not begin until May 25, 1880, as men and supplies were held up by ice conditions in the Straits. Pile driving commenced on a new dock at St. Ignace on June 29. Labor shortages quickly set in, and by mid-July grading had only progressed 6 miles. Two new DM&M locomotives and more flat cars arrived in St. Ignace by lake vessel in late July 1880 and were unloaded on the company dock. There they awaited the arrival of the first rail, which came shortly thereafter. Work trains were put on, but after a month's time only 2 to 3 miles of steel were laid. By the end of October, 15 miles had been completed, and tracklayers were 35 miles out by the first of the year.

Conditions in the swampy, roadless wilderness were less than ideal. A half dozen men came down with typhoid, from which several died before reaching Marquette. The attending physician assured the remaining laborers that the fatalities were caused by "exposure met with on the trip to this city by boat, than by the fever itself." Relying on small boats traversing Lake Superior to bring supplies to the front was also hazardous, as witnessed by the swamping of the sail yacht *Starlight* on Sept. 29, 1880, with the loss of five men.[10]

The DM&M found itself short of funds to launch the next season's campaign, and on June 1, 1881, it negotiated a $3,000,000 loan from Central Trust Company of New York in exchange for a mortgage on the railroad property and its earnings. An additional $1,500,000 was lent based on the sale of 400,000 acres of swamplands to be received upon completion of the road. The DM&M issued still another $4,560,000 of land grant bonds that same day, backed by lands not covered under the Central Trust mortgage.

As the weather turned favorable in May 1881, tracklayers on the west end were putting down 1 mile of steel a day, and by early June they reached a point near Munising. With the completion deadline of December 1881 not far off, the DM&M contractors increased their pay rates in an attempt to attract more men. For terminal grounds at Marquette, the DM&M purchased a 40-acre tract of waterfront, between the Ely residence and Jackson Street, from the Champion Iron Company. A portion of the hillside to the west was blasted away and used to fill the lakeshore. Besides yard trackage, the DM&M built a temporary roundhouse at the east end of the property and a frame freight house on Lake Street, both of which went into service in early 1881.

Tracklayers on the east end reached Sage, near the prospective junction with the Sault branch, in mid-August 1881, and by mid-September were in the vicinity of McMillan. Labor shortages continued to hamper the work, as did a forest fire near Munising which destroyed some 15,000 ties destined for the road. Heavy rains came in the fall and caused great hardship. In September it rained for almost sixteen days straight. Though 100 miles of steel had been laid by the end of the month, 50 more remained to close the gap. Men had to stand in 3 feet of water while grading across the Tahquamegon swamps near Newberry. Their perseverance paid off, and only 3 miles of grading and 12 miles of steel remained by the first week of November. The track work on the west end reached the end of McDermid and Hendrie's contract, 92.5 miles east of Marquette, on November 25.

December 7, 1881, saw the long-awaited day arrive. A special train left Marquette headed for the Straits with contractor and now General Superintendent Thomas McKeown, Marquette pioneer and businessman Peter White, Land Agent William O. Strong, contractor John S. Hendrie, and other assorted guests and reporters. Their departure was premature, as it was not until the morning of the 9th that the gap was closed. Three of the dignitaries took turns giving speeches and driving spikes, after which Peter White was to deliver the final blows. White was about to utter some thoughts as well, but was told by one of the hundred or so laborers in attendance, "Dhrive that nail if yer goin' to—we've heard bosh enough." The special arrived at St. Ignace at six o'clock, where 2,000 people were on hand to watch it pull under an arch of evergreens decorated with flags and banners. With the train arriving in darkness, quite a show was created when thousands of rockets and Roman candles were shot from the arch in celebration.[11]

On December 20, 1881, Governor David H. Jerome, Railroad Commissioner J. H. Williams, and the DM&M directors journeyed across the Straits on the *Algomah*,

The old DM&M's Jackson Street freight house in the Lower Yard at Marquette was used until a new brick freight station was built on the hill near the passenger depot in 1912. The box car visible at the platform belongs to one of the South Shore's connections at Mackinaw City, the Grand Rapids & Indiana, later absorbed by the Pennsylvania Railroad. *Wesley Perron Railroad Collection, Peter White Public Library, Marquette, Mich.*

having viewed the newly completed Michigan Central road into Mackinaw City the day before. At St. Ignace, the party boarded a DM&M special which whisked them to Marquette in 7-plus hours. Everyone marveled upon arrival at how quickly the line had been carved out of the wilderness. The Board of Control met on December 29, authorizing transfer of the full swampland grant to the DM&M.

To dispense the land grant and fill up the surrounding country, the DM&M land department, under William Strong, was formed in October 1879. Land agents were sent to Canada and even England to encourage immigrants to come and settle along the line. The railroad built wagon roads into the country and donated property for schools, churches, and cemeteries. Locaters met the new arrivals and took them to their sites. They put a positive spin on the land's agricultural value, saying the numerous swamplands were mainly due to beaver dams. When these were removed, the water would be confined to natural streams and the exposed land could be made extremely productive. The territory's average growing season of 108 days and its 40 degree mean temperature were probably not emphasized. Squatters who had occupied the land before the DM&M was given control were sold their land at unimproved prices. Speculators were discouraged, and the DM&M land department was noted for being liberal in times of hardship.

The DM&M founded seven experimental farms and spent $42,000 draining 75,000 acres of swampland in an attempt to make it suitable for agriculture. In spite of these efforts, land sales and settlement were slow to develop. It remained to be seen whether settlers could make a living, given the soil conditions and short growing season. The conditions east of Newberry were especially troublesome, with numerous swamps and morasses. Following lack of interest from the farmers, it was said that there were likely iron deposits along the line, and that the hardwood lumber would make fine charcoal for the furnaces that would follow. The DM&M even began planting wild rice in the lakes and marshes along its route in hopes that ducks would remain throughout the summer months to provide targets for hunters.

Although the line met requirements for the grant, there was still much to be done. Ballasting was not completed until early 1882 and track speed in some places was only 15 miles per hour. The DM&M instituted regular passenger service on December 19, 1881, but the run took almost 12 hours on account of track conditions. As the Michigan Central had yet to start service into Mackinaw City, all business was local in nature. The telegraph line along the DM&M was ready for use December 29, bringing further civilization to the eastern UP.

Early freight traffic consisted largely of charcoal shipments to the furnaces along the line. The recently opened Martell furnace at St. Ignace received a seventeen-car ore shipment from a new mine just west of Champion, called the Dalliba, during the first week of operation. Although the Martell would close in 1893, a more important operation was constructed at Newberry by the Vulcan Furnace Company, with funds from the DM&M syndicate. Nearby woodlands provided fuel, while the DM&M hauled iron ore from the Marquette Range and finished products to St. Ignace. Just to the west of Newberry, Robert Dollar, who bought a sizable tract of pine from the DM&M in 1882, constructed a large mill at Dollarville. Dollar's Peninsular Lumber Company mill came to produce 6,000,000 feet of lumber per year, and, as it was an interior mill lacking lake access, it ensured a lumber haul to the DM&M. Some traffic was also received at St. Ignace off regular Lake Superior Transit and New England Transit Company vessels bringing freight shipments from Detroit.

MACKINAC TRANSPORTATION COMPANY

Large additions to the DM&M's traffic hopefully were to come from the exchange of goods and raw materials with the Lower Peninsula via connections with the Michigan Central (MC) and Grand Rapids & Indiana railroads at Mackinaw City. In order to bridge the 8-mile gap over the Straits of Mackinac, a contract was let in 1880 with the Detroit Dry Dock company to construct a side-wheel ferry capable of breaking foot-thick ice at 4 miles an hour. The new ferry, the *Algomah*, 127 feet long, 33 feet

DM&M 2038 was one of a large series of freight equipment delivered to the road by the Michigan Car Company, President McMillan's firm in Detroit. *Wesley Perron Railroad Collection, Peter White Public Library, Marquette, Mich.*

wide, and with an 11-foot draft, had steel plates for dealing with the ice. It was thought that if the *Algomah* proved wanting in the depths of winter, tracks could be laid on the ice itself.

Boat operations would be under the Mackinac Transportation Company, which was formed on October 10, 1881, by James McMillan, Hugh McMillan (James's brother), and Henry Ledyard (general manager of the MC), with a capitalization of $65,000. The boat company never came to own dock facilities, using those of the MC at Mackinaw City and the DM&M at St. Ignace. The steamer *Algomah* arrived at the end of October and started regular service on January 9, 1882. The ice at the Straits was notorious and many times got the better of the *Algomah*. Ice packs, called windrows, were sometimes found up to 40 feet thick along the shore. The current and wind conditions at the Straits could quickly close paths created just a short time before. The *Algomah* would sometimes become stranded for weeks at a time and the passengers would be forced to walk across the ice to complete their journey. Drays would come out for the freight and haul it to shore.[12]

By the end of June 1882, the *Algomah* was pulling a scow, known as *Betsy*, fitted with railroad tracks. Although the scow only had room for 4 cars, it allowed the first movement of freight cars between the two peninsulas, without expensive break bulk at St. Ignace and Mackinaw City. *Betsy*'s limited capacity badly handicapped the operation and created quite a bottleneck at the Straits. Winter conditions proved especially trying. When *Algomah* became slowed by ice, *Betsy* would continue unimpeded and hopefully stopped before a rear end collision ensued. The crew on the *Betsy* had no protection from the elements, and a seaman manned its tiller on an open deck.

Through passenger service between Marquette and Detroit was inaugurated on May 1, 1882. Trains left Marquette at 1:30 PM, and, after passengers embarked on the *Algomah* for the ride across the Straits, sleepers were available at Mackinaw City for the rest of the 22-hour journey to Detroit. The westbound Michigan Central train, which left Detroit at 5:30 PM, took 21 hours to make Marquette. In the summer of 1882, the Marquette Express and the Detroit Express were put on an overnight 8½-hour schedule between Marquette and St. Ignace, and daylight mixed trains were added over the route. A new connection was made at Mackinaw City on July 3, with the opening of the Pennsylvania (PRR)–affiliated Grand Rapids & Indiana, from Fort Wayne, Indiana.

Initial traffic on the DM&M was handled by six 33-ton Baldwin 4-4-0s (1–6), with 58-inch drivers. The first pair of these, as has been mentioned, arrived at St. Ignace in July 1880. Two more (to power the west end work trains) were shipped via the C&NW and MH&O, and arrived at Marquette on February 17, 1881. The last pair were received in time for the line's opening. The new through service to Detroit was made possible by the addition of seven passenger engines from Manchester Locomotive Works in 1882. These 4-4-0s (7–13) weighed almost 38 tons, and, with 63-inch drivers, were the largest passenger engines on the UP. Known as "Blood" engines, they were highly spoken of on the road. Another Manchester engine, an 0-4-0 saddle tanker (17), was added to the DM&M for switching service. Passenger equipment included two brand new baggage-mail combines, two new coaches, and a couple of secondhand second-class cars, all received in interchange off the MH&O on November 26, 1881.[13]

MARQUETTE & WESTERN

One of the ways the McMillan syndicate hoped to secure business for the DM&M was by handling iron ore off the MH&O interchange at Marquette to St. Ignace. In the spring of 1881, the DM&M purchased 1,500 feet of lake frontage at its eastern terminus, and announced it would be the site of a new pocket ore dock. A circular sent to Marquette Range mine owners informed them that St. Ignace had a much longer shipping season than other upper lake ports and would enjoy lower vessel rates to steel-producing areas. The DM&M backers envisioned 300,000 to 500,000 tons of iron ore moving to St. Ignace, and 800 ore cars were optimistically ordered from Michigan Car Works in anticipation of large ore traffic.

McDermid and Hendrie were given the contract for the St. Ignace ore dock, which called for a 900-foot-long dock of 100 pockets and a 600-foot approach to reach the hill behind Main Street. The dock was to be three tracks wide, with the outer tracks over the pockets and a middle track for empties. The first of some 10,000 piles was driven on November 25, 1881, with work proceeding throughout the winter. Although work was still ongoing, the dock saw its first activity in late April 1882, when the Lake Superior mine sent down some 1,500 tons. Even in June only 50 pockets were fully operational, but lack of capacity did not prove a problem.

As the shipping season wore on, it became obvious that the DM&M management's hope of receiving ore off the MH&O for handling to St. Ignace had been unrealistic. Only

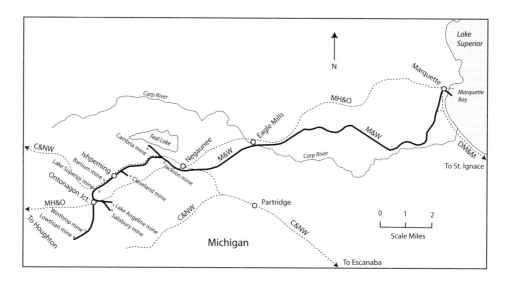

Marquette & Western Railroad, 1884

60,000 tons had been sent off the St. Ignace dock by the end of 1882, a small sliver of the trade compared to the 1,013,490 tons in lake shipments handled by the MH&O. Many thought it was foolish the DM&M had constructed an ore dock on the east end of its 150-mile line while stopping 15 miles short of the mines on the west end. Building of a second road to the Marquette Range received strong endorsement from mine owners hoping to obtain rate relief from the MH&O monopoly. High ore prices had allowed for a profit even with high tariffs, but lately prices had fallen, and, without a corresponding drop in freight rates, the owners were having difficulty getting a return on their investments.

The DM&M took the first steps towards meeting that want when Chief Engineer Charles Musson surveyed a line in October 1882 from the east end of the DM&M's waterfront yard in Marquette to Negaunee. The new road, which followed the Carp River for most of its 13-mile journey, was pronounced to be free from heavy grade and curvature and to lend itself advantageously to the economical handling of ore. The ruling grade would be quite moderate, 95 feet to the mile westbound, compared to the 142-foot grade on the MH&O.

After the DM&M and MH&O failed to come to an agreement on ore traffic over the winter, the Mackinac road was left with little choice but to try and capture some on its own. Although the DM&M's articles were initially revised to accommodate the new construction, on October 12, 1883, a new corporation, the Marquette and Western Railroad Company (M&W), was incorporated to construct the 25 miles of line between Marquette and Ishpeming. The Marquette press rejoiced that the DM&M had finally realized the folly of shipping ore to St. Ignace. With the completion of the Weitzel Lock at the Sault in 1881 for the accommodation of larger and heavier vessels, it was hoped that even the Escanaba ore business would be redirected to its rightful place at Marquette.[14]

The contract for grading, bridging, and fencing the M&W was let to the Buffalo firm of Craigie, Rafferty and Yeomans, with the roadbed to be ready for ties and rail by

February 1, 1884. Actual work began on September 3, 1883, with 200 men. The work was carried out in three segments simultaneously, with one crew working out of Marquette, one from Eagle Mills, and another from Ishpeming. Right of way had all been cleared and grubbed by September 15, with some 600 men employed. The contractors hoped to have the more open stretches of grade completed by the time the snow arrived, leaving the protected areas in the woods until later in the season.

A bitter confrontation soon developed at the proposed M&W-MH&O crossing in Negaunee. The M&W envisioned crossing at grade, while the MH&O insisted on a bridge, due to heavy traffic. The bridge was opposed by M&W, as the necessary property in downtown Negaunee would command heavy prices. In spite of the lack of an agreement, the M&W confidently graded up to the proposed crossing, and the dispute headed off to the Michigan Board of Control for arbitration. After inspecting the site on November 14, 1883, the Board ended up supporting the MH&O, forcing the M&W to cross overhead.

That same month, Craigie, Rafferty and Yeomans were given the contract for laying rails and ties. One thousand tons of steel rails were docked at St. Ignace and put down wherever possible, including on some mine branches west of Ishpeming. Although construction had gone well, in November heavy snows and cold weather began to slow the work. By mid-January 1884 all grading had been completed, except for the disputed site at Negaunee. The first work train arrived at Negaunee on February 23, where work was held up awaiting completion of the overpass over the C&NW and of the disputed span over the MH&O. The latter would require 1,900 feet of trestle with a 120-foot iron bridge over the railroad itself. Not everyone in Negaunee thought the massive trestlework was an asset to their community. The *Negaunee Iron Herald* remarked that the "unsightly trestle . . . will prove damaging to all interests involved, even to the victors of the conquest." A site for the 24′ × 92′ Negaunee depot was reached by a spur off the main line.[15]

At Ishpeming, property owners demanding what was felt to be excessive compensation held up M&W forces. The railroad took matters into its own hands early Sunday morning, April 6, 1884, laying tracks across Main and First streets before residents had even gotten out of bed. The courts were left to decide what value should accrue to the property owners, and track laying proceeded without incident. Wahlman and Grip received a contract to build the M&W's downtown Ishpeming passenger depot and a 4-stall roundhouse near the Barnum mine, west of town.

The arrival of an officer's special at Ishpeming marked the first official trip over the entire line on May 26, 1884. The Cleveland mine, which was reached by a 1.84-mile spur off the main line at Ishpeming, had the honor of making the first shipments over the M&W on June 6. Other mine spurs completed in 1884 included one of 1.48 miles to the Lake Angeline mine and another 2.15 miles long to the Winthrop mine. The entire line officially opened for business on June 9. Although an economic recession took over the nation in 1884, depressing the ore market, the M&W's business steadily increased as new spurs were completed. That summer saw shipments being made over the M&W by the Jackson mine at Negaunee; the Cambria, Cleveland, Barnum, Lake Superior, Salisbury, and Pittsburgh and Lake Angeline mines at Ishpeming; and the Lowthian and Winthrop mines at Winthrop.

Although the DM&M would have preferred to obtain the long haul on iron ore traffic to St. Ignace, the road realized it would never be able to compete with Lake Superior vessel rates out of Marquette. In August 1883, negotiations were completed with the Cleveland Iron company to purchase its waterfront property at the west end of the DM&M's yards, including the ore dock. Although still in use, the facility was not up to the present standards, and a contract was let to Craigie, Rafferty and Yeomans in January 1884 for a new Marquette ore dock.

The new dock, located just south of the old Cleveland dock at the foot of Baraga Street, was to be 41.5 feet above the water and composed of 100 60-ton pockets, giving a total capacity of 6,000 tons. Three tracks traversed the length of the dock, with unloading to take place on the outer two tracks. The DM&M, realizing the St. Ignace dock would never meet expectations, cannibalized fifty of its inside pockets for use in the new construction. The M&W dock was filled with iron ore for the first time on the evening of July 2, 1884, and two days later the steam barge *Hiawatha* with her consort *Minnehaha* began taking the first load out of the chutes. The new dock was even equipped with lights for night loading. The M&W also laid trackage that month into its new coal dock, which paralleled the shore starting at the old Cleveland dock and running under the new M&W ore dock. Steam hoists were used to unload lake coal from the vessels right into rail cars. The old Cleveland dock was replanked for use as a merchandise dock by the M&W.

The entry of the Marquette & Western into the field saw ore freight rates drop from 65 to 40 cents per ton, with the MH&O cutting its charges to several cents a ton below the newcomer's. Although good news for the mine owners, the competition certainly reduced the profit margins for the railroads involved. The 8-ton ore cars in use at that time required the operation of a large number of trains to move the iron ore. Crews, on the other hand, were more productive, with a monthly salary and no hours of service law. Each crew generally made three round trips to the range each day. The M&W could handle 75 empties up the hill, although difficulty was experienced getting out of Marquette yard on the heavy grade up to the Carp River. Eastbound was not a problem, and, on June 14, 1884, 70 loaded ore cars were taken by one engine out of Negaunee. Train size increased throughout the summer and by the end of August, 117 cars had been brought down in one train.

The M&W provided further competition for the MH&O on July 27, 1884, when passenger service was instituted. Three round trips a day were made out of Marquette to Ishpeming, and the service proved quite successful given the more convenient location of the Ishpeming depot compared to the MH&O facility in South Ishpeming. The MH&O compensated by cutting its fare 10 cents under that of the M&W on the round trip to Ishpeming. At Marquette, the Tremont House property was purchased for use as the road's depot and general offices, replacing the former DM&M depot near the gas works and giving more convenient access to the city center.

Other improvements necessary at Marquette included enlarging the DM&M roundhouse from 6 to 10 stalls to accommodate the M&W's fleet of locomotives. The seven Moguls (50–56) and three 0-6-0s (57–59) had been delivered from Baldwin in early 1884. The Moguls' 18,432 pounds of tractive effort was superior to anything in use on the rival MH&O. Considered "crackerjack" engines, they were a favorite with enginemen and, until larger Moguls came along, were the "pride of the fleet." The 34½-ton 0-6-0s were also considered large for their day. The Moguls were engaged in freight and passenger service, while the 0-6-0s held down yard assignments. M&W rolling stock included 2 coaches, 2 baggage cars, and 500 ore cars.[16]

—DETROIT—
Mackinac & Marquette
and
Marquette & Western
RAILROADS.

WEST				EAST		
FIRST-CLASS 5.	FIRST-CLASS 3.	2ND CLASS 1.	STATIONS.	2ND CLASS 2.	FIRST-CLASS 4.	FIRST-CLASS 6.
P.M. 4.50	P.M. 1.05	A.M. 7.50	Arr.....Ishpeming.....Dep	A.M. 8.10	P.M. 1.30	P.M. 5.20
4.40	12.55	7.37	.....Negaunee.....	8.20	1.40	5.30
4.00	12.15	A.M. 7.00	Dep.....Marquette.....Arr	8.55	2.15	6.10
		P.M. 6.30	Arr.....Reedsboro	9.00		
		2.45	.....Seney.....	P.M. 12.27		
		12.55	.....Newberry.....	2.22		
		11.30	Dep.....St. Ignace.....Arr	4.00		
		A.M. 8.10	Arr..Mackinaw City..Dep	P.M. 8.10		
		A.M. 3.41	Dep.....Detroit.....Arr	P.M. 10.10		
		A.M. 9.35		P.M. 3.30		

Connections made at Marquette and Negaunee with the M. H. & O. R. R. for the Iron, Gold, Silver and copper districts; at Reedsboro with a daily stage line for Manistique, etc.; at Seney with tri-weekly stage for Grand Marais; at St. Ignace with the M. C. R. R. and G. R. & I. R. R. for all points east and south; also daily stage line to Sault St. Marie.

D. McCOOL,   F. MILLIGAN,
Gen'l. Supt.   Gen'l. Pass. Agt.,

In its first abbreviated ore season the M&W wound up sending 250,866 tons of ore off its new dock and the old Cleveland dock. The DM&M handled an additional 51,109 tons out of St. Ignace, no doubt most of which came off the M&W. The MH&O was still firmly in command, handling 667,623 tons of ore via Marquette and 64,420 tons through L'Anse. Operations for the year ending December 31, 1884, saw the M&W earning $131,765, of which $123,958 was from freight operations. Operating expenses totaled $61,612, leaving a net of $72,716. Although over $1,000,000 in bonds were issued to pay construction costs and provide new equipment, it was hoped the M&W would have no trouble in meeting interest payments if operating trends continued.

During the summer of 1884, the M&W surveyed a line from near Ontonagon Jct. to Champion, where the company hoped to tap that mine's large output. Some predicted the Champion line would form a connection with the Milwaukee, Lake Shore and Western (MLS&W), then building north through the new Agogebic (later Gogebic) Iron Range, near the Montreal River, to Ashland, Wisconsin. The M&W extension achieved paper status with the forming of the Ishpeming, L'Anse & Ontonagon Railroad Company on January 13, 1885, to build an 80-mile line from Ishpeming to Ontonagon. Capitalization was set at $1,000,000, and the company's directorate consisted of DM&M and M&W backers. Other than nuisance value, it was questionable why the M&W would parallel the MH&O to L'Anse, especially as there would be no land grant. L'Anse would be an excellent outlet for ore off the new Agogebic Range, but a line change away from Ontonagon would have to be authorized and would meet with bitter opposition from that quarter. The coming spring would see the Ishpeming, L'Anse & Ontonagon project become moot, further depressing Ontonagon's hopes.[17]

THE M&W IS LOST TO THE MH&O

After the success the M&W enjoyed in 1884, the announcement that the DM&M had sold the line to the rival MH&O came as quite a shock. The transaction provided badly needed funds to the DM&M and relieved the MH&O of what was becoming a real threat to its viability. The M&W also fit well into the MH&O operating scheme, creating a double track between Marquette and Ontonagon Jct., as well as two ore docks in Marquette. Rate pressure was done away with as the MH&O regained its monopoly on Marquette ore shipments. As the M&W had recently raised $400,000 in New York to pay for its westward extension to Champion and Republic, the threat to the MH&O of losing traffic from its best-paying mines was also eliminated.

The MH&O issued 6 percent bonds, backed by a mortgage on the two properties, and 6,000 shares of common stock to make the purchase. Although the new bonds increased the MH&O's fixed charges by $84,000, it no doubt seemed a small price to pay. It was said that if the MH&O raised its ore rates to 50 cents, the increase could be recouped. As the ore market was still unhealthy, any excessive increase was said to be "suicidal." The transaction was made effective April 1, 1885, with the Marquette & Western remaining a paper shell under MH&O ownership.[18]

James McMillan tried to put on a good face, saying the road had been leased so as "to unite the interests of the M&W, MH&O and the DM&M."[19] The DM&M picked up two seats on the MH&O directorate as a result of the sale. McMillan said this would serve to represent Michigan's interests on the MH&O board, including the building of a line west to a connection with the Milwaukee, Lake Shore & Western or the NP. The westward expansion remained alive when the state granted a two-year extension of the MH&O land grant. The MH&O was required to complete 10 miles out of L'Anse by July 1, 1886, with the entire line to be completed a year later.[20] Regardless of the prospects for the westward extension, Peter White wrote, "In such strife and reckless competition as prevailed last year neither company [MH&O or M&W] could have lived—both would sooner or later have gone to the wall."[21]

The MH&O slowly integrated the M&W into its property, creating changes that were viewed positively for the most part. The M&W agency at Negaunee was closed on

This rendering of Negaunee in 1885 shows the Pioneer Furnace covering most of the lower area, with the kilns to the right and furnace to the left. Running behind the furnace is the Marquette, Houghton & Ontonagon main line with the joint MH&O-C&NW depot located near the upper left hand margin. The Marquette & Western main line, or south main line of the MH&O, is visible for only a short distance in the lower left hand corner. Paralleling it to the north, where the passenger train is seen leaving for Escanaba, is the Chicago & North Western main line. After passing its engine terminal and connection with the MH&O, the C&NW goes under the MH&O, along its freight house in the middle of town, and then curves to the west and Ishpeming. *Paananen Collection*

May 20, 1885, with all business being handled at the MH&O station. Crews had set to work at Winthrop Jct. (formerly Ontonagon Jct.) and Negaunee the day before, making connections between the former M&W and MH&O. Under the new operating scheme, the only traffic using the M&W line between Marquette and Negaunee consisted of two passenger trains each way. The MH&O line saw some twelve scheduled ore trains plus one freight each way. M&W trackage west of Negaunee took the freight and passenger trains of the combined roads, with the MH&O line between Negaunee and Winthrop Jct. used only for ore traffic. This brought all passenger trains into the more convenient Ishpeming depot of the M&W. Negaunee residents said they would be "profoundly thankful" if one of the consequences of the takeover would be the demolition of the "Mackinac trestle" over the MH&O. The bridge remained for some time until a bridge crew, salvaging its white pine, took several weeks to bring it down in December 1902.[22]

At Ishpeming, the M&W depot was moved a short distance to the south to eliminate the stub arrangement. The MH&O closed its agency in South Ishpeming and moved into the M&W depot in March 1886. The M&W roundhouse near Barnum mine was abandoned and its work transferred to the MH&O facility at South Ishpeming. The

In this undated photo, the joint depot at Negaunee is seen with an MH&O or DSS&A passenger train stopped on the north side. C&NW passenger trains either headed or backed up the incline off their main line to reach the south side of the depot. This situation was rectified on November 15, 1910, when the C&NW track was extended west along the DSS&A, a little over 2 miles, and rejoined the C&NW main line near the DSS&A diamond. The former Marquette & Western depot is visible on the extreme right. *Paananen Collection*

M&W Moguls, judged superior to any power on the MH&O, required the placing of a new 50-foot turntable at the MH&O Marquette roundhouse in December 1886, as they would not fit on the old table.

MH&O passenger trains started operating into the Tremont House depot on June 28, 1885, affording better connections with DM&M trains, and creating a true union station for Marquette. The new summer schedule saw the MH&O running a morning and evening train as far as Michigamme, and running a midday mail train the entire length of the road to Houghton. Another round trip operated over the former M&W trackage, leaving Marquette at 12:30 PM and connecting with the C&NW at Ishpeming. The MH&O placed a new 2-stall brick engine house and turntable at Michigamme in 1886 to service passenger power at that point.

As ore prices stayed low for 1885, the MH&O did not see an increase in tonnage despite the M&W takeover. Given its earlier ice-out date, St. Ignace was responsible for the season's first shipment of Lake Superior district ore to Lake Erie, and it continued to receive three to four trains a day until navigation opened at Marquette. Marquette wound up shipping 750,047 tons in 1885, a drop of 168,442 tons from 1884. Tonnage at L'Anse fell from 62,086 to 20,027 tons, causing the MH&O to discontinue further use of the dock.

MH&O earnings improved dramatically in 1886 due to an increase in ore business. New iron ore finds east of Negaunee resulted in spurs being laid off the former M&W

An eastbound DSS&A passenger train straddles Front Street as it makes its station stop at the old Tremont House depot in Marquette. The structure had originally been built by James Pendill as a hotel in 1858.   *Paananen Collection*

An 1886 drawing of the Marquette waterfront depicting, from right to left, the Grace Furnace dock (formerly the original Jackson dock), the merchandise dock, the MH&O ore dock, the Cleveland ore dock, and the Marquette & Western ore dock. *Paananen Collection*

A pair of small former Marquette, Houghton & Ontonagon switch engines spot
ore cars on the dock at Marquette shortly after the DSS&A merger. Loaded ore
cars at this time were dropped down to the docks under the control of switchmen
from the Upper Yard, but then spotted over the pockets with the aid of engines
like these tiny 0-4-0s.   *Paananen Collection*

trackage into the Negaunee, Buffalo, and Pioneer mines. An additional spur was laid into the Blue mine, also a part of this group, the following summer. The new business provided a real boon to Negaunee, and, by the end of August, there were five switch engine assignments working around town. Two were employed in the yards and two on the "new finds," as well as one at night. The MH&O was also helped in March 1886 by the extension of the Mineral Range Railroad across the Portage Lake into Houghton. This narrow gauge railroad, serving the Copper Country on the Keweenaw Peninsula, had been built in 1873. Transfer between the narrow and standard gauge cars was made at the MH&O yards in East Houghton.[23]

THE MACKINAC ROAD GOES BANKRUPT

The DM&M, unable to match rates with boats operating on Lake Superior, continued to struggle with an inadequate traffic base. Iron ore moving east out of Marquette to the St. Ignace dock and local furnaces remained the DM&M's principal business, accounting for 42 percent of its traffic in 1882. Of the 86,611 tons of iron ore moved that year, the St. Ignace dock received 60,657 tons, with the remainder going to the furnaces. The next largest traffic category was lumber and forest products at 73,029 tons or 36 percent, followed by charcoal at 16,103 tons or about 8 percent. Merchandise traffic, handled at higher rates than ore and lumber, was largely the province of the boats during the navigation season. Detroit jobbers were also unable to phase out Chicago suppliers in serving the UP, due to longer shipping times and higher rates. Shipments of pig iron and blooms did provide some needed revenue following the opening of the furnace at Newberry.

Passenger business made up almost a third of the DM&M's total revenue. The Marquette paper commented, "Gradually the two peninsulas of Michigan are coming into closer relations with each other, as a result of the opening up of better means of communication between them through the DM&M line, and the feeling hitherto existing among their people, that they belong to different commonwealth begins to wear away." The question remained whether enough "communication" existed to make the DM&M a viable institution. The DM&M looked for traffic wherever it could and for years even ran huckleberry trains out of Marquette to the plain between Chocolay and Sand River, some 10 miles to the east. The fare for the round trip excursion was but 20 cents.[24]

As the DM&M operated through newly opened country, its employees sometimes had to take justice into their own hands. Seney, a backwoods community named for DM&M director George I. Seney, did not have a bank, and lumberjacks were given just enough money to get to St. Ignace, where they could cash their checks. One day a dozen lumberjacks decided to drink their train fare before heading off for St. Ignace, confident the trainmen would choose to avoid an encounter with twelve such men. Conductor James Connell was not impressed and took on all twelve men, one at a time. Within 10 minutes he had collected all the woodsmen's checks, and upon reaching St. Ignace he escorted them to the bank, where, after cashing their checks, he deducted their fares.

The DM&M directors did what they could to create a more favorable financial position. During 1882, capital stock was reduced and first mortgage bonds were paid off through liquidation of assets. This allowed the Mackinac road to reduce its capitalization from unacceptably high levels. Even with the restructuring, the DM&M's net revenues, which amounted to only $25,000 in 1883, fell well short of covering the annual interest payments of $136,000. The road was able to find some money left over from construction to make up the balance.

McMillan said that the country the railroad served was still largely wilderness and that revenues were bound to improve as development took place. The DM&M's potential role as a vital transcontinental link in conjunction with the Northern Pacific and the Canadian roads out of the Sault still held promise. The DM&M, however, could ill afford the effects of the 1884 recession, and on October 1, it defaulted on an interest payment. It was said that the road had yet to sell some of its bonds and that the failed interest payment was mainly due to an error on the part of the road's treasury. Many thought the DM&M would purchase the MH&O, and the yearly promises to build the Sault branch were not viewed with scorn.

Reality could not be glossed over indefinitely, however, and most were shocked to see the DM&M declare bankruptcy. Although some traffic increases had occurred with the end of the 1884 recession, they proved insufficient to put the road into the black, and Central Trust Company foreclosed on the 1881 mortgage for non-payment of interest. A U.S. Circuit Court ruled on July 10, 1886, that the road was to be put up for sale, with all bids due by October 20, and no bid of less than $500,000 to be considered. Hugh McMillan, secretary-treasurer of the DM&M, came in as high bidder and was awarded the property for $1,010,000. McMillan was also required to assume DM&M's current obligations of $3,040,000. This seemed quite a bargain for a road that cost slightly over $12,000,000 to build and equip. The two McMillans now controlled almost 100 percent of the DM&M.[25]

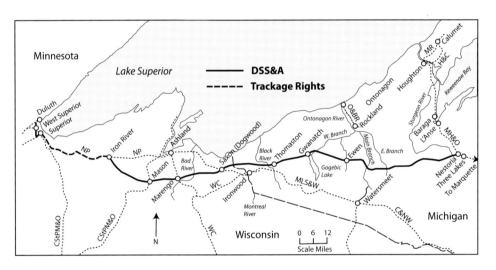

Western Division, June 22, 1888

4

FORMATION OF THE DSS&A—CANADIAN PACIFIC SEIZES POWER

The failure of Detroit suppliers to reassert their dominance in the UP, the inability to turn the tamarack swamps of the eastern UP into agricultural land, and the failure to divert Marquette Range ore from its closest lake port (Marquette) to one further east at St. Ignace left the DM&M with but one remaining hope: that it could be made part of a transcontinental link between the Northern Pacific to the west and connections to the east at the Sault and Straits of Mackinac. On December 18, 1886, the DM&M was reorganized as the Mackinaw & Marquette Railroad Company (M&M), which in turn, four days later, was consolidated with three other paper companies controlled by the McMillan syndicate—the Sault Ste. Marie & Marquette Railroad Company, the Wisconsin, Sault Ste. Marie & Mackinac Railway Company, and the Duluth, Superior & Michigan—to form the Duluth, South Shore and Atlantic Railway Company (DSS&A).[1]

The Sault Ste. Marie & Marquette, as already mentioned, had been formed in 1880 by the DM&M to build off its main line to the Sault. The Wisconsin, Sault Ste. Marie & Marquette was formed by these same interests on September 7, 1886, to build 130 miles of road between Marquette and the Wisconsin border at the Montreal River, near Ironwood. The remaining 125 miles from West Superior, Wis. to the Montreal River was the domain of the Duluth, Superior and Michigan (DS&M), incorporated August 13, 1886. The DS&M was originally formed by West Superior interests, with John H. Hammond as president. Hammond, a civil engineer by trade, was involved with the Manitoba & Southwestern Railroad before becoming the founder of West Superior. The McMillans had come to own 58 percent of the DS&M's stock at the time of consolidation.[2]

After consolidation was authorized at meetings of the various predecessors, the approved articles were filed with the secretaries of state for Michigan and Wisconsin on March 9 and March 14, 1887, respectively, officially creating the Duluth, South Shore & Atlantic Railway. The resulting merger used franchises and existing trackage for a line from Duluth to the Straits of Mackinac and the Sault. Capitalization of the DSS&A was set at $22,000,000, or approximately $40,000 per mile.[3]

John Hammond expressed Duluth-Superior's enthusiasm for the DSS&A, saying, "the northwest will have an eastern and southern outlet by way of the South Shore and the lower Michigan lines without paying tribute to Chicago, and it's a fact that a man can't get through Chicago now without leaving part of his worldly possessions behind him. He's got to buy something, if only a glass of peanuts."[4] I. I. P. Odell, on a director's special passing through Minneapolis on November 21, 1886, reinforced the importance of Duluth, saying the DSS&A would get most of its business there, "though they may come into Minneapolis over some other lines."[5] Everything seemed possible at this early juncture.

The first South Shore board of directors consisted of James and Hugh McMillan; Columbus R. Cummings and Norman B. Ream, Chicago; George I. Seney and August D. Julliard, New York; and Calvin S. Brice of Lima, Ohio. Additional members of the DSS&A syndicate included Francis Palms, George H. Hammond, William B. Moran, and John S. Newberry of Detroit; and F. P. Olcott and Samuel Thomas of Chicago. Cummings, president of the Union National Bank, and four other members of the board had been involved in the construction of the Nickel Plate Road and had funds to invest after a profitable sale. The syndicate was given authority to raise by subscription $8,000,000 or more to pay the contractors, and to purchase the Mackinaw & Marquette at a price not to exceed $20,000 per mile. The syndicate was to receive, in return for each mile of completed road, $12,000 in first-mortgage 5 percent South Shore bonds, $30,000 in preferred stock, and $36,000 of common stock. Cummings was elected the South Shore's first president with Brice as vice president.

On the west end it was hoped to run over NP trackage from some point west of Ashland into Duluth to cut down on construction costs. This had been made possible when the NP built from Northern Pacific Jct. into Superior in 1881, with a further extension into Ashland three years later. The direct link between Ashland and the Twin Ports effectively settled lawsuits brought by the State of Wisconsin to force the road to abide by its charter and complete to the Montreal River.

Further mileage could be done away with by using the MH&O between Marquette and Three Lakes. The syndicate attempted to purchase that road, but these efforts ran into difficulty when some of the syndicate members, including Seney and Brice, were unable to raise their share of the funds. Samuel Thomas agreed to make up the difference, and by November 1, 1886, the DSS&A syndicate had come to own the great majority of MH&O common and preferred stock, giving them "practical control."[6] James McMillan, and others with Detroit connections, hoped acquiring the MH&O would see their community once again come to the forefront in the Upper Peninsula. "The trouble all along has been that the MH&O has worked in the interests of Chicago and against Detroit," said McMillan. "Now things will be changed."[7] This wishful thinking remained a part of McMillan's strategy, in spite of the earlier failure of the DM&M to counteract Chicago economic interests in the UP.

On February 15, 1887, the DSS&A made a 99-year lease of the MH&O. Under the terms of the agreement, revenues would accrue to the MH&O on a mileage basis, with the South Shore guaranteeing payment of fixed charges and 6 percent dividends on MH&O preferred stock. MH&O operations were integrated into those of the South Shore on May 1, 1887, with all business being conducted under the new name effective that date.

The remaining 166-mile gap between the NP connection and Three Lakes was to be dispensed with under a contract signed on October 18, 1886, with Brown, Howard and

Company of New York. President C. R. Cummings and Samuel Thomas were both heavily involved in Brown, Howard & Co., the former Nickel Plate contractor, and naturally stood to benefit. The contract also called for the building of the long-discussed branch off the old DM&M main line near Sage into Sault Ste. Marie. The contractors were to be paid $20,000 for each mile of completed trackage, with additional payments for building side tracks and line side structures, and for fully equipping the road. J. A. Latcha, construction superintendent for Brown, Howard and Co., was appointed chief engineer of the DSS&A.

The contract with Brown, Howard & Co. provided that conditions existing on the DM&M on October 18, 1886, were to form the standard for new construction on the South Shore, except that 60-pound steel was to be used on the main line. The ruling grade on the new construction was not to exceed anything on the MH&O and Milwaukee, Lake Shore & Western. This would not be too difficult a feat considering the horrendous grades the MH&O experienced climbing out of Marquette and L'Anse and those on the Birch Hill east of Ashland on the MLS&W.

THE WESTERN EXTENSION

Latcha soon had several survey parties engaged in the uncompleted territory. John F. Stevens, who later went on to fame with the Great Northern Railway (GN) and Panama Canal, was employed as assistant chief engineer and did most of the fieldwork. The first party started west off the MH&O at Three Lakes in mid-November 1886. Two other parties headed each way out of Lake Gogebic. Supplies were accumulated at Superior and other points for an early start to construction the coming year. There was an urgency to get the line located before the spring thaw so that contractors could move their supplies into position while the ground was frozen, rather than having to traverse miles of swamp before starting work. Stevens recalled that that winter was exceptionally cold, with 3 feet of snow on the ground in most places. The snow had to be cleared away before surveyors could set the locating stakes, and all work was done on snowshoes. Between the MH&O at Three Lakes and the Milwaukee, Lake Shore & Western at Dogwood was a true wilderness, with the only access being provided by the old military road between Watersmeet and Rockland.

By the first of the year, the route had largely taken shape. From a junction with the MH&O at Three Lakes, the line headed for the top end of Lake Gogebic, then skirted the north end of the Gogebic Iron Range. After crossing over the Wisconsin Central at Marengo, and under the Chicago, St. Paul, Minneapolis and Omaha (CStPM&O, or Omaha Road) near Mason, the line ran northwest to a connection with the Northern Pacific at Iron River, some 30 miles west of Ashland. Serving Ashland had been ruled out on account of heavy grades. A ruling grade of 52.8 feet per mile or 1 percent was maintained for the entire route.

The 1 percent grade necessitated a great deal of extra expense, especially climbing east from the south branch of the Sturgeon River, and at the crossings of the Ontonagon River Middle Branch and the Black River. The divide between the WC at Marengo and the CStPM&O crossing near Mason also proved troublesome. Stevens was especially proud of the 12-mile tangent between the Main Branch of the Ontonagon River and Lake Gogebic. Such a tangent was unheard of anywhere on the UP. The line was run as

The massive wooden bridge over the Bad River consisted of a 150-foot Howe span and 1,196 feet of trestle approaches. The bridge was replaced with steel spans in 1913. *Paananen Collection*

near the confluence of the various branches of the Ontonagon as possible so that the pine timber between Three Lakes and Lake Gogebic could be floated down and handled by the South Shore.

By spring the locating parties had completed their work and things were largely in readiness for construction to begin. The 166-mile extension was divided into three segments called the Western, Gogebic, and Summit divisions. The subcontract for the Western Division, Dogwood to Iron River, was awarded on January 27, 1887, to Henry and Balch. They started west off the MLS&W connection with 100 Italian workmen in late February, and by the end of July they were grading across the Indian reservation at Odanah. Construction went comparatively smoothly, and by September 10, men were being paid off with the work largely completed. A steel gang working west out of Dogwood laid 12 miles by mid-November and reached the Bad River bridge before suspending for the winter.

The 57-mile Gogebic Division subcontract, awarded in February to Harrison and Green, of Milwaukee, ran east of Dogwood to the East Branch of the Ontonagon River. Grading on this stretch was made difficult by the presence of "stiff clay" or "loon shit" so prevalent in northern Wisconsin and the western UP. The lack of swampland greatly aided construction, however, and the first rails were put down by a work train going east off the MLS&W connection in July. This segment had some fine belts of hardwood and pine and "as good farming land as there is on the peninsula."[8]

The Summit Division, between the new town of Nestoria (at the junction with the MH&O near Three Lakes) and the East Branch of the Ontonagon River, was under subcontractor F. C. O'Reilly. Clearing on this division was completed in mid-April and some grading begun, although handicapped by deep snow. The first 20 miles west of Nestoria proved to be the toughest stretch on the western extension, having to be blasted out for almost the entire distance due to heavy rockwork. Latcha pronounced the rest of the division to be "easy sailing."[9] Some 2,500 men, largely Italian, were employed on this division by summer, with attempts made to recruit more men throughout the country. O'Reilly's efforts were hampered by several strikes, all of which were put down with the assistance of the Baraga county sheriff. After the leadership of the "discontented dagos" was rooted out, the other men would usually return to their jobs.[10]

Grading on the entire western extension was completed on October 29, 1887. The largely Italian work force was for the most part glad to be paid off, not caring much for the uncivilized UP. By mid-November rail had been laid eastward from Dogwood as far as Lake Gogebic (for a total of 37 miles), and also westward for 20 miles out of Nestoria. In spite of work being held up by occasional rail shortages and incomplete bridge work, by Christmas only an 11-mile gap remained. By this time there was over 2 feet of snow on the ground, but the contractors used plows to clear the grade. The closing of the Summit and Gogebic divisions occurred on December 29 at the bridge over the West Branch of the Ontonagon. Calvin Brice wired, "Contractors closed our track yesterday if Bridge [at Sault Ste. Marie] is swung there is continuous line of rail from Montreal to Duluth." Of course, this was not continuous DSS&A trackage, as the MLS&W would have to be used west of Dogwood and the NP west of Ashland.[11]

Negotiations were not going well with the NP for use of its Ashland line between the DSS&A junction at Iron River, Wisconsin, and Duluth. In preparation for a breakdown in talks, the South Shore put several survey parties in the field for an independent line north of the NP. Terminal grounds, 6,000' long by 360' wide, were purchased on the West Superior waterfront between the NP and CStPM&O trackage. The South Shore also acquired a one-quarter interest in the Lake Superior Terminal and Transfer Railway Company (LST&T), a terminal company in its beginning stages at West Superior. The DSS&A even petitioned the U.S. government for approval to construct a new bridge across the St. Louis River between Rice's Point (Duluth) and Connor's Point (West Superior).

In preparation for an early resumption of work, the line to Dogwood was cleared of snow in February 1888. Of the 166 miles from Nestoria to Iron River, 40 miles of track remained to be laid, while ballasting was required on some 130 miles. Bridging and grading had been completed for the entire distance. The first steel gang was put on in early May and by the middle of the month over 1,000 men were employed laying track and ballasting. The last rail on the Western Division, tying the South Shore into the NP at Iron River, was laid on June 22, 1888. All resources were then shifted to ballasting the new line, with crews working east out of Iron River, west and east from Dogwood, and west from Nestoria. Three steam shovels were put to work getting out ballast for the remaining trackage. It was thought the line would be ready for operation on September 1, unless the men were unable to survive the terrible infestation of mosquitoes.

Thomaston, named for Samuel Thomas and located 87 miles west of Nestoria, was to be the headquarters of the Western Division (Nestoria-Duluth) and serve as the crew change point between Marquette and Duluth. Mine runs to the Gogebic Range

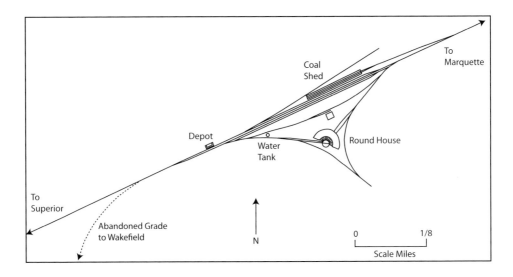

Thomaston, Michigan, December 1912

would also be based at this terminal. Originally the DSS&A envisioned locating this terminal at the picturesque head of Lake Gogebic, but after local property owners tried to hold up the railroad, the site was moved 15 miles west. As was often true of booming construction camps, Thomaston in its early days had an unsavory reputation. *The Ironwood Times* reported, "Thomastown [*sic*] on the DSS&A road is undoubtedly one of the toughest little places on the Upper Peninsula. There are no police officers there and law and order are comparatively unknown. Gambling places and houses of ill-fame are open and unchecked, and men are held and robbed with impunity."[12]

Facilities constructed at Thomaston included a depot, freight warehouse, 16-stall roundhouse, 50′×60′ blacksmith shop, coaling station, water tank, supply warehouse, and master mechanic's office. A four-story, forty-room company hotel was built for the accommodation of train crews, and, for permanent residents, four double cottages were erected. Before the hotel was finished, six long tents were put end to end to serve construction workers and also for a time to serve as a public eating facility. At that time no one could envision what kind of traffic would be handled over the South Shore, and, although a 26-track yard was laid out, only 4 tracks were put down to start.

The building of the South Shore stirred other railroad activity in the UP, often using the same contractors employed on the Western Division. The Milwaukee & Northern built into Republic and to a connection with the South Shore at Champion, arriving at the latter point on November 12, 1887. The first M&N freight trains arrived at Champion two days later, with the first passenger service being offered on November 21. Two daily M&N trains to Chicago made close connections with the DSS&A. In an agreement signed July 25, 1887, the M&N became a joint owner of the South Shore Champion depot, and transfer tracks were constructed for interchange. The M&N provided still another avenue for Chicago and Milwaukee business interests to dominate the UP and further dampened Detroit jobbers' and McMillan's hopes. The DSS&A was left to fend for short hauls from UP points to Champion and the C&NW interchange at Ishpeming.

Thomaston, Michigan, between 1888 and 1935, served as the crew change point between Marquette and Duluth-Superior. This photo shows the original depot looking east, August 7, 1912.   *Paananen Collection*

Champion, Michigan, was an important junction point with the CM&StP, or Milwaukee Road. This eastbound DSS&A passenger train is seen along the north side of the joint depot; Milwaukee tracks ran along the south side. The two lines joined just to the west, allowing for through Chicago-Calumet passenger movements and for DSS&A crews to pick up and set out freight cars in the joint interchange yard.   *Paananen Collection*

A view of the Champion passenger station as seen from the CM&StP side. A separate freight house was maintained by the DSS&A for less-than-carload traffic.
Paananen Collection

In late 1887, the C&NW started its long-talked-of extension from Ishpeming to Republic and Michigamme. A dispute soon developed with the South Shore over right of way along the north shore of Lake Michigamme. The conflict was settled around the first of the year when the South Shore agreed to let the North Western cross its line near Fan Bay and parallel it into Michigamme. The new service into Republic saw South Shore car loadings from the productive Republic iron mine drop. In an agreement dated May 1, 1888, the South Shore sold the C&NW and M&N one-third interests in the Republic mine trackage. The South Shore continued to maintain the joint tracks, although switching was divided equally among the three roads.

THE SAULT BRANCH

On the east end, the DSS&A faced a threat from the Minneapolis, Sault Ste. Marie and Atlantic Railway Company (MSSM&A, or Soo Line), a line backed by Minneapolis flour milling interests and headed for the Sault. As a potential competitor for traffic off the Canadian roads, the South Shore wanted to establish itself at the Lock City ahead of the MSSM&A's expected New Year's Day 1888 arrival. Rexford Bros. and Hodge, of New York, received the subcontract for clearing, grading, bridging, and tieing the 46.8-mile-long branch, and set up a camp near the main line junction in December 1886. Known for a short time as Sage Jct., the location took the name Sault Jct. (later spelled Soo Jct.) after the first of the year.

Final surveys on the Sault branch were completed on January 13, 1887, allowing the first grading to take place on a swampy 15-mile segment out of the Sault. Matters pro-

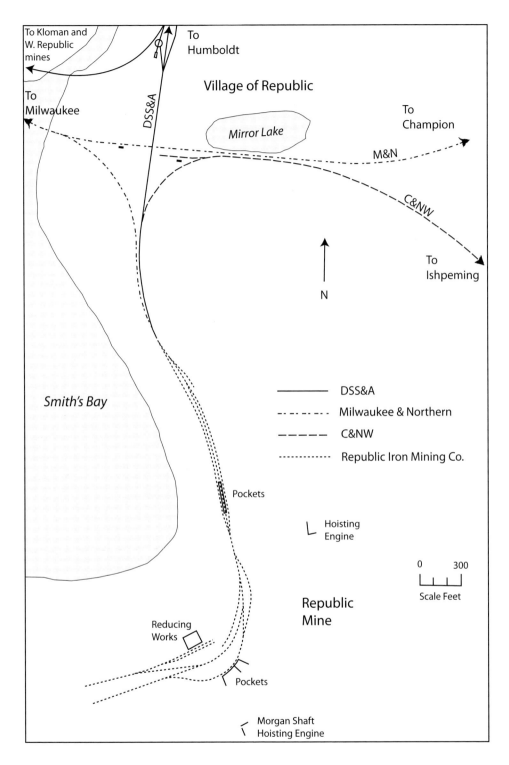

To Kloman and
W. Republic
mines

To
Humboldt

Village of Republic

To
Milwaukee

DSS&A

Mirror Lake

To
Champion

M&N

C&NW

To
Ishpeming

N

Smith's Bay

DSS&A
Milwaukee & Northern
C&NW
Republic Iron Mining Co.

Pockets

Hoisting
Engine

0   300

Scale Feet

Republic
Mine

Reducing
Works

Pockets

Morgan Shaft
Hoisting Engine

Republic, Michigan, February 16, 1888

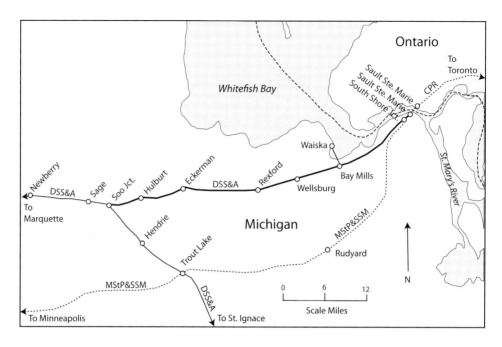

Sault Ste. Marie Branch, May 1891

gressed to the point where track laying commenced in mid-June. The swampy conditions made work difficult, but by mid-July, 13 miles of track were laid, with crews averaging ¾ mile a day at the most. Despite periodic storms and rail shortages, a South Shore work train pulled into Sault Ste. Marie on September 16, 1887. With the last spike, cannon brought over from Fort Brady fired a 21-gun salute, causing the Sooites to become "crazy with enthusiasm" over their first rail service and a year-round connection to the civilized world.[13]

The South Shore was also busily constructing terminal facilities at the Sault, including a 12-stall brick roundhouse, 56-foot turntable, and water tank. Forty yards from the roundhouse, a 16′×40′ "temporary" depot was erected. Plans were drawn for a "magnificent" union station, which had trains arriving under cover, but it was judged to be too late in the season to start construction.[14] Regarding the temporary depot, about all the local scribes could say was "well it is finished."[15] Upon completion of the depot, the carpenters moved to construct a 24′×80′ freight house. The facilities were judged to be far enough along to begin regular service on October 10, 1887, with scheduled trains making connections with Nos. 1 and 2 at Sault Jct. After what seemed like a long period of pointless delay, the mail contract was taken from the stages and given to the South Shore on January 9, 1888.

On the other side of the St. Mary's River, the arrival of the first Canadian Pacific train at the Canadian Sault on November 30, 1887, proved the cause for another celebration and salute from the Fort Brady artillery battery. The rails of the Minneapolis, Sault Ste. Marie & Atlantic reached the city limits of Sault Ste. Marie on December 6. Owing to the difficulty in securing right of way at the Sault, the MSSM&A decided to run into

Before being replaced with steel, bridging was typically done with Howe deck trusses such as this 128-foot span over the Waiska River at Bay Mills, Michigan, later Brimley. *Paananen Collection*

town over the South Shore trackage from a point just south of the roundhouse, and "temporarily" use the DSS&A facilities over the winter months. "Soo" General Manager F. D. Underwood said his road would build a roundhouse and side tracks as soon as conditions allowed in the spring to care for the "enormous business" that would be forthcoming.[16]

Connecting the DSS&A and MSSM&A with the CPR still required a bridge across the St. Mary's River. The Sault Ste. Marie Bridge Company had been formed for this purpose on February 19, 1881, during the still-formative days of the DM&M. Its capital stock was set at $100,000, and its seven directors (James McMillan, George Hendrie, Francis Palms, Fred E. Driggs, Hugh McMillan, William B. Moran, and William K. Muir) were all DM&M men. On July 8, 1882, Congress authorized construction "whenever due authority shall have been given to any person or corporation by the Dominion of Canada with the sanction of the British Government to build or join in the building of a bridge for such purpose."[17]

The project languished due to the state of the DM&M's finances, and the fact that the Canadian Pacific did not begin active work on its Sault branch from Sudbury until early in 1887. CPR bridge engineers began taking measurements for the new International Bridge in the fall of 1886, and bids were sought for the 2,500-foot span just after the first of the year. Charters for the St. Mary's bridge were secured from the American and Canadian governments by two separate corporations, both using the name Sault Ste. Marie Bridge Company. These companies were consolidated on February 28, 1887. Negotiations between the South Shore, CPR, and MSSM&A concluded that the CPR would own 50 percent of the structure and the American roads each 25 percent. The same percentages would govern the bridge's organization and maintenance expenses. If tolls were insufficient to pay expenses, the three participating roads would make up the deficit in proportion to the traffic they enjoyed crossing the bridge. James McMillan assumed the presidency of the Sault Ste. Marie Bridge Company, with William C. Van Horne, of the Canadian Pacific, vice president.[18]

The New Jersey Bridge Construction Company, organized by the Canadian Pacific and the DSS&A, came to an agreement on May 26, 1887, with the Sault Ste. Marie Bridge Company and Central Trust Company to build the span. The Minneapolis, Sault Ste. Marie & Atlantic entered into the project in a supplemental agreement dated June 29. Capitalization was set at $10,000, with the CPR owning half the shares and the American companies splitting the remainder.[19] The Construction Company agreed to turn over the completed span on or before November 1, 1887, ready for "passage of railway trains and vehicles and foot passenger[s]."[20] Upon completion, the Bridge Company would pay the Construction Company $1,900,000 for the span, to be financed by 5 percent bonds and stock.

Robert G. Reid, a well-known Canadian bridge builder, received the contract to construct the massive bridge on April 4, 1887. American steel prices were judged to be excessive on account of high tariffs, and fabrication of the bridge superstructure, except the draw span, was let to Dominion Bridge Company of Lachine, Quebec. The contract called for a fill on the American side leading to a 400-foot draw span, which would be constructed by Detroit Bridge and Iron works. Only the first 200 feet of the draw, towards the American side, would span water, with the other half available in case another canal was dug. Beyond the eastern abutment of the draw was another fill, about 350 feet long, followed by the main bridge consisting of ten spans, each 239 feet in length. These spans were to be pin-connected trusses in the American style. There would then be another 500-foot fill on the Canadian side and finally two 104-foot spans over a slough before reaching solid ground. The entire structure and approaches would be some three-quarters of a mile in length. Engineers finished the work of locating the bridge on May 10, 1887, and construction started immediately thereafter on masonry work.

The first bridge iron arrived from Montreal at the end of August 1887, with work beginning from the Canadian side. Iron for the swing span arrived on November 12, 1887, and a crew from Detroit Bridge and Iron began to assemble the pieces on the American shore. Winter weather then moved in and for a time progress was "hardly apparent."[21] By mid-December, however, the flooring system reached the U.S. main land abutment and work was being started on the last of the ten spans. Engineers received instructions to have the bridge ready for train movement by January 2 "at all hazards," and the draw was swung for the first time on December 26.[22]

The last rail on the great connecting link was laid December 31, 1887, on the fill between the main spans and the draw. Minneapolis, Sault Ste. Marie & Atlantic engine 26 was waiting to make the first crossing, while on the other side CPR engine 209 pulled up with similar intentions. Engineer A. M. Thompson on the 26 told the CPR crew that it had better clear the way or be pushed back. The CPR relented and the Soo Line went down in history as making the first trip. Some braved the cold by occupying the pilot, tender, and flat cars in order to be able to say "they were on the first train to cross the great international bridge." The span opened the only rail connection between the U.S. and Canada for some 1,400 miles between the Red River of the North and Port Huron, Michigan.[23]

Sault Ste. Marie brimmed with optimism. The *Detroit Evening News* prophesied, "A wonderful change will the new year bring to the Soo. A year ago it was a frost bound,

This 1911 view, looking east, shows the swing span over the canal leading to the American Weitzel and Poe Locks at Sault Ste. Marie closed for railroad traffic. In the distance on the right is the 156-foot swing span over the Canadian lock.
Paananen Collection

snow-buried hamlet, and in a month or so will be a city, situated upon one of the greatest trunk lines of the country, a flourishing railroad center, past whose doors will thunder through trains bound from the plains of Dakota to see the seaboard."[24]

As was often the case with new carriers needing to draw attention to their service, the Minneapolis, Sault Ste. Marie & Atlantic instituted lower freight rates to the East, which the Chicago lines were required to meet. The former launched a counterattack before the newly created Interstate Commerce Commission (ICC), arguing that freight from one part of the U.S., going through Canada to another part of the U.S., in bond, should pay duty. This idea would have put a serious crimp in the South Shore's aspirations to be part of a transcontinental system. The Michigan Central and the Chicago & Grand Trunk in the Lower Peninsula, also negatively affected by the proposal, were able to effectively campaign against the amendment, which never came to pass.

Ten 239-foot pin-connected trusses bridged the St. Mary's Rapids between the swing
spans leading to the American and Canadian Sault locks.   *Paananen Collection*

EQUIPMENT FOR THE SOUTH SHORE

In 1886, vessels traversing the Sault locks between Lake Superior and Lake Huron handled 487,600 tons of freight, and the South Shore optimistically hoped to handle one-half
of that traffic upon completion. To handle such a massive business would require large
increases in equipment over what had been inherited from the predecessor companies.
To complement the 16 locomotives the DSS&A took over from the DM&M and the 52
off the MH&O, Brown, Howard and Co. ordered 20 Mogul engines (67–86) from Brooks
Locomotive Works in February 1887. The first three of the new engines arrived at Marquette on May 6, and were pronounced heavier and more powerful than anything in use
on the predecessor roads.

The need for improved passenger power was made evident by the poor showing the
South Shore had made during the 1887–1888 winter season. The Ishpeming *Iron Ore,* in
an editorial titled, "The Delay, Short Steam and Antiquated Line," did not speak highly
of the new road. Calling its time table "a hollow mockery," the *Iron Ore* thought the road
would be better off using "a Scottish bag piper who will run ahead . . . and 'bla' merry
blasts to arouse the inhabitants." The main difficulty in getting over the road was the
small power then in use. The MH&O had formerly run two-car locals composed of a
combination baggage-smoker and a coach, while through trains contained a small baggage car, smoker, and coach. The South Shore promptly added parlor cars and sleepers,
which proved more than the 30-ton engines could handle. Freight power could be used,
but could not keep the schedules. As the parlor cars were as heavy as two coaches, they
were pulled off at Marquette and limited during the winter to the lighter grades of the
Mackinaw Division (former DM&M trackage).[25]

Engine 303 goes for a spin on the 50-foot hand-operated turntable located at the Fifth Street roundhouse in Marquette. The Brooks Mogul was part of the large locomotive order placed following the DSS&A's formation in 1887. *Paananen Collection*

One of the engines acquired from the MH&O was this 0-6-0 seen performing yard duty in Marquette at the east end of East Yard (Lower Yard) in 1911. The semaphore in the background governs the LS&I diamond at the east end of the yard. *Paananen Collection*

The Lake Superior Limited, still in Marquette yard limits, heads up Bagdad Hill for Calumet. It will be some time before the ore cars in the foreground are put back in service. *Wesley Perron Railroad Collection, Peter White Public Library, Marquette, Mich.*

To overcome this difficulty, fifteen American Standards (102–116) with 5½-foot drivers were ordered from Baldwin for delivery in the summer of 1888. Even though they were Standards, they exceeded anything in use on the UP. The *Mining Journal* commented, "The immense size of the engines can hardly be understood. . . . Standing on the ground at the level of the rail, any man of average height can look right through under the engine boiler, while he can stand on the running board in the cab and not touch the cab roof. From the foot board to the cab roof is about eight feet. These engines, it is expected, will pull seven loaded coaches up the L'Anse hill easily, and can make their 50 miles an hour whenever it is desired."[26] The order also contained another fifteen Moguls (87–101), comparable to the earlier Brooks locomotives.

The South Shore's first new passenger car order totaled twenty coaches (210–229), five baggage and express (10–14), and four mail cars (40–43). Pullman was so backlogged that the order went to Jackson and Sharpe, although the former did build a private car, *Marquette,* No. 100, for President McMillan. Ten of the new coaches were smokers, the first of which arrived in early July painted a "peculiar maroon."[27] The new mail cars, which went into service on July 30, 1888, brought Railway Post Office service to the Mackinaw Division for the first time. The South Shore also ordered five sleepers (*Sault Ste. Marie, St. Ignace, Boynton, Gogebic,* and *Houghton*) from Wagner Palace Car Company which went into service June 3, 1888, and ran through between Detroit and Houghton in conjunction with the Michigan Central. The *Detroit Sun* congratulated James McMillan "in his great and successful efforts to unite the upper and lower peninsulas of Michigan."[28] Another improvement made to South Shore passenger service in 1888 was the use of automatic air brakes.

The initial South Shore order for freight equipment was made on February 1, 1888, with Lafayette Car Works for 250 25-ton, 34-foot boxcars (3600 series), 500 20-ton ore cars (03700 series), and 40 30-foot cabooses (540 series). These were the first long cabooses to be used on the South Shore, as the DM&M had used only the short 4-wheeled variety and the MH&O had not used any. On the same date a contract was signed with McMillan's Michigan Car Works for 500 additional 25-ton, 34-foot boxcars (3600 series) and 10 short cabooses (500 series) for ore service. The Michigan Car Works boxcars, the first of which arrived in Marquette on August 7, 1888, were marked Duluth, South Shore & Atlantic, and carried the slogans "Through Line," and "The Soo-Mackinaw Short Line."[29] To deal with winter snow conditions, the South Shore ordered a big Leslie rotary snow plow (711) in August 1888. After the plow was set up in the Marquette shops, a successful trial run held in the ore yard on January 16, 1888, saw it shoot snow into the gardens of homes along Washington Avenue.

THE CANADIAN PACIFIC ASSUMES CONTROL

During its short period of independence, the South Shore welcomed signs that other Canadian roads had their sights on Sault Ste. Marie. Grand Trunk surveyors arrived at the Sault in early December 1887, and with the purchase of the Northern and Pacific Junction Railway in early 1888, the road advanced west to Callander, Ontario. It was thought the DSS&A and Northern Pacific, at least for the present, would serve as a bridge for the Grand Trunk between the Sault and its isolated trackage in Manitoba and Saskatchewan. This would be just the type of bridge traffic needed to make the South Shore a viable institution. The *Toronto Globe* commented, "This is the most important movement in Canadian railway matters since the commencement of the Canadian Pacific. The Grand Trunk is on the march to the Sault and it is bound to get the shortest line to that important point. It will there make connection with the Northern Pacific system, and a large part of the trade of the American northwest must pass there on its way to New York."[30]

The Canadian Pacific took a dim view of the interloper. If the Grand Trunk made connections with the DSS&A and MSSM&A at the Sault, the CPR's line around the north end of Lake Superior would suffer from the new competition. Sir George Stephen, CPR president, was also concerned that the Minneapolis, Sault Ste. Marie & Atlantic might wind up in the hands of the New York Central (NYC). Stephen warned that this would be "a most potential instrument for diverting traffic from the Canadian channels and drawing it forever into U.S. channels."[31]

At the same time the South Shore was coming under increasing economic pressure as the syndicate started to unwind. As Thomas wrote McMillan, "I am at a loss to know what we ought to do. As you know I raised and paid for Seney and his friends, 1,460,000$. I was compelled to pay off Cummings and take his subscription. I took a larger part of the M.H. & O. int . . . In all I have individually, three-million dollars in securities and advances, and can not sell or use a dollar of them any where . . . Our road is new and unknown and does not command credit as it is, and I fear will not for sometime. I am free to confess my inability to raise the money needed this summer."[32]

These two forces came together in April 1888, and, in negotiations between Brice and Thomas, and Sir George Stephen and Sir Donald Smith (a CPR director), the two Canadians wound up with 51 percent of the South Shore's capital stock. Prices paid were said to be slightly over the quoted price, proving to be a second windfall on top of the construction profits for members of the DSS&A syndicate. Stephen and Smith went on to acquire the Minneapolis, St. Paul and Sault Ste. Marie (MStP&SSM, or Soo Line), a merger of the Minneapolis, Sault Ste. Marie & Atlantic and other roads, giving the CPR a monopoly on roads entering the Sault and shutting out the Grand Trunk in the process. Although matters were kept quiet for a time, on May 19, 1888, a private car full of high Canadian Pacific officials, including Stephen, Smith, and William C. Van Horne, showed up at Champion. The party made a thorough tour of the entire South Shore property and the rumor soon prevailed that the independent days of the DSS&A were numbered.[33]

Sir George Stephen resigned as president of the Canadian Pacific shortly thereafter, and one of his last acts was to officially transfer the South Shore stock to the CPR on August 2, 1888. Stephen optimistically predicted the new acquisitions' traffic "would be difficult to overestimate."[34] Van Horne, never enthusiastic about the purchase of the two American lines, was forced to assume their liabilities on being elected Stephen's successor. Others viewed the changed dynamics with dismay. James J. Hill of the St. Paul, Minneapolis & Manitoba (soon to become the Great Northern) found it alarming that his competitor, the Soo Line, was receiving help from Montreal. Smith wrote Hill that the purchase of the South Shore and the Soo Line was "entirely for the protection of the Canadian business of the CPR & not in the least with the object of adding to the extent of one cent to our own means."[35] Stephen had even tried to have Hill take hold of the two properties, but without success. In March 1890 Hill made an unacceptable offer for control of the Soo Line in exchange for an agreement to pool all traffic on the CPR and GN. The trouble was the GN would not be completed to Puget Sound for three years, and only CPR traffic would be divided until that time. Van Horne scoffed at the offer and wrote Stephen that Hill was "concealing his poison in friendly words."[36]

The CPR takeover also created worries of rate cuts among the Chicago roads, and concern on the part of the Michigan Central and Grand Rapids & Indiana as to what would become of traffic across the Straits of Mackinac. James McMillan assured them that the DSS&A would continue to operate independently and solicit traffic from all sources. With the high stock prices the CPR had been forced to pay, it was thought there would be no downward pressure on rates as the parent company tried to get all the revenue it could from its new subsidiaries. East Coast interests hoped that the purchase

William C. Van Horne assumed the presidency of the Canadian Pacific shortly after its takeover of the DSS&A in 1888. Through W. F. Fitch, his hand-picked manager of the South Shore, Van Horne largely set the road's policy until his retirement in 1899. *James J. Hill Reference Library, Reed Hyde Papers, RH 698*

would lead to development of the north country and the end of its dominance by Chicago jobbers in favor of their own. The shift was thought possible due to the close connection between the Boston & Lowell and the Canadian Pacific and the large amount of Boston money invested in the UP. Given the difficulty the Detroit jobbers faced in meeting Chicago competition, it is hard to imagine how parties in New England could have overcome their even greater separation from the UP. The real losers turned out to be the Grand Trunk and ultimately the DSS&A, as the CPR would never provide the bridge traffic promised by its competitor. The *London Standard* reported that the Grand Trunk stockholders were not at all pleased as the "policy of the company have allowed the Canadian Pacific to walk around them."[37]

At the annual meeting of the South Shore held in New York in early August 1888, CPR representation on the board become dominant with the election of Sir George Stephen, Sir Donald Smith, William C. Van Horne, Richard J. Cross, Thomas W. Pearsall, and John W. Sterling as directors. Of the old management, only McMillan, Thomas, Brice, Seney, and J. G. North were retained. The officers of the road remained largely the same, causing the Marquette *Mining Journal* to comment, "Those who predicted that everything was to be torn up by the roots and 'God save the Queen,' supplant the more aristocratic air of 'Yankee Doodle' just because of the transfer of a portion of the South Shore stock to new hands, must feel considerably and extensively left as they read the following list: James McMillan, of Detroit, president; Calvin S. Brice, of New York, first vice president; W. C. Van Horne, of Toronto, second vice president; W. A. C. Ewen, of New York, treasurer; L. M. Schwan, of New York, secretary."[38]

There was concern in Marquette regarding its status as the South Shore's headquarters. The community was reassured on August 23, 1888, when Van Horne arrived for a conference with James McMillan, Samuel Thomas, George Seney, and others. After the meeting McMillan told the *Mining Journal,* "We have been looking around today for a site for a fine depot and office building. You may say that it has been determined to locate the headquarters of the South Shore road at Marquette permanently, and steps will at once be taken to provide the necessary office accommodations and shops. The shops [DM&M and MH&O] will be consolidated, the MH&O being retained because [they are] provided with larger and more permanent buildings."[39]

THE DULUTH ENTRANCE

At the time of the CPR takeover, trackage on the Western Division to the Northern Pacific connection at Iron River was largely completed, with only surfacing remaining. The only question left unanswered was whether the South Shore would reach Duluth via the NP or go it alone. With negotiations at an impasse, the new owners opted for an independent line. McMillan told Van Horne, "we must make effort to get all grading completed by October twenty fifth at latest if we hope to get track down + ballasted this season."[40] Assistant Chief Engineer Stevens soon had a number of locating parties in the field, and the contract for the West Superior extension was let to Henry and Balch in mid-August.

The first through movement between Marquette and Duluth occurred on August 25, 1888, when a special containing President McMillan, Second Vice President Van Horne, directors Seney and Thomas, and Chief Engineer Latcha traversed the Western Division into Iron River, and then used NP rails to the Twin Ports. McMillan commented to the Duluth press that the Western Division was in good condition, except for ballasting in several places, and that speeds of 50 miles an hour had been attained. McMillan laid to rest rumors that the South Shore would build northwest of Duluth to Winnipeg, thereby forming a secondary CPR main line. He said the main advantage the CPR would give to the South Shore was traffic, apparently out of the Sault, a projection which unfortunately bore little fruit. The party then left for St. Paul and a conference with Vice President Oakes of the NP. Although the main topic was the Northern Pacific & Manitoba, whose rails were currently invading the CPR domain in the Winnipeg area, the use of the NP between Iron River and Duluth was temporarily brought to a resolution, with the South Shore to be charged $1 a train mile for use of the NP trackage between Iron River and Duluth.

The agreement brought a stop to the construction of the independent entry, the wisdom of which South Shore secretary L. M. Schwan said had been in doubt for some time, as it was felt the road's resources could be better utilized elsewhere. There was widespread speculation that the remarks of U.S. president Grover Cleveland, questioning the desirability of Canadian ownership of American roads and whether restrictions should be placed on U.S. commerce routed through Canada, had been the cause of the pullback. Schwan denied this, saying, "I do not believe that the policy as outlined in the message will be put into force. It was a great stroke of policy on the part of Mr. Cleveland and shows him to be one of the best and most original politicians in the country."[41]

The South Shore began limited mixed train service into Duluth on September 17, 1888, running west on Monday, Wednesday, and Friday and returning the next day. Connections were made at Nestoria with the Houghton passenger trains, and stops were made at Thomaston for meals. The train was said to be mainly for the benefit of the contractors, but business expanded to the point that a daily, if disjointed, service was offered beginning October 8. The Duluth car was attached to the 7:30 AM Republic passenger train out of Marquette and cut off at Humboldt, where another crew brought it into Thomaston. Out of Thomaston, the coach became part of a mixed run, with a scheduled arrival of 9:30 PM at Duluth. American Express began offering service over the route in early December 1888, followed by railway mail service on February 1, 1889. As the territory was desolate and had few open stations, a telegrapher was placed on each train and given a pocket sounder and key.

Service was considerably improved with the institution of a new through train between Duluth and Sault Ste. Marie on July 1, 1889. Close connections were made at the Sault with the through Soo Line–Canadian Pacific service for Montreal and Boston. The new DSS&A trains, known as the Boston Express and Duluth Express, usually had 5 cars and were pulled by a 45-ton Baldwin passenger engine. A Duluth–Sault Ste. Marie sleeper brought up the rear. The Humboldt-Duluth run was changed to a mixed following the start of the express runs.

Contractors Henry and Balch had been called off from their work west of Iron River on August 26, 1888. Due to the urgency of the oncoming winter season, the contractors had "not been letting grass grow under their feet," and with 1,000 men were at work along the proposed line.[42] Balch settled up with his dozen subcontractors as best he could, commenting: "While we are greatly disappointed as well as vexed at the way matters have gone, our firm will undoubtedly have all it can do in building eight miles on the cut-off line, and the several branch lines into the Gogebic mines."[43]

The DSS&A's 8-mile-long "cutoff line" was to be built to avoid paying valuation on the expensive NP terminal properties at Old Superior, South Superior, and West Superior. South Shore trackage would leave the NP's Ashland line near Cutter and head northwest. After going under the CStPM&O, the line would head north and cross Bluff Creek and the Nemadji River. Upon reaching Billings Ave. (later 28th St.) in Superior, the South Shore would swing west until it reached the NP short line. There it would head north to join the LST&T, making use of its Union Station. At the north end of the LST&T's yards, the South Shore would cross over the CStPM&O and terminate at its waterfront property.

Henry and Balch had a large force at work on the cutoff as early as mid-September 1888. After the settling of various right-of-way disputes, grading had progressed by the end of November to where the line was nearly ready for ties and iron. At noon on December 7, trackage between the NP crossing at Atlantic Jct. (19th Ave.) and the West Superior Union Depot, 3.75 miles, was completed, and the South Shore mixed began to use the new route. With grading complete on the entire 7.76 miles between the NP junction near Cutter and West Superior, Henry and Balch were paid off and work suspended for the winter. A big gap remained over the Nemadji River, which would require a draw span as the government considered it to be a navigable stream.

The independent South Shore entrance into Duluth was still a topic of discussion. Latcha advocated building a 4,000-foot bridge across the St. Louis River 0.5 miles west of the NP span and then paralleling the St. Paul & Duluth Railroad trackage into Duluth. This caused the *Duluth News* to comment, "It seemed from the beginning absurd for so important a road to reach its terminus over borrowed tracks."[44] Not all were in favor. West Superior interests said if the South Shore intended to make their community a "flag station on their way to Duluth as the NP has been doing for the past six years, we can see no reason, under heaven why people of Superior should help to ruin their harbor facilities just to help said road reach Duluth or any other point beyond us."[45] Van Horne felt it would be better to make use of the NP bridge across the St. Louis River and run alongside the CStPM&O trackage from Rice's Point to Fourth Street. With its large terminal property in West Superior, Van Horne did not feel the South Shore would require much trackage in Duluth.

At the same time that new construction was ongoing, the original properties were upgraded. The Mackinaw Division, never profitable to its previous owners, had begun to suffer from neglect. Under the South Shore management, the whole division received a beefing up in the spring of 1888. Trestlework was strengthened with additional bents, piles, and stringers. Twelve miles of iron rail east of Marquette were re-laid with steel and 120,000 ties were put in. By fall, the railroad had been rejuvenated to the point that train speeds were the highest on any road north of Grand Rapids, Michigan. Connections off the MC and GR&I typically left Mackinaw City 30 to 45 minutes late, but invariably arrived in Marquette on time. The burning of the St. Ignace roundhouse on May 5, 1888, necessitated further east end improvements, and a new 8-stall house was placed in service in November. St. Ignace also received a new iron turntable, ash pits, pump house, and incline coal dock.

A NEW BOAT FOR THE STRAITS

The problem of navigating the Straits of Mackinac still needed resolution, with winter ice conditions making for less than reliable service. McMillan held discussions with the Detroit Dry Dock Company, whose architect, Frederick Ballin, envisioned conquering the ice with the use of a bow propeller. The stern screws would propel the boat onto the ice, while the bow screw, mounted 8 feet below the water line and operating in reverse, would create a back current that would wash away the crushed ice under the vessel. If this idea proved practical, under the worst circumstances, the new ferry would only take one day to make the crossing, while the poor *Algomah* had been known to be stuck for lengthy periods. Frank E. Kirby designed the ship, known as the *St. Ignace,* and work was begun by the Dry Dock Company in the spring of 1887.

When completed the 1,200-ton *St. Ignace* measured 215′6″ long and 52′3″ wide, with a height of 15′8″. She came equipped with two compound engines running on 127 pounds pressure from three Scotch boilers. A cabin ran down the center of the ship with two tracks wrapped around it. The stacks were mounted on top of the cabins fore and aft. The hull, made of oak, had a spoon-shaped bow, which was designed to raise the vessel up on the ice and crush it. The *St. Ignace* started out from the St. Clair River on April 7, 1888, and took about 60 hours to make the trip to its home port, bucking ice most of the way. Captain Louis R. Boynton described the journey: "We had only twenty-five miles of clear water since leaving the river and the *St. Ignace* walked through the entire distance of ice, which varied from two feet in thickness to windrows nearly twenty feet thick. . . . I am satisfied that no ice that can collect in the straits can stop her."[46]

In preparation for the *St. Ignace,* a new 1,150′ × 50′ slip dock, three tracks wide, was constructed at her namesake port. The dock was also home to the new passenger station constructed over the summer. When these combined with its lumber dock, merchandise pier, and warehouse, the DSS&A came to have some impressive facilities at St. Ignace. The Marquette *Mining Journal* wrote that it was apparent St. Ignace "has the big end of the South Shore horn and Sault Ste. Marie the little."[47] The Sault Ste. Marie paper, in dismissing the new ferry, wishfully concluded: "its success is doubtful."[48]

Shovel 706 is seen loading a string of empty ore cars in this view of the large gravel pit at the West Yard in St. Ignace, Michigan. The coal trestle in the background serviced engines at the West Yard roundhouse. *Paananen Collection*

HANDLING THE ORE BUSINESS

Although the DSS&A was created in hopes of attracting large amounts of bridge traffic, its principal commodity, like that of its predecessors, continued to be iron ore. The 1886 and 1887 ore seasons were marked by lack of dock capacity and resulting car shortages. Dock pockets often became filled while waiting for vessels to arrive, leaving no place to unload cars, and this resulted in a shortage of empties for loading at the mines, much to the displeasure of the mine captains.

To help overcome the lack of dock capacity, the DSS&A awarded a contract in December 1887 to Thomas H. Hamilton of Toledo to add a 650-foot extension, containing one hundred 100-ton pockets, to the former M&W dock. With a new length of 1,700 feet, the dock's capacity grew to 17,000 tons. Although an additional 11,000-ton capacity was available at the old M&O RR dock, the M&W dock was the only one with chutes mounted high enough to efficiently load modern ore boats. Another improvement saw the resurrection of the old light plant of the Marquette & Western, which had been in service for only one season before the MH&O takeover, to light the two docks and allow nighttime operations. The new facilities greatly helped the dispatch of vessels at Marquette and boat captains no longer dreaded visiting the port.

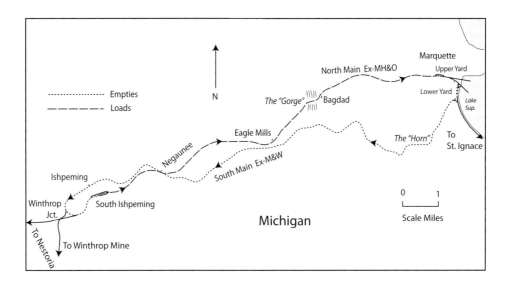

Routing of Ore Trains, June 30, 1887

The rail component was improved in June 1887 when westbound ore empties started using the former M&W trackage to Winthrop Jct. before returning as eastbound loads on the MH&O line to Marquette. This avoided turning the engines on either end of the line, and eliminated time-consuming meets on the MH&O line. To give increased flexibility on its double main line between Negaunee and Marquette, the DSS&A built a .62-mile cutoff between the north and south lines at Eagle Mills in 1889. If trouble developed on one of the lines, the segment as far as Eagle Mills could still be used as double track.

Conductors were used on ore trains for the first time in 1887, ending the MH&O practice of having the engineers in charge of the train. The trains were modern by today's standards in that they did not have cabooses. This bit of forward thinking was abandoned by the 1889 season, when cabooses came to be used on all trains. That year the South Shore also began to run ore trains at night to alleviate congestion. Because of crowded conditions in the Upper Yard at Marquette, a new coach yard was built closer to the depot to free up the old coach yard for ore. This required the removal of the old MH&O freight depot, near the depot, and less-than-carload business was transferred to the former DM&M freight house on Lake and Jackson in the Lower (East) Yard.

To reach new iron ore finds of the Pittsburgh and Lake Superior Iron Co., south of Negaunee, the South Shore organized the Negaunee & Palmer Railroad Company (N&P) on June 30, 1888. This company built a 4.45-mile branch, completed in August 1888, off the end of the old Rolling Mill branch to the Volunteer mine. The South Shore made advances to build the N&P and assumed stock control at its organization. The Volunteer mine, located near Palmer, was the site of an open pit siliceous ore deposit.[49]

Although the South Shore main line bypassed the Gogebic Iron Range a few miles to the north, it was envisioned the burgeoning region would be tapped with short branches. During the winter of 1887–1888, surveyors located a spur south from Thomaston to

Wakefield. Another branch survey left the DSS&A main line north of Bessemer, and, after reaching that community, headed west along the southern boundary of the Gogebic mining district, before turning north along the Montreal River to rejoin the main line. The L'Anse ore dock would provide an outlet for the Gogebic iron ore, and a cutoff was surveyed between that point and a junction with the main line at the crossing of the East Branch of the Ontonagon River. Transloading at L'Anse, instead of on the Wisconsin Central and Milwaukee, Lake Shore & Western docks at Ashland, would reduce vessel hauls by 200 miles. The shipping season would also be extended a month or two by avoiding the bad ice conditions in Chequamegon Bay.

Following completion of the grade for the independent entrance into West Superior, Henry and Balch shifted much of their equipment to the Gogebic Range loop line, and, by mid-September 1888, some 500 men were engaged a short distance from the main line at Bessemer Jct. After some dispute, agreements were reached at Bessemer to cross the Lake Shore on an overhead trestle and go under the WC. Work on the Thomaston-Wakefield branch started toward the end of September, with choppers clearing the right of way on the Thomaston end. By the end of November, bridge timbers were being sent up the branch, although it was said no rails would be laid until spring due to shortages.

Latcha wrote Van Horne that they were sure to have trackage into Bessemer before 1888 was out, and, if not too much delay was encountered in bridging the Lake Shore, it might be possible to complete the line all the way into Ironwood. Depot grounds were graded at the foot of Monroe Street in Bessemer and tracks reached this point on October 24. A depot was erected at the site the following month. Grading was completed to the Montreal River by November 22, and before winter closed down operations, rails were laid to within a couple of miles of Hurley. The South Shore hoped to attain 25 percent of the Gogebic Range tonnage in 1889, or some 325,000 tons of ore. The question remained whether the South Shore could handle a traffic increase of this magnitude. Although the mining captains on the Marquette Range agreed that the DSS&A had improved service since the MH&O days, it still was found lacking compared to the C&NW.

Projects such as the Gogebic loop line, Thomaston-Wakefield branch, L'Anse cutoff, and Superior cutoff were not rejuvenated with the start of 1889, and the close of the 1888 construction season brought an end to the expansionist era of the South Shore. The Gogebic Range mines were largely owned by principals or friends of the MLS&W or WC, and how much tonnage the DSS&A could have secured was open to question. New tonnage would have been gained only through DSS&A, or more likely CPR, financial support for new finds being explored on the east end of the range near Wakefield. It was also rumored that the MLS&W threatened to build off its Choate Branch into Houghton unless the South Shore incursion was stopped. South Shore rails were pulled up beyond Bessemer, and the Wakefield branch never got beyond the grading stage.

The value and earning potential of the South Shore route itself was also still open to question. Some thought that the South Shore would assume a large portion of the grain and flour trade on the lakes. J. O. Hayes, a mine owner on the Gogebic Range, predicted the completion of the South Shore would have a marked effect on the vessel charters, taking many boats out of the grain trade, and making them available for hauling ore. Others saw the South Shore receiving much of the Northern Pacific's

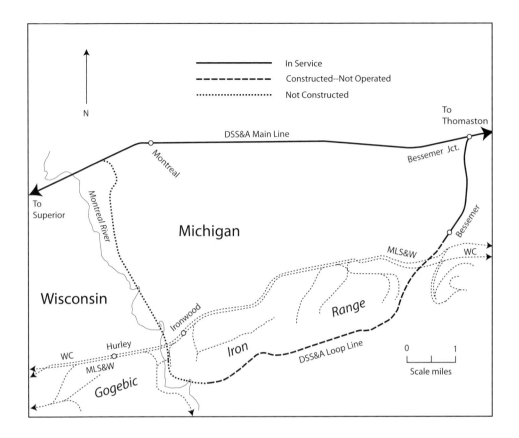

In Service
Constructed--Not Operated
Not Constructed

N

To
Thomaston

DSS&A Main Line

Montreal

Bessemer Jct.

To
Superior

Montreal River

Michigan

Bessemer

MLS&W

WC

Wisconsin

Ironwood

Range

WC

Hurley

Iron

DSS&A Loop Line

0   1

MLS&W

Scale miles

Gogebic

Gogebic Range Loop Line, 1889

transcontinental traffic, which would be routed via Duluth instead of St. Paul. The latter community had largely taken over as the NP's principal eastern gateway for non-lake traffic.

The DSS&A was truly a short cut from the Head of the Lakes to New York and especially New England. The shortest route between Duluth and New York via Chicago totaled 1,394 miles, while routing over the South Shore via St. Ignace cut this down to 1,373 miles, and going via the Sault only totaled 1,292 miles. Considering freight trains of this period usually took 8 hours or more to run 100 miles, this was not an insignificant mileage. Even more beneficial was the ability of the South Shore to avoid the congested Chicago gateway. On the other hand, Chicago roads would fight any solicitation via the CPR and the Sault, which would result in a diminished line haul. Moreover, given the limited population at Duluth-Superior and beyond, there was little demand for a high-speed service to the East Coast. The area's jobbing needs could be more quickly and cheaply met by Minneapolis, St. Paul, or Chicago firms. Duluth's heavy shipments of outbound grain, flour, lumber, and ore, and inbound coal, were handled expeditiously enough by lake boats capable of reaching almost 2,000 miles of navigable water on the Great Lakes.

Perhaps the most discouraging evaluation of the South Shore property was offered by Assistant Chief Engineer John Stevens: "The road was one that as an engineer I did not take pride in building. It was understood that one basic, if not the principal, reason was to make money for some of the members of the syndicate and I was so advised when I took charge."[50] The new Canadian owners also began to entertain suspicions that the South Shore had been "skinned" by Brown, Howard and Co.[51] The Michigan Railroad Commission seemed to agree, saying in its report for 1888, "The new line from Nestoria to state line was built by contract, and was not constructed as well as railroads usually are by parties who expect to operate them."[52]

A large number of South Shore box cars, some equipped with the "Marquette Route" herald, are spotted for loading at the Sparrow-Kenton mill near Kenton, Michigan. The mill lasted from 1891 until 1910. *Paananen Collection*

5

THE ZENITH CITY SHORT LINE

The Canadian Pacific further solidified its influence on the DSS&A when Van Horne brought in an outsider, William Foresman Fitch, to fill the new position of general manager, effective November 1, 1888. As Van Horne wrote Fitch, "The object of the Ex. Com.'s action is to invest you with fullest power and to make you responsible to the Board alone. It may be well for you to know this confidentially before you meet Mr. McMillan as he is personally interested in some men and measures which you may probably find not entirely to your liking."[1] Fitch, who had begun railroading in October 1871 as a clerk on the C&NW, had risen through the ranks to become general manager of the affiliated Fremont, Elkhorn & Missouri Valley and Sioux City & Pacific companies before coming to the South Shore.

Fitch proceeded to make some needed economies, causing short-lived superintendent George Jarvis to comment to McMillan, "From present indications I do not think Mr. Fitch is satisfied with my services and forces have been so materially reduced and duties enlarged that will no doubt be compelled to resign."[2] Another change Fitch wrought was to give the DSS&A a new slogan of "Zenith City Short Line." This change from "Soo-Mackinaw Short Line" eliminated confusion with the CPR's other American subsidiary, and the South Shore's main competitor, the Soo Line. "Zenith City" was Duluth's moniker, and although a rather tiny amount of DSS&A revenue came from that point, Fitch felt that was where the road's future lay.

The first coordination with the Soo Line, which would plague the South Shore's interests in later years, came shortly thereafter. F. N. Finney, president of the Soo Line, was appointed second vice president of the DSS&A in June 1890 with the resignation of Van Horne. On September 14, 1890, the passenger departments of the Soo Line and South Shore were consolidated, with headquarters in Minneapolis. C. B. Hibbard, the DSS&A's general passenger agent, who was viewed by Van Horne as "ambitious and zealous,"[3] was given control of the consolidated department. Passenger agents were given the difficult task of representing two competing roads in soliciting traffic.

Local freight business on the Western Division began to take hold during the winter of 1888–1889 as the new DSS&A opened up previously inaccessible pine lands. By March 1892, there were thirteen sawmills in operation or under construction between Nestoria and Iron River, as well as several shingle mills. Iron River and Ewen were each

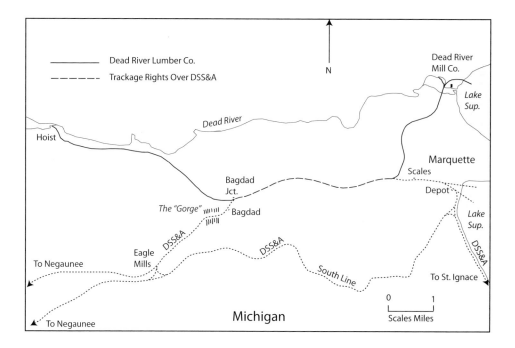

Dead River Lumber Company, 1895

home to three pine mills, with others located at Matchwood, Kenton, Kitchie, and Sidnaw. Trout Creek Lumber Co., at the community of the same name, operated the largest of the Western Division sawmills. Cedar mills were located at Sanborn, Marengo, Saxon (formerly Dogwood), and Matchwood. On the Houghton Division, or former MH&O trackage, additional mills were found at Eagle Mills, a mile west of Champion, and Three Lakes; there were several at Baraga (including the huge Nester mill), and Sturgeon River Company had a new plant at Chassell. The mills at Baraga and Chassell contributed little to the South Shore car loadings given their location on the L'Anse Bay of Lake Superior and their access to cheaper lumber schooners.

The DSS&A was formed at the peak of Michigan's lumber production and its 1890 cut of 4,245,177,000 feet led the nation in total output, as had its cut every year since 1880. This total would never be equaled, however, as the pace could not be sustained due to diminishing forest reserves. The pine loggers began to move west into Wisconsin, Minnesota, and eventually the Pacific Northwest, a trend that would be reflected in the South Shore traffic base.

A major source of log traffic for the South Shore developed when T. H. McGraw and R. K. Hawley of Cleveland purchased timber at the headwaters of the Dead River. To harvest this timber, the Dead River Railroad was organized on November 11, 1889. The road was constructed in two parts, with the DSS&A functioning as an intermediary. A 4-mile branch off the South Shore at Bagdad Jct. (near the top of the hill west of Marquette) was built in the spring of 1890 to a log hoist on the Dead River. Another branch, 2.98 miles in length, was constructed off the DSS&A, just west of the Marquette ore yard, north to the site of the Hawley mill at the mouth of the Dead River. Logs could not be floated the entire length of the river because of waterfalls, deep gorges, and a dam.

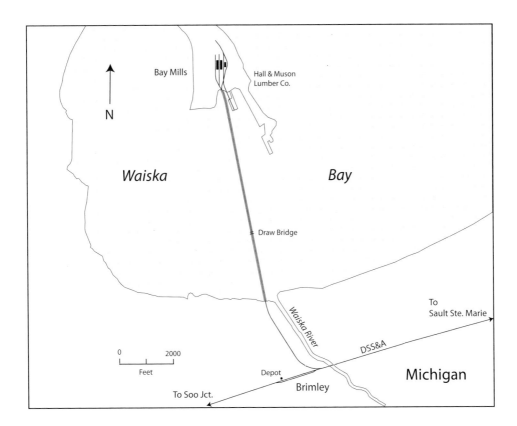

Bay Mills Spur, July 1896

The South Shore contracted with Hawley and McGraw to handle the logs, and the first trains, manned by South Shore equipment and crews, were run on August 11, 1890. The log trains were run in conjunction with the mill season, with up to six a day being operated in 1891 and as many as eight trains a day the following year.

On the Mackinaw Division, the South Shore enjoyed a contract with Robert Dollar to handle logs to the dump at St. Ignace for towing to a mill at Bay City on the Lower Peninsula. Smith Bros., at Eckerman, had a similar contract. The South Shore also operated log trains from Walker's Pit (later Fiborn) to Bay Mills (later Brimley) on the Sault branch. At Bay Mills the logs were dumped into the Waiskey River and floated down the river to the Hall and Buell (later Hall and Munson) mill. The South Shore let a contract in late 1890 to Henry and Balch to build a 2.25-mile spur to directly serve the mill. Other log traffic could be found 7 miles east of Seney, at Danaher, where a spur served Danaher and Melindy Lumber Co. During the winter of 1891–1892, the DSS&A handled some 75 cars of logs a day on the Mackinaw Division and 125 on the Western Division.

Non-log traffic would be needed to compensate for the diminishing forest reserves. A 1-mile spur was laid in June 1894 to reach the site of the new state asylum, awarded to Newberry the year before. Besides ordinary supplies, the South Shore received healthy coal traffic to the asylum from the Sault Ste. Marie coal dock. Another 0.4-mile spur in South Marquette was constructed in 1889 to handle coal and supply shipments to the new state prison.

A drawing of the Furst, Jacobs & Co. quarry, which was located just south of the wye at the Lower Yard in Marquette. In this view looking north, the south main line is seen at the upper left headed toward Negaunee. *Paananen Collection*

The brownstone trade also held great promise in the 1890s. The Detroit and Marquette Brownstone quarry received a nearly mile-long spur in 1889 off the old M&W trackage in Marquette, adding some $125,000 in freight revenue to the DSS&A the following year. On the Houghton Division, the Lake Superior Red Sandstone quarry opened at the turn of the century at the new station of Arnheim. A 0.6-mile branch built to serve the quarry was abandoned in September 1917, by which time brownstone had fallen out of favor as a building material.

Additional short-haul traffic was realized when the Ontonagon & Brule River started operating into Sidnaw on October 10, 1889. The DSS&A ferried cars back and forth to the Champion connection with the O&BR's parent, the Milwaukee & Northern, some 38 miles to the east. The M&N eventually constructed its own line to Sidnaw by building northwest off its Milwaukee-Champion line at Channing. This link opened January 1, 1893. On July 1 of that year, the Milwaukee & Northern officially became the Northern Division of the Chicago, Milwaukee and St. Paul (CM&StP, or Milwaukee Road).

Besides local shipments, South Shore general freight agent William Orr actively solicited through business. In mid-November 1888, Orr successfully pressured the Chicago roads to give Duluth the same rates as the Twin Cities on New York traffic. Then in early December, those rates were reduced 25 cents when traffic was routed via the Canadian Pacific to Boston. This made Duluth and Ashland lumber rates to New England very close to those out of Chicago. While many of the mills intended to ship lower grades of lumber by water, it was said the higher grades would be sent east by rail.

One negative Orr had to deal with was that the long-promised South Shore branch to Ashland had not materialized. Ashland shipments had to begin with a short haul on the CStPM&O to Bibon, or Wisconsin Central to Marengo, or Milwaukee, Lake Shore &

A view of the Sidnaw, Michigan, depot looking east in 1911 shows the Chicago, Milwaukee & St. Paul tracks in the foreground, while the South Shore tracks heading for Marquette are seen to the rear of the depot. The two lines crossed just to the west of the depot, with the crossing being governed by an interlocking plant. *Paananen Collection*

Western to Saxon. Agents for these companies did all they could to avoid a short haul. In the early 1890s, there was a move at Ashland to build a belt line railroad around the city, which would bring the South Shore into town. This was felt to be very desirable as the DSS&A was viewed as the "great rate maker."[4] The other roads in Ashland saw no need for such a belt line and certainly were not interested in having the "great rate maker" come to town. A logging road, with the grand title of the Minneapolis, St. Paul & Ashland, built out of Ashland to a connection with the DSS&A at Chequamegon Jct. (west of Bibon) in 1898, but furnished little in the way of traffic from the lumber mills that lined the Ashland bayfront.

The flour and grain traffic out of Duluth-Superior and the Twin Cities was also actively pursued. Henry D. Minot, the head of Hill's Eastern Minnesota Railway Company, sought Chicago rates on grain for Duluth and helped his new road by funneling Minneapolis traffic to the Twin Ports and the DSS&A. Minot also promoted the 23-cent "export grain" rate from Minneapolis to Boston in December 1889. Much of this traffic was not designed for export at all, but was used locally in New England. The principals behind this rate were Governor Smith of the Central Vermont and others who had a number of private cars. They did not really care what the rate was, so long as their cars were actively employed. Van Horne largely put a stop to such schemes, saying, "While I am disposed to cooperate in almost every way with connecting lines and carry in connection with them any business which they may wish to handle, I do not like to see our line or any line in which we are interested, carrying freight which does not pay the expense of hauling it, simply to put money into pockets of individuals who are practically robbing the roads with which they are connected." Van Horne did agree to allow the export rate to continue as long as it did not apply to more than 25 percent of the total grain shipments and was used strictly for export traffic.[5]

The Eastern Minnesota also pursued East Coast passenger traffic to be routed via Duluth and the South Shore. Van Horne warned Fitch, "I will be glad if you will make the necessary enquiry to satisfy yourself as to whether or not the D.S.S. & A. is gaining enough by the permission which seems to have been given to Mr. Minot to cut the eastern passenger rates from St. Paul and Minneapolis to justify the demoralization that has resulted from it and that is likely to grow out of it. It cannot continue long without affecting business from which you otherwise would get full rates."[6]

Another brake on lower rates was the federal government's continuing suspicion of Canadian ownership of American railroads. During U.S. Senate hearings held in the spring of 1889, senators were anxious to find out whether Canadian involvement did more harm than good, and if their exemption from the Interstate Commerce Act gave them an unfair advantage over the U.S. roads. Some even felt the two-year-old act should be revised. The Senate committee also wondered whether U.S. traffic was being diverted to Canada. The question most commonly asked of Van Horne at the hearings was, "What would be the result if Canadian roads were shut out from doing business in the United States?"[7] Although the senators were pacified, Van Horne warned Fitch regarding rate reductions, "There is some danger of adverse legislation at Washington during the present session of Congress and our enemies there should not be given any more ammunition to be used against us than can be helped."[8]

The Canadian Pacific was also faced with a question of fairness regarding its other property, and the South Shore's chief opposition, the Minneapolis, St. Paul & Sault Ste. Marie. Van Horne wrote, "It should not be forgotten that the Canadian Pacific cannot allow the D.S.S. & A. and its connections between Minneapolis and the 'Soo' any greater division of the through rate than it allows to the M.St.P. & Ste.M. and this by reason of the greater mileage of the D.S.S.& A. reduces its earnings per ton-mile. In such matters the Canadian Pacific must treat the two lines west of the 'Soo' precisely as if it had no interest in either—as if they were two perfectly independent and competing lines."[9]

During the winter of 1889–1890, the South Shore handled some 90 cars of eastbound bridge traffic daily through Marquette. Grain trains often ran in more than one section. The Duluth Imperial Mill Company and the Duluth Roller Mill Company sometimes sent complete trains over the South Shore. One of the more noteworthy trains, which ran in January 1890, was composed of 15 cars of flour for Boston, and was brightly decorated with slogans. The flour had been made at the Imperial mill, and the freight cars built at the Minnesota Iron Car Works in West Duluth. Thus, with the exception of the locomotive and caboose, the entire consist and its contents were of Duluth manufacture.

Unfortunately, the grain and flour traffic returned to the lakes with the spring breakup, there being no way to compete with water rates to the East Coast. The rail rate to New York was 32½ cents a hundred on flour, with the water rate just over half that at

$17\frac{1}{2}$ cents. The Eastern Minnesota, although willing to help the DSS&A during the winter months, became solely interested in filling the holds of Hill's Northern Steamship Company's Great Lakes fleet during the season of navigation. The big Minneapolis flour mills even got around having to use the rails during the winter months by building large warehouses in the East, which enabled them to ship a full year's supply of flour to market by boat during the season of navigation.

Although an enormous tonnage was handled into the Twin Ports by the NP, CStPM&O, Eastern Minnesota, and St. Paul & Duluth for export down the Lakes, the South Shore received but a few crumbs. This is amply demonstrated by 1894 figures, which show that of the 221,811 loaded cars handled in and out of Duluth-Superior, the DSS&A accounted for only 3,582. South Shore bridge traffic was further negatively affected with the lease of the Wisconsin Central by the Northern Pacific on April 1, 1890. Although the lease was broken following the Panic of 1893, the arrangement tended to funnel NP freight and passenger business out of the Twin Ports to Ashland and down the WC.

Van Horne remained optimistic about the South Shore's passenger business, writing Fitch in the fall of 1889, "I would like to see you soon about next season's campaign. We should make a strong pull for passengers and the arrangements should be as perfect as possible when spring comes."[10] Business improved on the Western Division to the point that one of the Marquette-Michigamme locals had its run extended into Bessemer beginning June 8, 1890. The other Michigamme local had its origin changed to Republic, from which point it made a morning turn to Marquette. A daylight Marquette-Houghton run was added later that year, affording much better connections with CM&StP at Champion. A further service improvement saw the addition of a daylight run between Sault Ste. Marie and St. Ignace, which enabled passengers out of the Sault to make connections for the Lower Peninsula at Mackinaw City and passengers out of St. Ignace to connect with the Duluth Express at Soo Jct.

Westbound connections with the Michigan Central continued to be a problem. Fitch went to Detroit in December 1892, ostensibly for the purpose of "jacking up" that road and trying to find out why their trains were always an hour or two late into Mackinaw City. The Marquette *Mining Journal* commented, "Had Upper Peninsula people been assured that such was the purpose of the visit of the South Shore's general manager and general passenger agent to Detroit they would have fitted them out with some first-class hardwood clubs for use on Ledyard [Michigan Central president] and the superintendent of his Mackinaw Division."[11]

Express traffic on the South Shore passenger trains began to be handled by a new company, Northern Express, on November 1, 1889, as the result of a breakdown in negotiations with American Express. Van Horne, expressing dissatisfaction with American, wrote, "I have never heard of an Express Co. offering for a line half of what it was worth to them."[12] Northern Express Company, renamed Western Express on October 30, 1894, took over duties on most of the CPR's American properties and its allies, including the Soo Line. Western Express would handle the South Shore's express traffic until the formation of American Railway Express Company during the First World War.

A doubleheader with engines 101 and 36 works a westbound passenger train up Bagdad Hill, past the ore yard in Marquette. The 101 was one of the new Baldwin 4-4-0s received by the South Shore in 1888, while the smaller 36 was of Detroit, Mackinaw & Marquette origins. *Wesley Perron Railroad Collection, Peter White Public Library, Marquette, Mich.*

An eight-car passenger train powered by a small Standard is seen on Bagdad Hill near the Dead River connection switch, west of Marquette. *Wesley Perron Railroad Collection, Peter White Public Library, Marquette, Mich.*

Soo Jct. was an important exchange point, with the South Shore main line out of Marquette splitting into two segments for Sault Ste. Marie and St. Ignace. In this view looking west, the main track to St. Ignace curves in the foreground, while the main track to Sault Ste. Marie is behind the depot. Freight cars were exchanged in the freight yard in the background, just beyond the junction switch.   *Courtesy of Roy Paananen*

Au Train, Michigan, lost much of its significance when the county seat for Alger County moved to Munising in 1901. In 1911 this eastbound is about to cross over the Au Train River and then climb 6 miles to Ridge station, which straddled the divide between the Lake Superior and Lake Michigan watersheds.   *Paananen Collection*

THE LAKE MICHIGAN & LAKE SUPERIOR
RAILWAY COMPANY

The South Shore continued to enjoy healthy ore traffic in the early 1890s as a result of its continuing monopoly at Marquette. Thirty-four mines shipped 1,376,335 tons of iron ore through Marquette and 51,853 tons through St. Ignace during the 1889 season, with the Republic being the leading shipper at 221,219 tons. Mines only stood to become more productive as time went on. New explosives and power drills became commonplace on the Marquette Range, and, in 1889, Lake Superior Iron Company made use of the first steam shovel to load stockpile ore into cars. This was a great advance over the old method of loading cars with wheelbarrows. The miners resented the machine and called it "The Finn," in honor of the Finnish laborers it displaced.[13] This work was the most grueling of the miner's hard lot and most of the layoffs were only temporary.

Capacity problems still haunted the South Shore's iron ore hauling. During the 1889 ore season the South Shore was handling between 1,000 and 1,500 cars of ore a day. Things quickly became stretched to the limit when a gale blew for five days, during which time the South Shore docks did not see a boat. As the Marquette breakwater did not provide protection to vessels loading at the ore docks during stormy weather, they were forced to cast off and seek shelter until the weather passed. This resulted in all the pockets and ore cars being filled with ore and no empties being available at the mines for loading. President Grover Cleveland did not help matters any when he vetoed a $100,000 authorization to extend the Marquette breakwater.

To overcome the continued lack of ore dock capacity and resulting car shortages, the South Shore let a contract to M. J. Peppard for a further 600-foot extension of the M&W dock over the winter of 1889–1890. A new approach trestle, curving to the south, was also added, allowing empty ore cars to be dropped toward the Lower Yard without traffic tie-ups on Front and Superior streets. Empties could then be easily dispatched up the former M&W main line to the mines. Most of the material for the new construction came from the underemployed ore dock at St. Ignace, with some 600 feet being removed. The extension ran into problems in March 1890 when the Board of the United States Engineers ordered the work stopped for violating the harbor line. The dock had advanced 385 feet at this point, resulting in a 64-pocket addition instead of 100 pockets as originally planned.

An even more major project at Marquette that winter saw Henry and Balch begin work on a brand-new ore dock at the foot of the old Jackson cut. This dock, No. 4, was constructed with 200 pockets, each capable of holding 135 tons of ore, for a total capacity of 28,000 tons. Standing 46.5 feet from water to rail, No. 4's loading length measured 1,200 feet, with a 560-foot approach. The first ore was dumped into the pockets on June 20, 1890, and the next day the steamer *Pontiac* took out the first cargo. With the new dock and the extension of the M&W, the South Shore's dock capacity at Marquette almost doubled. The South Shore further shored up its ability to handle ore traffic by building 200 20-ton, 22-foot-long ore cars in its Marquette shops during the winter of 1889–1890.

Mining activity on the Marquette Range was confined for the most part to the area east of Champion. On the west end, things were quiet, waiting for higher prices which

The 427-foot-long James Watt, a bulk freighter of 1896 vintage, takes on iron ore from the south side of the DSS&A Dock 4 in Marquette in 1905. The Spear coal dock is to the right. *Library of Congress, Prints & Photographic Division, Detroit Publishing Company Collection, LC-D4-18248*

would make the mining of low-grade ores profitable. A major development in the South Shore's ore hauling future came in 1890 when the Cleveland Iron Mining Company took over the holdings of the Iron Cliffs Company. This resulted in the formation of the Cleveland-Cliffs Iron Company (CCI) the following year. Cleveland-Cliffs soon become the dominant player on the Marquette Range, with the Iron Cliffs, Cliffs Shaft, Barnum, Salisbury, and Foster mines being added to the Cleveland, Cleveland Lake, Moro, and Michigamme mines under Cleveland management. The 1890 season saw 968 boats load an average of 1,360 tons at the Marquette docks for a total of 1,316,351 gross tons. With the end of the ore season came the resulting layoffs. During the summer the South Shore had some ninety engine crews, which dropped to fifty during the winter with the loss of mine runs and dock switch engines.

The healthy car loadings were threatened by a potential intrusion of Ferdinand Schlesinger, who was about to construct a railroad from Escanaba to Iron Mountain, Michigan. Only a short extension of the Schlesinger road would put the line into South Shore territory. The South Shore began to seriously entertain an extension of the Negaunee & Palmer branch to the Lake Michigan port of Gladstone to protect their interests. The Lake Michigan and Lake Superior Railway Company was formed on

The curving track in the foreground off Dock No. 1, or the old Marquette & Western ore dock, was put in by the DSS&A in 1890 to provide direct access to the Lower Yard without trains having to block Front and Superior streets when handling empty ore cars. Trains made up in the Lower Yard could then head right up the south main line to Negaunee and the Marquette Range. Load ore cars for Dock 1 were pulled up the hill and shoved straight out on to the dock. The lumber dock is seen in the foreground. *Library of Congress, Prints & Photographic Division, Detroit Publishing Company Collection, LC-D4-10883*

November 10, 1890, to build the 90-mile line, with a capitalization of $500,000. As Finney wrote Van Horne, "Their line must for a portion of the way I think of necessity run identically with ours, or very close to it. I believe if we can get this piece of line under way it would put a stop to their building and we will thus command their business as well as the other business in the Marquette district."[14] Schlesinger's Escanaba, Iron Mountain and Western soon wound up in the C&NW fold and the danger passed.

In spite of a 25 percent decline in ore prices during the summer, the South Shore handled 1,027,323 tons of ore through its Marquette docks in 1892. At that time the Lake Superior district accounted for 55 percent of the iron ore mined in the United States, with 86 percent coming from the Michigan ranges. One casualty of the decline in iron ore prices was the Iron Range & Huron Bay Railroad (IR&HB), which had been formed in July 1890 to build from Champion directly north to Huron Bay on Lake Superior. Detroit men invested over $2,000,000 in the project, which had just completed its 42-mile line when the fall came. Hounded by creditors from the start, the IR&HB received its death blow when the DSS&A and C&NW reduced rates for Champion-area mines from 60 to 45 cents. Unable to operate at such a margin, the IR&HB never began operations, and rotted away until scrapped in 1900.[15]

The drop in ore prices was a prelude to the bank Panic of May 1893, which caused heavy suffering on the Marquette Range. With over 2,000,000 tons of iron ore remaining on the Lake Erie docks from the previous season unsold and furnace men only offering $3.75 and $4.00 for the best ores, most mine owners did not consider operating worthwhile. Cleveland-Cliffs shut down all but one of its mines in May 1893 and Republic Iron suspended operations for sixty days. Unemployment reached 80 percent in the mining regions, and the DSS&A brought in relief supplies without charge. The South Shore ore business did receive a boost when vessel charters out of Marquette weakened to where they were only 5 cents more than Escanaba. With the 20 cent differential in rail rates to Escanaba, many of mining companies which usually shipped via the C&NW found it was cheaper to send their ore to Marquette.

The ore business rebounded dramatically in 1894 and reached an all-time high that year, with 1,424,409 tons being handled through Marquette. Much of this ore was off stockpiles from the slow 1892 and 1893 seasons. The Marquette Range resumed its former role as the leading ore producer in the Lake Superior District, retaking the title from the Gogebic Range. This title would be lost forever in 1895 to the new Mesabi Range in Minnesota, which began to provide stiff competition to the older ranges as its ore lay close to the surface and could be worked in open pits more economical than the largely underground workings found on the Marquette Range.

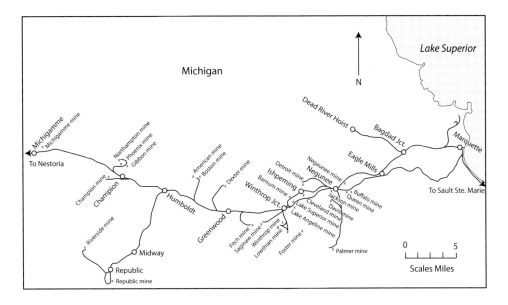

Marquette Iron Range, 1896

The Sault Locks were becoming a negative to the ore trade, and some of the larger boats could not even enter Lake Superior. The opening of a 900-foot lock by the Canadian government in 1895 took some of the pressure off the American side. The construction of the Canadian lock required the Sault Ste. Marie Bridge Company to erect a new 156-foot swing span to accommodate the new traffic lane. The U.S. Government's new lock, known as the Poe, was not far behind and was placed into service in 1896.

THE TRAFFIC AGREEMENT

With a healthy ore season and a large business hauling construction supplies, the South Shore had started out profitable enough, clearing $600,000 on revenues of $1,500,000 in 1887. At that point, bonding had been held to $12,000 per mile with an issue of 5 percent first mortgage bonds. Carrying construction supplies did not guarantee fiscal well-being to a railroad, and upon assuming the MH&O debt and pledging 6 percent on MH&O preferred stock, Samuel Thomas soon realized the DSS&A had taken on "an obligation it was unable to carry out."[16]

Although under Fitch's management South Shore's operating ratio fell to 60 in 1889, it was still not enough. Van Horne pressed Fitch for more revenue: "Can you twist the tail of your coat enough to make her yield something over $800,000.00 net? That will enable us to sell the bonds we are now carrying and put the property in a healthy condition financially."[17] Thomas felt the problem was the "ruinous rates" negotiated to secure traffic for the road without allowing much in the way of profit.[18] As he wrote Van Horne, "It is a fact, that the owners of this property should agree upon some plan of re-adjustment of its securities at an early date, in order to furnish hope for those who are assisting it with money in its difficulties."[19] The yearly payment of over $500,000 to holders of MH&O securities proved impossible without advances from the CPR. By mid-1890 the South Shore had incurred a floating debt of nearly $3,500,000 compared with $1,200,000 in 1888, causing Van Horne to write McMillan, "The DSS&A isn't starting off quite so well as we hoped this year."[20]

In an attempt to bring order to the chaos, on May 27, 1890, the DSS&A and CPR entered into the "Traffic Agreement." Under the agreement the South Shore would issue $20,000,000 in 4 percent bonds to be used to retire the MH&O stocks and bonds as well as the DSS&A 5 percent first mortgage bonds. The CPR would guarantee the interest on the new 4s, which would be the only indebtedness faced by the DSS&A.[21] The Marquette, Houghton & Ontonagon became a permanent part of the South Shore under a purchase agreement dated July 17, 1890, and the lease was rescinded. The MH&O land grant was transferred to John Sterling and Samuel Thomas as trustees to keep it out of the South Shore mortgage. Also enveloped into the South Shore fold was the Negaunee & Palmer Railroad.[22]

In exchange for guaranteeing interest on the 4s, the DSS&A agreed to give to the CPR, at Sault Ste. Marie, all passenger and freight traffic reached by the latter road or its connections. Unfortunately for the DSS&A, no similar restrictions were placed on the CPR. The DSS&A was required to use all available earnings to meet interest payments on the new 4 percent bonds and prior bonds. Any deficit was to be made up by the Canadian Pacific; however, they could not use a default to start foreclosure proceedings. It was thought the excellent credit rating of the CPR would generate a strong demand for the South Shore bonds, particularly in London. The DSS&A directors at their meeting of July 17, 1890, hoped "a large portion of the consideration thus paid to the Canadian Pacific Company would speedily return to the treasury of the company through the increased price which would be obtained for the bonds, as the result of the guaranty."[23] Samuel Thomas optimistically predicted, "I have great hopes that in the future the road will be able to earn its fixed charges, and a small surplus besides."[24]

Another development at the July 17, 1890, meeting saw James McMillan resign from the presidency of the South Shore. McMillan, as head of the state Republican committee, had been nominated by the legislature to represent Michigan in the U.S. Senate from January 2, 1889, and holding both positions proved too great a burden. Peter White praised McMillan's work in building a railroad across the UP, saying, "I now am of the opinion that the whole matter would have remained dormant until now, had there been no James McMillan to awaken to the importance and the necessity of such a road. His courage, his pluck and skill, his diplomacy and largely his money, poured forth in unstinted volume, did the business."[25]

Samuel Thomas feared that F. N. Finney, in whom he lacked confidence, would be the CPR's choice for the new opening. As he wrote McMillan, "It strikes me that the time has arrived when my financial position with these people is such that I can step forward and demand the head of these properties, and take the place in order to protect my own financial interest in the stock and debts and be of service to you as my personal friend and political associate in the Senate in the future. If the management of the Road, which runs though your state, should fall into the hands of a person unfriendly to you, your interests might be sacrificed as well as my own."[26] Thomas, already a CPR director, was successful in his pursuit and was appointed McMillan's successor.

The refinancing of the South Shore in 1890 turned out to be less than a complete success. The failure of Baring Brothers investment house in London in October, due to unwise Argentine securities holdings, made sales of the 4 percent bonds difficult. The Canadian Pacific purchased over three-quarters of the South Shore 4s in 1892 and 1893, using them to retire the MH&O stock and bonds, DSS&A unfunded debt, and a small portion of the DSS&A 5s.[27] Although the CPR's annual report for 1890 assured stockholders that the terms of the "Traffic Agreement" were "so favorable that no loss or expense to your Company is to be feared," CPR management in the 1890s grumbled that it was not receiving nearly the traffic off the South Shore that it had expected in return for the drain on its treasury.[28]

If it had not been for the benevolence of the CPR, the DSS&A surely would not have survived the Panic of 1893, which took some 200 railroads, including the Northern Pacific, into the hands of the receiver. The Panic's effects, which took some five years to overcome, caused the South Shore's financial picture to remain unsatisfactory, and in 1895 the South Shore defaulted for the first time on its 4 percent bond payment to the CPR. The South Shore continued to meet interest payments on the remaining first mortgage 5s to prevent the DSS&A from being foreclosed by outsiders.

Some of money received from the sale of 4 percent bonds also went for improvements, including a new car ferry for the Mackinac Transportation Company. The car ferry *St. Ignace,* with only 10 cars capacity, generally faced a backlog of traffic waiting to move across the Straits. In December 1892 a second switch crew was placed in St. Ignace yard, and the ferry was said to be "churning the straits at all hours in order to transfer the great quantities of copper, flour and lumber passing east by the South Shore route."[29]

To alleviate the congestion, Detroit Dry Dock Company received a contract for a new ferry-icebreaker in March 1892. The *Sainte Marie* was similar to the *St. Ignace,* but it had three tracks on the main deck for a capacity of 18 cars, as well as a third more power. With separate compound engines and four Scotch boilers producing 4,000 horsepower to drive the forward and aft propellers, the designers felt the boat capable of keeping "a passage open to the North Pole."[30]

The 1357-ton *Sainte Marie,* 288 feet long and with a 53-foot beam, had enclosed sides which afforded better protection in rough weather. Said to be the heaviest vessel ever constructed aside from warships, the new ferry arrived at St. Ignace on June 9, 1893. This allowed the *St. Ignace* to be sent down for a general overhaul, at which time she was believed to have been rebuilt with enclosed sides like her new counterpart. The original *Algomah* was sold two years later to Island Transportation Company, where she lived out her years serving the resort community of Mackinaw Island.

The Soo Line came to help share in the expenses of the ferry when it entered into a contract on April 26, 1890, providing for exchange of traffic between that road and the Michigan Central and the Grand Rapids & Indiana at Mackinaw City. Under the agreement the Soo Line paid 24 percent of the Mackinac Transportation Company's costs, while the South Shore was responsible for 22 percent. The Soo Line also paid the DSS&A a car haul charge between the interchange at Trout Lake and St. Ignace.

Still another use of the new 4 percent bonds was to purchase the capital stock of the Mineral Range Railroad, an important narrow gauge road running on the Keweenaw Peninsula from Houghton to Calumet. This insured that Mineral Range traffic would continue to come into the hands of the South Shore at Houghton, and not become a part of any expansion plans of the Chicago & North Western or Chicago, Milwaukee & St. Paul.

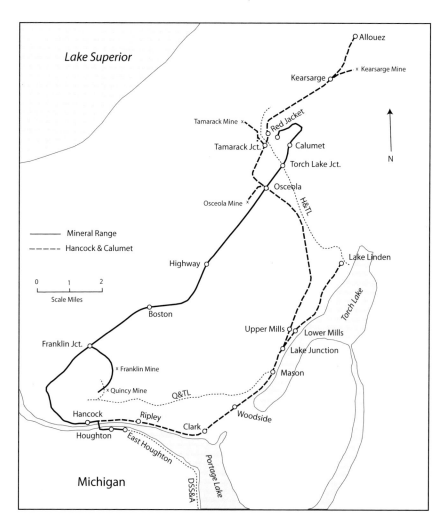

Combined Mineral Range and Hancock & Calumet Systems, November 1, 1887

Lake Superior

Allouez

Kearsarge Mine ×

Kearsarge

Tamarack Mine ×

Red Jacket

Tamarack Jct.

Calumet

Torch Lake Jct.

Osceola

Osceola Mine ×

H&TL

N

Lake Linden

Mineral Range

Hancock & Calumet

Highway

Torch Lake

0   1   2

Scale Miles

Boston

Franklin Jct.

Upper Mills

Lower Mills

Lake Junction

× Franklin Mine

Mason

× Quincy Mine

Q&TL

Woodside

Hancock

Ripley

Clark

Houghton

East Houghton

Michigan

DSS&A

Portage Lake

6

THE MINERAL RANGE
AND L'ANSE BAY
RAILROAD

The mining of copper in the 80-mile-long Keweenaw Peninsula, north of L'Anse, formed the basis for some of the earliest development on the Upper Peninsula. Although some commercial mines operated as early as 1844, transportation difficulties limited the mines' success, which only improved, like that of the iron mines of the Marquette Range, with the opening of the Sault Locks. Lake Superior thereafter met the region's transportation needs for the most part, except during the winter months when navigation ceased and left the lakeside communities in a very isolated state, sometimes for five months or more.

After several false starts, residents of Hancock decided during the winter of 1870–1871 to pursue a railroad venture that would end the isolation and promote better communication with the mining regions farther up the Keweenaw. Charles E. Holland, a Hancock hardware merchant then serving in the Michigan legislature, was approached to lead the enterprise. Holland doubted whether Hancock, with a population of only 2,700 people, had the resources to back such a railroad, but decided to find out by asking for $100,000 in subscriptions. Holland started the process by writing a check for twenty $100 shares. Within a few weeks the entire amount was taken up, mostly by Hancock residents, but with several Houghton people also coming on board.

As a result of these initial steps, the Mineral Range and L'Anse Bay Railroad Company was incorporated on April 18, 1871, with a capitalization of $200,000. The company was to build a line, not exceeding 3'6" in width of T rails, from the "head of Keweenaw Bay . . . by the way of Houghton and Hancock to the north line of Houghton County in the Township of Calumet . . . about forty five miles in length."[1] The head of Keweenaw Bay would take in L'Anse, proposed terminus of the Houghton & Ontonagon. Holland was elected president and Richard M. Hoar, vice president. The name of the railroad was shortened to the Mineral Range Railroad Company (MR) at the board of directors meeting held October 25, 1872, and the idea of building to L'Anse was abandoned when the MH&O let it be known it was headed for Houghton. Instead, the MR would head southwest and build 100 miles from the tip of the Keweenaw Peninsula at Copper Harbor to an imaginary connection with the Northern Pacific on the Ontonagon River.[2]

Surveys were conducted during the spring and summer of 1871, and although the initial destination of Calumet was only 12.5 miles from Hancock, there were some formidable obstacles. The area along Portage Lake was fully developed with various mills and warehouses, forcing the MR to start over the water, at the Bendry dock, and then head up the side of the bluff on a 4 percent grade for 1,200 feet. The grade then moderated to 2.76 percent for another 2 miles until the top of the bluff was reached, from which point a ruling grade of 1.14 percent was maintained to Calumet. All this climbing was necessary to gain the 630-foot elevation between Hancock and Calumet.

Holland was given authority to purchase the necessary rails, a locomotive, and a few cars with which to begin construction at a board of directors meeting in February 1872. J. C. Sharpless, who had been chief engineer of the Pennsylvania Central, was hired to oversee the work. Bids were sought for the first 6 miles of road between Hancock and Boston Location, but all were rejected, and it was decided to do the work with company forces. Grading on 5.5 miles of the line was completed by November 9, 1872, when work succumbed to the winter conditions.

Grading was resumed in May 1873 on the remaining 7 miles into Calumet. To provide the necessary funds, 8 percent first mortgage bonds totaling $200,000 were issued June 1, 1873. Grading by mid-July had been largely completed from the Hancock dock up to the county road crossing at mile post 8, and that same month the first locomotive, a few flat cars, and rails were received. Unfortunately, it was realized that the $62,400 in stock and $130,000 in bonds sold thus far would be insufficient to complete the line. Rather than go into floating debt and endanger the incomplete line, it was decided to halt construction when the money ran out and wait for the remaining bonds to be sold. The available funds would allow the grading to be completed into Calumet and rails to be laid to M.P. 8. The press urged people to put their "shoulders to the wheel" and take up subscriptions to allow the road to be completed for the entire distance.[3]

By mid-August the road had been cleared for the entire 12.5 miles, grading was being undertaken at the twelfth mile, and 35-pound iron rails had been laid 2 miles out of Hancock. When the money ran out on September 8, 1873, the line was opened as far as Midway, 8.1 miles from Hancock. An agency was established at Midway, and arrangements were made to deliver freight to that point. The grade was within a few days' completion into Calumet, and iron for the final 4½ miles was on the dock at Hancock.

The residents of the Copper Country were able to dig a little deeper, and by September 25 work had been resumed. Track laying was delayed by rainy conditions early in October, but with improving weather, crews were able to complete the 4.4 miles into Calumet. The ballast gang was close on the heels of the tracklayers, and the first freight was brought into Calumet on October 6, 1873. Regular passenger service started two days later, with two daily round trips out of Hancock. Running time was 1 hour, and passengers were charged 65 cents for the entire distance. Although there was no fanfare to mark the occasion, Orrin Robinson, the line's first treasurer, recalled years later, "It was a Hancock enterprise throughout, projected, financed, constructed and run by Hancock men, who felt justly proud of their achievement."[4]

Right from the beginning the Mineral Range was "taxed" trying to handle the business offered.[5] Some 175 passengers a day used the line, and the road added another pair of passenger trains in May 1874. American Express Company contracted to handle express shipments, and $34 a month was received for hauling U.S. mail. Freight business

This scene, at the foot of Tezcuco Street in Hancock, is alive with activity as the *Joseph L. Hurd* unloads goods for transloading into Mineral Range cars for forwarding to the Copper Country. *Michigan Technological University Archives and Copper Country Historical Collection, Roy Drier Coll., Neg. 00877*

was booming and the Mineral Range depot and dock at the foot of Tezcuco Street in Hancock, as well as other docks, were filled with goods awaiting shipment to the booming Copper Country. At the Mineral Range Calumet depot, it was necessary to lengthen the main line and put in another siding to care for the increasing traffic.

Soon after starting operations, the Mineral Range entered into a contract with the Calumet and Hecla to haul copper concentrate, during the winter months, to the Lake Superior Smelting Co. on Portage Lake. C&H had built its own railroad, the Hecla and Torch Lake (H&TL), in 1867 to haul copper-bearing rock from their Calumet-area mines to their stamp mill on Torch Lake. After the rock was separated from copper at the stamp, the concentrate was normally handled by boat to the Lake Superior smelter (Torch Lake and Portage Lake were connected by the Torch River). The smelter would then melt the copper into bars for shipment east by Great Lakes vessel. To facilitate the wintertime rail movement, the MR built a short extension east out of Hancock to reach the smelter, and, in Calumet, a transfer platform was erected at the junction with the H&TL. Direct interchange was not possible due to the 4'1" gauge employed by the H&TL. The Mineral Range also began to participate in the movement of copper-bearing stamp rock with the opening of the Osceola mine near Calumet, in late 1873, taking the rock to Osceola's stamp just west of Hancock.

The Mineral Range's first locomotive, a 17½-ton Mogul from Baldwin, received the No. 1 as well as the name *Portage Lake,* although employees soon took to calling her *Peggy.* As bond sales mounted in September 1873, a 19-ton Mogul (*J. C. Sharpless*—2) was ordered from Baldwin so as to arrive before the close of navigation. The slightly heavier *Sharpless* was generally used for freight, while *Peggy* held down the passenger assignment. Another Baldwin Mogul (*Kee Wee Nemo,* later renamed *Keweenaw*—3), completed in June 1875, lacked the pulling capacity of the *Sharpless* and saw service as a spare engine. *Sharpless* was capable of handling 10 empty rock cars up the heaviest part of the grade out of Hancock. Coming back down the hill she usually would handle 12 loaded rock cars and 6 to 8 cars of copper concentrate (300 to 330 tons). The freight crew would usually make two round trips a day between Hancock and the mines. To care for the increasing business, a fourth locomotive, a 22-ton Baldwin Mogul (*O Te Ti Ani,* later renamed *Calumet*—4) arrived at the Hancock docks on August 28, 1880.

The Mineral Range passenger equipment, a baggage-smoker and a coach, were received in mid-September 1873. Both cars were 35 feet in length and 7 feet in width. Due to their narrow width, the cars had double seats on one side and a single row of seats on the other. To keep the weight distributed this pattern alternated halfway through the car. Growing passenger traffic saw the Mineral Range receive another passenger coach and an additional smoker on June 30, 1874. As part of the Osceola Mining Company's rock hauling agreement, that company purchased the equipment, with the Mineral Range being responsible for all maintenance. The 40 Osceola cars were of 12-ton capacity, had a hopper bottom dump, and were the first to be equipped with 4-wheel trucks. The Mineral Range's own complement of freight equipment had grown to 18 cars by mid-1874, mostly "platform" cars.

These were good times on the MR given its Copper Country monopoly. In its first abbreviated year of operation in 1873, the Mineral Range earned $19,422 with expenses of $11,447. Net earnings grew to $28,863 in 1875, allowing a 10 percent dividend to be declared. This was thought to make the Mineral Range the most profitable narrow gauge road in the country. Although paying no dividend in 1876, the MR followed with one of 5 percent in 1877. The financial picture darkened in 1878 due to a downturn in the copper region. Passenger business was particularly hard-hit. Expenses were correspondingly cut to ensure a net income equal to that of previous years. The high freight rates necessary to ensure profitability would haunt the road in the future.

Indicative of the harsh UP winters, 26 percent of all costs in 1874 were related to snow removal. After the worst storm of the season, on March 8, 1874, caused the morning train to be 2 hours late in Calumet, the *Portage Lake Mining Gazette* commented, "This was the second long detention this winter. When we consider the long waits on outside railroads, which encounter snow in abundance, the praise for fighting snow so well on the line of the Mineral Range is all the more deserved."[6]

President Holland described the wintertime plight of the Mineral Range: "The snow commences falling in November usually, and continues to fall steadily until January or February, with occasional heavy storms after that time, with high winds and heavy drifts. . . . By the 1st of January we have from 1½ to 3 feet of snow, and it is not an unusual thing to find 3½ to 4 feet of snow in the woods on the 1st of April. . . . During the winter of 1875, with very heavy snows, high winds, and the mercury ranging from 0 to 35 below

(Fahrenheit) for over 40 days, we were only delayed, all told, about 3 days; that is the Smelting Works and Stamp Mills, to which we brought their daily supplies of material, were stopped, on account of our inability to get trains through, only about 3 days. In exposed places on the 146 feet grade the snow often drifts to the depth of 3½ to 5 feet on the track, and becomes so hard that one could walk upon it as easily as upon a floor."[7]

The Mineral Range operation was fairly constant over its first decade. Most of the passenger runs were mixed, handling general commercial traffic as well as passengers. The rock trains operated separately. Inbound commodities included mining equipment and support timbers, cordwood, and general merchandise. The Mineral Range handled 161,447 tons of stamp rock in 1881, which accounted for 86 percent of its tonnage. With its 5 cent per mile rate, the Mineral Range received 21 percent of its earnings from passenger traffic. A lot of the region's prosperity was due to Calumet and Hecla. In 1880 it was the largest and richest copper operation in the world, employing over 2,000 men. Indicative of the mineral wealth was a 3½-ton piece of mass copper brought in for shipment from the Central mine at the far north end of the Copper Country, in May 1881. When met with competition from western producers, C&H periodically would give them "a blow below the belt," arranging large copper sales at 10 cents a pound and forcing many of them to the wall. C&H thus retained the status the "imperial mine holds among the world's producers of copper."[8]

Civilization took another step forward on the Keweenaw Peninsula in 1880, when Lake Superior Mineral Range Telegraph Company, a Mineral Range subsidiary, installed a line between Calumet and Hancock. The company was purchased outright on January 16, 1886, and continued as the Mineral Range Telegraph Line. The region became physically connected to the rest of the civilized world on a year-round basis with the arrival at Houghton in 1883 of the Marquette, Houghton & Ontonagon Railroad. Business was exchanged across Portage Lake by the Portage Lake Transfer Company, a subsidiary of the MH&O. Ferries were used in the summer, and sleighs over the ice in winter. Passengers were transferred at no extra cost.[9]

The good times for the Mineral Range became clouded when the stamp mills along Portage Lake started to encroach on the shipping lanes with their waste rock. A study conducted by the War Department in 1883 concluded "the evil should be corrected."[10] This created quite a problem for the allied Osceola and Tamarack mining companies, which took immediate steps to locate a site on Torch Lake for a new stamp mill. The move boded ill for the Mineral Range as the Osceola and Tamarack rock traffic was its major source of revenue. The mining companies had long been after the Mineral Range for a reduction in rock hauling rates. With $11,636 in profits to put towards a 10 percent stock dividend in 1883, the railroad, however, was anxious to see this pattern continue. Negotiations with the mining companies for the Mineral Range to serve the new stamp mill location on Torch Lake proved unsuccessful.

With trouble ahead, the Mineral Range management decided it was a good time to get out. Several parties expressed an interest, including the Marquette, Houghton & Ontonagon railroad, but the line ended up being sold in early 1885 to the New York banking house of Henry S. Ives and Company. The new board took over on July 14, 1885, electing George H. Stayner president and Henry S. Ives vice president and secretary-treasurer. Charles A. Wright was appointed local manager. The Ives syndicate quickly made a rule that directors meetings could be held in New York, with the executive committee having the power to take actions outside of the regular board meetings.[11]

THE HANCOCK & CALUMET RAILROAD

The new management faced an immediate problem with the Osceola and Tamarack mining companies' response to high Mineral Range freight rates: the Hancock and Calumet Railroad Company (H&C), formed on January 14, 1885, had a capitalization at $300,000, and, using a gauge not over 3.5 feet, was to run approximately 18 miles from the north end of the wagon bridge in Hancock, along Portage Lake, and then north to Red Jacket (a district of Calumet) and the mines. The H&C directorate was largely made up of members of the Bigelow syndicate which controlled the Osceola and Tamarack mines.[12]

A contract to build the line was let on February 27, 1885, with the H&C treasurer being authorized to deliver $300,000 in capital stock and $200,000 in bonds to the contractors in payment. Construction between Osceola (just outside Calumet) and Torch Lake began in May and made use of a 2.4 percent ruling grade to reach the bluff overlooking the lake. The line then descended on a 3 percent grade to the stamp mill, with three ravines requiring major trestles 150 to 210 feet long. The line leveled out upon reaching the future site of the Tamarack and Osceola stamp at Upper Mills, where copper rock would be dumped into pockets. Past the stamp, the line continued down to Portage Lake, which it paralleled for the remaining 14.5 miles to Hancock. As the line bypassed Lake Linden (site of C&H's stamp mill on Torch Lake), a 2.5-mile H&C branch was built to serve that community from Lake Jct. This H&C branch would also come to serve the new C&H smelter at Hubbell (just west of Lake Linden) upon its completion in 1887.

Enough grading had been done by July 1885 for the H&C to start laying 3-foot gauge trackage out of Osceola, using a leased Mineral Range work train. The following month, the first rails were put down on the south end with the delivery of the H&C's first locomotive (*Torch Lake*—1), a used Brooks Mogul, at its Ripley dock. The main H&C yard and roundhouse were located at the north end of the line at Tamarack (just south of Calumet), with smaller facilities behind the stamp at Upper Mills. Trackage was all in place in October. After the H&C took possession of the 40 Osceola rock cars from the Mineral Range, regular service began on December 1, 1885, with up to three rock trains daily being sent out from the Tamarack and Osceola mines to the new stamp in the early stages. Rock hauling was performed by two new Baldwin 2-8-0s (*Tamarack*—2, *Osceola*—3), which were delivered in September 1885.

A 30′×90′ two-story depot was constructed in Red Jacket, and at Hancock a 30′×50′ structure was erected on a vacant lot east of the Lake Superior smelter. A similar building was erected a half mile west of Lake Linden. Although passenger equipment was not scheduled to arrive until March, the H&C agreed to provide a mixed train, based out of Red Jacket, beginning on New Year's Day 1886. This job made a Red Jacket–Hancock–Lake Linden–Hancock–Red Jacket cycle each day, with 50 minutes being required between Red Jacket and Hancock, and 45 minutes between Hancock and Lake Linden. In spite of the "inconvenient location" of the Hancock depot, the H&C found considerable merchandise business to handle as well.[13] Service was increased to two trips daily, making the same cycle, on February 15. Beginning in August 1886, passenger service was provided by a new 4-6-0 from Baldwin (*Kearsarge*—4), said to be "the largest narrow gauge engine in the district."[14]

MINERAL RANGE EXTENSIONS

The Mineral Range lost almost all its rock traffic as a result of the construction of the Hancock & Calumet and the shift of the Osceola and Tamarack stamps from Hancock to Torch Lake. In an attempt to avoid further hemorrhaging, Ives and Company quickly launched a project to protect them at Calumet. Robert Hall was given a contract to build a 1.5-mile extension from the Mineral Range's Oak Street depot in the Laurium district to the Red Jacket district, circling the Calumet and Hecla mines. This would prevent the H&C, with its depot at Red Jacket, from taking away Mineral Range passenger traffic.

Mineral Range rails reached the new terminus on November 11, 1885, with a new turntable, temporary roundhouse, and depot either finished or nearing completion. The first trains started operating out of Red Jacket on December 1. As Laurium and Red Jacket were only a half-mile apart, it was said that if you missed the train at Red Jacket, you could cut across the mining company property and still catch it at Laurium. A short distance out of Laurium, at Opechee (Osceola), the Mineral Range crossed the Hancock & Calumet at grade, and a Pennsylvania Steel Company interlocking plant was installed to protect the crossing. This was only the second interlocking plant in Michigan and the first in the UP.

Another Mineral Range extension, built in October 1885, was a 1.8-mile branch to serve the Franklin, Pewabic, and Quincy mines. These mines were in the process of converting from cordwood to coal, and the Mineral Range looked to handle the fuel from the Hancock docks to the mines. The MR branch, although completed in 1885, did not see any service until the summer of 1886. The Mineral Range lost some of this business in 1902, when the Quincy Mining Company built its own coal dock at Mason near its stamp mill along Torch Lake. This allowed the coal to be moved over the company's own railroad to the Quincy mines, shortchanging the Mineral Range.

The final Ives expansion saw the Mineral Range bridge Portage Lake to connect with the MH&O at Houghton. Final plans called for the existing wagon bridge to be rebuilt with the roadway occupying a top deck and the railway below. On account of the bridge's dual use, the Mineral Range split the cost of the span with Houghton County. The new bridge would consist of Howe trusses supported by rock cribs and curved trestle approaches for a total length of 1,100 feet. A 180-foot-long center swing span, operated by a stationary steam engine, would allow Portage Lake vessel traffic to pass. This would occur frequently as the span was only 6 feet above the water.

The driving of piles for the new span started on November 2, 1885, but was later held up due to thin ice conditions. Work on removing the draw span of the old wagon bridge began on January 5, with all traffic across Portage Lake being moved on the ice until completion of the new span. After struggling to sink cribs in the 70-foot depths of Portage Lake, a new contractor resorted to driving piles, allowing construction to proceed. The first train went over the new bridge on March 23, 1886. Some four or five hundred people gathered on the ice of Portage Lake to watch the historic event, with the locomotive *Portage Lake* designated to do the honors. All the whistling and tooting that accompanied the move brought another five hundred people to the scene to take part in the celebration.[15]

At Houghton, the Mineral Range graded along the south shore of Portage Lake to a connection with the MH&O in East Houghton. The new trackage was laid with three rails to accommodate both narrow and standard gauge equipment. The line into East

This photo was taken from the stack of the Calumet and Hecla mine. The Mineral Range depot at Red Jacket is in the middle right. Further west, up the street and beyond the church are the depot grounds of the Hancock & Calumet. The Tamarack mine is in the upper left-hand corner. *Michigan Technological University Archives and Copper Country Historical Collections, Roy Drier Coll., Negative 00171*

Houghton opened for business on March 25, 1886, with the first morning train out of Red Jacket and the last train in the evening making connections with the MH&O at East Houghton. The midday run only ventured as far as the Mineral Range depot in Houghton, which was remodeled from an old hotel and was much closer to the central business district. The new facility was much appreciated by Houghton residents, as it did away with the mile-long walks to Hancock and East Houghton.

Mobility was further increased on April 19, 1886, with the inauguration of commuter service between Hancock and Houghton. Beginning at 8:00 AM, from the foot of Reservation Street in Hancock, 21 trips to Houghton were made. An additional 6 trips

An eastbound South Shore passenger train prepares to depart from the East Houghton depot for Marquette. The dual gauge trackage accommodated the narrow gauge Mineral Range trains which began venturing across the Portage River into Houghton in 1886. *Michigan Technological University Archives and Copper Country Historical Collections, Roy Drier Coll., Negative 00576*

were added May 16, as well as a fourth train to Red Jacket for the summer and fall months. A used standard gauge steam dummy for the commuter run arrived in May and was paired with a standard gauge coach, which arrived two months later. The commuter service, known as the "ferry train," was done away with on December 1, 1887, due to lack of patronage.[16]

RECEIVERSHIP

The Ives era was tainted by dubious financial arrangements. Under the original owners, the Mineral Range had a capital stock of $120,000 and a bonded debt of $198,000. Ives and Stayner, forming a majority of the executive committee, authorized an additional

$450,000 in bonds in 1885 and 1886, many of which were sold to the Ives banking firm at 75 cents on the dollar, even though they were selling on the open market in the $130 to $146 range. Ives also took a stock issue of $272,000 at par value, even though shares were selling for $130. The moves were highly controversial in that they were not authorized by a majority of the board. The Mineral Range soon found itself in debt to Henry Ives & Co. for $410,000, and the days of paying 10 percent dividends were over.

One reputable way Ives was able to put the new financing to use was to gain control of the Hancock & Calumet. The Mineral Range, realizing the threat the H&C posed to its existence, began talks with the Bigelow interests regarding a possible purchase. After the syndicate protected themselves with a 10-year hauling contract, the sale was arranged in March 1886. The mining company also had the option of extending the contract for an additional 10 years. The purchase price was $250,000, with the Bigelow syndicate's Tamarack, Osceola, Iroquois, and Kearsarge mining companies retaining $100,000 in H&C stock. After the Mineral Range takeover, Henry Ives was elected president and Charles Wright appointed general manager of the H&C, in addition to their duties with the Mineral Range. The H&C continued to be operated independently for the most part, although some equipment became mixed with that of the Mineral Range. An extension of H&C trackage across the smelting works yard in Hancock was completed on November 25, 1887, which, combined with 0.95 miles of trackage rights, allowed the H&C to reach the Mineral Range depot.[17]

Ives, accused of taking $328,000 worth of MR securities without credit to the railroad, lost control on August 23, 1887, with the election of a new board of directors. *Railway Age* commented, "Hitherto the little road has paid 10 percent dividends. Mr. Ives evidently considered this an excessive rate and proceeded to cut it down, but his summary ejection has doubtless saved the property from being wrecked."[18] At the directors meeting held August 31, Stayner and Ives were voted out and Francis B. Loomis, of New York, was elected to head the road. Charles Wright kept his position as local manager. The first task of the new management was to get rid of the Mineral Range's inflated value and do something about the million dollars in debt hanging over the road.

With the Mineral Range unable to meet its interest payments, a suit brought by J. N. Wright, acting for the first mortgage bonds holders, forced the road into receivership. Charles Wright was appointed receiver on June 1, 1888. The receivership proved very short-lived and an agreement was reached with the creditors allowing the MR to return to the old ownership on December 1, 1889. Business had improved so dramatically that all parties agreed that "continuance of the receivership would further none of the interests involved."[19] Wright was given back his old post as general manager, with executive decisions now in the hands of President Charles Bard. Mineral Range finances were put in shape on January 1, 1891, with the issuance of $600,000 in bonds to retire the old Ives issues.

The H&C picked up additional traffic with the start-up of Bigelow's Iroquois and Kearsarge mines at Allouez (north of Calumet). These companies contributed the necessary funds for construction, which started out of Calumet in July 1886. The 3.36-mile extension opened for regular service on March 12, 1887, with the two H&C Calumet passenger trains having their runs extended to Allouez for a short time. These were taken off the time card in October 1887, and in fact by the summer of 1889 all H&C passenger service to Calumet was gone—a needless duplication of Mineral Range service. It was still possible to ride on a "rock train, with caboose attached" connecting with the H&C Shore Line runs between Hancock and Lake Linden.[20]

The H&C's wood business expanded with the growth of the copper mines. A 3-mile branch southeast off the Shore Line near Woodside was completed in time for the 1888–1889 logging season. This branch, which was extended to 6 miles in length by the fall of 1889, was used to get out wood for the Bigelow mining operations. Another logging enterprise saw the Hancock & Calumet extend its line north 1.25 miles from Allouez to Fulton, with service beginning October 28, 1891. That same year the H&C built extensions from the Tamarack mine to the North Tamarack and from the main line to the Tamarack Jr. and the Kearsarge mines, totaling some 3.18 miles. To keep up with the expanding traffic, three new Consolidations (*Iroquois*—5, *Ahmeek*— 6, and *Opechee*—7) and a Mogul (*Delaware*—8) were added to the fleet between 1887 and 1891.

Wood replaced copper rock as the largest commodity handled on the Mineral Range after the latter traffic went over to the H&C. As more mines used coal for fuel, this commodity took over in prominence. With expansion of mining activity in the Red Jacket area and the need to serve an expanded population, Mineral Range business grew to record levels in 1889. In October 1888, the Mineral Range purchased a used 24-ton Consolidation (*Hancock*—5), and a new 33-ton Baldwin Tenwheeler (*Houghton*—6) was added the following year. The new Baldwin, much larger than anything then in service on the MR, was used mainly in passenger service and proved its mettle getting through snow drifts. Another improvement made by the Mineral Range in the spring of 1889 was the building of a new passenger station at Hancock.

A 36-ton Baldwin Consolidation (*Superior*—7) was added to the Mineral Range ranks in February 1891. This engine, built to the same pattern as several in use on the Hancock & Calumet, performed very well in the Copper Country and was soon the crew's favorite assignment. The Mineral Range added its last narrow gauge locomotive in May 1892. This Baldwin Consolidation (*Red Jacket*—8) was one of the first Vauclain Compounds, capable of using steam twice. The road also acquired additional boxcars and platform cars to care for the increasing wood and merchandise traffic, bringing the total to 86. Many of these came from the Cincinnati and Eastern, which had converted to standard gauge. A second interlocking plant was added at the crossing with the Hecla & Torch Lake road at Calumet, and in 1892 a new enginehouse and water tank were placed at Tamarack.

The most trying times for the H&C and Mineral Range crews were during the winter months. Blizzards would sweep into the Keweenaw Peninsula, which stuck like an appendage into frozen Lake Superior, bringing temperatures of twenty and thirty degrees below zero. Huge drifts would form as high as the tops of the equipment. It was not possible to shut down, as the stamps were dependent upon the delivery of copper rock to continue production. At times it became a real struggle to keep the trains running between the Osceola, Kearsarge, and Tamarack mines and the stamps at Torch Lake. While in the summer months over 30 rock cars could be handled over the H&C by one locomotive, in the winter months, three engines would struggle with 12 to 15 empties. Even the short little passenger trains on the Mineral Range, consisting of only a baggage car and a coach, required two of the Mineral Range's heaviest locomotives to get through the drifts and up the hill to Red Jacket.

Mineral Range No. 6 powers a narrow gauge passenger train near Calumet on June 1, 1911. No. 6, also known as *Houghton*, was delivered to the Mineral Range from Baldwin in November 1889. *Michigan Technological University Archives and Copper Country Historical Collections, Roy Drier Coll., Negative 00571*

The Mineral Range adapted well to its changed role on the Copper Range, and in what turned out to be its last year of independent operation, 1892, it carried 139,147 tons of freight and 120,102 passengers. Expenses were kept well in line, with an operating ratio of only 60. Tonnage remained largely wood products and general merchandise.

DSS&A CONTROL

The DSS&A had long been aware of the strategic importance of the Mineral Range and the H&C. Samuel Thomas had sought to gain control of the properties in 1888, but it was not until December 1892 that the South Shore, using the new 4 percent bonds, was able to garner a majority of the Mineral Range stock. General Manager Fitch confirmed this to the Marquette *Mining Journal* on December 31: "Our people in New York have, within the past few days, bought a large majority of the stock of the Mineral Range, thereby getting control of that property." The Canadian Pacific directly purchased a majority of the MR's 1891 5 percent consolidated bonds, further solidifying control.[21]

The DSS&A instituted its own slate of directors at the Mineral Range annual meeting held on July 11, 1893, and at the stockholders meeting that followed on August 8,

The last Mineral Range narrow gauge locomotive was a Baldwin Consolidation and one of the first Vauclain compounds, capable of using steam twice. Here it is seen at Calumet after its sale to the Hancock & Calumet, lettered as their No. 40.
Paananen Collection

William F. Fitch was elected president. General offices of the narrow gauge road were moved to Marquette on October 1, 1893, with the only office remaining in Hancock being that of General Manager Charles Wright. After Fitch assumed that role, Wright was offered the position of superintendent. Wright declined and Mineral Range trainmaster John C. Shields was promoted to fill the vacancy. Shields, a longtime employee of the Mineral Range, had started as a fireman shortly after the road began operations. DSS&A trains began to use the more centrally located Mineral Range Houghton depot effective November 1, 1893, and the South Shore station at East Houghton was converted for use as a freight house.

Most of the Mineral Range freight business continued to be located on the Hancock & Calumet segment; some 75 percent of this was hauling copper rock to the stamps at Upper Mills. Although originally starting out with one stamp, by the end of the 1890s this complex had grown to four mills, requiring 28 rock trains a day to keep the stamps busy. On the lower level, spurs off the Lake Linden branch fed the stamp's boilers with coal and wood and took out loads of copper concentrate for the Bigelow syndicate smelter at Dollar Bay, which was constructed in 1888. The Dollar Bay site (some 4 miles east of Hancock) was later expanded to include a rolling and wire mill and sawmill complex. This facility, the only copper manufacturing operation in the UP, was dismantled in 1925. The Hancock & Calumet picked up another rock customer in 1897 when

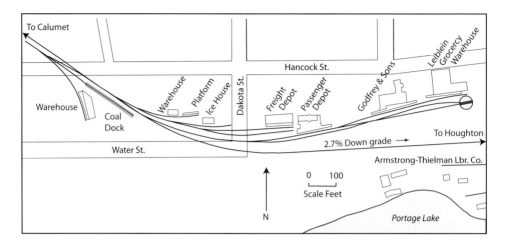

Hancock-Lakeview Station, 1917

arrangements were made with the Wolverine mine (north of Calumet) to handle some of its output to the inactive Allouez stamp (2 miles north of Allouez). The H&C exercised 2.15 miles of trackage rights over Allouez Mining Company's narrow gauge line to reach the mill.

Passenger service in the late 1890s consisted of three trains each way on both legs of the system. Trains left at 7:45 AM from both Red Jacket and Lake Linden. At Hancock, a connection was made and the train from Red Jacket continued across the bridge to Houghton. After a quick turnaround at Houghton, connections were again made at Hancock with the Lake Linden train for H&C points. Trains departed from Red Jacket and Lake Linden again at 12:15 PM and 5:00 PM. The businessmen of Hancock were pleased when a new freight depot was built in 1899 near the MR's Lakeview passenger depot, saving the difficult climb off Portage Lake. The passenger depot, originally at the foot of Tezcuco Street, had been moved to the Lakeview location when the South Shore assumed control. This also made it possible for patrons to get their bills and freight all in one location and centralized the agency force.

One of the northbound Mineral Range passenger trains experienced some excitement when it was held up by four masked robbers on September 15, 1893, at a road crossing near Boston Location. Two men held revolvers to the engine crew, while two others ordered the express messenger to fill a bag with the contents of his safe. The train was carrying some $70,000 to meet the Calumet and Hecla payroll. After the money was handed out, the men in the engine cab told the engineer to "go ahead damned quick." Houghton County sheriff William A. Dunn and the Pinkertons were soon on the case and quickly arrested a few unsavory types who had been frequenting the vicinity. It was discovered the plan had been devised by Ed Hogan, a disgruntled former express messenger who was familiar with the operation. His brother Dominick was the messenger in the express car that day and had the money ready when the holdup took place. All the money was recovered and those involved were arrested.[22]

STANDARD GAUGE

Calumet and other points in the Copper Country enthusiastically greeted the announcement in July 1897 that the Mineral Range was about to be converted to standard gauge. It was thought the change would speed up passenger service by 30 minutes by doing away with the change of trains. Freight service would see a more drastic improvement. Currently cars arrived on the South Shore evening freight and were spotted at the transfer platforms at East Houghton. Their lading was transloaded into the narrow gauge cars during the night, and they would be sent on their way to Calumet and Lake Linden the next day. With the new arrangement, Calumet would become the real terminus of the Houghton line, and freight traffic would go right through.

Changing over the excellent Mineral Range trackage, with its 65-pound steel, many standard gauge ties, and copper rock tailings for ballast, would be a relatively simple matter. The last narrow gauge movements were made over the Mineral Range trackage on September 22, 1897. Trains were then shifted to the Hancock & Calumet line until the change was completed. The next day work started on widening out the rails on the Hancock end. At Calumet, the trackage arrangement was considerably altered, as the Mineral Range trackage north of the H&C diamond was abandoned and a new standard gauge track laid along the H&C into Red Jacket. The H&C Calumet depot facilities were not very large, but Fitch said the building was in too good a shape to tear down and start over. Beyond the depot, a small coach yard was built to service the passenger equipment laying over between runs. The change in depot location did not win favor with the people who lived in Laurium, the site of the earlier Mineral Range depot, but Fitch said the curvature was too sharp to effect standard gauging on that part of the line.

The first run of standard gauge passenger equipment over the Mineral Range was made as far as Osceola on September 26, 1897, to check the new alignment. Three days later thousands were on hand at Calumet to witness the arrival of No. 3, the first through train from Marquette. General Manager Fitch, himself at the throttle of engine 107, and others aboard the train were greeted by shrieking whistles, Calumet village mayor Henry J. Vivian, the Red Jacket brass band, and a banner reading "Welcome D.,S.S.&A." To many, this event marked the end of the Mineral Range and its envious record of 26 years without a serious injury to any of its passengers. The Mineral Range local, Nos. 5 and 6, continued to be handled by the old crew, with a smoker and a first class coach. With the South Shore trains running through to Calumet, the parent company agreed to pay the Mineral Range 40 cents a train mile between East Houghton and Calumet. The South Shore kept all the revenue on those trains except for local mail and express, which went to the Mineral Range. With the conversion of the Mineral Range to standard gauge, DSS&A freight trains 31 and 32 (Marquette–East Houghton) had their runs extended to Calumet.[23]

Standard gauge power for the Mineral Range was initially contributed by the South Shore. Three former DM&M American Standard engines (34–36) were purchased in 1897, along with an ex–Marquette & Western 0-6-0 switcher (71) and an elderly MH&O 4-6-0 (83). Other power from the South Shore included the three former M&W Moguls (200–202) and four Moguls the South Shore had purchased in 1888 (402–404, 409). As the Mineral Range became standard gauge, the Hancock & Calumet inherited the most powerful of the MR's narrow gauge power and other equipment. The wood business on

No. 3 is seen at the Calumet depot on September 29, 1897, the first standard gauge train to arrive from Marquette. General Manager Fitch himself was at the 107's throttle as the historic train was brought into town.   *Michigan Technological University Archives and Copper Country Historical Collections, Roy Drier Collection Negative No. 00569*

East Houghton, Michigan, September 20, 1918

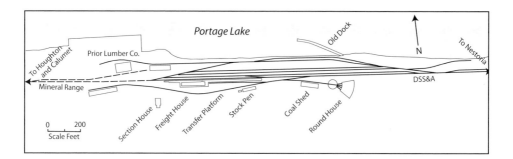

the H&C was booming and it was thought the Mineral Range boxcars could be cut down for that service. What equipment could not be used was gradually sold. As the roundhouse facilities on the north end were only capable of handling two standard gauge locomotives, another 3-stall house was added to the Tamarack facility in 1899.

With plenty of narrow gauge equipment available for non-interchange traffic, the Hancock & Calumet amended its articles on June 3, 1899, to build 50 miles from the present northern terminus to "a point on Lake Superior." New trackage was necessary to get at the timber currently being cut in back of the old Allouez mine. Contractor Ernest Bollman's pursuit of support timbers and cordwood for the Bigelow syndicate mines had the H&C trackage reaching some 15 miles north of Allouez by February 1901.[24]

The H&C picked up some additional traffic along the Shore Line in 1898 when it started handling the concentrate of the Quincy Mining Company from its stamp at Mason to its newly constructed smelter at Ripley. This traffic was handled in cars provided by Quincy. The H&C and Mineral Range also continued to handle concentrates from various mills to the independent Lake Superior smelter at Hancock. In the summer of 1900, the two roads were hard-pressed trying to deal with the heavy inbound shipments of coal and merchandise as well as rock hauling. Coal boats lined up in Portage Lake, waiting for their turn at the Mineral Range dock. On October 12, 1901, the DSS&A brought 100 cars into East Houghton, mainly building materials consigned to the Copper Country.

Some days it was difficult to get a seat on the regular passenger trains, and rarely a day went by when there was not a special movement of some sort. Some of the local passenger business lessened as the Copper Country joined the interurban craze sweeping the nation with the construction of the Houghton County Traction Company. This firm completed from Houghton to Laurium in June 1901, while the Lake Linden extension started operations in December 1902.

The Mineral Range constructed its first standard gauge extension to the newly opened Arcadian mine. This 3.3-mile spur took off the main line at Arcadian Jct., just north of Boston Location, and was ready for service on October 29, 1898. To enable the mine to reach its stamp, a 3.8-mile extension from Arcadian wye (1.3 miles east of Arcadian Jct.) to a connection with the H&C Shore Line at Woodside was opened on July 28, 1899. In addition, the 4.36-mile narrow gauge segment from Woodside to Grosse Point, which had been constructed by the H&C as a wood spur, was converted to standard gauge. The Arcadian, Franklin, and Centennial (at Calumet) mines all came to have stamps located at Grosse Point. Loaded trains for Grosse Point were typically over 500 tons, in spite of the heavy grade and curvature encountered on the run down to Torch Lake. The Grosse Point job was based at Arcadian Jct., where a 2-stall enginehouse was built inside the wye.[25]

Detour over CStPM&O and StP&D, Bibon to Duluth, June 20, 1892, to November 29, 1892

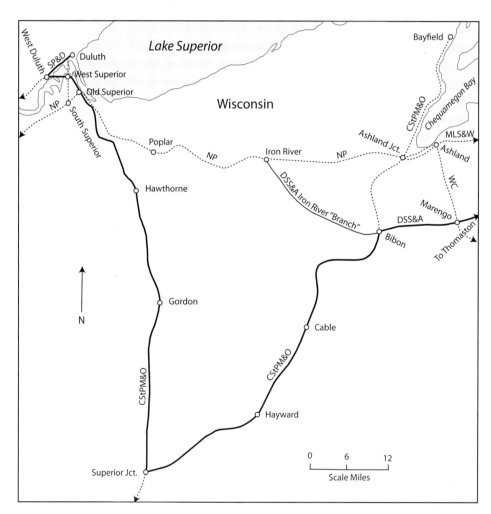

7

AN INDEPENDENT ENTRANCE TO SUPERIOR

Although the DSS&A had been running over the Northern Pacific between Iron River and Atlantic Jct. (Superior) for several years, a trackage rights agreement had never been finalized. The NP wanted rental based on a valuation of $20,000 a mile, while the South Shore felt $15,000 was more realistic. The DSS&A believed it would be more economical to build and construct its own line rather than continue to use trackage rights if forced to pay the NP's figures. Additional payments to the NP included rental for the Union Station in Duluth and for a roundhouse stall and trackage at NP's Rice's Point (Duluth) yard, maintenance expenses on the NP main line, and tolls over the St. Louis River bridge between Duluth and Superior.

By the end of 1891, the lack of an agreement was causing the NP to run out of patience. NP president Thomas Oakes felt the South Shore would need a year to build a new line and the "loss of business in that year will more than compensate for any saving . . . in rental."[1] On March 17, 1892, Oakes wrote General Manager W. S. Mellen, "In the event of their refusing to execute the contract or continuing the delays of the past you are authorized to give immediate notice that they must discontinue using our tracks, and if necessary, spike the connection at the junction."[2]

Continued stonewalling on the part of the South Shore saw the NP follow through with its threat, and, on June 20, 1892, the DSS&A made its last regular run out of Iron River via the NP to Duluth. Roundabout trackage arrangements were made with the CStPM&O from Bibon southwest to Superior Jct. and then northwest to West Superior. At that point, South Shore passenger trains backed into the Lake Superior Terminal & Transfer's Union Station, while freight trains made pickups and setouts in their nearby yard. Instead of using the NP bridge over the St. Louis River to reach Duluth, the DSS&A ran over 8.4 miles of St. Paul & Duluth trackage, using its Grassy Point bridge to reach the Zenith City.

Iron River sat forlornly at the end of a South Shore branch. Up until this time Iron River had provided no revenue to the South Shore, as the NP trackage agreement prohibited the DSS&A from doing business at that point. The South Shore was now free to solicit traffic, which was good from the start as public sentiment was against the NP.

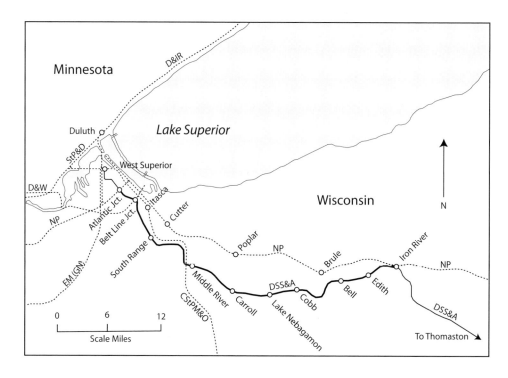

Independent entrance to Superior, November 29, 1892

Effective July 17, 1892, the South Shore even extended the Bessemer passenger local to Iron River, connecting with the Houghton and Detroit Express at Nestoria.

Iron River's branch line status proved temporary, as Henry and Balch were awarded a contract on June 28, 1892, to once again take up the independent entrance to Superior. To obviate the 125-mile-long CStPM&O reroute, the contract called for completion of the grading by October 1, with all steel to be laid one month later. A new survey placed the South Shore line through the center of Iron River, 150 feet south of the NP. This led to still another dispute, as the NP claimed a 400-foot right of way based on its land grant. After discovering on the morning of July 15 that the DSS&A had started laying track, NP Wisconsin division superintendent F. Greene rushed in on a special from Duluth, tried to get the work stopped, and then headed off to Ashland to obtain an injunction. By that time a mile of track had been laid, and the South Shore obtained another injunction preventing the NP from tearing up the new line. Agreements were reached later in the summer, allowing the DSS&A to retain its trackage on the disputed right of way.

By September 1, 800 men were employed on the independent entrance. P. F. Smith of Iron River received a contract to build a temporary wooden bridge across the Nemadji River at Superior, with a permanent steel drawbridge to be constructed later to meet the requirements of the War Department. With the old scheme of branching off the NP near Cutter no longer a possibility, that portion of the old grade was abandoned and the South Shore swung over the CStPM&O near Middle River, instead of under it at Itasca. On September 25, the first rails were laid across the NP at Atlantic Jct. towards

Iron River. A track laying machine then set to work, laying 12 miles before being sent to Iron River to finish up from that end.[3] Rails were joined on Thanksgiving Day 1892, and General Manager Fitch arrived in West Superior on a special in time for a turkey dinner. Although ballasting had kept up with the track laying on the eastern segment, there was no ballast at all on the 12 miles out of Atlantic Jct.

Depots were built at Iron River and between Stinson and Thompson Avenues on 19th Street to serve Old Town Superior residents. With the DSS&A now crossing the NP at Atlantic Jct., an interlocking tower was placed in service at that point on May 8, 1893. After surfacing was completed, freight trains began using the line on November 29, 1892, with passenger service following on December 4. Besides the night run, a daylight service was instituted over the entire Western Division beginning January 8, 1893. This train originated at Houghton, making connections at Nestoria with the westbound Lake Superior Limited (St. Ignace–Houghton) before proceeding to Duluth. The westbound run connected with the eastbound Lake Superior Limited at Nestoria before going around the west leg of the wye to Houghton.[4]

The new service resulted in a healthy increase in business, and the South Shore brought more new immigrants to Duluth in 1893 than all other roads combined. The day passenger was not long-lived, however, falling victim to the Panic of 1893. It was replaced in part by a mixed service between Nestoria and Thomaston, later Nestoria-Ewen. Reflecting the improving economy, the west end passenger local was reinstated between the latter points in July 1894, and, on April 27, 1896, resumed running all the way into Bessemer.

Even though the independent entrance had been completed just the year before, surveyors were put into the field at Superior in 1893 to correct several deficiencies. The bridge over the Nemadji, a pile trestle, did not meet the requirements of the War Department for a swing span. Secondly, the South Shore crossing of the Superior Belt Line and Terminal at Belt Jct. (south of Old Superior) ran through the heart of what was hoped to be the future ore yard of the Duluth and Winnipeg Railroad (D&W). Lastly, the community of Old Superior was dissatisfied with three railroads cutting swathes across their community. By shifting east, parallel to the CStPM&O, the DSS&A would also be closer to the business district of Old Superior.

Property was purchased in July 1893 to allow an eastward extension of the DSS&A's 28th Street line to a connection with the CStPM&O trackage at Old Superior. Trackage rights over the Omaha road were then obtained for 1.64 miles to the Superior Belt Line & Terminal crossing, avoiding independent crossings of the Nemadji River and Northern Pacific. From the Belt Railway crossing, the South Shore would use 0.38 miles of that road to reach Belt Jct. There the DSS&A would branch off onto its own rails to a connection with the old 19th Street line just south of Bluff Creek. Henry and Balch received a contract to fill in the missing pieces, and operations began over the new route on August 1, 1894. Old Superior passengers were served by a new depot at Ninth and Becker.

Still another revision in the Superior routing occurred when the DSS&A established a grade crossing over the Great Northern, successor to the Superior Belt Line & Terminal, at the east end of its Allouez yard (the old Duluth & Winnipeg facility). The South Shore main line was extended north to a connection with the CStPM&O at Allouez, just south of the Nemadji River bridge, eliminating the run over the Belt railway.

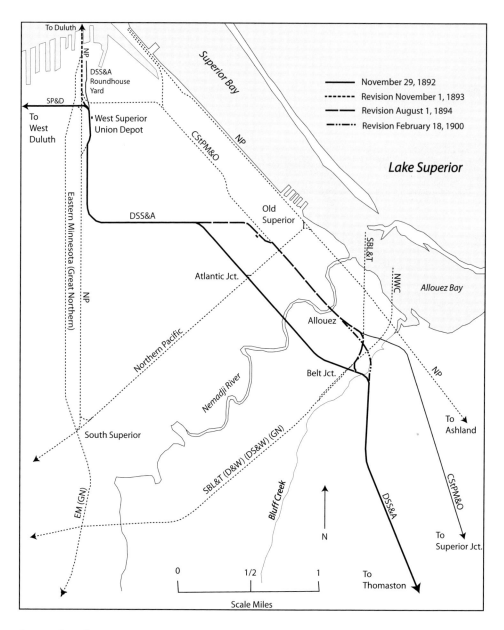

Routing through Superior, Wisconsin, November 29, 1892, to February 18, 1900

Under an agreement dated February 18, 1901, South Shore trackage rights over the Omaha road were shortened to 1.35 miles.

With only 15 percent of its Twin Ports freight business going to Duluth, the South Shore had long desired for this traffic be handled by the NP out of West Superior. This would allow DSS&A freight trains to tie up at the latter point and reduce expensive terminal charges and bridge tolls. The South Shore was able to mend fences with the NP,

This view looks north off the roof of the DSS&A's 5-stall engine house at the Roundhouse Yard at Superior in August 1912. The Northern Pacific's double-track main line to Duluth is seen to the left, while the Omaha Road's Superior Yard is on the right. *Paananen Collection*

and this practice was instituted on November 1, 1893. DSS&A passenger trains also resumed running over the NP between West Superior and Duluth under the new agreement. To accommodate the new operating scheme, the South Shore resurrected its undeveloped terminal property in West Superior, building a small 4-track stub yard at the site, as well as a 3-stall engine house. Another 4-track double-ended yard was built along 28th Street east of Tower Avenue.

Superior was a hotbed of activity during the American Railway Union strike in 1894. Supporters of Eugene V. Debs, seeking to aid strikers at the Pullman Palace Car Company plant, organized a boycott of Pullman cars and put heavy pressure on DSS&A men at the Twin Ports to back their cause. Finally, on the evening of July 17, a South Shore crew refused to pick up their train at the LST&T yards in West Superior. Fitch arrived in West Superior the following morning, and, after discussions, the DSS&A men agreed to call off the strike in return for being reinstated.

The South Shore enjoyed good labor relations for the most part. When a wage cut had to be made in 1895 due to continuing effects from the Panic of 1893, employee committees were invited to a conference. They were given statements showing the road's earnings and expenses for the three previous years. An agreement was made to cut wages for all those making over $65 a year, from General Manager Fitch on down. Salaries over $3,000 a year received a 20 percent cut, and those over $1,200 were cut 10 percent. All other employees received cuts ranging from 3 to 7 percent depending upon their rate of pay. These cuts were restored by a 10 percent raise handed out in January 1896 as times improved.

Forest fires, exacerbated by lax logging methods, played serious havoc with the South Shore's Western Division on several occasions. On September 2, 1894, the DSS&A's mammoth 148-bent timber trestle over the Wisconsin Central at Marengo was consumed by one such fire. Rather than rebuild the bridge, the South Shore made a line change which resulted in them going under the WC. Another serious disruption occurred on June 29, 1900, when the DSS&A's half-mile trestle over the Middle River and CStPM&O at Rockmont burned, resulting in a detour move over the NP between Iron River and Superior.

As this arrangement isolated the trackage west of Iron River, beginning July 8 the DSS&A started running over the Hawthorne, Nebagamon & Superior (a Weyerhaeuser logging railroad) between Lake Nebagamon and Hawthorne, and used the CStPM&O for the remaining distance into Superior. The South Shore immediately began work on a new bridge and fill, but traffic was not restored until September 9, 1900.

Even though the South Shore now had an independent entrance to the Twin Ports, the slogan "Zenith City Short Line" had grown wearisome and had been painted over for some time on the sides of the South Shore's rolling stock. In the summer of 1892 a new trademark, "The Marquette Route," was introduced and quickly found favor, especially in the DSS&A's headquarters city. A much larger black box soon appeared on the South Shore rolling stock with "The" and "Route" in roman and "Marquette" in script.[5]

Evidence of over-optimistic traffic predictions in the road's early years led to the South Shore selling a number of locomotives to the Soo Line in 1892. These included the former MH&O American Standards and eight of the 1888 Brooks Moguls. The South Shore also sold five Dickson 4-4-0s to the Duluth & Winnipeg. The sale of power came to haunt the South Shore during the severe winter of 1892–1893, which required the running of a number of plow extras, leaving little slack to care for regular traffic. The rotary received quite a workout, proving its worth. Some had come to view the machine as a "white elephant" due to the mild winters that had prevailed in previous years.[6]

To care for dressed lumber shipments, the DSS&A added 400 33-foot, 25-ton boxcars (8000–8598 and 45000–45198, even nos.) built by Wells and French in 1893 and 1895. These were augmented by the purchase of another 600 cars (11000–11599) from American Car and Foundry in 1905 and 1909, bringing the first 36-foot boxcars to the road. The DSS&A continued to experience a shortage of ore cars, but the problem with the ore traffic was that several thousand cars stood idle during the winter months. The same could be said for log flats, since the logging business was largely inactive during the summer. To get around this problem, South Shore master car builder D. C. Mulvihill devised a 25-ton car that had a diagonal floor, which could be folded down flat to cover the hopper opening. The ends could also be laid down for loading of lumber and logs. With the building of some 400 "combination ore cars" (7000–7500) between 1895 and 1899, the DSS&A was also able to quit leasing ore cars from other roads—a common practice in previous years.

The South Shore's Leslie rotary plow No. 711 is seen at Grand View, 2½ miles west of Marquette, clearing snow off the siding.   *Wesley Perron Railroad Collection, Peter White Public Library, Marquette, Mich.*

THE DULUTH & WINNIPEG RAILROAD

The Duluth and Winnipeg Railroad (D&W), started by local Duluth interests in 1878, played an important part in the Hill–Van Horne struggle of the 1890s. The line, dormant for many years, did not lay its first trackage until the fall of 1888, and by the end of 1890 it had been extended northwest 82 miles out of Cloquet, Minnesota. The focus then shifted east, and, in 1891, 12.7 miles of line were completed from Cloquet to Short Line Park. The D&W joined the St. Paul & Duluth main line at that point and used 11.6 miles of trackage rights to reach Duluth.[7]

With potential revenues from the embryonic Mesabi Iron Range in sight, the D&W entered into an agreement on July 22, 1891, with the Superior Belt Line & Terminal Railway to use 12 miles of its line from New Duluth, Minnesota, to Allouez, Wisconsin. The D&W agreed to build an ore dock at Allouez over which it would ship not less than 100,000 tons per year. During the summer of 1892, the Duluth, Missabe and Northern (DM&N), another embryonic Mesabi Range ore carrier, built from Mountain Iron to a connection with the D&W at Stony Brook Jct. As the DM&N had no dock facilities of its own, the D&W would handle its ore to the lakefront. The first ore off the Mesabi Range arrived from Mountain Iron on November 1, 1892, upon the partially completed Allouez ore dock. The D&W handled 4,245 tons of ore that first year, but Duluth interests felt the business was rightfully theirs and provided incentives for the DM&N to build into their community. On July 22, 1893, the first DM&N ore train arrived on their new Duluth ore dock, cutting the D&W out of the process.

North Star Construction Co., builder of the D&W, had received $20,000 in 5 percent bonds and $25,000 stock for each of its 97.7 miles. Bond sales had not gone well, and, facing a half million dollars in floating debt, the Construction Co. was looking to get out. Successful negotiations were conducted by the DSS&A's Samuel Thomas, who took over as president. James J. Hill, eyeing the D&W for some time, had purchased much of the line's indebtedness with the idea of foreclosing at an opportune time. He was no doubt taken aback when the Canadian Pacific purchased the line outright for $1,316,924. Fitch took over as general manager of the D&W in June 1893. Unfortunately settling the D&W's debt proved no easy task, given its control by Hill. Van Horne also had a hard time receiving support from the CPR executive committee, some of whom had ties to both the CPR and Hill's Great Northern.[8]

As the D&W main line was but a short distance from the Mesabi Range, it would be a simple matter to gain access. The D&W also had a controlling interest in or outright ownership of 18,420 acres of cutover lands believed to be rich in iron ore. Some even thought the D&W, in combination with the DSS&A, would serve as a possible alternative route for the CPR between Winnipeg and the Sault. As part of the new westward shift, the DSS&A's general freight office was moved to Duluth Union Depot on November 1, 1893. General Freight Agent Orr optimistically announced that the D&W would be completed to Winnipeg early in 1894. Fitch said CPR traffic would not be routed over the D&W extension, but the line would bring Red River Valley wheat and Mesabi Range ore to Superior and handle lumber west from the mills along the DSS&A. Chief Engineer H. J. Payne, a gang of men, and considerable quantities of steel rails were sent out early in December 1893 to bring the existing D&W trackage into shape. Payne also led a survey party off the end of track at Deer River in January 1894, but they were called back after reaching Bemidji.

The calling in of Engineer Payne was no doubt due to the effects of the Panic of 1893. After the DM&N shifted its ore business to its Duluth dock, the D&W business dried up, with only 6,950 tons being handled in 1894. Low grain prices and a poor crop added to the CPR's troubles during the Panic, leaving little money for D&W improvements, much less extensions to Winnipeg or into the Mesabi Range. The D&W expenditures were said to be one of the major reasons the CPR was unable to make a dividend payment in the second half of 1894, drawing the ire of the directors, particularly Sir George Stephen. Stephen, however, could not convince Van Horne to rid himself of the D&W. Hill continued to apply pressure, announcing his intentions of building a parallel line east out of Fosston, Minnesota. When Van Horne attempted to fund the D&W extension by selling construction bonds in the small towns along the proposed route, Hill's agents were soon on the scene paying off prospective D&W bond purchasers with cash. Hill also took on the D&W every chance he could in the courts as a major D&W debt holder. Due to lack of support, the Duluth & Winnipeg went into receivership on October 13, 1894, with Fitch appointed as receiver.

After a foreclosure sale, the D&W was reorganized as the Duluth, Superior and Western Railway (DS&W) in July 1896. The offices of the road continued to be in Marquette, with Fitch remaining as president and general manager. Van Horne continued to profess optimism over the road's prospects. As he wrote CPR director Thomas Skinner, "The D & W is the best property we have & this year will demonstrate that. It is moreover our only weapon against the Great Northern and Northern Pacific."[9] Traffic reawakened on the D&W when the first cars of Mahoning mine iron ore came off the Duluth, Mississippi River and Northern Railway (DMR&N) connection at Swan River on July 4, 1895. This allowed the Allouez ore dock to go back into service after a long hiatus. The 250 ore cars owned by DMR&N were soon insufficient to handle the business offered, and that winter the D&W ordered 600 25-ton cars from Michigan-Peninsular Car Co.

Unfortunately, the price of ore fell in August 1896, and the Duluth, Superior & Western had little business. Even Van Horne admitted that the road's debts "have piled up shockingly."[10] The CPR board then made its move and told Van Horne that if he did not get rid of the DS&W they would fire him. Van Horne finally gave in, and CPR vice president Thomas Shaughnessy and director Richard B. Angus went to New York to negotiate a deal with Hill. The DS&W was turned over to the Great Northern on April 17, 1897, for the same price the CPR had paid for the property 4½ years before. Although the Great Northern was to aid the Soo Line and South Shore with traffic, Van Horne acidly wired Stephen, "You will be glad to hear D. and W. matter settled satisfaction everybody."[11]

The traffic agreement with the Great Northern was largely ignored by Hill, who continued to use his Northern Steamship Company vessels whenever possible out of the Twin Ports. The year 1897 saw the GN handle 94,504 loaded cars in and out of Duluth-Superior, compared to only 5,987 for the DSS&A. Just four years after the DS&W purchase, GN iron ore shipments through Allouez pulled even with those of Marquette and during the fifth season exploded to over 4 million tons, almost double Marquette's total. With the Mesabi going on to become the dominant range in the Lake Superior District, a line such as the DS&W would have ensured financial health to the DSS&A and allowed it to balance its strategically weak link along the south shore of the lake. The loss for the DSS&A was especially troubling considering it was about to lose its monopoly on the Marquette ore business as well.

LAKE SUPERIOR & ISHPEMING PROVIDES NEW COMPETITION

Mines on the Marquette Range had long complained of the rates and service provided by the DSS&A and its predecessors. The lack of ore cars, always a problem with the iron ore roads, was especially acute on the South Shore. As Superintendent George Jarvis wrote Van Horne, "Our car equipment is not sufficient to allow of the delivery of cars at the mines in the evening for the following day's loading, as is the practice in vogue on the Chicago & North-Western Railway; aside from this, our coal shipments from Marquette generally cause a delay of twelve (12) hours to cars, and it frequently occurs that we are obliged to fill a mine's order for empty cars with cars loaded with coal for the mine, which must be unloaded before the cars are available." The C&NW, with its

The 412, one of the 1888 Baldwin Moguls, wheels an empty ore train up what is believed to be the south main line out of Marquette toward the Marquette Range. *Paananen Collection*

greater car supply, could also continue to provide empties to the mines even if its ore dock pockets at Escanaba became filled due to late-arriving boats.[12]

The 45-cent iron ore rate from Ishpeming to Marquette was also a frequent topic of complaint and felt to be "fully one-half higher than the rate should be." While the rate could be tolerated in good times, the reduction in ore prices in 1892 "will not warrant the payment of such freight charges as has been given in the past."[13] The principal mining company on the Marquette Range, Cleveland-Cliffs Iron, decided the time had come to control its own destiny and surveyed an independent line from Presque Isle, north of Marquette, to Ishpeming the same year. With additional backing from Pittsburgh and Lake Angeline Iron Company, this effort became officially known as the Lake Superior and Ishpeming Railway Company (LS&I) on February 21, 1893. Even though the ore business would only get worse with the Panic of 1893, CCI decided now was a good time to build for the future: "The advantages of building in this Columbian year are many and manifest. Railroad material, supplies and equipment are lower than they have been in several years and lower than they may be again for several years to come while money can be obtained in the East on more favorable terms than ever before."[14]

Many in Marquette cheered the building of the new road, and its promoters, seeking the donation of the terminal grounds at Presque Isle, claimed the LS&I would be constructed to such high standards that its low freight rates would end the hauling of Marquette Range ore to Escanaba. Some questioned whether Marquette would benefit from a competing line, given its probable effect on the South Shore. The building of the

LS&I was not likely to cause ore to be diverted from Escanaba to Marquette, given the inherent efficiency of the C&NW route to Lake Michigan points. The DSS&A paid out over $50,000 per month in salaries in Marquette, and wouldn't the splitting of the DSS&A ore traffic mean less work for the Marquette shop employees? Wouldn't fewer train miles affect the South Shore trainmen and enginemen? If the rates were cut would not this have to be made up largely on the backs of the employees? Reduced ore rates would accrue benefits mainly to the absentee mine owners.

The absentee owners clearly thought there would be benefits and construction began on the LS&I in December 1895. The new 21-mile line was completed on August 12, 1896, and the first cargo of Cleveland-Cliffs ore taken off the new LS&I ore dock a week later. Owing to its late start, the LS&I only handled 300,000 tons of ore in 1896, compared to 1,274,000 tons over the South Shore. In its first full year of operations in 1897, however, LS&I's tonnage mushroomed to 1,036,594, already exceeding the South Shore's total of 903,736 tons. As well as reducing the DSS&A's ore tonnage, the new line brought reduced rates, with the two roads hauling to Marquette for 32 cents a ton. This resulted in a further drain on the DSS&A's bleak finances. Besides considerable ore traffic, the DSS&A also lost out on the Dead River log business when the LS&I built a connection to the Dead River branch near its crossing with the South Shore at Bagdad Jct. in 1903. The Dead River mill was located just south of the LS&I ore yard at Presque Isle.

Whether Cleveland-Cliffs ever gave the DSS&A a chance to preserve its monopoly to Marquette is unknown. With the South Shore's balance sheet in the red, there was little opportunity for additional ore car purchases without further advances from the CPR, which was facing its own bleak financial problems with the Panic of 1893. Reducing the tariff was not always felt to be the answer, either; as the CPR's Shaughnessy once wrote Fitch, "I would not, however, be inclined to enter into the contract for the mere glory of handling the tonnage."[15]

An additional road that wound up the in LS&I fold was the Munising Railway, which got its start in 1895. Beginning at the community of the same name on Lake Superior, the line went under the DSS&A at Munising Jct., 5 miles to the south, before heading into the woods and a connection with the C&NW at Little Lake. A nearby DSS&A-served community, also known as Munising, became Wetmore on January 1, 1896, under a directive from the U.S. Post Office. The LS&I took control of the Munising Railway on July 1, 1901, and constructed another subsidiary, the Marquette and South-eastern (M&SE), to tie it into the LS&I system.

The M&SE built out of the LS&I Marquette yard at Presque Isle and went south along Lake Superior, eventually paralleling the DSS&A's Lower Yard. At the east end of the yard, the M&SE crossed the South Shore main line on a diamond and ran alongside before turning off to the south near Chocolay. The LS&I was required to maintain an interlocking at the busy Marquette crossing, which was used as a switching lead for the Lower Yard. As the M&SE passed by the state prison, it was allowed to jointly serve the facility by purchasing a half-interest in the South Shore spur effective December 31, 1901. The M&SE opened its 26.96-mile line from Marquette to Lawson (junction with the Munising Railway) on July 1, 1902.

Traffic for the new LS&I extensions was provided when Cleveland-Cliffs purchased much of the remaining acreage of the Detroit, Mackinac & Marquette swamp land grant on June 26, 1902. Until that time only about 7 percent of the swamp lands had been sold.

After the lands' tax-free status expired in 1897, the quality of the remaining swamp lands was such that many acres were allowed to revert back to the state to cover back taxes. The Detroit, Mackinac & Marquette land grant income bonds only earned 1 percent interest during the early years of the 20th century. As these bonds were coming due on October 1, 1911, with no revenue to pay for them, it was decided to reorganize the land holdings into a new firm called the Detroit, Mackinac & Marquette Land Company.[16]

The remaining MH&O land grant lands and those acquired by tax deeds had been in the hands of trustees Samuel Thomas, his wife, and John Sterling since the MH&O lease of 1890. This property was passed on to the South Shore Land Company Ltd., organized on December 19, 1898. The main purpose of the organization was to keep the lands exempt from the general mortgages of the DSS&A. Although some one-quarter of the total land area of the Upper Peninsula of Michigan had been donated to the South Shore or its predecessors (1,871,707 acres) and the C&NW (801,386 acres), the land was of such questionable value that the roads did not accrue nearly the land grant revenue attained by roads in other parts of the country.[17]

The building of the Manistique and Northwestern (M&NW) into Shingleton on the DSS&A's Mackinaw Division in late 1898 created another new connection. The M&NW hoped to act as a bridge route between the South Shore and the ferry port of Manistique on Lake Michigan, 40 miles to the south. Such routing was discouraged by the DSS&A as the rate division was much less than that on the longer line haul to St. Ignace or the Sault. The M&NW passed into the hands of the GR&I in 1902 and was reorganized as the Manistique, Marquette and Northern Railroad Company, using a ferry connection on the Lower Peninsula at Northport. A still later reorganization into the Manistique and Lake Superior (M&LS) occurred on July 23, 1909, when control passed to the Ann Arbor Railroad, which connected with it by ferry from Frankfort. The M&LS was extended 4.5 miles west of Shingleton to a direct connection with the Marquette & Southeastern at Evelyn in June 1911, saving shippers $1 per thousand pounds over having the South Shore involved in the routing.[18]

At nearby Seney the South Shore connected with the Manistique Railway, a common carrier logging road, which made its first run some 31 miles north to the Lake Superior community of Grand Marais on October 8, 1893. Another branch ran 8 miles south of Seney to Germfask. Although an interchange was maintained at the crossing, the South Shore realized little traffic, as the logs transported over the Manistique were milled at Grand Marais and then handled by lumber schooner down the Great Lakes. The Manistique discontinued operations on November 5, 1910, with the end of the pine era.[19]

Many of the country's businessmen awaited the outcome of the 1896 presidential election between Republican candidate William McKinley and Democratic populist William Jennings Bryan. Bryan had been campaigning in the UP and on the night of October 14, 1896, was en route from Marquette to St. Ignace with no stops planned. The lumberjacks of Seney, on hearing of their favorite candidate's passing, thought he should make a stop there as well. Taking matters in their own hands, they "borrowed" some torpedoes from the railroad and set them on the track. On exploding these torpedoes, the train would be required to stop, and the woodsmen hoped to get a chance to see their candidate. The agent at Seney, W. G. Miller, caught wind of the plan and telegraphed the dispatcher, who told the train's engineer to ignore the warning. This was done and the lumberjacks were treated to nothing more than loud noises as train passed through.[20]

With the election of McKinley as president and the uplifting of business prospects, 1899 proved to be the biggest season ever at Marquette, with over 2,720,000 tons of ore being shipped. Unfortunately, the LS&I had over half of the tonnage and the South Shore's totals would only diminish as the newcomer built spurs into additional territory. New promising finds were opened on the Negaunee & Palmer branch, and half-mile spurs were also laid into the Mary Charlotte mine and Breitung Hematite mine in 1903. This new trackage was for the joint use of the C&NW and South Shore, with the LS&I later sharing the traffic under an agreement dated October 1, 1912.

The good market for ore caused renewed interest in some of the long-idle west end mines and saw the reopening of the Michigamme, Imperial (formerly the Wetmore), and Beaufort mines. The Beaufort spur was relaid in 1900, with the C&NW being given trackage rights from Michigamme to access the mine on October 4, 1902. As the market for low-grade ores declined, all this activity, except at the Imperial, shut down for good by 1905. The Beaufort's machinery was hauled over to a more promising site at the nearby Ohio mine, which joined the shipping list in 1907.

Among the big mergers that took place during the McKinley administration was the massive consolidation of steel interests under J. P. Morgan to form U.S. Steel in 1901. The Marquette Range, at 37.8 percent, was the only iron mining region in the Lake Superior District in which U.S. Steel ended up with less than 50 percent ownership. This was due to the heavy concentration of Cleveland-Cliffs mines, which remained outside the conglomerate. U.S. Steel's influence was especially dominant in the Mesabi Range, where it controlled 71.8 percent of the output. The same year saw Minnesota pull ahead of Michigan for the first time in total ore shipments. This output was led by the Mesabi Range, which now sent out 46 percent of the Lake Superior District's ore.

The South Shore launched a big capital improvement in the fall of 1905 with the building of a new ore dock (No. 5) on the original Ely dock site. The dock approach branched off just east of Third Street, passing through the passenger yards, and then crossed Front Street on an overpass. Another overpass bridged Lake Street and another went over the James Pickands coal sheds. The massive dock reached a height of 70'8", taller than any other dock in existence at that time except for one owned by the Great Northern at Allouez. This allowed the South Shore to service the new and larger ore boats coming on line, which required higher chutes to afford a proper angle for delivering ore into their holds. The length of the dock from the water's edge to the end of the dock was 1,350 feet, with 200 pockets of 200 tons capacity.

Although the dock was supposed to be ready for the opening of the 1906 navigation season, construction lagged due to timber shortages, and it was not until August 2 that the first ore was dumped into the dock. The *Edwin F. Holmes* took out the first cargo nine days later. Because of the height of the new dock, it was no longer possible to let ore cars drift down out of the Upper Yard to the street-level docks. The South Shore continued to let the loaded ore cars roll down to the approach under the control of two switchmen, but when they reached the approach a switch engine would couple on and shove them the rest of the way. This practice was done away with in later years and a Consolidation would handle 10 to 12 cars right out of the Upper Yard. A running start was required to make the dock without stalling as there was a steep 2.4 percent ruling grade between Third and Front streets.

Dock No. 5 had a maximum unloading capacity of 675 tons per hour, figuring a 10-hour day. If the ore dock pockets became filled, the 14-track storage yard up on the

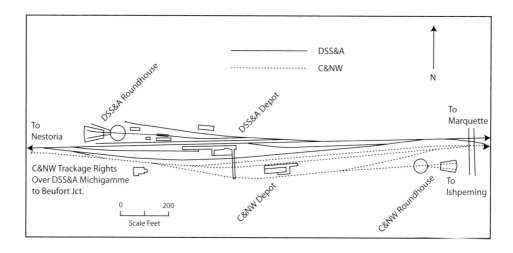

DSS&A ——————
C&NW - - - - - - - - -

N ↑

To Nestoria

DSS&A Roundhouse

DSS&A Depot

To Marquette

C&NW Trackage Rights
Over DSS&A Michigamme
to Beufort Jct.

C&NW Depot

C&NW Roundhouse

To Ishpeming

0   200
Scale Feet

Michigamme, Michigan, 1902

Michigamme in 1900 was busy as the site of a lumber mill and an iron ore mine. The shaft house of the latter can be seen to the left of the mill's refuse burner. *Paananen Collection*

The Imperial mine shaft No. 2, in October, 1909. The Imperial was one of the westernmost iron mines on the Marquette Range. This district's ore was not as rich as that found in the mines around Ishpeming and Negaunee, and west end mines were generally operated only in times of strong ore prices.   *Paananen Collection*

Marquette, Michigan, 1912

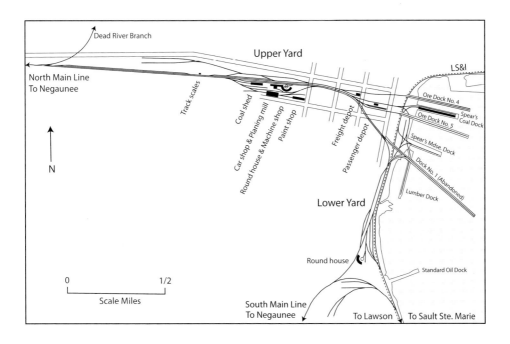

hill between Fifth Avenue and the scales had a capacity of 435 cars. As an ore dock pocket could hold 4 cars of ore, it was common for furnace operators to request a certain mixture of ore to be placed in a boat's hold. Thus the first ore dumped into a pocket might be a certain grade from a certain mine, on top of which would be dumped a different grade from another mine. This entailed much additional switching for the yard crews. The practice was eventually done away with when lower freight rates were offered in lieu of mixing. Even then boats sometimes would move up and down one side of the dock, or even to the opposite side, to take on different compositions of ore. The receiving yard west of the scales was only used to hold inbound ore until it was weighed. The Lower Yard was reserved for commercial cars, unless it happened to contain ore routed all-rail.

After the completion of Dock No. 5, the old Marquette & Western dock was taken out of service due to rotting upper timbers. Although 2,400 feet long, it only stood 45 feet high, incapable of loading modern ore carriers. Salvage work began during the winter of 1907–1908. During the 1913 season, ore Dock No. 4 started to show its age and the engineering department advised that the pockets should not be loaded to more than half their capacity. This limited the 20,000-ton dock to 10,000 tons. The outer end of the dock was taken down in the spring of 1914, and the balance was removed the following winter. This left No. 5 as the only South Shore dock remaining in service.

The effects of the bank Panic of 1907, although not nearly as long-lasting as those of the Panic of 1893, resulted in a dismal 1908 ore season, with shipments off almost one-half from 1907 totals. After a small shipment of 430 tons in April, there were no further ore shipments off the Marquette docks until June. The cyclical nature of the ore business was evident as, by 1909, car shortages were again in evidence on all three roads serving the Marquette Range. M. A. Hanna opened the American mine in 1906, and the 2.06-mile Boston mine branch, abandoned in 1901, was relaid in 1908 to provide service. The South Shore crossed the C&NW's Michigamme branch to reach the American, and, under an agreement dated June 30, 1910, the DSS&A came to split the ownership of the mine spurs with the C&NW. After the mine closed, all trackage was removed in 1927.

THE LUMBER BUSINESS

Lumber continued to be the South Shore's second-leading commodity, although the focus shifted from Michigan to Wisconsin, the latter reaching its peak of lumber production in 1898, when it led the nation. The South Shore's independent entrance into Superior took part in this trend, enjoying a large local business. The big Weyerhaeuser mill at Lake Nebagamon opened on May 22, 1899. Although much of Weyerhaeuser's business went down their Hawthorne, Nebagamon & Superior (HN&S) railroad to a connection with the CStPM&O, the South Shore found it necessary to employ a road switcher at Lake Nebagamon during the summer months when the mill was in operation. The road switcher operated out of Iron River during the winter when the mill was shut down. Besides Nebagamon Lumber Co., Lake Nebagamon also was the site of several ice houses which supplied customers as far away as Marquette and the Copper Country.

The westbound Lake Superior Limited passes Marquette Scales, a mile west of the downtown depot. Inbound iron ore trains were left west of the scales and then weighed by yard crews before being placed on the docks for unloading. *Paananen Collection*

Edward Hines came onto the northern Wisconsin lumber scene in a big way during the summer of 1905, purchasing the White River Lumber Company mill at Mason and the Alexander and Edgar mill at Iron River. The DSS&A built a 1.68-mile spur from Bibon to Mason to serve Hines's White River operation in 1905. Although the mill had been in existence since 1882, White River Lumber Company, founded by John Humbird and other men closely involved with the CStPM&O, had relied almost exclusively on that road to handle its business. As much of Hines's timber was near the DSS&A at Gund's Siding (later Cusson), arrangements were made to lay a third rail on the South Shore from Mason to Iron River to accommodate Hines's narrow gauge equipment. By mid-November 1905, Hines was sending 70 cars of logs a day to the Iron River mill pond. Additional Wisconsin lumber mills along the South Shore included the big Gurney Lumber Company at Gurney, as well as smaller operations at Sanborn, Bibon, Leclair, and Bell. The Wisconsin lumber traffic was also fleeting, and by 1918 the state ranked eighth in U.S. lumber production.

In Michigan, G. A. Bergland moved his mill from Sidnaw to Lake Gogebic in 1902 to be nearer his timber holdings. The South Shore constructed a good-sized depot at the new station of Bergland and a trestle out into the lake for a log dump. South Shore log flats were used on the Bergland logging branch, which ran north of town, as well on the main line hauls. Although the pine was gone, new hardwood mills were opened at Ewen and at Tula near the Wisconsin border. Trout Creek was home to three mills, including the extensive Weidman & Son mill which opened in 1912.

Just east of Ewen, Holt Lumber Company bought timber from the Diamond Match Company on Baltimore Creek in 1901. In preparation for development, W. F. Fitch, Chief Engineer H. J. Payne, and William Holt went out to visit the site in 1902 aboard

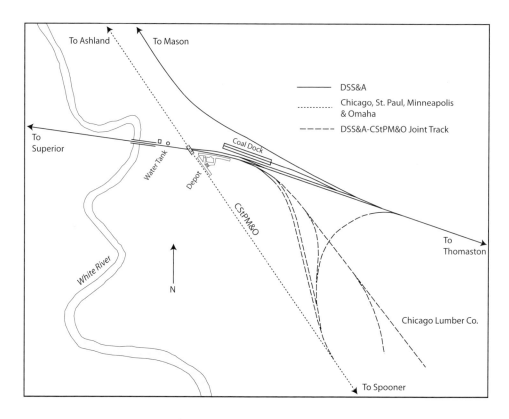

To Ashland

To Mason

DSS&A

Chicago, St. Paul, Minneapolis & Omaha

DSS&A-CStPM&O Joint Track

To Superior

Water Tank

Coal Dock

Depot

CStPM&O

To Thomaston

White River

Chicago Lumber Co.

N

To Spooner

Bibon, Wisconsin, 1913

Fitch's car *Marquette*. Fitch's participation ended at that point, and, as Payne and Holt tramped over the red clay, the general manager, off the back platform of his car, hunted partridge flushed up as the locomotive shoved the *Marquette* down the track. To harvest the Holt timber, the South Shore went on to construct, between 1902 and 1905, a branch which grew to 6 miles in length off the main line at Baltimore. DSS&A crews operated over the branch, with the logs going to Ishpeming, and over the C&NW to the Holt mill at Oconto, Wisconsin.

On the Houghton Division at L'Anse, the Marshall Butters Co. opened a large mill at the old mill site, which received a number of spurs off the DSS&A in 1912 and 1913. This company also operated its own logging railroad. The DSS&A secured other lumber business beginning in the spring of 1910 by opening a ferry service between Baraga and the Charles Hebard and Son mill at Pequaming, just across L'Anse Bay. A 152-foot ferry dock, with apron, was put in at the foot of Ontonagon Street in Baraga, allowing rail cars to be loaded onto scows for the trip to the mill. Even with the new ferry service, 90 percent of Hebard's lumber continued to go out by boat.

At Marquette, the Dead River branch, owned by the Dead River Railroad but operated by the DSS&A, was sold to the South Shore on July 25, 1907, for $15,000. Although the old Hawley mill at the end of the branch was inoperative, the spur was used by South Shore passenger specials to reach the Marquette County fairgrounds each year during the first week of September. The branch also attracted a number of new milling opera-

Besides the ferry service across the Straits of Mackinaw, the DSS&A barged railroad cars across L'Anse Bay from Baraga to Pequaming, Michigan, for loading at the Charles Hebard and Sons lumber mill. This arrangement was put into effect in 1910. *Paananen Collection*

tions, including the Brunswick-Balke-Collender mill, which manufactured bowling equipment, and Piqua Handle and Manufacturing Company, which made a wide array of hardwood products.[21] On the Mackinaw Division, the South Shore built a branch some 5 miles north out of Soo Jct. to serve the Hunter and Love Lumber Co. mill, on the Tahquamenon River, in 1911. At the new station of Raco, a new hardboard mill was built by Richardson and Avery around 1914.

Despite the new additions to the lumber industry, many more outfits, mainly old pine mills, went out of business. Fire consumed the largest of the UP operations, that of Hall and Munson at Bay Mills, on January 22, 1904. The Michigamme mill closed in 1906, and the big Defer mill at Saxon, Wisconsin, burned on May 27 of that year. The Dollarville operation shut down in 1909.

Traffic to the Keweenaw remained active thanks to the booming copper industry. Duluth jobbers, anxious to participate in this expanding market, were rewarded with a speeded-up freight service out of the Twin Ports effective April 27, 1902. The new service provided deliveries in 24 hours to Marquette and Houghton and in 36 hours to the Sault. Many Duluth jobbers established branch houses in the Copper Country, and the new schedule gave them a competitive edge over their Chicago counterparts, whose goods required some 30 hours to make the distance. Detroit jobbers were still out of the picture, since it took almost a week for goods to travel from Detroit to the Copper Country. The DSS&A also added a new freight run, No. 39, which ran on Mondays and Thursdays from Champion to Houghton. It was on these days that most of the perishable freight for the Copper Country arrived off the CM&StP road from Chicago and Wisconsin jobbers.

An emblazoned 20-car train of Gold Medal flour consigned to the E. M. Lieblein
wholesale grocery, in the left background, rests on the Hancock hill after its arrival in
the late fall of 1900.   *Wesley Perron Railroad Collection, Peter White Public Library,
Marquette, Mich.*

One special movement that emphasized the importance of the jobbing business of
the Copper Country was a 20-car shipment of 5,000 barrels of Gold Medal brand flour
from the Washburn-Crosby company mills in Minneapolis to E. M. Lieblein, a wholesale
grocer in Hancock. This train, received off the CStPM&O at Bibon, was specially decorated and made quite a scene at Hancock and stations along the way in the late fall of
1900.

Passenger travel between Duluth and the Copper Country also became more feasi-
ble with the reestablishment of day passenger runs (Nos. 5 and 6) between Duluth and
Michigamme on May 29, 1899. No. 6 made connections at Nestoria with trains 1 and 4
running between the Copper Country and Marquette. No. 5 would receive Calumet
passengers off train No. 9 at Nestoria. Both Nos. 5 and 6 stopped for dinner at Lake
Gogebic at the "company's new dining room overlooking the lake."[22] New trains, Nos. 9
and 16, made a nighttime run between Calumet and Nestoria, connecting with trains 7
and 8 in addition to bringing down passengers for No. 5. The Nestoria-Bessemer local
was a casualty of the new arrangement, and its discontinuance marked a permanent end
to passenger train service on the Bessemer branch.

The DSS&A engineered what was considered quite a coup when it signed an agreement with the Chicago, Milwaukee & St. Paul to inaugurate through service between
Chicago and Calumet. It had been thought the Copper Range Railroad (CR), then

building into Houghton off the CM&StP at McKeever, would be used, but the CR still lacked an outlet to Calumet. The new through service, begun on November 26, 1899, reduced the running time between Chicago and Calumet by nearly 2 hours and resulted in four trains daily out of the Copper Country. The Lake Superior Limited left Calumet at 7:45 AM for the St. Ignace and Lower Peninsula connections. The Chicago Mail followed at 2:30 PM, making connections with the C&NW at Ishpeming before continuing on to Marquette. The new CM&StP Chicago Limited, which did not leave until 4:00 PM, still arrived in Chicago at 7:00 AM, 25 minutes earlier than the Chicago Mail. No. 16 left at 9:30 PM, making connections at Nestoria with 7 and 8 between the Sault and Duluth. Calumet-Chicago service was further integrated with the start of a through fast freight service in conjunction with the CM&StP on December 4, 1899.[23]

Under the new agreement, the CM&StP was also allowed to provide passenger service over the DSS&A between Republic and Marquette. Unlike the Champion-Calumet operation, the Republic-Marquette service was manned with Milwaukee Road crews. To facilitate the new service, a connecting track was placed between the CM&StP and South Shore tracks at Milwaukee Jct., just north of Republic, in December 1899, with the switches controlled by the interlocking at that point. No. 5 started backing down from Michigamme and connecting with these trains at Humboldt before heading to Duluth.

The Copper Range Railroad was completed into Houghton on December 27, 1899, and rumors swirled that the Chicago & North Western would form an alliance with the new road. A C&NW connection would be made possible by building a 30-mile connecting link off its Interior branch to a Mass or Rockland connection with the CR. Although the new connection would cut some 30 miles off the present route via Negaunee, it would still entail a 490-mile run to Chicago as opposed to only 410 miles via the DSS&A and CM&StP. The rumored alliance did not come to pass, but the South Shore did face increasing competition, beginning in October 1906, when the Copper Range and CM&StP began a through Chicago passenger service via McKeever. The two roads also offered a 36-hour freight service between Chicago and points in the Copper Country.

The Chicago & North Western did improve its Copper Country service by instituting a through Wagner sleeping car between Chicago and Calumet, which the South Shore handled on the Chicago Mail. The DSS&A and C&NW also entered into an arrangement on January 18, 1900, allowing the North Western to handle its own passenger train between Ishpeming and Marquette. This train, connecting with the morning passenger train from Chicago at Ishpeming, used North Western engines and crews. By running down the south main line into Marquette, the C&NW train came into the Tremont House depot facing west, and quickly left at 8:05 AM with a day run south over the North Western. The C&NW and CM&StP trains added variety to the consists at the Tremont House depot at Marquette, with the yellow North Western cars and darker yellow "St. Paul" equipment standing out in contrast to the vermilion of the South Shore.[24]

The height of C&NW passenger service to the Copper Country came about on May 15, 1910, with the start of the new Iron & Copper Country Express. A DSS&A connecting train left Marquette at 5:15 AM and, after setting out its coaches at Negaunee, picked up the C&NW consist. The South Shore mail car went through and was painted yellow to complement the North Western equipment. The C&NW's

In this photo taken in the link and pin coupler days around 1890, a short eastbound train sits on the Duluth-Superior main line at Nestoria, Michigan. The original depot at right burned on September 9, 1903, due to an overturned stove. *Michigan Technological University and Copper Country Historical Collections, Herman Page Collection, Negative 00567*

Chicago-Marquette sleeper was set out at Ishpeming and brought in by the C&NW's own service, while the diner operated as far as Houghton. This new train, designed to compete with the CM&StP service, was the first Copper Country train scheduled to arrive in Chicago each morning.

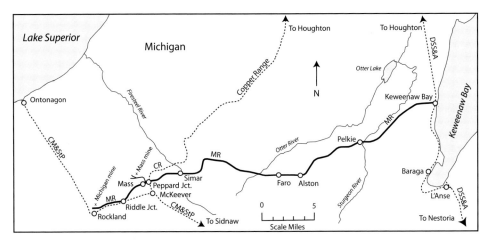

Mineral Range South Range Line, November 17, 1903

8

THE SOUTH RANGE LINE

The announced construction of the Copper Range Railroad out of McKeever, through the South Range of the Keweenaw Peninsula to Houghton, motivated the South Shore to revive its long-envisioned cutoff between the Houghton Division and the Western Division. In addition to improving service between Duluth and the Copper Country, the cutoff would serve the Michigan Copper Company and the Mass Consolidated Mining Company, both of which became active in this region in 1899, opening up long-idle mines. A DSS&A surveying party started out early that year from a junction with the Houghton Division some 12 miles north of L'Anse, passing the mining properties and then heading to Lake Gogebic, where connections were made with the Western Division. The new connection would shorten the distance between Duluth and Calumet to 242 miles versus 277 miles via Nestoria. The layover at desolate Nestoria had a tendency to discourage Duluth passenger traffic and most Copper Country business gravitated toward Marquette.

The DSS&A decided to let its Mineral Range subsidiary own and operate the new construction, and its articles of association were changed on February 20, 1899, to provide for a standard gauge line from Copper Harbor to some point on the Ontonagon River. Mass Consolidated contracted with the Mineral Range to handle copper rock from its mine to a stamp mill to be located at the junction with the Houghton Division along Keweenaw Bay. The junction took the name of the adjoining body of water, and by mid-November 1899 a joint MR-DSS&A two-story 24′×56′ depot had been completed at this point. A new 50,000-gallon water tank was also built, with water supplied from Kelsey's Creek by means of a 6,000-foot gravity-fed pipe.[1]

A contract for building the South Range line was let in late 1899 to Balch and Peppard, and a start was made on the heavy rock work west of Fire Steel River in January 1900. The Fire Steel bridge, one of the largest in the Upper Peninsula, would tower 70 feet over the river and span some 2,400 feet. All the piling for the bridge had been driven by the first week in June, by which time graders, working out of Keweenaw Bay, were said to be nearly "in the sight of the Mass."[2] By June 16, 56-pound rails had been laid out of Keweenaw Bay as far as the Sturgeon River, and the track reached Laird in early September. The bridge over Otter River, 7 miles west of Laird, was completed in mid-October, but the Fire Steel River trestle remained under construction. In mid-November the steel gang

Keweenaw Bay was the junction between the Mineral Range South Range line and the DSS&A main line between Nestoria and Houghton. Looking north, one sees the Mineral Range trackage along the left-hand platform, while the South Shore main line is down in the hole to the right. At the far right is the stamp mill of the Mass Copper company, where copper rock is being dumped into the bunker from an overhead trestle. The trestle fed off the Mineral Range South Range line and made an overhead crossing of the South Shore main line. Just to the north of the rock dump, one can see the bunkers for the locomotive coal chute built into the trestle bents. *Thomas A. Wilson Collection*

was shifted to Riddle Jct., a connection with the CM&StP just west of Mass, to allow work to continue. Mass, which would serve as the base of operations, received an engine house, with power being turned on the wye at nearby Peppard Jct. At Peppard Jct., a 1.81-mile spur split off to serve the Adventure and Evergreen locations. A further 0.96-mile extension of this spur was made in 1905 to serve the Mass C shaft. Work on the western segment between Riddle Jct. and Lake Gogebic was left for another season, forcing Duluth–Copper Country business to continue to be exchanged at Nestoria.

The first through train over the South Range line, a special containing General Manager Fitch and General Superintendent Lytle, was run on December 18, 1900. Upon reaching the end of the line at Riddle Jct., the special continued over the rails of the CM&StP to Ontonagon. One of the contract provisions of the CM&StP running between Champion and Calumet was that the DSS&A would be allowed to use the Milwaukee road's rails into Ontonagon. The official opening of the 36-mile line, on December 23, 1900, saw the establishment of through passenger service between Calumet and Ontonagon. To reach its isolated South Range line, the Mineral Range was given trackage rights over the DSS&A for the 19.36 miles between Houghton and Keweenaw Bay.[3]

Spring was often late making an appearance in the Copper Country, as witnessed by this scene on the South Range line near Mass City on April 17, 1907.   *Paananen Collection*

Freight service on the branch was provided by a daily local freight, Nos. 92 and 91, which made a round trip from Mass to Keweenaw Bay and return daily, except Sunday. Mineral Range engines 34 and 36 were the first to see regular service on the South Range line. The Mass mine made its first shipment on January 3, 1901, and that summer the copper rock movement began in earnest. At Keweenaw Bay, the Mineral Range reached the stamp by crossing over the DSS&A main line on a trestle, and the copper rock was gravity-dumped into the mill's bins. The trestle also served the pockets of the Mineral Range's locomotive coaling facility. Copper concentrate from the stamp was sent via the DSS&A to the Quincy smelter at Ripley or the Coles Creek smelter operated by the Copper Range west of Houghton.

The Mineral Range did not serve the Michigan mine directly until November 17, 1903, when a 3.38-mile branch from Riddle Jct. was put into operation. The Michigan mine used one of the stamp heads at the Mass mill at Keweenaw Bay to process its rock. In addition to the mines, the opening of the South Range line was of great benefit to local homesteaders. The copper mines created a great demand for timber and the railroad provided a means of economical transportation for the stuhls and lagging. There were also stands of virgin white pine that brought new logging activity. Even in the areas where the pine had been floated downstream, the hardwood was still standing, as it was too heavy for that form of transport. Lumber mills were built at Alston (formerly Laird) and Faro (later Nisula). Cream, cabbage, and potatoes also provided traffic, and there were always shipments of cordwood for fuel. The South Shore did its part to help settle the South Range, and J. H. Jasberg, DSS&A colonizing agent from Hancock, is given credit for bringing many Finnish residents to settle on the cutover pine lands.

In constructing the South Range line and Arcadian branch, the Mineral Range took on floating debt from the CPR along with other bills. It was decided that the best way to handle this situation would be to make the Mineral Range part of the "Traffic Agreement" of 1890 between the Canadian Pacific and the DSS&A. A contract was signed between the three parties on January 1, 1901, under which the Mineral Range would sell its remaining 5 percent bonds and issue up to $1,000,000 in new 4 percent bonds. The Canadian Pacific would guarantee the payment of 4 percent interest on both issues, while the Mineral Range in turn would give the CPR as much traffic as possible via Sault Ste. Marie.[4]

STANDARD GAUGING THE HANCOCK & CALUMET

Part of the funding received by the Mineral Range was used for improvements to its subsidiary—the Hancock & Calumet. A freight rate dispute between the H&C and the Tamarack and Osceola mining companies in 1900 caused the latter to survey their own line down to Torch Lake. It became clear the H&C had to become more efficient to retain the rock haul. Under an agreement reached June 1, 1901, the H&C was leased to the Mineral Range, with the latter guaranteeing payment on the H&C consolidated 5 percent bonds. The MR would also standard gauge 22.8 miles of H&C trackage, which would greatly improve productivity through the use of larger locomotives and rock cars.[5]

In May 1901, the Mineral Range traded its shares for $100,000 in Hancock & Calumet stock held by the Tamarack and Osceola mining companies. Another $250,000 in MR stock was issued to the mining companies in exchange for a like amount of demand notes. This gave the mining companies a 47 percent stake in the Mineral Range, with the DSS&A owning the remainder. In subsequent years, the mining companies would continue to advance funds to the Mineral Range in exchange for stock in order to maintain its equity share. The Hancock & Calumet lingered as a paper shell until December 27, 1934, when its 50-year charter expired. The entire property was conveyed to the Mineral Range Railroad Company on January 1, 1935.[6]

The first segment of the H&C to be standard gauged was from the Mineral Range main line at Calumet to the Centennial mine. This was done in July 1901 to allow coal shipments to be handled from the Mineral Range coal dock to the mine, with the first such shipment taking place in mid-October. Preparations for the changeover of the main line began in April 1901 with the distribution of a number of standard gauge ties. The roadbed was widened as necessary and 80-pound steel distributed along the heavy traffic area between the Tamarack and Osceola's Union coal dock on Torch Lake and Calumet.

The last narrow gauge train pulled into Hancock from Lake Linden around noon on November 8, receiving "an ovation all along the line."[7] The train was not sent back, and the steamer *Thomas Friant* provided temporary service between Hancock and Lake Linden during the changeover. She continued to do so for three days, until regular standard gauge service was instituted on the 11th. Under its new standard gauge operation, the H&C provided four passenger trains each way between Hancock and Lake Linden. On the second trip out to Lake Linden, the crew made a round trip to Calumet and back. The Mineral Range saw four passenger trains each way—the Calumet-Ontonagon run, plus three South Shore trains.

As the H&C logging trackage near Fulton would not be long-lived, it continued to operate as a narrow gauge, as did the Wolverine rock haul to the Allouez stamp. Wolverine rock continued to be handled to the Allouez mill until August 1902, when a new stamp at Traverse Bay, on the east side of the Keweenaw Peninsula, went into operation. The Traverse Bay operation was a joint effort between Wolverine and Mohawk Mining Company. Mohawk purchased the old Mohawk & Traverse Bay narrow gauge road, which had formerly handled stone from the Hebard quarry to a dock on Traverse Bay. New narrow gauge trackage was laid between the quarry and the Mohawk mine in June and July 1901, and a connection was made with the Hancock & Calumet trackage at Fulton. On September 3, 1901, the Hancock & Calumet leased the Mohawk Mining Company trackage for five years, and the Mineral Range contracted to handle its rock and coal shipments between Gay, on Traverse Bay, and the mine. As the new stamps at Gay neared completion, the Mohawk trackage was changed to standard gauge in August 1902. These standard gauge runs made use of 26-foot, 30-ton rock cars (1000–1198 even nos.) instead of the 40-ton equipment in use on other parts of the Mineral Range system.[8]

The narrow gauge Bollman branch beyond the Mohawk mine was torn out in the summer of 1902. This former logging branch, which extended 17 miles into Keweenaw County, saw little use except to store the two roads' largely unneeded narrow gauge equipment. After the equipment was sold off, the need for the steel caused the line itself to be picked up. Some of the Bollman branch rail was scheduled to go into new logging spurs to be built out of Mohawk (formerly Fulton) easterly towards Traverse Bay. These logging operations, also under Bollman's control, cut lagging and logs for the Osceola and Tamarack mines. The H&C was also busy laying standard gauge spurs into new copper developments, including the Ahmeek and reactivated Allouez mines in 1904, and the Kearsarge Shaft No. 4 the following year.

Power for the new standard gauge Hancock & Calumet was provided by four Rogers 100-ton Consolidated engines (MR 190–193) and two 60-ton Brooks switch engines (MR 160, 161). The 160 arrived at the end of January 1902 for use as the Hancock yard engine, while the others were put into service the following month. Rock hauling was accommodated by ordering 175 new 30-foot, 40-ton rock cars (2–350 even nos.) from American Car and Foundry; the first of these arrived at Hancock on October 12, 1901. This all-wooden fleet would grow to over 600 cars by 1910. Standard gauge commercial traffic was taken care of with the addition of 50 36-foot, 30-ton boxcars (2000–2098 even nos.), 25 30-ton gondolas (1 to 49 odd nos.), and 75 41-foot flats (51–199 odd nos.). A dozen 4-wheeled short cabooses (600 series) were used, as none of the runs tied up at outlying points. Two of the narrow gauge coaches used on the Hancock–Lake Linden run were sent to Marquette and equipped with standard gauge trucks and steam heat.

Mineral Range No. 192, a standard gauge Rogers Consolidation, is engaged in hauling copper rock to the stamps. One of the Mineral Range 4-wheel cabooses sits on an adjacent yard track. Dual gauge trackage is still in evidence in the foreground. *Paananen Collection*

The main link to the Keweenaw, the Portage Lake bridge, received a major rebuilding over the winter of 1899–1900. The height of the span was increased to 8 feet above the water and the bridge was strengthened with steel. Changes were also made at the abutments to allow easier passage for vessel traffic. The Portage Lake Bridge Company, which owned the bridge, ceased to exist on February 15, 1901, with its rights being turned over to Houghton County. With the change in ownership, the Copper Range sought permission to use the bridge in common with the Mineral Range. The county and the two carriers came to satisfactory agreement on February 18, 1902, enabling the Copper Range to launch its Calumet extension.

The new competitor began work on its Calumet line on April 8, 1902. After crossing the Portage Lake bridge, the Copper Range paralleled the Hancock & Calumet Shore Line to Lake Linden. Several crossovers were put in between the two lines and the CR was granted rights to jointly serve the Lake Superior smelter and the Quincy Mining Co. warehouse spurs. Upon reaching Lake Linden, the CR climbed the bluff before terminating at Calumet. Within a few years the Copper Range assumed half the commercial business moving into the Keweenaw, to the detriment of the Mineral Range.

In an attempt to thwart such losses, the Mineral Range constructed a 3-mile extension from the Red Jacket district of Calumet into Laurium in the summer of 1902. The Mineral Range's new depot, located at the corner of Florida and Third streets in Laurium, officially opened for business on January 1, 1903, with the Lake Superior Limited (1–2), Marquette Local (3–4), and Ontonagon Local (9–12) all running into Laurium under the new arrangement. The Laurium service was not successful, and the trains went back to terminating at Red Jacket shortly thereafter. Nos. 1 and 2 again took up a Laurium layover for a year's time beginning in the fall of 1906, but the practice was not repeated after that.[9]

Other new railroad service in the Copper Country was provided by the Keweenaw Central Railroad Company (KC). This line began operating in December 1906 from a connection with the Hancock & Calumet at Mohawk into the far northern reaches of the Keweenaw Peninsula at Lac la Belle. Although initially trackage rights were enjoyed over the H&C into Calumet, in early 1908 KC passenger service south of Mohawk was discontinued and connections were made at the latter point with the new morning MR passenger between Calumet and Gay. After arriving back in Calumet, this MR run made an additional turn to Mohawk in the afternoon to bring passengers to Calumet for the No. 4, and still another turn to Gay in late afternoon. The copper mines in the far northern reaches of the Keweenaw were not successful and the short-lived KC was abandoned on March 7, 1918.[10]

The Mineral Range passenger service between Calumet and Ontonagon was yielding mixed results. Although it was fairly well patronized out of Ontonagon, patrons discovered that by getting off at Peppard Jct., they could board a Copper Range train for Houghton and make better time than by staying on the Mineral Range service. Patrons even started complaining about the lack of facilities at Peppard Jct., and the Michigan Railroad Commission ordered a platform to be built for the transfer of passengers. The Mineral Range pulled the train off on January 18, 1903, but decided to try again that summer. The run was reduced to Houghton-Ontonagon by 1905, and the following year the job started operating out of L'Anse. The same equipment was used in conjunction with Nos. 5 and 6, which began operating between L'Anse and Duluth instead of out of Michigamme as before.

This practice was short-lived and service on the South Range line was reduced to a mixed train in early 1907. The job left Mass at 7 AM and made a turn to Keweenaw Bay, connecting with trains 2, 3 and 103. By this time the Copper Range had instituted a more direct Calumet-Ontonagon run of its own. The South Range line began to take on a branch line character, with worn 56-pound rail and poor ballast. An inspection made by the Michigan Railroad Commission in August 1909 did say that tie renewals were being made and stamp sand applied in an effort to recondition the line.

Mineral Range and Copper Range operations on the Keweenaw were severely disrupted when the Portage Lake drawbridge was rammed by the steamer *Northern Wave* and pushed off its turret into the water on April 15, 1905. Bridge engineer Dan Hardiman thought the *Northern Wave* gave only three blasts of her whistle instead of the four required for opening the bridge. After Hardiman realized the boat was coming through, a frantic effort to open the draw failed when mechanical difficulty set in. A temporary span was installed by laying heavy timbers across barges where the swing span once stood; this arrangement was capable of handling freight and passenger cars, but not locomotives.

President Fitch met in conference with government and Copper Range Railroad officials on April 18, and it was quickly decided that the present bridge was not worth repairing and that a new span with larger openings was required. The new draw would be built with openings of 108 feet on each side of the center pier, as opposed to the 64- and 65-foot openings on the old span. As the temporary bridge would soon have to be removed for navigation purposes, it was decided to equip a scow with trackage and start a car ferry operation between the South Shore yards at East Houghton and the old Lake Superior smelter grounds east of Hancock. This ferry operation, used jointly with the

Copper Range, began the morning of April 24, 1905, and was capable of handling 60 to 70 cars a day. Perishables were given priority, and, if there was any room left, regular freight was handled.

In mid-July, Prendergast and Clarkson were given the contract for the new span. Plans called for the old south pier to be retained and a new center and north pier built. The new bridge ended up taking longer than anticipated, and work dragged on through the winter. A temporary bridge was put in place upon completion of the center pier, allowing rail service to begin. The new draw was swung into position for the first time on April 8, 1906. DSS&A No. 3, the "Northwestern train," delayed 2 hours by the removal of the temporary track, made the first trip across the new draw, and as it passed it gave a long whistle, which was picked up by the other mills along Portage Lake in an ovation that lasted for several minutes.[11]

GLORY DAYS ON THE MINERAL RANGE

During the years before World War I, Calumet and Hecla and the region as a whole saw its glory days. C&H stock reached $1,000 a share for a time in 1907. Following the passage of a bill in the Michigan legislature allowing mining companies to own each other's stock, Calumet and Hecla purchased the Bigelow holdings in the Copper Country, including the Osceola, Tamarack, and Ahmeek mines, on February 26, 1909. Through this purchase Calumet and Hecla also came to own 47 percent of the Mineral Range stock.

The Mineral Range shared in this prosperity, working some thirty crews and hauling some 15,000 to 16,000 tons of copper rock daily from twelve mines, or a little more than half of the total tonnage generated in the district. The next largest carriers were the Copper Range, which handled some 6,000 tons daily for Copper Range Mining, and Calumet and Hecla's Hecla & Torch Lake, which handled another 6,000 tons a day. The Quincy & Torch Lake, operating from the Quincy mine to its Mason stamp, and a private railroad which served the Isle Royale mine, south of Portage Lake, handled the remaining 3,000 tons.

A record amount of rock was handled on January 9, 1909, after the railroad fell behind due to the winter cold and snow. That day the Mineral Range handled 598 loads of rock, or around 21,420 tons. The Mineral Range at that time was hauling to the Tamarack and Osceola stamps at Mills, the Centennial and Franklin stamps at Point Mills, and the Mass stamp at Keweenaw Bay, as well as taking Michigan mine output to the Copper Range interchange. New power obtained to handle the increasing rock business included six Consolidations (194–199) and two 0-6-0 switch engines (162, 163) from American Locomotive Company's Brooks Works. On September 21, 1910, Mineral Range officials took out one of the new "hogs" on a test run over the Grosse Point line and some of the other branches that had received the new 80-pound steel rail and strengthened bridges. It was thought that 1911 would see even heavier rock tonnages than 1910, and the Mineral Range was now in position to handle full-blown production from the mines.[12]

The Michigan mine's output was now given to the Copper Range interchange as a result of that company's leasing a head in the Atlantic mill at Redridge on the east side

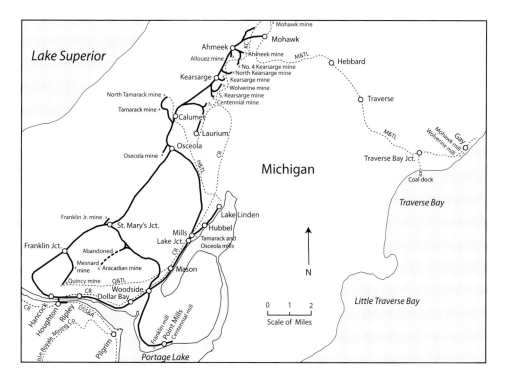

Mineral Range Railroad, 1912

of the Keweenaw Peninsula. The Mineral Range hoped to regain the Michigan haul, as the company was building its own stamp just north of the Mass mill on Keweenaw Bay. Construction started in 1906, but after $175,000 had been expended the Panic of 1907 saw the bottom fall out of the copper market, and the project was stopped. Although some work carried on after the copper market improved, the mill was never finished despite being 80 percent complete. It was said that the stamp could not be worked at a profit due to high freight rates from the mine to the stamp. With the closing of the mine, the Mineral Range pulled up its spur from Riddle Jct. to the shaft in May 1913.

The South Range line was badly cut when a train dramatically fell through the Fire Steel trestle on May 18, 1912. The eastbound mixed run, with a combine, four boxcars, and eleven rock cars from the Mass mine, made a stop at Simar to pick up a flat car. Most of the train hung out on the trestle when engineer Archie Bishop heard the ten bents give way. He hung on the whistle to warn the passengers and crew on the combine, but fortunately one of the trucks on the rear part of the train became wedged in the damaged bridge, preventing further equipment being drawn down into the river below. Nine cars ended up going into the chasm, while the engine and two cars remained upright on the east end as did three cars and the combine on the west side. The damage took some time to repair, and copper rock traffic out of the Mass was rerouted over the Copper Range to Houghton.

The troublesome Fire Steel trestle, just west of Simar on the Mineral Range's South Range line, gave way under the weight of an eastbound mixed train on May 18, 1912. Fortunately no one was hurt, as the locomotive and occupied combine did not follow the nine freight cars into the abyss. *Paananen Collection*

World War I saw increased demand for the copper and wood products along the Mineral Range. At White Siding, on the South Range line, Rubicon Lumber Company shipped out 1,000,000 feet of logs in 1915. The demand for copper rose as industry raced to manufacture war materials. With copper hitting 30 cents a pound, a record 270 million pounds were produced by the Michigan mines in 1916, or 13 percent of the nation's total copper output. The Mineral Range worked 26 crews daily during the winter of 1916–1917 to keep the stamps fed with rock. It was during this spike that the last Mineral Range equipment was obtained. The first steel rock cars (1500–1599), 28 feet in length and with a capacity of 50 tons, were obtained in July 1913. These were followed by an additional order (1600–1699) during the winter of 1915–1916. Two massive Consolidations (300, 301), weighing 112 tons, were also received that winter from American's Brooks works.

SAINTE MARIE DEPOT COMPANY

After the turn of the century, the South Shore put considerable emphasis on improving its passenger facilities to replace "temporary" frame structures and ward off increasingly vociferous complaints from local communities. The first of these projects, in conjunction with the Soo Line and Canadian Pacific, took place at its important eastern gateway of Sault Ste. Marie, Michigan. The Sainte Marie Union Depot Company was formed on March 15, 1900, to replace the small frame depot at that point with new passenger and freight facilities. Capitalization was set at $750,000, with stock to be equally owned by the Canadian Pacific, South Shore, and Soo Line.

In the spring of 1900 work began on a new 187′ × 44.5′ sandstone passenger depot at the corner of Magazine and Canal streets. A 40′ × 100′ frame freight depot was

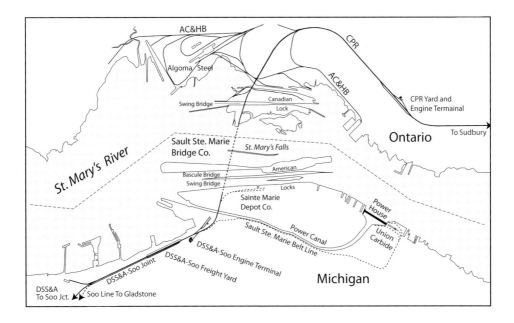

Sault Ste. Marie, Ontario and Michigan, 1917

also constructed, along with a separate concrete immigration building. The site, reached by a half-mile spur off the DSS&A main line at Superior Jct., just west of the International Bridge, brought the depot much closer to the central business district. The new facilities opened on January 2, 1901, with DSS&A No. 18 from Soo Jct. being the first to use the new arrangement. *Railroad Gazette* wrote, "With a neat little park at each end, the station is an interesting and attractive waiting place for travelers."[13]

The Canadian Pacific was a short-time participant in the affairs of the Sainte Marie Union Depot Company, withdrawing from the firm in November 1901. The CPR continued to use the station, however, and entered into a separate contract with the Depot Company on January 1, 1902, outlining its share of the costs. Operating expenses were based on total number of cars handled by each of the roads.

The Soo Line and South Shore entered into another contract governing use of remaining facilities at Sault Ste. Marie, effective May 31, 1901. The Soo Line had never come to construct its own facilities at the Sault, and under the agreement the DSS&A purchased a half-interest in the MStP&SSM's holdings, primarily land, and the Soo Line bought a half-interest in the South Shore property and facilities. The Soo Line gained a half-interest in some 7 miles of main line and yard trackage as well as industrial spurs serving the Bradley-Watkins mill, Peninsula Bark and Leather, Northwestern Leather Company, and the Union Carbide Works. The South Shore's 16-stall brick roundhouse, turntable, clinker pit, coal derrick and shed, track scales, oil house, and icehouse also became jointly owned. The DSS&A continued to run the yard at the Sault with its personnel. To accommodate the larger locomotives coming into use, the 56-foot table was replaced by one of 70 feet in 1907.[14]

This imposing sandstone passenger depot was used by the Canadian Pacific, Soo Line, and South Shore at Sault Ste. Marie, Michigan, and served as the terminus for the trains of all three roads. The DSS&A, as the senior road, handled all operations at the facility. The 24´ × 38´ immigration building is partially seen on the left-hand side of the photo. *Paananen Collection*

A DSS&A passenger special heads across the St. Mary's river between the American and Canadian Sault. Regular DSS&A passenger trains terminated at the American Sault, with cross-border movements being made by the Canadian Pacific passenger trains until 1948. After that, international travelers were required to use a ferry to reach the respective depots. *Collection of Harold K. Vollrath*

Tedious delays at Soo Jct., and the threat of a new short line railroad running direct from the Sault to St. Ignace, saw the DSS&A enter into a trackage agreement with the Soo Line on February 15, 1901, to run passenger trains over the latter's tracks between Trout Lake and the Sault. As a result, passengers coming out of the Lower Peninsula on No. 15 (St. Ignace–Sault), or out of the Copper Country on No. 2, could take DSS&A No. 92 from Trout Lake and arrive in the Sault at 7:55 PM instead of 9:50 PM as before. Another pair of trains that operated over the Soo Line made connections at Trout Lake with No. 1 from Mackinaw City. Connecting service also continued to be provided via Soo Jct. The Trout Lake service lasted for several years, whereupon the DSS&A went back to making all connections at Soo Jct.

The new summer passenger schedule that went into effect May 4, 1903, provided for improved connections at the Straits, allowing quicker transit times between the UP and Detroit. A new sleeping car service was also implemented between Sault Ste. Marie and Detroit. This sleeper came out of the Sault on train No. 7 and was passed off to No. 2 at Soo Jct. From the Detroit end, train No. 1 brought the sleeper out of Mackinaw City, giving it to No. 18 at Soo Jct.

Operations on the Mackinaw Division were severely hampered by several events which took place in the late spring of 1902. On June 6, the steamer *Douglas Houghton*'s tow *Madeira* collided with the swing span over the American channel at the Sault, knocking it off its turret and into the shipping channel. The bridge tender thought the *Houghton* was alone and swung the span into the path of the *Madeira*. All boat traffic was required to use the single Canadian lock until repairs were completed. The *International* was chartered from the Soo Ferry Company to make passenger connections between the two Saults, with freight being diverted to St. Ignace. The American channel reopened on June 11, and train service resumed with CPR No. 9 the following day.

As traffic was being rerouted through St. Ignace, disaster struck there as well. Switch crews had to be careful while loading the ferries to keep the load balanced. Cars were carefully shoved in, part way on one side and then on the other, so the list would not become too great. The switchmen could watch a pendulum mounted on the ferry's bridge so things did not get out of hand. The captain was also on the bridge ready to hurl epithets if things got too uncomfortable from his perspective.

Things normally went smoothly, but on June 10, 1902, the St. Ignace switch crew, loading cars of iron ore into the big ferry *St. Ignace,* pressed their luck too far and caused her to roll over onto her side and down into 24 feet of water. Fortunately the crew was able to escape without injury. As luck would have it, the Mackinac Transportation Company's backup ferry, the *Sainte Marie,* was undergoing overhaul at Detroit at the time. Arrangements were made to have her leave the following day. The old *Algomah* was brought out and used to transfer passengers and baggage over to Mackinaw City. A wrecking train was sent from Marquette to fish cars out from the overturned ferry, allowing the *St. Ignace* to be re-floated and the slip to be freed for the *Sainte Marie.*

OTHER NEW DEPOTS

One day a traveling man asked a local resident if he could direct him to the South Shore depot at Marquette. When the local man pointed at the Tremont House, the visitor responded, "I think you would have the decency to answer a civil question." The Marquette resident assured the man that it really was the depot, causing the salesman to respond, "That, why the Pennsylvania road wouldn't put coal in that building."[15] The old Tremont House, built in 1858, had come to be regarded as an "eye sore" by many Marquette residents.[16] Finally in 1901, the DSS&A came through with a depot reflecting the importance of its headquarters city. After businesses were unable to come up with a free site further west along Washington Avenue, the DSS&A decided to place the depot midway between Front and Third. Grading was completed in May 1901, and a contract was let to David Hood of Duluth.

Upon completion, the two-story depot stood 35′ ×105′ in size, with the upper floor being reserved for the South Shore's operating and purchasing departments. General Manager Fitch continued to reside in the general offices, located in the Nester Block, along with the accounting, engineering, and legal departments. The depot, built of sandstone, had stone trimmings and a slate roof. All around the structure was an 8-foot awning, providing protection from the elements. The South Shore began use of the $25,000 facility on January 11, 1902, with the arrival of the Chicago, Milwaukee & St. Paul No. 10 from Republic. The new facility was located on a stub off the main line, and outbound passenger trains, starting from a dead stop, often had difficulty backing or heading west up the grade to the main line junction switch just east of Fourth Street. Sometimes a switch engine would be called upon to lend assistance. At the very least, the heavy throttle action made quite an impact on the adjoining residences and businesses.

Fitch, as a director of the Lake Superior Terminal & Transfer, was also heavily involved in construction of the new Union Depot at Superior, Wisconsin, after the old structure succumbed to fire in June 1904. The Great Northern wanted the new permanent depot to be located farther east in conjunction with the GN's Interstate Bridge at Connors Point. Most preferred the old location at Broadway and Oakes. Fitch, acting as a mediator, made several trips to St. Paul, finally gaining a consensus to build at the former site. Superior officials expressed their gratitude, saying they were "convinced that not only the speedy construction but the increase of the appropriation from $15,000 to $40,000 were largely due to his efforts."[17] The new two-story brownstone station, opened to the public on December 8, 1905, was widely acclaimed for its "beauty of design." West Superior, having eclipsed Old Town or East Superior in recent years, was renamed Superior on July 1, 1903, with stations at Old Superior taking the name Superior, East End.[18]

The city of Houghton, possessing a small converted hotel for a depot, reminded President Fitch of that fact whenever possible. Following the completion of the new stations at Marquette and Sault Ste. Marie, it became Houghton's turn, with David Hood again being given the contract for a new sandstone depot. Using plans based on Fitch's sketches, a new 24′ ×110′ single-story depot was constructed along the Mineral Range trackage on the same site as the earlier one. Sandstone from Traverse Bay Red Stone Co.

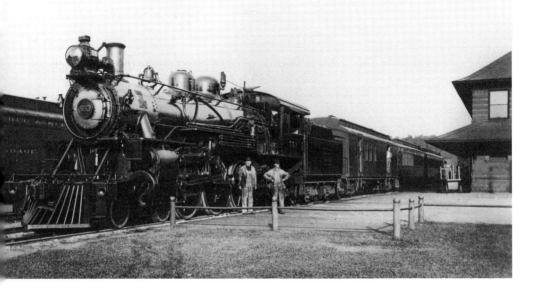

An eastbound passenger is seen on one of the stubs at the Marquette passenger station, no doubt shortly after the delivery of Pacific-type locomotive No. 553 in 1913. The Milwaukee Road head-end car on the next track is probably part of one of the CM&StP through trains then running directly into Marquette from Republic over South Shore rails.   *Paananen Collection*

was used, and the structure was given a slate roof. The new depot was officially opened to the public by President Fitch on November 2, 1903, with South Shore No. 4, the "Northwestern train," making the first stop. The local media spoke of the new depot as a "gem," and although "small" it was "complete."[19]

The large increases in traffic to the Copper Country saw several long yard tracks being laid at East Houghton in October 1900. Part of the bluff was cut away by the South Shore's steam shovel to create room for a new track. The resulting fill material was taken over to the north side of the yard and placed along Portage Lake. This allowed a new main line to be laid, bypassing the yard trackage for the most part, with less interference from the Houghton yard engines.

Natural causes further altered the scene at East Houghton when fire consumed the roundhouse on October 15, 1906. The flames spread so rapidly that only one of the three engines inside could be brought out part way before being overtaken. East Houghton lacked high water pressure connections and it was necessary to resort to a bucket brigade to save surrounding buildings. The South Shore suffered again when the temporary house took fire on March 7, 1908. This time the fire department was able to string hoses together from the nearest hydrant before the conflagration made too much headway. To prevent further catastrophes, a 4-stall reinforced concrete roundhouse was put into use in December 1908.

Calumet, as well as Houghton, had for a long time been after the South Shore to improve its depot. The local press grumbled that the locomotives at Calumet received

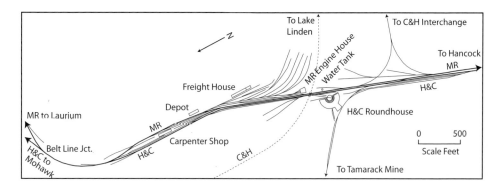

Mineral Range, Hancock & Calumet, Calumet, Michigan, June 30, 1916

better treatment than the passengers, and the community had grown tired of "apologizing for the appearance of the barn like looking building." The "decrepit, decayed" structure was said to be the most "unsightly thing in Red Jacket."[20] Finally in 1908 it was announced that a new $25,000 two-story depot would be built using Ohio hydraulic compressed bricks, with sandstone trimmings and an asbestos roof. The second story of the new depot would contain offices for the Mineral Range superintendent, chief dispatcher, and accounting department. The new facility, located just east of the present depot, was opened to the public on January 26, 1909. Calumet on the whole seemed pleased by the new depot as was President Fitch, who "did not believe it possible to erect such a beautiful building and so substantial appealing one on such a small outlay of money."[21]

Hancock was the last major point on the Mineral Range to receive a new depot. Contractor Archie Servile began work on the single-story 30′ × 76′ structure, up on the bluff at the Lakeview location, on June 15, 1916. The "dark rose colored brick" building with cement trim had both ladies' and men's waiting rooms and "sanitary drinking fountains and lavatories." Hancock Agent Charles S. Jones and his clerks transferred over to the new depot on November 29, 1916.[22]

The South Shore also entered into several joint projects with the Chicago & North Western during this time. To keep up with increasing merchandise shipments, the C&NW and DSS&A constructed a joint transfer station at Ishpeming in 1897. The new shed, just east of Third Street, was 304 feet long and 12 feet wide, with doors and tracks on both sides of the building. Merchandise off the C&NW was segregated into DSS&A waycars for points all over the UP. This work had previously been done at Negaunee.

Ishpeming had long complained of the condition of its separate C&NW and DSS&A passenger depots. After indoor plumbing was placed in the South Shore passenger depot, the Ishpeming *Iron Ore* wrote: "The lavatory followed the Northwestern's new chimney top, and what may follow the lavatory can only be told by waiting. In the meantime, after a wait of forty years, we are requested to be patient."[23] Continued complaints saw a contract let for the construction of a modern joint passenger station in June 1906, with completion taking place that December.

In Ishpeming, unlike Negaunee, the C&NW and DSS&A each maintained separate depots until June 1906 even though they were in extremely close proximity, as shown in this photo. The DSS&A depot is in the rear, with the C&NW facility in the foreground. *Courtesy of Superior View*

Nearby Negaunee continued to be put off in regard to the condition of its joint DSS&A-C&NW depot. Mayor Joseph H. Winter became frustrated at the continual "dodging" and "shifting the blame for the delay on the other [railroad]," and described the depot as "a disgrace to the city as well as to both railway companies."[24] In March 1910, Winter let it be known that unless quick action was taken, he would take steps to require flagmen at each public crossing, and a marshal would be on hand with the arrival of every train to ensure that streets were not blocked longer than the law allowed.

These pronouncements woke up the two roads, and in April 1910 the C&NW announced plans for a new 24′ × 100′, single-story, fireproof depot, to be located a few feet west of Gold Street. The North Western also constructed a new line parallel to the DSS&A west from the Negaunee depot to the C&NW crossing west of town. This allowed North Western passenger trains to cut off their main line, go up to the depot, and, rather than back down to the main line, continue on the new line to the diamond crossing, where the cutoff would rejoin the old main line for the remainder of the trip to Ishpeming. This new scheme was put into use on November 15, 1910. North Western trains made use of the south side of the passenger depot, while DSS&A trains held down the north side. The new brick and stone depot opened for business on December 25, 1910, and was viewed as a tremendous improvement.

A new depot at L'Anse came about not as the result of complaints, but due to runaways on the steep grade into town. On June 11, 1891, train No. 35 was coming down into L'Anse when brake chains broke on several flat cars after having been set too tight. Soon the train was hurtling down the 8-mile hill out of control. Engineer Con Harrington stuck to his post until a mile and a half out of L'Anse, when he leapt and was badly injured. At the bottom of the grade, the line took a sharp turn to the west, which caused the runaway to fly off the track and crash into the depot, completely demolishing it. Fortunately the depot had been cleared of people before the crash. Besides the locomotive, 14 freight cars were derailed.

Another deadly runaway occurred on September 27, 1900. The L'Anse pusher, engine 408, bringing 14 cars of logs and cordwood into L'Anse, was soon making too much headway, which engineer James Farrell was unable to check. Farrell and fireman Ed Delaney jumped to safety a half-mile from the L'Anse depot, while the brakemen hurried back to the caboose, which was cut off just before the train started to derail. A boy who was playing about the depot saw the runaway and quickly ran into the station to tell Agent McKee and Telegrapher Rebec. They barely had time to escape with their lives. The engine and first two cars made it around the curve and then the train broke in two. The third car hurled through the depot and the other cars followed. The Fall River trestle some 200 feet from the depot was also damaged, with broken timbers and twisted rails. The overturning of the depot stove added to the problems, as the damaged depot and two nearby boxcars were soon in flames.

A couple of sheds were brought in to act as a temporary freight and passenger station, but as the location had been susceptible to runaways, the South Shore decided to erect a new permanent structure a quarter-mile west, where a new siding was installed in the summer of 1901. As the town fathers vehemently opposed having the new depot so far from the commercial center of L'Anse, the controversy dragged on for some time. The DSS&A finally went ahead and erected the new 20′×56′, two-story frame depot where it had intended in 1906.

Runaways were not exclusive to the South Shore, and the federal government finally took action in 1893, passing legislation requiring that all cars used in interstate transportation be equipped with air brakes and automatic couplers in five years' time. In 1893 only 23 percent of the nation's fleet of 1.3 million freight cars were so equipped. The railroads complained that five years was insufficient time and, after several extensions, the law did not take effect until August 1, 1900.

Although the use of air brakes provided safer operation, runaways were not unheard of. On October 3, 1905, engine 100 was bringing fifteen cars of ore down the hill into Marquette, but when engineer McNulty attempted to set the air, he found it had no effect, and the loaded train quickly picked up momentum as it neared the Upper Yard. Unfortunately the ore extra came upon engine 207 on the main track as it brought up a cut of ten empties. The engineer on the 207 saw the runaway approaching, reversed direction, and got up to 15 miles an hour before the collision occurred. Both engine crews jumped in time to avoid serious injury, but the 100 and twelve of its cars derailed. The 207 also derailed, but after bouncing along on the ties for 500 feet, it regained the rails when passing over Fifth Street. The unmanned 207 and its ten empties continued backing towards the Lower Yard. At Third Street more misfortune followed when the 207 and its cars came upon engine No. 60 pulling an empty gondola. The engineer of the 60 barely had time to reverse the engine before it was time to jump. In the subsequent crash several of the empty ore cars attached to the 207 were telescoped by the 60, which became the third runaway train in the process. No. 60's fireman managed to board the 207 and brought it to a stop. Phillip Trombley, a passerby who was a former railroader, noticed the cab of the 60 was empty at Baraga Ave. and climbed aboard, stopping the third runaway before any more victims were encountered. Besides the equipment carnage, the accident tore up several hundred feet of main line.

NORTH COUNTRY MAIL

In keeping with the new depot facilities, the South Shore's passenger equipment also received improvements. In the summer of 1899, two vestibule-equipped trains were put into service on the Duluth–Sault Ste. Marie run. The vestibules, of the Gould patent, had been constructed and fitted to the existing cars in the Marquette shops, the first use of this type of equipment in the South Shore territory. Wagner kept up the pace by providing new sleepers for trains 7 and 8.

Nos. 7 and 8 went on to receive two entirely new consists in 1901. General Agent Mart Adson praised the new cars: "The new trains will be the best equipment that money can buy. It is the policy of the South Shore to show appreciation of its growing business by giving high class service. The passenger business of the road has grown to such an extent in the past few years that additional equipment is necessary, and while getting it the company has placed an order for two of the finest trains in the country."[25] The two baggage cars (500, 501), two second-class coaches (600, 601), and two first-class coaches (700, 701) were ordered from American Car and Foundry and came equipped with Gould wide vestibules, steam heat, and electric lights powered from a dynamo in the baggage car. The equipment had Allen paper wheels with steel tires, considered to be state-of-the-art at that time. It was thought the Pullman Company, which had taken over Wagner, would round out the consists with new sleeping cars.

This was not to be the case, as a policy shift instead saw the DSS&A order five new sleepers from Barney and Smith in early 1902. Emulating the practice of its sibling Soo Line and other roads, the South Shore chose to operate its own sleepers in what was felt to be a cheaper option than the Pullman contract, which required the payment of a mileage fee plus a charge for each occupied berth. The new sleeping cars, modern in every respect, came equipped with non-telescoping ends and measured 4 inches taller than conventional cars, allowing 2 inches additional headroom in each berth. The 10-section design also had a stateroom, a ladies' dressing room, a smoking compartment, and lavatories. The sleepers were given local names: *Duluth, Superior, Ishpeming, Houghton* and *Sault Ste. Marie,* and were painted in the usual South Shore vermilion with black and gold ornamentation.

The new equipment was instituted on June 1, 1902, with the expiration of the Pullman contract. The new Nos. 7 and 8, called the North Country Mail, operated a 4-car consist between the Sault and Nestoria, and 5 cars between Duluth and Nestoria with the addition of the Duluth-Calumet sleeper. The remaining sleeper was kept as a spare. The old equipment from Nos. 7 and 8, after a thorough overhauling, was put on Nos. 1 and 2 between St. Ignace and the Copper Country.[26]

The DSS&A and Canadian Pacific decided to implement the long-discussed through sleeper between Duluth and Montreal in June 1906. The South Shore ordered two 79-foot, 12-section sleeping cars (*Negaunee, Newberry*) from Barney and Smith to facilitate the run. The service, which was not heavily patronized, only lasted until early 1908, and passengers went back to connecting with the through CPR–Soo Line service at the Sault. The passenger car roster was further augmented in 1908 by the addition of a 60-foot first-class coach (702), three 75-foot second-class coaches (602–604), and a 50-foot baggage car (502). These cars, from Barney and Smith, were necessary to handle the increasing immigrant traffic the road was facing, and they also enabled the DSS&A to change out a set of equipment on Nos. 7 and 8 for repairs.

The South Shore added nine locomotives to its fleet in 1907, three designed to care for the longer passenger consists, and six for the iron ore and freight hauling trade. The three passenger engines were 85-ton Baldwin Tenwheelers (500–502). The 502 completed its first run January 1, 1908, on the "Northwestern train," and was described by the *Calumet News* as a "mammoth piece of machinery."[27] Another engine of this class (503) was put into service the following year. The six freight engines received in 1907 were the South Shore's first Consolidations (600–605). These Baldwin 2-8-0s weighed 86 tons and were the first of a series that would be the mainstay of the road's freight service for the next 30 years. Another new engine the South Shore received in 1907 was a 0-8-0 switcher (90) from Baldwin which was designed to boost ore onto Dock No. 5. Without a pony truck, this engine was of limited usefulness after the ore season ended, and one was soon added, allowing it to perform in road service. The new purchases brought the South Shore's locomotive fleet to 87 engines. The line also owned 67 passenger cars and 2,846 freight cars.

"THE SOUTH SHORE"

When Thomas Shaughnessy took over as Canadian Pacific president from Van Horne on June 12, 1899, he was also made first vice president of the South Shore. W. F. Fitch was elected to a dual role of second vice president and general manager on August 1, 1899. Samuel Thomas remained president of the DSS&A, with offices in New York. Thomas began to suffer from health problems a few years later and resigned on November 19, 1902, relinquishing his post to Fitch, who also retained the rank of general manager. Although there were frequent rumors at the turn of the century that the South Shore would move its general offices to Duluth, the plans were never carried out. In fact, William Orr, the South Shore's general freight agent, moved his office back to Marquette on May 1, 1899, after a six-year stay in the Zenith City. The combined passenger department with the Soo Line proved unworkable with agents representing both competing roads, and the DSS&A came to have its own general passenger agent once again on June 18, 1896, when George W. Hibbard assumed the post.

The DSS&A slogan "Marquette Route" had come to mean little other than specifying a point on the system and at the end of 1905 was replaced with "The South Shore." Mart Adson, who replaced Hibbard as the DSS&A's general passenger agent that same year, was credited with designing the new herald, featuring "The South Shore" in white, on a black background. The background was rectangular with a section taken out of the lower left and upper right hand corners. Beginning in 1906, the new herald, which would last for the remainder of the road's existence, was in general use on the sides of the road's rolling stock and stationary. With the coming of Adson, the South Shore's passenger traffic department returned to Duluth. Freight traffic offices had returned there in 1901 following the resignation of William Orr and his replacement by Wayland W. Walker.[28]

Even though the South Shore's operating ratio was only 73 in 1905, its tremendous indebtedness of over $28,000,000 never gave it a chance to earn a profit. Record net earnings of $1,000,349 were posted in 1906 but were still not enough to meet fixed charges. Along with capitalization of $22,000,000, the South Shore carried a debt of $86,120 for each mile of railroad. A striking comparison could be made with its sibling, the Soo Line, which had a debt of only $33,050 per mile. This allowed the Soo Line to earn a profit even with higher operating ratios. Another Michigan operation, the Detroit & Mackinaw, somehow got by with a capitalization of $18,929 per mile. Many complained that the high passenger and freight rates in the UP, after navigation closed, were due not to the high cost of operation, but to the amount of "water" in railroad finance, especially the DSS&A. *The Evening News* at the Sault wrote, "When the history of weird, crazy, frenzied, ruthless financing is written, undoubtedly the Duluth, South Shore & Atlantic railroad is entitled to be described as 'Exhibit A.'"[29]

Calls for more stringent regulation to deal with railroad finance, shipper rebates, and rate discrimination had resulted in the passage of the Interstate Commerce Act of 1887, creating the Interstate Commerce Commission. Federal oversight was needed as the result of a ruling by the U.S. Supreme Court in 1886 that state regulatory agencies could not oversee the 75 percent of rail commerce that was interstate. Even the ICC had been initially restrained by conservative judicial interpretation, but it received a needed boost with the passage of the Hepburn Act, which took effect on January 1, 1907, and provided the ICC with additional authority to carry out its mandate.

At the state level, the Michigan legislature created a new three-man railroad commission on June 19, 1907, with power to regulate intrastate freight rates. South Shore passenger revenue took a hit on April 18 of that year when a law was passed reducing intrastate rates from 4 cents a mile to 3 cents. Roads on the Lower Peninsula were allowed to charge only 2 cents a mile. The UP roads had successfully argued that they needed higher rates due to sparse population and heavy winter operating expenses. While population in the Lower Peninsula averaged 54 people per square mile, in the UP it was only 12. The UP roads also lacked the profitable freight business enjoyed by those on the Lower Peninsula to compensate for a loss in passenger revenue. Winters on the UP were much more severe than on the Lower Peninsula, requiring higher maintenance expenses.[30]

The differential was of short duration, and the Michigan legislature sought to implement the 2-cent-per-mile fare statewide in early 1909. Arch B. Eldredge, DSS&A general attorney, argued that even now the South Shore was not earning 6 percent on its valuation and could ill afford to take a further cut. He also countered proponents' claims that increased ridership from lower rates would make up for any lost revenues. DSS&A passenger earnings in 1907 were $953,256, but fell to $780,157 in 1908 with the 3-cent fare. This was in spite of the fact that 31,640 more passengers were carried in 1908 than the year before. Not everyone agreed the 2-cent fare would be beneficial. One Marquette businessman said paying 3 cents a mile "with well equipped trains and up-to-date service looks a lot better to me than two-cent fare with second rate engines and coaches and curtailed schedules."[31] The Marquette *Mining Journal* commented,

A 1906 DSS&A advertisement from the *Agora*. *Paananen Collection*

"The DSS&A in particular serves a bleak and forlorn territory from which the bulk of the pine was cut years ago, and there are many miles of this road on which the local business has never netted a dollar."[32]

The 2-cent fare legislation did pass in the 1911 session, whereupon the South Shore immediately sued the State of Michigan, saying the intention of the law had been exceeded. A restraining order was granted on July 26, 1911, with the South Shore continuing to charge 3 cents per mile and issuing rebate slips in case the road suffered an adverse decision in the courts. U.S. District Court Judge Sessions, in his ruling issued January 8, 1918, came out against the state, backing the South Shore's contention that the 2-cent fare was "confiscatory."[33] This put the dispute to rest, letting the DSS&A off the hook for some $750,000 it had allocated to pay the rebate checks. These checks were now worthless unless one took the advice of the *Newberry News:* "In spite of the high cost of paper, by deft application of those South Shore rebate checks to your walls, a very tasty effect can be secured with little expenditure."[34]

The 1907 Railway Hours Act, which went into effect on March 4, 1908, also had a major effect on the expense side of the equation, limiting dispatchers and telegrapher operators to a 9-hour shift. As some stations only had one man on duty for 12 hours, it was up to the railroads to see whether they could get by with fewer hours or needed to add more men. The always progressive State of Wisconsin tried to limit telegraphers to an 8-hour shift, but the statute was ruled unconstitutional by the Wisconsin Supreme Court. Train service employees also benefited from the federal law, which limited their tour of duty to 16 hours and mandated rest periods. This put an end to the 30-hour slogs between terminals that had not been unknown to freight crews. Crew change points on the South Shore remained at Thomaston and Marquette, although the length of time on duty became more of an important factor in getting trains over the road.

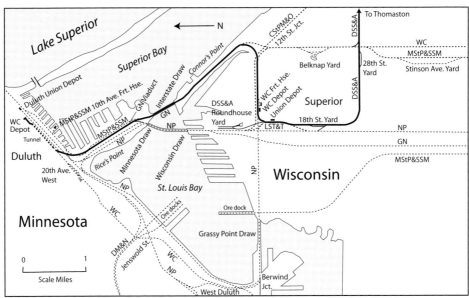

Routing of DSS&A Passenger Trains through Duluth-Superior, January 1, 1911, to July 11, 1915

9

BRIDGE ROUTE REVISITED

The construction by the Soo Line of the Brooten line (1909) and Plummer line (1910) from origins in western Minnesota to the Twin Ports was felt by some to be a great thing for the South Shore and likely to do much to increase its fortunes. The Canadian Pacific's single track main line around the north shore of Lake Superior was greatly overburdened with traffic. Rather than doubletracking, it was natural the CPR would make use of its subsidiaries and start routing traffic from Winnipeg to the border, over the Soo Line to Superior, and then via the DSS&A to Sault Ste. Marie. This routing was 80 miles shorter and had better grades than the CPR.

The *New York American* said, "The shortest and easiest line of travel from any points of New England to any points on the Missouri west of Duluth will lie over the Canadian Pacific and the Duluth, South Shore & Atlantic when its connections are completed on the west. Those who buy this stock for mere speculation will probably be disappointed. Those who buy it now and stow it away and forget it will wake up some morning and find Duluth, South Shore & Atlantic selling at five or ten times what they paid for it."[1] It was hoped the new bridge traffic would bring a higher class of freight to the South Shore and thus more revenue. In 1908 fully 42 percent of the DSS&A's traffic was hauling iron ore.

For a brief period, it was even considered that the South Shore might take part in the Minnesota extensions. The development of the Cuyuna Iron Range in Minnesota, and the desire of interested parties there to have a railroad other than the NP or GN haul their ore to the Head of the Lakes, caused these men to approach President Fitch in 1908 about building a line to the new range. Shaughnessy told Fitch the CPR would be willing to advance funds for construction, but in the end it was agreed by all parties that the new line would fit much better into the Soo Line system than the DSS&A. With the Soo's Brooten line largely completed, it was thought the South Shore would make use of this trackage for the first 40 miles towards the Cuyuna. The Soo's proposed Plummer line would also pass near the Cuyuna, resulting in an isolated South Shore segment among those of its sibling.

Not everyone shared a rosy view of the DSS&A's prospects. The *Wall Street Journal,* countering the views of the *American,* wrote that the South Shore went "through a thinly populated territory, while its tonnage is of low grade.... traffic connections amount to little; in fact, it is so situated that it must compete with the water route for long haul traffic." With "a gross capitalization of $84,947 per mile . . . It is hard to see anything bright in the road's future. Left to its own resources, it would speedily pass into receivers' hands. Its very existence depends upon the Canadian Pacific. How much longer the Canadian Pacific may elect to support the South Shore is problematical."[2] Although the South Shore stock price rose in 1909 on rumors of the DSS&A being flooded with CPR traffic, these speculations would prove optimistic. The Soo's Brooten and Plummer lines largely hauled Dakota wheat to the Twin Ports, where the commodity was transloaded onto more efficient boats plying the Great Lakes. The South Shore incurred its last surplus in 1902, and it would be 40 years before it saw another.

The efficiency of the Great Lakes for transport was due in large part to government subsidy. The United States decided the Sault needed a new lock capable of handling three large lake vessels at one time. The $7,000,000 project, which saw an additional canal built just north of the American lock, required the Sault Sainte Marie Bridge Company to build, at its own expense, a bascule bridge providing at least a 318-foot opening. This portion had formerly been on fill. An existing fixed span just north of the new bascule bridge was replaced with fill material provided by the government. A contract for the bascule bridge over the north canal, with two 168-foot leaves, was let to the Pennsylvania Steel Company and funded by the Canadian Pacific. The bridge, the largest of its type ever constructed, saw a test opening on November 9, 1913, although the canal itself was not placed in full operation until the following September.

In 1910 rumors became widespread that the Canadian Pacific was about to have the Soo Line lease the South Shore in order to reduce the smaller road's deficit. W. F. Fitch would retire and his duties would be assumed by his counterpart on the Soo. A South Shore official said that rumors of this nature were ridiculous given the recent Northern Securities decision. As the Soo Line was the main competitor of South Shore, antitrust action would be quickly brought by the government against any such move, as had been the case in James J. Hill's attempt to coordinate the Northern Pacific and Great Northern.

Although far from the coordination rumored earlier, the coming of the Minneapolis, St. Paul & Sault Ste. Marie and the Wisconsin Central (leased by the Soo in 1909) into the Twin Ports did result in some efficiencies in conjunction with the South Shore. Under a contract dated July 1, 1910, the South Shore shifted its Superior-Duluth freight business from the NP to the Soo at quite a savings. The DSS&A's less-than-carload business began to be handled at the Soo's Duluth freight house, located along the bayfront at the foot of 10th Ave. West. Similarly the South Shore freight house and team track near the Lake Superior Terminal & Transfer's Union Station in Superior was done away with in 1911, with the work subsequently handled at the Wisconsin Central's Superior freight house.[3]

On January 1, 1911, DSS&A passenger trains shifted from the Duluth Union Depot to the new Wisconsin Central depot, which had been built two years earlier. DSS&A trains continued to run into the LST&T depot at Superior before swinging east to a connection with the WC just east of Tower Avenue. After making another stop at their Superior depot, DSS&A trains used WC and MStP&SSM rails to Connors Point and then over the Interstate Bridge of the Great Northern's Duluth-Superior Bridge Company. On the Duluth side of the bridge the elevated viaduct of the Duluth Terminal, another GN subsidiary, was used. At the north end of the viaduct, the DSS&A trains branched off the GN trackage and used a short connection to join the WC trackage leading to

In 1911, DSS&A passenger trains shifted from the Duluth Union Depot, whose turrets are seen to the right of Michigan Ave., to the Wisconsin Central station in the foreground, which was used for the duration of South Shore passenger service. Just below the photographer the track entered a tunnel, on the other end of which was the WC's 20th Ave. yard, where passenger power and equipment was serviced. All switching and servicing in Duluth was done by Soo Line crews and personnel.
Lake Superior Railroad Museum Collection

their depot. DSS&A equipment and power at Duluth was serviced in the nearby WC yard at 20th Ave. West, where the South Shore rented one stall in the roundhouse.[4]

Passenger train routing in the Twin Ports received another change on July 11, 1915, when DSS&A movements quit using the Interstate Bridge. Instead the South Shore began using a combination of LST&T, WC, and Northern Pacific trackage and the NP's Grassy Point Bridge to reach Duluth. Just west of the Grassy Point draw, at Berwind Jct., the South Shore used an isolated segment of the WC to reach the latter's Duluth depot. As a result of the change, the DSS&A also quit making a station stop at the WC depot at Superior and only used the LST&T's Union Station. In December 1916, the WC completed a new depot in West Duluth, and South Shore trains started making a station stop at this point shortly thereafter.

CHANGES IN THE ORE BUSINESS

As commonly occurred in mining regions, South Shore operations in the Upper Peninsula were troubled on a number of occasions by cave-ins from underground workings. On August 26, 1902, one such cave-in undermined the south main line, or former Marquette & Western trackage, near the Queen mine east of Negaunee. Some 200 feet of track plummeted into the 100-foot-deep hole. The line was not rebuilt, reducing the

South Shore to one main track between Negaunee and Eagle Mills. The bottleneck proved to be a dispatching headache, especially during the ore season. To provide an element of safety, a staff system was instituted between those two points in February 1906. Trains could only leave Eagle Mills or Negaunee after the last opposing movement brought a key which operated the staff machine. The insertion of the key into the machine allowed traffic to flow in the other direction.

Another 200-foot segment of the south line between Winthrop Jct. and South Ishpeming succumbed to a cave-in from the Lake Angeline mine in December 1907. Before the opening of the 1908 shipping season, a connecting track was laid around the north end of the opening, but it suffered from adverse grades which greatly handicapped ore operations. Thus most of the ore from Winthrop Jct. was pulled over the north line. After it appeared that the cave-in had stabilized, the DSS&A decided to fill the opening, restoring the main line to its original configuration. This work, begun in late fall of 1909, allowed the south main line to reopen in April 1910.

As the activities of Cleveland-Cliffs Iron's Negaunee and Maas mines began to intrude on the DSS&A right of way east of Negaunee, steps were taken in 1908 to relocate the main line between Negaunee and Eagle Mills. CCI dedicated this work to its subsidiary Lake Superior & Ishpeming. The 3.65-mile relocation was put in about a half-mile south of the original right of way from just west of Eagle Mills to near the Pioneer Furnace in Negaunee. The new South Shore trackage was built on the LS&I right of way, closely paralleling the latter's line. The new main line went into service on July 26, 1910, and allowed for a double track by still using the old line. This brought an end to the staff system between Negaunee and Eagle Mills. The DSS&A completed an additional parallel track along the relocation a few days later, which allowed the old line to be abandoned to the encroaching miners. South of Negaunee, the Negaunee & Palmer branch, near the Rolling Mill mine, suffered the effects of a cave-in around December 1916, making it necessary to shift over to a nearby LS&I track. In the process the South Shore pulled up its own line to the Rolling Mill and Mary Charlotte properties, and henceforth utilized LS&I spurs to reach those mines.

The rebirth of the national economy following the Panic of 1907 saw the South Shore's ore business recover nicely in 1909, with tonnages only 20 percent below those of the LS&I. The 1910 ore season proved to be even stronger when almost every mine on the Marquette Range joined the shipping list. Final tonnage through the South Shore dock totaled 1,383,206 tons. The 1912 ore shipping season was a record-breaking year for the Wisconsin and Michigan iron ranges, with the DSS&A handling 1,072,544 tons, followed by only a slight decrease for 1913. As often was the case, this rush of ore business was followed by a lull in 1914, as the steel mills worked off large stockpiles.

The strong growth in iron ore markets before World War I saw a revival in activity along the Negaunee & Palmer branch. Trackage which had been pulled up just after the turn of the century was reinstalled at the Volunteer property. The C&NW jointly served the Volunteer, owning a 50 percent stake in the mine spurs under an agreement dated November 6, 1911. Other mines joining the shipping list along the N&P branch at Palmer were the Empire in 1907, the Isabella in 1916, and the Maitland in 1918. At the far south end of the branch, the South Shore entered into an agreement with the North Western on March 19, 1917, for 2.2 miles of trackage rights to reach the Richmond mine, east of Palmer. The South Shore also bought a half-interest in the C&NW trackage at the mine itself. On the west end, large tonnages out of the Republic became a thing of the past when the mine was acquired by Cleveland-Cliffs on May 1, 1914 and ore started to be routed over the LS&I. DSS&A shipments were limited to all-rail movements, primarily to the Sault. The LS&I also made inroads into other DSS&A-served mines by acquiring rights to serve the Lake Superior and Breitung Hematite mines.

CHIEF WAWATAM

The car ferry operation at the Straits of Mackinac underwent a major revision in 1910 when it was decided to invest in two all-steel ferries like those being used across Lake Michigan by the Ann Arbor and Pere Marquette. Frank E. Kirby, creator of the *St. Ignace* and *Sainte Marie,* designed the first boat and Toledo Shipbuilding Company received the contract. Christened the *Chief Wawatam,* the new boat was 338.8 feet long, 62 feet wide, and 20.7 feet deep, with a gross tonnage of 2,990 tons. The *Chief* had four tracks on her main deck and was capable of holding twenty-six 36-foot cars. Loaded from the bow like the *Sainte Marie* and *St. Ignace,* its stacks split the middle of the four tracks. Above deck were cabins for passengers and crew. The new vessel had three propellers, one on the bow and two astern, which were powered by three triple expansion engines and six Scotch boilers. *Chief Wawatam* had the usual spoon-shaped bow to ride up on the ice and crush it. The *Chief* was launched at Toledo on August 26, 1911, and left for the Straits on October 16, 1911, under the command of 77-year-old L. R. Boynton, who had brought both the *St. Ignace* and *Sainte Marie* up from the shipyards on their first runs.

The need for a better spare boat caused the Mackinac Transportation Company to order another steel boat from Toledo Shipbuilding in the spring of 1912. The new steel *Sainte Marie,* also designed by Frank Kirby, was 250 feet long, 62.2 feet wide, and 21.7 feet deep, with a capacity of 2,383 gross tons. The wooden *Sainte Marie* was taken out of service and left June 9 under tow to Toledo, where as much of her as possible would be scavenged. The old *Sainte Marie*'s machinery was used in the new vessel, with her six boilers and two engines developing 3500 horsepower. In keeping with her status as a spare boat, the *Sainte Marie* had a capacity of only 14 freight cars, but given her short length, maneuverability, and powerful engines, she was an excellent ice breaker, better than the larger *Chief.* The *Sainte Marie* entered service in March 1913. Because of her excellent ice breaking capabilities, the *Sainte Marie* was often chartered by the Lake Carriers' Association in the spring of the year to get an early jump on the navigation season or to free vessels caught up in the ice.

On October 10, 1911, with the expiration of its 30-year charter, the boat company was reorganized as "The" Mackinac Transportation Company for another 30 years. Most of the expenses of the Mackinac Transportation Company were covered by cash advances by the owners, as operating revenues never covered expenses and the parents were billed monthly for the deficits. From the beginning of operation in December 1881 to December 31, 1917, the Mackinac Transportation Company's operating ratio averaged an astonishing 234.5 percent.[5]

By this time the automobile was beginning to make its presence felt on the UP, especially during the resort and hunting seasons. Much of this business came from the more populous Lower Peninsula, and the Mackinac Transportation Company found new business. Initially the automobiles were treated as rail traffic and required to be

The 108 unloads her passenger train off the *Chief Wawatam* upon its arrival at St. Ignace. The *Chief* had brought the cars across the Straits of Mackinaw after making connections with trains of the Michigan Central and Grand Rapids & Indiana at Mackinaw City.   *J. Foster Adams, Wesley Perron Collection, Peter White Public Library, Marquette, Mich.*

loaded on flat cars with their gasoline tanks drained. A one-way crossing was subject to an $18 freight rate in 1916. Considering a new Ford only cost $575, this was quite steep. Due to widespread complaints, Mackinac Transportation announced in 1918 that it was prepared to handle autos without the use of flat cars or having to drain the gas. Rates were set at 17.5 cents per hundred, with a 2,000-pound minimum. The complaints continued, and the lack of capacity caused long tie-ups. The *Chief* had space set aside for 51 autos, with the remainder reserved for rail traffic.

With Mackinac Transportation Company not up to the task, the State of Michigan entered the automobile ferry business on August 6, 1923, leaving the *Chief* to carry only the larger makes of cars, which had trouble fitting aboard the new state ferry, *Ariel*. When the *Ariel* laid up for the winter, Mackinac Transportation resumed its temporary monopoly, charging $5.50 a car and $1.10 per passenger, much higher than the state fares of 25 cents per passenger and around a dollar for a car. In 1931 the state started offering winter service by agreeing to pay the difference between the railroad rates and their own fares. This created heavy losses, and beginning in 1936, the state leased the *Sainte*

Marie for the winter months under a bare boat charter arrangement with Mackinac Transportation.

THE WALKER ERA

W. F. Fitch retired from the presidency of the South Shore in November 30, 1911, after a 23-year stay with the road. As Fitch put it, "I want to get out and give some of the younger fellows a chance."[6] Fitch undoubtedly arrived on the scene with hopes of turning the South Shore into a major player on the railroad scene. He suffered disappointments in the course of his stewardship, with most of his steps closely monitored by Montreal. The Marquette *Mining Journal* wrote, "that his plans failed to materialize was due in large measure not to his lack of ambition or foresight, but to conditions over which he had no control."[7] Fitch remained a director of the South Shore and was elected a vice president and director of the Wisconsin Central in 1912, although still living in Marquette. With no pension available, Fitch was still active when he passed away on September 16, 1915.

Rumors again surfaced that the road was about to pass into Soo Line control, but Archibald Eldredge, the South Shore's first vice president and general attorney, was elected to replace Fitch. While President Fitch had also acted as general manager, Eldredge had no operating experience, and the general manager post was given to General Freight Agent Wayland W. Walker, who also took over the vice presidency. Under an organization scheme worked out by CPR President Shaughnessy, Eldredge was the chief officer of the DSS&A, having charge of the law, finance, accounting, and land departments. Walker, as the company's chief executive, would lead the operating and traffic departments. Shaughnessy decided that the two principal officers would remain separate, with Eldredge residing in the corporate offices at Marquette while Walker stayed in the Fidelity Building at Duluth. With Walker in Duluth was E. R. Lewis, who oversaw the South Shore's engineering department, which had moved to Duluth early in 1913.[8]

Arch Eldredge, 58 years old and a native of Fond du Lac, Wisconsin, had come to the UP in 1882 as an attorney for the C&NW at Ishpeming. In 1890 Eldredge had begun work on the South Shore as general attorney at Marquette, and had been given the title of vice president and general attorney in May 1910. Walker had been with the South Shore traffic department since 1891.

Upon assuming his duties Walker found that, as was typical of many Class I railroads built in the 1880s, the DSS&A needed rehabilitation in the new century. The *Duluth Herald* commented, "The South Shore has taken a new lease of life. The roadbed, buildings and equipment are being replaced, restored and rehabilitated. As rapidly as work can be financed and carried out, the road is taking its place among modern railroads, with modern equipment and service."[9]

The revitalization of motive power included ordering needed replacements for the 4-6-0 500-class passenger engines, whose narrow fireboxes made for poor steaming. One South Shore engineer remembered, "They were the poorest excuses of steam locomotives I have ever run."[10] The South Shore kept up with modern practice by ordering two new 92.5-ton Pacific class (550, 551) engines from American's Schenectady works. These were delivered in 1912.

Instead of going with the 2-8-2 Mikado freight power then in vogue on American railroads, the South Shore elected to remain with 2-8-0 Consolidations, and twelve of this class were received in 1913 from American's Brooks works, along with three more Pacifics. The Consolidations (700–711), which increased the DSS&A's ownership in this class of power to nineteen, weighed a little over 93 tons. The new Pacifics (552–554) had 67-inch drivers, 3 inches larger than found on the 550 and 551, and were also slightly heavier than the other Pacifics. The new 700s took over most of the South Shore freight hauling duties, reducing the 200-, 300-, and 400-class Moguls to yard duty. The average freight train size on the South Shore grew by almost 65 percent with delivery of the new power. The new passenger engines were used in Calumet–St. Ignace service.

Improvements to the passenger fleet included the purchase of two diners and two cafe-observation cars from Barney and Smith. The short 68-foot diners (305, 307) were to be used on the night trains between the Sault and Duluth, and the 75-foot cafe-observation cars (306, 308) on Nos. 1 and 2 between Calumet and St. Ignace. The cafe cars were placed in service in late June 1912, with the diners seeing their first runs later that summer. With 1913 expected to be another heavy year, the South Shore ordered 400 50-ton steel ore cars (9000–9399) in December 1912. These cars, from American Car and Foundry, were the South Shore's first all-steel cars and would remain in service until the road's demise. They were also the last new ore cars ever bought by the road.

To house its new power, the South Shore completed work in 1913 on a new 15-stall brick roundhouse, turntable, power house, and ash pits at Park Avenue in the Marquette Upper Yard. In addition, a March 1913 contract with American Bridge Company called for new larger turntables at Thomaston and St. Ignace. At Superior, two new long stalls were added to the engine house, making five in all. An earlier improvement at the Fifth Street shop complex at Marquette resulted from a bad fire on September 13, 1910, when the carpenter and car shop were consumed. Construction on a new fire-proof 95′×265′ building was started soon after, and it was put into use a few days before

The South Shore's problems with its passenger power were finally solved with the purchase of the H- and H-1 class Pacifics. Here the 552 is being serviced alongside the coal dock at the Park Ave. facility in Marquette. *Collection of Harold K. Vollrath*

On May 20, 1948, the 702 is bringing a cut of cars from uptown industries in Marquette down to East Yard for forwarding onto outbound trains. The statue of Father Marquette watches over the proceedings.   *Wilbur C. Whittaker*

One of the South Shore's two cafe-observation cars trails a westbound passenger consist, probably No. 1, at the depot at Marquette in 1911.   *Paananen Collection*

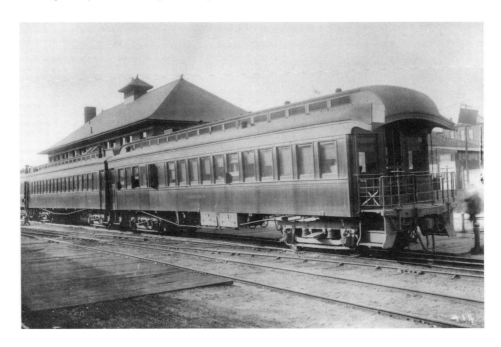

No. 9269, a U-2 class ore car, was one of the 400 purchased from American Car and Foundry in 1913. It is pictured at Marquette on May 20, 1948. *Wilbur C. Whittaker*

Christmas 1910. It was thought the new facility, with sixteen shop machines, would be capable of turning out twice the work of the old building. Another Marquette addition was a new brick freight house located just west of the Third Street crossing. The 127′×40′ structure gave draymen a much more central location than the old frame building in the Lower Yard.

The joint facilities at Sault Ste. Marie also received a thorough overhauling to accommodate the larger power coming into use. A new frame roundhouse with twelve 80-foot stalls was built, as well as a 36′×48′ boiler house, a two-pocket McHenry coaling tower, and a sand house. These facilities were all completed in December 1912, with the Soo Line covering half the expense.

To improve running times with the new 550-class Pacifics, the South Shore upgraded its line between Nestoria and Duluth with heavier rail and new ties. Walker believed "that the most effective way to increase patronage of the road is to improve the service so as to give the traveling public the most possible return for their money."[11] The roadbed, which the public had come to view as "rocky," received its most extensive rehabilitation since construction.[12] American Bridge Company also received a contract to replace, with steel, four wooden spans over Bad River, Vaughn Creek, Montreal River, and Culver River. This massive project required the use of some 93 cars of assembled bridge material. The new Bad River bridge made use of a 121-foot girder, one of the largest ever placed in the Northwestern U.S.

Local residents were pleased with the South Shore's efforts. *Skillings' Mining Review* commented, "Earnings show substantial increase, which doubtless encourages the management when putting a substantial part of them back into betterments and new equipment. If holders of South Shore securities should notice a falling off in net revenue they will find satisfaction in the fact that gross revenues are increasing and that the management is paying for extensive and permanent improvements."[13] It was true that this new work was taking money the South Shore did not have. The South Shore was some 12 years behind in meeting interest payments on its 4 percent bonds,

The 719 goes for a spin on the 75-foot turntable at Marquette's Park Ave. roundhouse in this May 1939 photo. These facilities were erected in 1913 to replace the outmoded former MH&O roundhouse at Fifth Ave.   *Harold K. Vollarth Collection*

and even had to ask the CPR to return $100,000 in interest payments made in 1912 to pay for the new improvements. No interest payments on the 4s were made after this time.

Walker felt the only way the "business of the railroad can be permanently built up," and its financial shortcoming overcome, was through agricultural development, and he intended to do everything possible to attract farmers to DSS&A territory.[14] A "demonstration farm" was established along the South Shore at Experiment, Wisconsin, near Lake Nebagamon. This 40-acre site, although transformed by agricultural graduates of the University of Wisconsin, was given a typical budget of a new immigrant to the area, and served to show what could be accomplished by an average citizen just starting out in the country.[15] Although sugar beet growing showed some initial promise, dairying turned out to be the only real possibility in the cutover lands of northern Wisconsin.

The South Shore ran a series of agricultural specials in conjunction with other UP roads. The first six-car train toured the system in 1912, promoting "all around" farming. A larger special, operated in conjunction with the Lake Superior & Ishpeming in the fall of 1913, carried cars of purebred cattle, sheep, pigs, and poultry in an attempt to introduce better-quality stock. Additional trains were run during the spring of 1914 and 1916. The 1916 train, designed to introduce better seed varieties to the farmers of the UP, was participated in by the Soo Line, C&NW, LS&I, and South Shore. Still another special in 1918 covered food preservation. Three women demonstrated canning, with a female Finnish interpreter providing help as needed to the large number of immigrants from that country. In the summer of 1919, the South Shore operated a stump pulling special, which eradicated thousands of stumps from the logged-over pine country.[16]

Shipments over the DSS&A continued to be dominated by ore and lumber at 40 percent and 25 percent respectively. Coke, cement, brick, and coal were the next-leading commodities, all well under 10 percent. Agricultural products, despite promotional efforts, totaled only 5 percent, and the great majority of these were imported. Agricultural commodities originated by the DSS&A in 1909 totaled only 16,680 tons, almost half of which was hay.

In the period before World War I, the South Shore operated both through and local freights over its entire territory. On the Mackinaw Division, Nos. 21 and 22 provided through freight service between Marquette and St. Ignace along with extras, which often handled all-rail ore to Newberry and St. Ignace. Nos. 23 and 24 operated as locals between Marquette and Soo Jct. Train 23 was assigned to work the Asylum branch at Newberry, and 24 might have as many as 10 cars of L.C.L. merchandise for the many small communities and logging camps along this stretch. On Mondays, the Armour meat car out of South St. Paul, Minnesota, was a part of No. 24's consist and its contents were distributed along the way. Logs for Newberry were picked up at McMillan from Lake Superior Iron and Chemical Co., whose engines worked the Northern Cooperage branch as well as the Danaher or east spur.

Lake Superior Iron & Chemical, a Detroit syndicate, had taken over the furnaces at Newberry and Chocolay in 1910. The Newberry plant was largely rebuilt and a new building erected for making wood alcohol and acetate of lime. Lake Superior Iron and Chemical also constructed a lumber mill at Newberry, sawing the good logs into lumber and using the poor logs for charcoal. The Chocolay furnace operation shut down for good in 1912, having made very little money for its investors during its various stages of operation since 1859.

Between Soo Jct. and St. Ignace trains 28 and 29 did the work, including servicing the Fiborn Quarry. The quarry, located on a 4-mile branch off the main line between Trout Lake and Soo Jct., furnished much of the limestone for area furnaces and started operations in 1905. The property was named after its chief investors, William F. Fitch, president of the South Shore, and Chase S. Osborn of Sault Ste. Marie. Algoma Steel purchased the property in 1910, and at the height of its production some 40 cars a day were forwarded to the Algoma works at Sault, Ontario. Later it was found more economical to bring the stone in by boat, and the quarry closed for good in the late 1930s.

Nos. 37–38 and 35–36 hauled Sault Ste. Marie cars to and from connections with main line through freights at Soo Jct., as well as working the Bay Mills branch and the new Seewhy logging branch and Fuller's Mill spur, built in 1911 and 1912, respectively. The Sault at the turn of the century held great promise as a manufacturing center, with the 19-foot drop between Lake Superior and the St. Mary's River thought to be an excellent source of water power. A 5-mile canal project, taken hold of by the Canadian promoter F. H. Clergue, finally opened in the fall of 1902. It was said to be the largest power canal in the world at the time, but engineering defects in the construction of the powerhouse meant it would need so much water that the level of Lake Superior would be affected. Although the project brought Union Carbide of Chicago to the Sault, water use restrictions put a stop to further development.

On the Ontario side, Clergue began construction of the Algoma Central & Hudson Bay railroad (AC&HB) in the spring of 1900 from the Canadian Sault north to

An eastbound passenger train pulls into Newberry, Michigan, station. The concrete block depot replaced a frame structure destroyed by fire in 1907. Newberry was an important point on the DSS&A, with the State Asylum and Lake Superior Iron and Chemical charcoal furnace being major customers. *Paananen Collection*

the Michipicoten region to serve mines and forest lands owned by his Consolidated Lake Superior Company. Algoma Iron Works (later Algoma Steel) built a mill at the Canadian Sault that was fueled by the iron ore and abundant hardwoods along the AC&HB. Wood pulp off the AC&HB was manufactured at the Sulphide Pulp Mills (later Abitibi Power and Paper) and given in interchange to the DSS&A and Soo Line for American paper mills in central Wisconsin. The fast-growing poplar trees used for wood pulp were also found along the South Shore and generated a large traffic. Another heavy industry on the Ontario side was the Nickel Ore Reduction Works, built to manufacture ores of the region. As a result of these heavy industries, a great majority of the freight traffic over the International Bridge was delivered or received from the AC&HB. For the years 1926 to 1932 the DSS&A received 532,295 tons of freight from the AC&HB and only 73,142 from the Canadian Pacific. The South Shore delivered 1,586,688 tons of freight for the same period to the AC&HB and 419,148 to the CPR.

The St. Ignace gateway remained a far more important source of interchange to the DSS&A, handling almost three times the traffic that went through Sault Ste. Marie. Between 1923 and 1932, the South Shore received 971,576 tons of freight off the Michigan Central and an additional 560,845 off the Pennsylvania Railroad, which had leased the Grand Rapids & Indiana in 1922. Deliveries were much heavier to those roads, with 2,653,222 tons being given to the Michigan Central and 2,702,795 to the PRR. Of the southbound traffic, 41 percent was lumber, 6 percent pig iron, 5 percent flour, and 4 percent copper.

Trains arriving at St. Ignace would leave their cars in the West Yard about a mile from the ferry dock before tieing up at the nearby roundhouse. The switch engine would remove the St. Ignace cars in the West Yard and sometimes separate the loads and empties for Mackinaw City, although often this was done right on the dock itself. Cars for the ferry were then shoved down, with a man riding the top of the first car with a long air hose in hand to whistle for the crossings and stop the train if necessary. A clerk would flag the busy U.S. 2 highway crossing by the depot as the cars were brought onto the ferry slip. During loading, cars were required to be balanced, as mentioned earlier, and care also had to be taken that the first car shoved into the corners did not have a high brake wheel, which might get caught up in the boat's deck supports. The switch crew could not take their engine onto the ferry apron, but used a couple of old flat cars as idlers. These were kept in the corner, a track that ran beyond the apron, alongside the ferry. The inbound caboose would be kept on the house track in back of the depot.

After being loaded, the ferry would usually take 3 hours to make the round trip between St. Ignace and Mackinaw City. One hour was required to transit the Straits and another hour for the Michigan Central switch crew to unload and load the ferry. The MC yard crew also handled the work for the PRR at Mackinaw. After pulling the inbound ferry, outbound DSS&A trains at St. Ignace were made up in the small four-track stub yard near the ferry slip, with the power backing down from the West Yard to pick them up. If there was only one switch crew, it usually worked at night, requiring the daytime passenger trains to load and unload their own trains on and off the ferry. DSS&A passenger train crews went over on the boat and got their rest at Mackinaw City, although the engine crews tied up in the West Yard after loading.

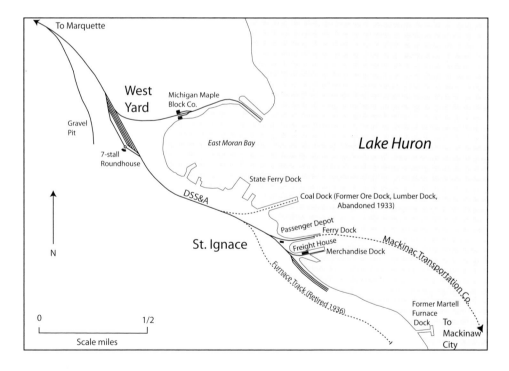

St. Ignace, Michigan, July 1943

Detroit wholesalers were still trying to make greater inroads to supply the iron and copper ranges. The Michigan Central time freight left Detroit at 1 AM and arrived at Mackinaw City at 8:30 PM. Merchandise cars were then brought over to St. Ignace and worked at the freight house, where they were consolidated into larger shipments. If the cars could get out of St. Ignace in decent shape, a two-day service into Marquette, Negaunee, and Ishpeming, with three days to the Copper Country, was possible. Merchandise totaled about 4 percent of the DSS&A's total tonnage.

Another major east end interchange took place at Trout Lake with the Soo Line. The DSS&A received between 25 to 30 cars daily, mainly of forest products, destined for Lower Peninsula points, and it delivered another 15 to 20 cars, mainly of the same commodity, daily to the Soo. There were connecting tracks on all four corners of the diamond. At Shingleton, the South Shore interchanged with the Manistique & Lake Superior, but the traffic did not amount to more than 3 or 4 cars a day. The exception would be if the Manistique furnace was receiving ore off the Marquette Range, in which case 25 to 30 cars of ore could be set out.

The South Shore had interchanges with the Munising Railway at Munising Jct. and at Evelyn. The track arrangement at Munising Jct. made it difficult for westbounds to pick up, but the business was small and only amounted to 12 cars a week in and out. At Evelyn the exchange averaged 7 or 8 loads a day to the Munising and only empties coming back to the South Shore.

Marquette typically had two switch engines on days and one at nights during the winter months. This increased dramatically during the ore season, when there might be three to six during the daytime and two at night. The ore switch crew often shoved empty ore trains up to the top of the hill at Bagdad. The commercial switch engines worked the Dead River branch as well as the quarry and prison spurs on the Mackinaw Division. The downtown freight house, which received three switches a day, and company material from the DSS&A shops and bridge and building yard in the Upper Yard, also provided traffic. Considerable coal traffic was generated from the new Pickands facility, located on the former DSS&A merchandise dock, which was placed in operation with the opening of navigation in 1914.

Pickands and F. B. Spear and Sons, the other major coal dealer in town, grew tired of handling coal on the old wooden docks and started operating at a brand new facility on the north end of the lower harbor on November 7, 1925. Ten-year contracts were signed with the South Shore, LS&I, and Cleveland-Cliffs Iron to handle all their local coal. The LS&I came in on the east end of the dock, while the South Shore pulled their loads out from the west end using their Lake Street Branch. The South Shore also had an interchange with the LS&I in back of the Spear dock. The LS&I would occasionally deliver iron ore for mixing on the South Shore dock, and this proved quite challenging due to the steep grade to the Upper Yard. A Texaco bulk oil operation was also located along the Lake Street branch, receiving oil off the lake which was sent out in tank cars. On the other end of the Lower Yard, by the old Marquette & Western main, was the Marquette Gas Company, which received cars of coal off the Spear dock for making coal gas.

Freight service on the Western Division was provided by through freights 53 and 54 between Marquette and Thomaston, which connected with trains 63 and 64 for the remainder of the distance to Superior. These trains lined up their own setouts at

An old MH&O Mogul, bumped into yard service by heavier Consolidations, is probably coming around the wye from the south main line and across the highway in Marquette's Lower Yard. This engine will have two more years of South Shore service before being sold to Lake Superior Iron and Chemical in 1913. *Paananen Collection*

Thomaston as there was no yard engine at that point. Marquette Range ore traffic was handled largely by extras. These jobs also brought coal up the hill for mine use. Nos. 55 and 56 provided local service between Michigamme and Thomaston. No. 56 did the switching at the Weidman mill at Trout Creek and the Bergland logging spurs. In the winter, when the logs were moving, an extra engine did the switching at Ewen and worked the Baltimore branch. West of Thomaston, the local work was handled by trains 67 and 68 as far as Iron River, and by trains 61 and 62, which made the Iron River Turn out of Superior.

Up on the hill at Negaunee, the South Shore received quite a few cars of iron ore off the LS&I for the furnaces at Newberry, and for Antrim on the PRR in Lower Michigan. The DSS&A also received most of its interchange with the North Western at Negaunee, while making its deliveries at Ishpeming. All C&NW interchange was considered Ishpeming business on paper, with some twenty loads being interchanged each way daily between the two roads in the Negaunee-Ishpeming area. These consisted mainly of manufactured and agricultural goods inbound for the distributing houses on the Marquette Range and in the Copper Country. During the daytime hours the Ishpeming and Negaunee switch engines would pull and set the interchanges, but at night road crews would attend to this business. Smaller interchanges also existed with the North Western at Michigamme and Republic, but these did not average more than a car a day. The C&NW abandoned service to these points in 1929 and 1932 respectively.

The switch engines at Negaunee and Ishpeming also worked the local mine branches during the ore season. The Negaunee engine worked the Negaunee & Palmer branch, while Ishpeming switch engines served the Teal Lake, Lake Angeline, and Winthrop mine branches. The Winthrop mine branch was home to the Pluto Powder Company (later Hercules Powder) plant, which had begun operations in February 1909. Further west, the American mine was served by local freights, while the Imperial mine branch was handled with ore extras, as was the Ohio mine on the Beaufort mine branch. The old Champion mine (the second largest hard ore producing mine in the Lake Superior district) had closed in 1910 and the Ohio would do the same in 1918.

The major interchange with the Chicago, Milwaukee & St. Paul took place at Champion. Two tracks were used for interchange; one was called the St. Paul track and one the South Shore track. Under ten loads, mainly inbound manufactured and agricultural

Engine 73 is spotting cars for a shovel loading stockpile iron ore on the Marquette Range. Stockpile ore was not immediately loaded into cars upon being taken out of the shaft, but taken to piling grounds by dump cars. *Paananen Collection*

commodities for distribution on the UP, were given to the South Shore each day, with a like quantity of mainly forest products being given to the Milwaukee. The CM&StP interchange at Sidnaw consisted mainly of logs going to mills served by the Milwaukee. This averaged several dozen cars a day during the winter months. The Milwaukee rarely had anything for the South Shore to pick up except empties.

In Wisconsin, the South Shore interchanged with the C&NW (former Milwaukee, Lake Shore & Western) at Saxon and the Wisconsin Central at Marengo. These interchanges saw a lot of wood products moving south to the paper mills in Grand Rapids (later Wisconsin Rapids) and other central Wisconsin points. At Bibon an important exchange was made with the Chicago, St. Paul, Minneapolis & Omaha. The CStPM&O ran an overnight train into Ashland and set out cars at Bibon for DSS&A points. Some of this traffic was very hot, such as meat out of the South St. Paul packing houses and fruit from the southwest. The South Shore spur to Mason was torn out in 1915, following dissolution of the White River Lumber company.

Superior was another major interchange point for the DSS&A. Coming into town the South Shore crossed over the Duluth, Missabe & Northern at Peyton, which saw occasional shipments of all-rail iron ore from the Mesabi Range. Inbound DSS&A trains would set out cars at 28th Street for the Soo Line, including anything for Duluth. At another three-track yard, between 18th and 21st streets, the DSS&A delivered cars for the Northern Pacific. Usually the remainder of the train would be left in the Lake Superior Terminal & Transfer yard. The engine and caboose and perhaps a few empties would then clatter across the Wisconsin Central and CStPM&O diamonds and tie up at the small South Shore yard. The process was reversed for outbound trains. The DSS&A had an assigned track to pick at the LST&T yard and then went on to the 18th Street and 28th Street yards for the rest of its train. The DSS&A maintained a rip track and carmen at 28th Street, where a final air test was made prior to leaving for Thomaston. As there was no switch engine at Superior, the few industries along the DSS&A in Superior were handled by the Iron River Turn, which did the switching at 18th Street yard and 28th Street yard and Superior East End, and then ran up the Northwestern Coal Railway to an interchange with that company alongside the GN's Allouez ore yard.

Continuing east, road crews blocked their own trains at Thomaston. A reduction of tonnage was often necessary at Ewen to make the hill east of town. The trains were again reclassified at Marquette into blocks for the Sault and St. Ignace, and the local cars were removed. As most of the eastbound tonnage went to St. Ignace, cars for the Sault were set out at Soo Jct. for movement to the Lock City.

The Houghton Division between Marquette and Houghton was home to through freights 31 and 32 and local trains 33 and 34. No. 34 switched the Arnheim quarry tracks and also the Baraga mill spur. A pusher engine was stationed at L'Anse to help the six eastbound (four passenger and two freight) trains up the 3 percent grade to Summit. At Keweenaw Bay, the South Shore interchanged with the isolated South Range branch of the Mineral Range. This traffic totaled 20 cars a day when the logs were moving in the winter, while in the summer the business would dwindle to practically nothing, except for a little bark.

The major interchange with the Mineral Range took place at Houghton. Most of this business was westbound with some 15 to 20 cars going daily to the MR, mainly

At Negaunee, a 600-class Consolidation handling a loaded ore train pauses to take water before heading across Silver Street and down the hill to Marquette.   *Louis Ruel photo, Wesley Perron Railroad Collection, Peter White Public Library, Marquette, Mich.*

Bibon was a major interchange between the Chicago, St. Paul, Minneapolis & Omaha and the South Shore, with traffic out of the Twin Cities destined for the Marquette and Copper Ranges. This view looks west along the South Shore main line from the Omaha overpass in 1911.   *Paananen Collection*

finished goods and agricultural commodities for the Keweenaw Peninsula, and with only 5 cars a day, mostly copper and lumber, coming back as loads to the South Shore. The Houghton switch engines brought most of these cars over to Hancock for the Mineral Range. No. 31, however, would also set out at Hancock on its way to Calumet. No. 32, out of Calumet, picked up at Hancock off the MR and again at Houghton any cars brought over by the switch engine. The Copper Range interchange at Houghton was also good for about 5 cars daily. This exchange took place by the bridge over Portage Lake, about ⅛ mile west of the passenger station. The Houghton switch engine also handled the local businesses in Hancock and Houghton, including a planing mill, a foundry, and Weber's packing house.

A typical DSS&A section house, used to house section foremen and often laborers at remote outposts, is seen on the right in this view of Groesbeck, Michigan, in 1911. *Paananen Collection*

10

WORLD WAR I—SOO LINE CONTROL FOLLOWS FEDERAL CONTROL

The leadership of the South Shore underwent profound changes with the entry of the United States into World War I. As the private rail network was unable to cope with the increasingly heavy movement of goods to the East Coast to prosecute the war in Europe, President Woodrow Wilson directed the federal government to take control of the nation's railroads on December 28, 1917. The single system, headed by William Gibbs McAdoo, was to be operated under the United States Railroad Administration (USRA). W. W. Walker was appointed federal manager of the South Shore and, as he was prohibited from having a dual role, resigned his position as DSS&A vice president and general manager. Arch Eldredge continued as president. Under the new arrangement, railroads were compensated by the government for the use of their properties on the basis of their average operating income from June 30, 1914, to June 30, 1917.[1]

During the period of federal control, DSS&A expenses grew dramatically as the result of the McAdoo Award, which gave railroad employees large wage increases. Low wages were said to be claiming a large part of the railroad work force as men left to work in the shipyards and munitions factories. By 1918, labor costs were said to be greater than the gross operating revenues of the U.S. roads a decade earlier. Later in 1919, the USRA gave employees an 8-hour day.

The South Shore and Mineral Range saw many of its men go off to war, with 275 men serving in the armed forces during the conflict. Women were brought in to fill the ranks, perhaps the most notable being Mrs. Robert Hendries, who worked under her husband on the Soo Jct. section. The *Newberry News* commented, "She was clad in over-alls and went about the work with the intelligence of one who has performed the labor for years."[2]

The South Shore suffered more upheaval with the passing of W. W. Walker on July 2, 1918, and Arch Eldredge shortly thereafter on September 9. George R. Huntington, federal manager of the Soo Line, was given control of the South Shore on July 10, and of the Mackinac Transportation Company that October. Edmund Pennington, Soo Line president, was elected president of the South Shore on October 1, 1918, and of the

Mineral Range seven days later. Huntington went on to order, in 1919, that the managements of the DSS&A and Soo Line be consolidated. This practice would have long-lasting effects, as it continued with the end of federal control in 1920. Under the consolidation, the Soo Line's president, vice president, secretary, comptroller, treasurer, purchasing agent, chief engineer, general mechanical superintendent, land commissioner, and a slew of other officials all assumed a like capacity on the DSS&A. From 1919 to 1925, the South Shore's purchasing, mechanical, engineering, stores, mail, and general passenger departments were all merged with those of the Soo Line in Minneapolis. South Shore Land Company affairs were handled by H. S. Funston, land commissioner of the Soo.[3]

This consolidation produced mixed results for the South Shore. The greater efficiency saved the DSS&A money over performing the functions independently and provided higher-quality department heads than it could afford, or require, for its size. Disadvantages to the DSS&A were that it became, in the eyes of many, a part of the Soo Line system, with the resulting loss of prestige. The South Shore was unable to leverage traffic, as supply purchases were made through the Soo Line's purchasing department. The DSS&A operating department and division engineering offices remained in Marquette, and this proved inconvenient when they were forced to deal with department heads in Minneapolis. When any type of conflict arose between the South Shore and the Soo Line, the Soo Line officers were not likely to take the side of the smaller road.

Some practices implemented under the USRA were of real benefit. Three railroads had previously maintained station facilities at Republic, but under the USRA, the South Shore and C&NW depots were closed and business was handled at the CM&StP station. This practice was continued after the end of federal control. The South Shore depot was moved to North Ironwood in December 1921 to placate the Ironwood Commercial Club, which had continued to press for the completion of the Gogebic Range branch.

Although the South Shore benefited from high traffic levels in the later years of World War I, the start of the war in Europe in 1914 initially disrupted the American economy, virtually halting all new building construction. This had a serious effect on the South Shore's lumber and ore business. For the fiscal year ending June 30, 1915, South Shore revenue fell under $3,000,000 for the first time since 1906. As the wartime economy kicked in in 1916, the Marquette Iron Range produced 5½ million tons of ore, an all-time record. Given the dominance of Cleveland-Cliffs on the range, the South Shore did not exactly share in the benefit and its tonnage actually fell slightly from 1915.

South Shore did pick up considerable bridge traffic during the war years with the closing of navigation on the lakes. Solid trains of grain moved out of the Twin Ports to Sault Ste. Marie, as well as to St. Ignace. The *Chief Wawatam* and *Sainte Marie* were engaged almost continuously ferrying cars across the Straits of Mackinac. The DSS&A also handled cars of silk during this period, sometimes by the trainload. These trains were usually routed via St. Ignace. Extra engines were rented from the Great Northern, Northern Pacific, and Canadian Pacific to keep up. A coal shortage during the winter of 1916–1917 saw the South Shore send 100 of its ore cars directly to the coal mines to help with the rail movement. Mackinac Transportation saw a rare coal movement of over 2,000 cars on its ferries in 1917 to alleviate the shortage at Algoma Steel.

In the midst of this traffic boom, the South Shore had to deal with a tremendous snowstorm which spread across the Upper Peninsula on March 16, 1917, and resulted in the annulment of every South Shore train between Duluth and the Sault. It was not until the 19th that a train finally made it into the Copper Country. The heavy wintertime traffic was again hit by a bad storm which started on Valentine's Day 1918 and tied up the Houghton Division between Marquette and Negaunee for 21 hours. Conditions were worse on the Mackinaw Division, and No. 2 became stalled between Marquette and Au Train, as did No. 14 in a cut near Trout Lake. Finally, on the third day the storm started to abate and a snow plow extra was ordered out of Marquette to "punch a hole" through to St. Ignace. The going was rough and the extra became stuck 2 miles west of Seney. Another plow extra was started east that night and managed to dislodge the earlier plow extra and shove it into Seney. After the plow reached St. Ignace, train No. 8, three days late, headed out and was the first train to make it over the Mackinaw Division. It was some days before the backlog of traffic was cleared up.[4]

Generally, however, the South Shore could take pride in its on-time operation, especially during the grueling UP winters. Veteran theatrical agent Charles Riggs commented, "In New York I have often told friends that it was something of a pleasure to run into a storm in northern Mi., just to see the railroad men take hold of things, and push their trains through. To be held up once in 41 years is a pretty good average and I'm not going to complain."[5]

An attaché of the U.S. mail service commented, "The engineers and trainmen of the Chicago lines that penetrate this region might well come up into the heart of the north country and spend some time learning the tricks of winter running from employes of the South Shore road. . . . It isn't accidental that the South Shore does so well. It is the result of the excellent arrangements of the management and of the experience of the train and engine crews. Most of the company's employes have been trying conclusions with northern winters for many years and they know just how to take them. I don't think there is a road in the country that makes better business of winter running than the South Shore."[6]

Lumber mills and other industries in the UP suffered severe car shortages with the booming wartime economy, and this was one of the major reasons for the government takeover. Mackinac Transportation Company business declined by 5,126 cars in 1917 from the year before, due to the inability to get empties in the UP. So much hay was on hand at Sault Ste. Marie that private residences were being used for storage until freight cars were available. The USRA took the complaints to heart and ordered 2,700 eastern road empties transferred to the UP, with 1,700 allocated to the DSS&A. This caused a rush of business on the Mackinac Transportation Company, and in May 1918 an all-time record was reached with 9,294 cars being ferried across the Straits. All this business was handled by the *Chief Wawatam,* which made 231 round trips that month. The crew of the *Chief* still found time to be patriotic, with 91 percent contributing to the fourth issue of Liberty Bonds.

A major change in the road's passenger service was implemented under federal control. DSS&A management had long felt it was a mistake to run Nos. 7 and 8 into Sault Ste. Marie when most of the South Shore's passenger business moved to St. Ignace. The USRA agreed and the change was made effective December 9, 1918. To placate the parent road, No. 117 ran out of the Sault after connecting with Canadian Pacific No. 17 and made an exchange with Nos. 7 and 2 at Soo Jct. The other connecting run out of Sault Ste. Marie, Nos. 17 and 18, met Nos. 8 and 1. The USRA also eliminated Nos. 105 and 106, the through Chicago, Milwaukee & St. Paul connection, which operated over the DSS&A between Republic and Marquette. This proved to be the last passenger service ever to operate over the South Shore Republic branch. The DSS&A

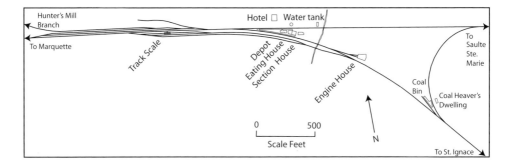

Soo Jct., Michigan, September 16, 1921

Republic-Marquette local had gone back to a Michigamme-Marquette schedule around 1905.

The DSS&A Marquette-Michigamme local and the Chicago & North Western manned Ishpeming-Marquette connection were combined under federal control, and their tasks were performed by one crew. The train started out of Ishpeming in the morning with the connection off the northbound C&NW overnight train for Marquette. At Marquette, the train made a quick turnaround before heading to Champion to connect with the northbound CM&StP overnighter. Upon return from Champion, a Marquette-Ishpeming turn was made in the afternoon to connect with a northbound C&NW run, and the final leg brought passengers and head-end business to Ishpeming for the southbound overnight C&NW train.

Residents on both sides of the St. Mary's River had long been after the railroads to run a short line passenger service over the International Bridge between the Canadian and American Saults. When the International Transit Company ferry quit running during the winter months, the two communities were entirely isolated aside from the CPR passenger train. The owning roads agreed to provide service from January 15, 1918, until the opening of the river to navigation. Although the service operated at a loss, it was much appreciated by the residents of the two Saults.

As the result of labor strikes in the coalfields, the USRA mandated cuts in passenger service to guard against a coal famine. Effective December 8, 1919, Nos. 5 and 6 between Michigamme and Duluth were run three days a week. On the days 5 and 6 did not run, night trains 7 and 8 added their local stops. The use of parlor cars, special equipment, and special moves was also eliminated to save fuel. With 7 and 8 having to cope with twice the business normally offered and the start of cold weather, the program proved to be a real hardship. Fortunately regular service was restored on December 18, 1919.

A 1916 valuation made by the Interstate Commerce Commission of the all railroad properties to determine a proper rate of return brought to light the sorry state of the DSS&A's finances. As of June 30, back interest payments on the 4 percent bonds owed to the CPR totaled over $9,000,000. The South Shore also owed its parent almost $1,000,000 for cash advances. These figures were quite remarkable considering the ICC placed a final value of only $17,250,000 on DSS&A property used for common carrier purposes. When preparing the contract for the South Shore, John Barton Payne, general counsel of the USRA, called the situation "eminently unsatisfactory."[7] The only redeeming factor was that the majority of the interest was due to the Canadian Pacific, which owned

51 percent of its stock. An agreement was reached with the CPR that none of the 4 percent bond interest could be expected during the period of federal control.

The period of federal control came to an end at midnight on February 29, 1920, although the railroads' income continued to be guaranteed until August 31, 1920. The railroads, although shedding one yoke, immediately came under the Federal Transportation Act, which took effect on March 1. Under that law, tariff changes could only be made after approval by the ICC or state regulatory agencies. Compensation for government use of the railroads was quite contentious, and final settlement with the South Shore and Mineral Range was not reached until November 1921. The agreement provided an annual payment of $562,348 to the South Shore and $144,006 to the Mineral Range.[8]

In spite of the heavy toll on the taxpayers under the USRA, many thought consolidation was a real benefit, and this idea was carried forward in ICC proposals put out in the early 1920s to consolidate the nation's railroads into 18 systems. The Commission felt the South Shore and the Soo Line were already part of a through transcontinental system (the CPR) and thus already a competitive force against the other area roads. The proposal was doomed to failure, as strong carriers were unwilling to combine with weaker roads, and the Commission also lacked authority to force its will on holding companies.

The end of federal control saw the Soo Line's top officials retain oversight over the South Shore. Edmund Pennington of the Soo Line remained DSS&A president, while former federal manager George R. Huntington was elected vice president and general manager. Still another Soo Line official, G. W. Webster, was elected treasurer. In 1920, the South Shore again came to have its own treasurer, W. J. Ellison, with offices in Marquette. C. E. Lytle, as general superintendent, was the top local operating official. S. R. Lewis oversaw what was left of the South Shore's traffic department from his offices in Duluth.[9] The South Shore underwent several quick changes of leadership in 1923. George Huntington took over Pennington's duties as DSS&A president in April, with Austin E. Wallace taking over Huntington's old job as vice president and general manager. Huntington's presidency was short-lived due to his sudden passing, at age 55, on November 3, 1923. C. T. Jaffray replaced Huntington as president on November 23.[10]

The country as a whole was hit by a severe recession in 1921, suffering deflation with the end of the war. The South Shore sought to cut costs by abolishing several freight assignments. Wisconsin state senator A. H. Wilkinson, complaining about the reductions, caustically remarked that the South Shore's "principal business is to haul water for the engines from Duluth to the Soo."[11] Iron ore mines could not find a market for their previous winter's stockpile and cut back operations to three days a week or closed altogether. The Marquette Range was said to be hardest-hit of all the ranges by the recession, with the DSS&A handling only 198,742 tons in 1921 compared with 704,017 tons the year before. Iron ore totaled only 11 percent of the South Shore's traffic in 1921, with logs being the principal commodity, followed by lumber products, and then gravel and stone. Total revenue for 1921 fell over $600,000 from 1920 levels, resulting in a net deficit of over a half-million dollars.

The nation was beset by a number of strikes following World War I as employees sought to hang on to wage gains and industry looked to cut costs. The South Shore was not immune from this trend, and a three-week strike by the crews of Mackinac Transportation Company over back pay occurred in February 1920. During that period little or no freight was transferred, and people were forced to go across the Straits on sleigh or by foot. After the parties reached a settlement, the *Chief Wawatam* made its first run on March 3. Even a three-week build-up of ice did not deter the icebreaker, and the trip to Mackinaw City was made without difficulty.

The *Chief Wawatam* was not always so lucky. On January 19, 1922, while handling No. 2's train, she became stuck fast about 2 miles from Mackinaw City and could go no further. After returning to St. Ignace on the 21st to take coal and provisions, she finally succeeded in reaching Mackinaw City. The following day the *Chief* headed back to St. Ignace only to be stymied once again about a mile out, fighting 20-foot-thick ice. Even pike poles and dynamite proved ineffective. The *Sainte Marie* headed out of St. Ignace on the 23rd, but had no better luck than the *Chief* and returned to St. Ignace on the 25th for supplies. The *Sainte Marie*'s second attempt brought her right up next to the *Chief,* freeing the vessel. A joint effort of the *Sainte Marie* and the *Chief* succeeded in opening a channel through the ice on the 27th. Both boats were used to clear up the backlog of traffic, and by January 30 things were back to normal and the *Sainte Marie* tied up.

The quick thinking of First Officer Fred Ryerse saved what might have been a catastrophic situation as the *Chief Wawatam* was loading in St. Ignace on April 26, 1922. During a heavy blizzard, the piles holding the *Chief*'s bow line gave way, allowing the boat to swing out just as a passenger train was being shoved across the apron. A Pullman hung suspended over the water with one set of trucks on the apron and another on the boat. As passengers in their night clothes rushed to safety, Ryerse ordered all ahead full, closing the gap between the ferry and the apron and keeping the car out of the 30-foot-deep water.

THE SHOPMEN'S STRIKE

Just as the South Shore was starting to emerge from the 1921 recession, along with most of the nation's carriers it faced additional labor difficulties. The largely pro-business U.S. Railroad Labor Board (RLB), formed under the Transportation Act of 1920, sought to reduce the excesses of the USRA by scaling back wages for clerks, section men, and shop craft workers. The employees were very agitated by the moves, but the RLB claimed the 3 to 5 cents an hour reduction for the section men still left their wages 69.4 percent above December 1917 levels, while the cost of living had only risen 17.2 percent. The shop crafts were particularly angered by the wage reduction, but pro-management journals did not see how the shopmen would ever go on strike, given that many of them had just returned from recession layoffs. The union sought time-and-a-half pay for Sunday and holiday work, discontinuation of the use of contract shops, and restoration of pay cuts of between 7 and 9 cents per hour. After the RLB rejected these demands, the South Shore employees joined a nationwide movement by walking off the job on July 1, 1922. The action affected about 40 men employed in Marquette's Lower Yard and 230 in the Upper Yard and adjacent shops.

In response, Vice President and General Manager Huntington let it be known that unless the men returned to their posts by July 10 replacements could be hired. Huntington justified this position by saying the grievances were not against the DSS&A but the result of actions by the RLB. Huntington's threat was ineffective and all the 270 South Shore

The *Chief Wawatam* and *Sainte Marie* do battle with ice conditions in the Straits of Mackinac in January 1922. The *Chief* was stuck for ten days off Mackinaw City during this period, with the *Sainte Marie* having been called out to free her. Fifty-four passengers led by Paddy Brown, a crew member, walked to St. Ignace over the ragged ice rather than wait it out.   *Wesley Perron Railroad Collection, Peter White Public Library, Marquette, Mich.*

The gang for section 47 is seen on their hand car near Kitchie. Employees such as these were subjected to heavy wage cuts during the 1921 recession, which resulted in massive strikes among carmen. *Paananen Collection*

employees remained off the job. The Soo then adopted a policy of not negotiating with the shop craft union, but only with the workmen as individuals. The railroad said it was up to the men whether they wanted to return to work and retain their seniority, or be replaced. On September 28, No. 4 pulled into the depot at Marquette and uncoupled a diner which contained thirteen replacement workers from Minneapolis. Four more replacements arrived on No. 2 from St. Ignace that same evening. A sleeper was coupled to the diner and the equipment placed under armed guard. In spite of these steps the South Shore shop men refused to break ranks, even though the railroad said more replacements were on the way.

DSS&A enginemen started complaining about the condition of the road's locomotives, claiming that of the 74 engines in service, 23 were now disabled, with many of the remaining engines in need of repairs. Enginemen claimed that most of the problems were due to lack of boiler washing, and that trains had to stop at practically every water tank because of leaky flues. Officials said the use of Lake Superior water, which contained very little lime, created little need for boiler washings. The company and the union continued their verbal sparring for several weeks until finally the Soo Line invited a strike committee to come to Minneapolis to negotiate. The committee returned to Marquette with an agreement giving all 371 men their jobs back with full seniority, and, after ratification, the first men returned on October 16.

Another set of workers who did not fare so well were the union ore dock workers. When these men refused to come to work in the spring of 1924 unless granted a wage increase, the DSS&A decided to contract the work with Addison-Miller, Inc., of St. Paul. The labor contractor instituted an "open shop," leaving the former employees out in the cold.[12]

In addition to its own labor problems, the DSS&A suffered from a nationwide strike of union coal miners in the spring of 1922. As shortages developed, a number of passenger trains were discontinued on July 30, including Nos. 9 and 12, the C&NW connection between Marquette and Winthrop Jct., and Nos. 3 and 4 between Calumet and Marquette. Trains 5 and 6, the Duluth local, losing their connection at Nestoria, were run all the way into Marquette on 3 and 4's schedule. The coal shortage was further aggravated by the rebound in freight traffic as the country emerged from the 1921 recession. A 10 percent rate reduction put into effect on July 1, 1922, caused traffic to almost double. Shippers had been holding back business waiting for the reduction to take effect and then saturated the rails. Using 500 tons of coal a day, the South Shore had sufficient supply on hand to last until September 15. Fortunately the United Mine Workers and bituminous operators came to an agreement on August 15, but it took a long time to replenish depleted stocks.

The Marquette Range began to show new life with the end of the recession, and by mid-August 1922 only the Cambria mine was inactive, and it reopened just after the first of the year. Still, shipments in 1922 totaled only 364,840 tons, barely half the 1920 figure. Most of this traffic came from the Richmond and Mary Charlotte mines on the Negaunee & Palmer branch. In April 1923 as the result of a petition brought by the Adriatic Mining Company and other independent mine owners, the ICC mandated that any rate over 54 cents per ton on iron ore from Ishpeming and Negaunee to Marquette, and 63 cents from more distant mines, was unreasonable.

The booming automobile age saw Henry Ford secure the Michigan Land and Iron company in 1920 to provide raw materials for his "Tin Lizzies." This was a hopeful sign to the Michigamme area, as the holdings included the nearby Imperial mine, which was soon bustling with activity. The South Shore put in new trackage to serve the mine in August 1921, and shipments started a year later. Initially, the South Shore did not receive the entire line haul, as the ore was routed via the C&NW to Escanaba, and then to Detroit by boat.

During the remainder of the twenties the Marquette Range saw considerable demand for siliceous ore, which averaged 35 to 40 percent iron and the same percentage of silica. Mines producing this ore, along the Negaunee & Palmer branch, included the Richmond, Maitland, Isabella, and Empire. Ore traffic on the South Shore for the 1923 season saw a healthy increase, with 848,303 tons being shipped over the Marquette dock and another 199,196 going all-rail. The 1924 ore season was depressed over most of the Lake Superior district, but the growing demand for the siliceous ore saw the DSS&A's tonnage over the Marquette dock actually rise to 1,051,996 tons. This was the first time the South Shore had handled over a million tons through the dock since 1913. This good fortune continued for the 1925 ore season, despite low ore prices.

Another new siliceous ore producer, the New Volunteer west of Palmer, began shipping in August 1926. An agreement dated December 1, 1925, provided the C&NW with trackage rights over the DSS&A to reach the New Volunteer and allowed them to purchase a half-interest in the mine trackage itself. The Ford Company, having trouble with an ever-increasing sulphur content in its Imperial ore, went on to find a large ore body at the Blueberry mine, north of Greenwood. To reach the Blueberry, the South Shore renewed its American mine branch and connected with the C&NW's Michigamme branch. After running over the North Western for 4,201 feet, the DSS&A branched off to the mine itself. The Blueberry mine tracks were owned jointly by the DSS&A, C&NW, and LS&I (which used the C&NW out of Ishpeming). All necessary trackage was completed in October 1928, and shipments began in the summer of 1929.

The South Shore ore traffic began falling in 1926 after its 1925 peak. The siliceous ore started moving heavily to the Chicago area, which meant routing over the North Western to Escanaba. The DSS&A's ore traffic improved slightly in 1927, but tonnage out of the Marquette dock actually fell due to Imperial mine ore being routed via Ishpeming and the C&NW. The 1927 season saw 826,304 tons of ore shipped over the Marquette dock and only 768,736 the following season. All-rail ore traffic remained constant at around 100,000 tons per year.

Further Ford activity brightened L'Anse's future with the purchase of the Stearns and Culver lumber mill in December 1922. While Stearns and Culver had employed 125 men at $2.25 a day in 1922, by 1925 there were 1,200 men employed at an average wage of $6 a day. All this was due to "Henry Ford, Ford-like, waving his magic wand."[13] The South Shore enjoyed 15- to 20-car daily movements of lumber from the L'Anse mill to the Ford automobile plant at Iron Mountain. This traffic was given to the CM&StP at Champion. In addition, Ford purchased two small lake freighters, which began to bring coal out of Toledo and other eastern coal ports to L'Anse, where it was transloaded into gondolas for Iron Mountain. Ford did its own switching at the L'Anse plant and interchanged to the DSS&A in a three-track interchange yard east of the main line.

Henry Ford brought his own train to L'Anse on an April 22, 1924, inspection trip. The train, made up of Ford's private car, a diner, and a Pullman, was handled by an immaculate Detroit, Toledo & Ironton locomotive. The enginemen were "dressed so spotlessly clean that they would not have been out of place waiting on table."[14] In typical Ford fashion, two crews were employed, thus allowing an 8-hour work day. The off-duty crew spent its time in the Pullman.

Ford contributed to the heavy hardwood log traffic over the winter of 1923–1924, with some 100 cars a day moving to his mills at L'Anse and Pequaming (Ford purchased the Hebard mill in 1923). In addition, Holt Lumber Company moved 8,000,000 feet of burned-over timber from its holdings in Ontonagon County to Saxon, Wisconsin, where Brown Land and Lumber Company had an active mill. The new Cadillac Lumber and Chemical mill, opened in August 1923, also greatly boosted the log business into the Sault. The following winter, the South Shore was hauling 150 to 200 cars of logs a day, including 60 or so for the Ford mill at L'Anse, 15 for the Cadillac mill at the Sault, and another 20 that were taken across the Straits of Mackinac for mills on the Lower Peninsula. Log trains were also being run from the Lake Gogebic area to the Piqua Handle and Manufacturing plant at Marquette, and from Tula to the Schroeder mill at Ashland, Wisconsin.

Although the hardwood and ore markets recovered nicely in the 1920s, other traffic losses were troubling. The virgin pine once sent to markets in New England, New York, and Pennsylvania had largely been cutover by 1912. The Duluth-Superior flour mills lost much of their eastern market with the construction of mills in Buffalo. Buffalo could

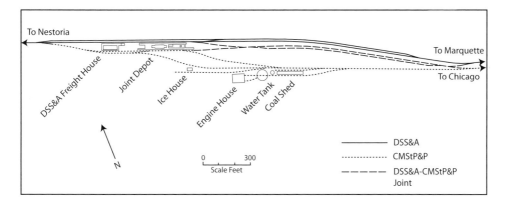

Champion, Michigan, September 25, 1928

sell flour 30 cents a barrel cheaper in the eastern markets than mills at the Head of the Lakes. The grain movements the South Shore had enjoyed during the winter months were largely a thing of the past, with boats handling this commodity from Duluth to Buffalo for as little as 2 cents a bushel. The copper market had also changed following World War I, with European markets and those in New York and Connecticut being served by water from mines in Arizona, New Mexico, Montana, and Chile. The copper from the UP mines was sent through St. Ignace largely to the Lower Peninsula, Ohio, and surrounding areas.

The UP continued to have difficulty converting to an agricultural community following the leveling of the pine forests in spite of the efforts of the South Shore's agricultural development agent, Joseph Jeffrey. Special trains continued to be operated to promote productive agricultural methods. A land clearing special was operated over the South Shore during 1923, showing what results could be obtained by dynamite and pyrotol. In June 1924, through the efforts of the agricultural extension office and five UP railroads, the "Cloverland Dairy Special" was run to encourage dairy farming and improve the stock of the region's dairy cows.[15]

A poultry train made a three-week tour of the UP over South Shore, LS&I, and Soo Line rails in 1925, and late that winter a Forest Fire Special was run on both peninsulas in conjunction with the State of Michigan, Federal Forestry Service, and the University of Michigan, as well as the Michigan Central, Detroit & Mackinac, DSS&A, and Soo Line railroads. A crop special, participated in by the C&NW, the Soo Line, the Chicago, Milwaukee & St. Paul, and the DSS&A, was run in the early spring of 1927 to promote homegrown dairy feed and also potato farming. This was followed by a sheep special which began touring on May 27, 1929, along the South Shore between Seney and North Ironwood. Although dairy farming did take hold around Bruce's Crossing, and some potatoes were shipped from Covington, Baraga, and L'Anse and along the Mineral Range's South Range line, agricultural development along the South Shore remained spotty at best.

A LITTLE MONEY FOR IMPROVEMENTS

During federal control, the South Shore's debt to the Canadian Pacific grew to astronomical proportions, reaching $1,521,213 in January 1920. After settlements were made with the USRA, these sums were turned over to the parent company, as well as funds set aside to apply toward rebate coupons in the passenger fare dispute. By February 1925, the interest on advances from the CPR had been narrowed to $147,846. At that point South Shore comptroller Arthur E. Delf told the parent company that anything over fixed charges, not including CPR bond interest, would have to go to improvements. Delf also reported that the ICC did not think the DSS&A should be making interest payments to the CPR. A frustrated I. G. Ogden, vice president of the CPR, did not see how "it is of any of their affair," and questioned how it could "be expected that this Company will use its free cash to loan out, without any charge of interest." As a practical matter, however, the CPR did not show interest on its South Shore 4 percent bonds as an asset, realizing this large sum would have to be eventually written off.[16]

Some of the line improvements made by the DSS&A during the 1920s included the relaying of parts of the main line with 80-pound rail, a ballast program, and lengthened sidings at Bergland, Thomaston, Au Train, Ridge, Creighton, McMillan, and Wetmore. Two new Consolidations (91, 92) for switching and two more Pacifics (555, 556) for passenger service were ordered from American Locomotive Company's Brooks works. The Pacifics, slightly heavier and more powerful than the earlier 550s, developed a solid reputation with the South Shore crews. The two Consolidations were also well liked and lasted until the end of steam. The superheated Consolidations' favorite haunt was the Marquette ore dock, where they performed the majority of the 494 yard shifts during the 1925 season.

The booming siliceous ore business caused the South Shore to purchase 125 former Duluth, Missabe & Northern 50-ton ore cars (9400 to 9524) in April 1925 and an additional 150 50-ton cars (9525–9674) from the same company in the spring of 1926. These turned out to be the last ore cars ever purchased by the DSS&A. The continuing heavy winter movement of hardwood logs caused the road to order 200 new 40-foot, 40-ton steel underframe flat cars (13100–13498 even nos.) from Pullman in the summer of 1924, allowing for reductions in rental to other roads. Later that year, the Soo Line built eleven cabooses (579–589) to their pattern to care for the South Shore's expanded freight business. These complemented a dozen similar cabooses (566–578) that had been constructed in the DSS&A's own Marquette shops between 1910 and 1919.

These were the peak tonnage years on the DSS&A, with freight business totaling over four million tons in 1924, 1925, and 1929, never to be equaled during the remainder of the road's existence. Passenger business, on the other hand, reached its zenith in 1920 and then started a steady decline due to increasing use of private automobiles and buses by the traveling public. The 1924 deer hunting season saw 1,200 automobiles cross the Straits of Mackinac, while only 200 cars had made crossing in 1923. This shift represented a $16,000 loss in passenger revenue for the South Shore. In an attempt to stem the tide, the DSS&A spruced up its passenger fleet with six new cars from Pullman. The new equipment included four 67′9½″-long, 82-seat coaches, two of which were first class (703, 704) and two second class (605, 606). Two 70-foot mail and express cars (102, 103) with a 30-foot working mail compartment made up the rest of the order.

Engine 92 is shown in a typical pose, making a run out of the Upper Yard for ore dock No. 6 at Marquette on May 29, 1948. *Wilbur C. Whittaker*

No. 572 is one of a dozen cabooses that were constructed from a Soo Line pattern at the Marquette shops between 1910 and 1919. Wilbur Whittaker captured it at Marquette on May 20, 1948. *Wilbur C. Whittaker*

No. 704 rests at the Fifth Street depot in Marquette in August 1947. This was one of a series of four new steel coaches purchased from Pullman and placed in service in May 1925. The purchase of these new cars failed to halt the declining passenger business, and they would be the last new passenger cars purchased by the DSS&A. *Wesley Perron Railroad Collection, Peter White Public Library, Marquette, Mich.*

The new equipment was put into service on trains 1 and 2 between Marquette and Mackinaw City early in 1925, but proved of little help in reversing the trend toward the private automobile.

Some additional expenditures were made necessary by natural causes. The South Shore's facilities in Marquette were hard-hit when a fire broke out in the old Marquette, Houghton & Ontonagon Fifth Street roundhouse on March 26, 1925. The solid stone walls, built in 1869, were immune from the flames, but everything made of wood, including the roof, succumbed. Although the fire was under control within 45 minutes, the blaze had a quick start and the very intense heat made it impossible to pull any of the seven locomotives from their stalls.

Another major blow to the South Shore's infrastructure occurred on July 16, 1926, when a tornado took three spans of the Bad River viaduct and blew them into the river. The twister also leveled a nearby section house, but its occupant was able to survive and flag down an approaching train which likely would have met with catastrophe. Two of the wrecked spans were found salvageable and put back into place with derricks. The remaining span was replaced temporarily in wood until a new one could be secured. The bridge went back into service in four days' time.

FURTHER CONSOLIDATION AT THE
HEAD OF THE LAKES

The DSS&A's Soo Line management sought to reduce expenses, or at least have them stay in the family, through a further consolidation of operations at Superior, Wisconsin. On April 1, 1925, the South Shore's yard and engine facility was closed and its freight trains began to use the Soo Line facilities at 21st Street. At the same time DSS&A passenger movements ceased using the Lake Superior Terminal & Transfer's Union Depot and began stopping at the Wisconsin Central depot. This was made possible by giving South Shore passenger trains trackage rights over the Soo Line from the 28th Street crossing to the depot.[17]

Eastbound DSS&A freight trains began to be made up in the Soo's Stinson Avenue yard in 1931, although crews still came out of the Belknap yard with their power and caboose. Inbound trains from Thomaston continued to be yarded at Belknap to speed interchange with the LST&T. Even so, the new arrangement greatly delayed the interchange of cars with the LST&T and Northern Pacific in comparison with the direct interchange that existed before 1925. The South Shore also claimed the use of Stinson yard added to its initial terminal delay costs. The Soo Line scoffed at these complaints, saying the South Shore had incurred plenty of terminal expense under the old setup by having its road crews switch out empties, defective cars, and industries, and by having them work three different interchanges. The South Shore's Iron River Turn, which had performed many of these duties, was extended to Thomaston as a result of the consolidation. Local business on the independent extension had fallen to the point that the local went out one day and came back the next.

The South Shore's once "valuable" Superior waterfront property was stripped of its trackage and buildings. The roundhouse and sandhouse were removed in 1925 and the remaining trackage the following year. Beginning in 1931 the DSS&A did not even bother to pay taxes on the land. The boom in Superior waterfront property had long since passed, with no new docks having been constructed since 1910, and the last extension having taken place in 1922.[18]

The joint Soo-DSS&A Superior freight house near the passenger station, consolidated in 1911, was closed on March 1, 1938, when all Twin Ports less-than-carload business started to be handled in the 10th Ave. freight house in Duluth. The final South Shore outpost at the Head of the Lakes, the agency at Superior East End, was closed on April 1, 1933.

PRUNING THE BRANCHES

Unfortunately for the South Shore, the lumber market fell off at the same time much of its siliceous ore business began going to Escanaba in 1926. As well as local log and lumber business, interline lumber from the Pacific Northwest also declined. Cutbacks were made in track maintenance and the DSS&A looked to get rid of some of its less viable branches. The Bessemer branch had managed to survive mainly through the efforts of Agent R. A. Marsh. Marsh had started a wood and coal business on the side at Bessemer and this proved to be the major source of traffic. Marsh also operated an auto service between Bessemer and Bessemer Jct., handling mail and passengers in connection with main line trains. The branch was an operating headache, as the Superior-Thomaston local, which handled the branch on its westbound trip, was forced to use a small engine because of weight restrictions between Bessemer Jct. and Bessemer.

Deferred maintenance caught up with the branch in 1927. The railroad claimed that it would take thousands of dollars to upgrade the line and that its traffic did not warrant rehabilitation. Although a number of government and business officials appeared in opposition at the ICC hearing, the body ruled that the average 2,200 tons of freight handled over the branch the last five years did not justify the South Shore service. An order authorizing abandonment was issued January 30, 1928, and the enterprising Agent Marsh was left without service to his fiefdom.[19]

The South Shore next decided to prune off its 8.7-mile-long appendage from Humboldt to Republic. Although this branch had been highly profitable when Republic ore moved to the Marquette dock, traffic had waned since 1912, when Cleveland-Cliffs took over the mine. Since then the DSS&A had only handled all-rail ore moving to furnaces along its route or connections. When the Republic mine ceased operating on June 1, 1927, even this traffic evaporated. All that was left was a little pulp, potatoes, Christmas trees, and some inbound coal. Service was provided twice a week with small classes of power. After the reorganized CM&StP, now known as the Chicago, Milwaukee, St. Paul & Pacific (CMStP&P, or Milwaukee Road), agreed to handle the DSS&A's Republic business at no higher rates, abandonment proceedings went smoothly, and ICC authorization was obtained on April 10, 1928.[20]

The 11.1 miles of the old south main line between Marquette and the Queen mine was put up for abandonment in 1930, as well as the half-mile connecting track between the north and south main lines at Eagle Mills. Since the cave-in at the Queen, all trains coming up the low-grade line had to go over the connecting track at Eagle Mills and resume their journey on the north main. The South Shore management felt that the South Shore's traffic could be handled over the north main without difficulty, and approval for removing the south line was received on October 28, 1930.[21]

Northern Wisconsin found itself in the national spotlight in the summer of 1928, when President Calvin Coolidge decided to spend his summer vacation at the lodge of Henry Clay Pierce, a St. Louis oil magnate. The lodge, located on Cedar Island in the Brule River, had its closest rail access 4.5 miles away at Winneboujou station on the DSS&A. South Shore forces undertook a flurry of activity to get the line ready for the presidential visit. The Winneboujou shelter shed was replaced by a new 60-foot depot, and a new platform was constructed. An 800-foot siding was built to hold the presidential special, as well as a 40,000-gallon water tank east of the depot. The route from Superior to Winneboujou was upgraded to ensure the president had a smooth ride. At Iron River, a wye was placed to turn the special. The South Shore's best passenger power, the 555 and 556, were sent out of Marquette on June 11 to protect the special. An entire crew was sent to Winneboujou for the summer to meet the needs of the presidential party.

All the preparations were largely for naught, as after the long trip from Washington the chief executive had had enough train travel and relied on a motorcade to take him from Superior to Cedar Island. Mrs. Coolidge remained on the train and arrived at Winneboujou about a half-hour after the president. A South Shore pilot train ran 30 minutes ahead of the special from the Allouez into Winneboujou with a speeder making

The Republic Mine was a strong revenue producer for the MH&O and DSS&A, in spite of additional service offered by the C&NW and CM&StP roads. By the time this photo was taken in October 1919, the traffic had largely disappeared due to its takeover by Cleveland-Cliffs in 1912. After that time, shipments were largely made over CCI's subsidiary, the Lake Superior & Ishpeming.   *Paananen Collection*

Iron River, Wisconsin, July 14, 1932

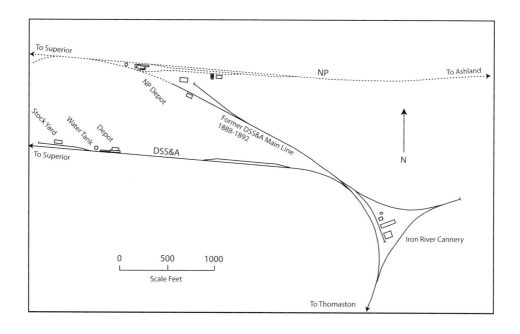

the same run a half-hour before that. The presidential party departed for Washington on September 10, and Winneboujou returned to its forgotten slumber.

HARD TIMES IN THE COPPER COUNTRY

The Mineral Range suffered the first of a series of setbacks when the Copper Range Railroad outbid them for the hauling contract between the Mohawk and Wolverine mines and the Gay stamp, effective December 15, 1917. The MR would never regain this important contract during the remaining 15 years of Mohawk operation. The MR did continue to handle the output from the Allouez and Ahmeek mines, with the latter now being the northernmost mine served by the MR, turning out around 5,000 tons of rock a day in January 1918. On the South Range line, the Mass was shipping 1,000 tons of copper rock a day to Keweenaw Bay. Given its grade, the Mass was having a difficult time producing copper at the government's price. After the Isle Royale mine was taken into the Calumet and Hecla fold, the Mineral Range began hauling its rock from Pilgrim (east of Houghton) to their stamp at Point Mills.[22]

The Mineral Range's Lake Linden–Gay passenger run, which replaced the Calumet-Gay run at the beginning of World War I, was discontinued with the Copper Range takeover of the Mohawk trackage. This train went back to making three trips between Lake Linden and Hancock before being eliminated altogether with the takeover of the Mineral Range by the USRA. Operation along the Shore Line was thereafter assumed by the Copper Range Railroad. The South Shore's CM&StP connection, Nos. 103 and 104, was also diverted to the CR, while the other three South Shore trains continued to run to Calumet on MR trackage. Shore Line service was not resumed following the end of federal control, but Nos. 103 and 104 were put back on the Mineral Range main line between Houghton and Calumet. This move was appreciated by Hancock residents, who preferred the more centrally located Mineral Range depot over the Copper Range station situated just north of the Portage Lake bridge.

Following the cessation of hostilities, the price of copper fell dramatically, as did that of most raw materials. Calumet and Hecla and its subsidiaries by 1919 were down to 50 percent capacity. Before the war, C&H had placed 70 percent of its copper output in Germany, a market which totally dried up with the war. C&H was forced to compete in the domestic market, where supply already exceeded demand. The branch from Arcadian Jct. to Point Mills fell on hard times as the Franklin mine and stamp shut down in 1918. The operation of the Centennial stamp was discontinued the same year, and the mines' output was transferred to the Calumet and Hecla mill. About all that was left to handle on the branch was an occasional car of supplies to the exploratory work of the Arcadian Mining Company.

The low price of copper forced the shutdown of the Mass Consolidated mine at Mass on December 8, 1919, with the stamp mill at Keweenaw Bay following suit four days later. Mass Consolidated said the price of copper was currently lower than the cost of production, and it had on hand some 1,250,000 pounds of unsold copper. The company hoped to resume operations when "conditions become normal," but normalcy would never return for the Mass mine.[23] With the loss of mine traffic, the major industry on the South Range line became the mill at Alston and various shippers of timber products. Ties and poles were rafted down the Sturgeon River in the early twenties to be loaded out at Pelkie. Pelkie was also the site of some potato loading for the Chicago market, along with nearby Kuro.

The South Range line service was officially cut west of Simar on October 5, 1923, as the result of the Michigan Public Utilities Commission condemning the Fire Steel bridge. If the Mass and Michigan mines reactivated, their preparation time was judged to be sufficient to build a new bridge over the Fire Steel. Rails on the west end were to be left intact. The Mineral Range constructed a 2-stall engine house and coaling platform at Keweenaw Bay to accommodate the required change in operation. On the west end, a wye was placed at Francis to turn the motive power. As resumption of South Range mining activity became increasingly unlikely, the Mineral Range was given permission to remove its rail west of Simar (MP 29.66) on August 26, 1926. The remaining portion of the line continued to more than meet operating expenses and provided needed interchange to the parent DSS&A at Keweenaw Bay.

Calumet and Hecla dealt a blow to the Mineral Range's remaining rock business by ceasing mine production entirely on April 1, 1921, due to the deep recession. In these difficult times, with copper selling for only 13 cents a pound, the mine owners were becoming increasingly frustrated by the high freight rates charged by the common carriers on rock and coal shipments. Coal could be brought up the lakes for 30 cents a ton to Torch Lake and Houghton, but from the docks to the north end mines, the railroads tacked on an additional 80 to 83 cents a ton. This was more than the cost of the coal itself. Rail rates, as a result of increases granted during federal control, were more than twice the pre-war levels.

After a one-year layoff C&H resumed mining operations, with negotiations continuing in regard to rock rates. At the end of federal control in 1920, the Mineral Range had been hauling rock from the Ahmeek to the stamps at 24.5 cents per ton, and at 18.5 cents from the Kearsarge. C&H wanted these reduced to 12 cents and 10 cents respectively. With the Mineral Range's actual cost estimated at 17.6 cents in winter and 14.5 cents in summer, the only way the Mineral Range could meet C&H's figures would be to operate at a loss. A counteroffer of 17 cents was refused by C&H, who decided it would be best to go it alone as a private carrier.

Calumet and Hecla proceeded to build a 9.3-mile line connecting Ahmeek mine shafts 3 and 4 with the Osceola stamp at Mills and the Ahmeek stamp just west of Hubbell along Torch Lake. Operations started on September 1, 1925, with Calumet and Hecla Consolidated purchasing the various H&C spurs serving their shaft houses at the Centennial, South Kearsarge, Kearsarge, North Kearsarge, No. 4 Kearsarge, Allouez, and Ahmeek mines. Trackage rights over the H&C main line from Kearsarge to Ahmeek were obtained to allow the C&H crews to reach these properties. Following ICC approval on October 19, 1926, and further negotiations, C&H made an outright purchase of this segment, as well as of trackage to reach the Ahmeek and Osceola stamp mills at Upper Mills. The transaction marked the end of Mineral Range's long career as a rock hauler.[24]

The loss of the copper rock and coal business was devastating to the Mineral Range. In 1925 the MR handled 1,377,519 tons of freight, but this figure dropped to 473,230 the following year. Copper rock totals fell from 841,139 tons in 1925 to zero in 1926. Coal tonnage fell from 106,999 to 76,942 as C&H started handling its own fuel to the mines. The

One of the former Mineral Range engines, Class F-5 Consolidation No. 715, is shown bringing an Extra East down along Marquette's Upper Yard in May 1948. On the hill to the right are several industries the DSS&A serviced along Washington Ave. *Collection of Harold K. Vollrath*

12.8-mile Hancock & Calumet line between Lake Jct. and Ahmeek lost 95 percent of its business and its reason for being. Following the sale of portions to C&H, the ICC approved abandonment of 2 miles of the line from Calumet to Kearsarge on August 5, 1927, and some 6 miles between Lake Jct. and Osceola on March 10, 1930. The only surviving H&C trackage from Hancock (Lake Shore Jct.) to Lake Linden remained valuable, generating $93,000 in revenue for the railroad in 1929, and continued to see daily service. In addition to the copper producers, the Shore Line was still home to two lumber mills, Dollar Bay Lumber Co. at Dollar Bay, and Bonifas-Gorman Lumber Company at Lake Linden.

The Arcadian Mining Company had been valiantly carrying on exploratory work at its property on the Point Mills branch, but finally gave up the work in 1926. This left no reason to maintain the Mineral Range branch between Arcadian Jct. and Point Mills, and permission to abandon was received from the ICC on September 22, 1927.

With the loss of almost all its business, the Mineral Range found itself with a large excess of power. The South Shore purchased four of the Mineral Range "hogs" (MR 195–198 to DSS&A 712–715) on August 15, 1924. Calumet and Hecla, in need of additional power to man its Trap Rock Valley Railroad, followed on February 1, 1926, by taking ownership of two more Consolidations (MR 194, 199). Although the South Shore tried to interest C&H in purchasing two Mineral Range 0-6-0 switchers (162, 163), they ended up going to the South Shore (50, 51) in 1926, as did two more Consolidations (MR 300,

The 604, an old F-1 class Consolidation, engages in some passenger car switching in the Upper Yard at Marquette on July 6, 1936. The 600s had been largely relegated to yard switching since the arrival of the Mineral Range Consolidations in the mid-1920s.   *Collection of Harold K. Vollrath*

301 to DSS&A 716, 717). The MR Consolidations were the largest power on the South Shore roster until arrival of the ex–New York Central Mikado types in the late thirties and were said to run quite well considering their small drivers. These larger Consolidations were quickly put into service on through freights between Superior and St. Ignace, with the smaller Consolidations being bumped onto 31 and 32 and local service.

No. 2 passes over the east siding switch as it comes into Trout Lake with a 550-class and three cars in May 1947. It will soon bang over the Soo Line diamond and make its station stop. One of the interchange tracks with the Soo Line is seen to the right of the engine pilot.   *Collection of Harold K. Vollrath*

11

DRASTIC CUTS— BANKRUPTCY

The South Shore's passenger business faced a number of detrimental factors in the 1930s. Even though the population of the Michigan counties served by the DSS&A had fallen from 234,184 in 1910 to 213,527 in 1940, automobile registration during the same period had risen from 2,130 to 9,522 in Marquette County and from 2,228 to 8,577 in Houghton County. To accommodate the new form of transportation, the State of Michigan had expended $52 million on road construction and maintenance in the Upper Peninsula. Even during the harsh UP winters the traffic did not revert to the rails, as the state became involved in snow removal in 1924 and in 1937 adopted a policy to keep all state roads clear at all times. All these factors, plus the personal freedom of the automobile, saw DSS&A passenger revenue plummet from $1,373,965 in 1923 to $248,224 in 1938.[1]

South Shore management had little choice but to keep pace by reducing passenger train miles. Trains 3 and 4 ("the Northwestern train") between Calumet and Marquette were discontinued on April 29, 1928. Losing their Nestoria connection, trains 5 and 6 had their runs extended from Michigamme into Marquette. As Nos. 5 and 6 were the last trains to tie up at the old Michigamme terminal, this allowed the closing of facilities at that point.

The Soo Line, and no doubt the Canadian Pacific, felt expenses were not being cut expeditiously enough, and General Manager C. E. Lytle was forced into retirement on April 1, 1929. As the South Shore had no pension for its employees, he was given a job as assistant to the vice president and continued to manage the Mackinac Transportation Company. The Soo Line brought in their own man, C. E. Urbahns, to take up offices in the second floor of the Marquette passenger station. Urbahns had started railroading with the Nickel Plate Road as a telegrapher in 1885, working his way up to become chief train dispatcher. He came to the Wisconsin Central in the same capacity on April 1, 1904, and within a year was made trainmaster at Abbottsford, Wisconsin. He went on to become superintendent at Stevens Point, Wisconsin, and on April 1, 1920, was made general superintendent of the Soo Line system.[2]

With Urbahns' appointment came another round of cuts in passenger service. The crew which handled the morning C&NW connection from Ishpeming to Marquette (No. 110), a Marquette-Champion turn (Nos. 111-10) to connect with the CMStP&P, an afternoon Marquette-Ishpeming turn (9–12), and finally the evening C&NW connection (No.

11) from Marquette to Ishpeming, saw its Champion and afternoon Ishpeming legs eliminated on May 26, 1929. This change badly delayed delivery of Chicago mail. Also eliminated were trains 117 and 118 between Sault Ste. Marie and Soo Jct., No. 2's connection. Thereafter the Detroit–Sault Ste. Marie Pullman was handled over the Soo Line between the Trout Lake and the Sault.

Urbahns made another major slashing on October 6, 1929. Nos. 5 and 6, the west end locals between Duluth and Marquette, were discontinued, leaving only night runs 7 and 8 west of Nestoria. Nos. 103 and 104, which formerly operated between Calumet and Champion, were extended into Marquette to provide some additional service to the range towns. In addition, Nos. 7 and 8 were discontinued east of Marquette, and trains 13 and 16, which came down out of the Copper Country to connect with 7 and 8 at Nestoria, were also pulled off. The last straight passenger service out of the Sault on the DSS&A, Nos. 17 and 18 (No. 1's connection at Soo Jct.), were given mixed train status. Thereafter connecting traffic with Nos. 1 and 2 was largely handled by Soo Line local passenger trains Nos. 86 and 87 between Trout Lake and the Sault.

Matters were exacerbated by the economic depression that began to sweep the nation following the stock market crash of October 1929. By the end of 1930 there were over 6 million unemployed in the U.S., with a resultant decline in the need for both freight and passenger transportation. On May 11, 1930, Nos. 11 and 20, the last pair of trains out of Marquette connecting directly with the C&NW at Ishpeming, were discontinued. To make better connections and improve delivery of Chicago mail off the CMStP&P's Copper Country Limited at Champion and off North Western No. 161 at Ishpeming, DSS&A No. 8 had its departure out of Duluth advanced from 11:45 PM to 8 PM. No. 7 brought up passengers and the Chicago Pullman for C&NW 162 at Negaunee and also connected with the Copper County Limited at Champion. Nos. 103 and 104, Marquette-Calumet, were renamed 9 and 10 under the new setup.

The scope of the Depression continued to widen as unemployment figures doubled in 1931 from 1930 and over 32,000 businesses failed. The bottom, however, was not reached until 1932, and further cuts in passenger service saw the last run of the Sault Ste. Marie–Detroit sleeper being made on September 25, 1932. The parlor cars were pulled off 1 and 2 the following year, and on July 1, 1939, those trains were discontinued in their entirety between Calumet and Marquette, leaving only Nos. 9 and 10 in Marquette-Calumet service.

UP residents complained that post office delivery had been set back at least a half-day as a result of the discontinuance of 1 and 2, and that passengers arriving at Marquette on No. 10 had to wait 16 hours before they could take No. 2 to eastern points. At a hearing of the Michigan Public Utilities Commission, Representative Charles Sundstrom of Michigamme maintained that the South Shore was a "Canadian concern . . . not trying to get business."[3]

Urbahns countered that new equipment had been placed on the trains in 1925 and ridership had continued to fall. Given its financial situation, Urbahns also said, the DSS&A could hardly be expected to operate the train at a loss. The Michigan Public Utilities Commission saw otherwise and ordered the trains reinstated on December 13, 1939. The state contended, "The public does not guarantee to those engaged in a public service that they will make a profit."[4]

The DSS&A took the matter to state court, which issued an injunction putting off the reestablishment pending trial. This proved but a temporary respite, as the court

Paynesville Depot

Paynesville, Michigan, was one of a number of South Shore stations to receive concrete block depots. This one had second-story living quarters for the agent and his family. The agency was closed during the budget cuts of 1931. *Paananen Collection*

ruled that the railroad had the burden to prove the Public Service Commission had acted unreasonably in its decision, and that the "plaintiff owe a duty of a public character, the duty to render reasonably adequate service to the public so long as the franchise of the Railroad Company is exercised."[5] Service was restored on August 4, 1941, nearly two years after its initial discontinuance. The DSS&A did manage to shorten the run of 9 and 10, eliminating the leg between Marquette and Champion on September 28, 1941. A South Shore crew based at Champion thereafter handled the CMStP&P's Copper Country Limited to Calumet, with a DSS&A steamer being kept at the Milwaukee Road's Champion engine house.

Urbahns also looked to reduce expenses by closing a number of open stations. One of the first to go was Humboldt in 1929. Humboldt had generated only $3,051 in freight and $1,157 in passenger revenue during 1928. At Sidnaw, the Milwaukee Road received permission to discontinue its manual interlocking, and color light signals operated in conjunction with gates were substituted. Agency stations at Au Train, Eckerman, and Paynesville were all closed in 1931, and Soo Jct., Kenton, Nestoria, Herman, and Keweenaw Bay followed the next year. An operator continued to be employed at the important junction at Nestoria. Chassell, Moran, Strongs, and Wetmore were closed in 1933.

The crossing of the South Shore and the Lake Superior & Ishpeming at the east end of the Lower Yard at Marquette, known as the Gas House interlocker, was converted to an unmanned interlocker in 1934. Another crossing with the LS&I, at Eagle Mills, was turned into an automatic interlocking in 1935, replacing the mechanical interlocking at

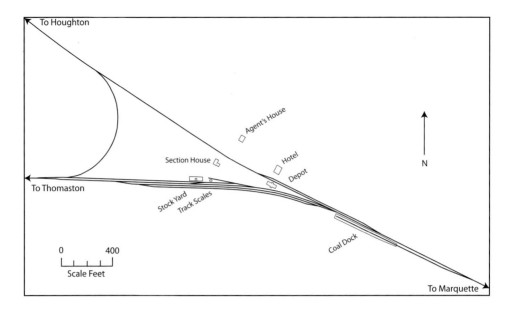

To Houghton

Agent's House

Section House

Hotel

Depot

To Thomaston

Stock Yard

Track Scales

N

Coal Dock

0   400

Scale Feet

To Marquette

Nestoria, Michigan, June 24, 1924

that point. A 1938 petition to the Michigan Public Utilities Commission resulted in the closing of the agencies at Michigamme, McMillan, and Shingleton, and the joint LS&I station at Munising Jct. The PUC ruled that Brimley had enough business to maintain an agency, but moderated its stand in 1943, allowing the agency to close as long as caretakers and "reasonable" service were provided.[6]

At Marquette's Lower Yard, the 14-stall roundhouse and turntable were removed during the spring of 1928, and all repairs and servicing were done thereafter in the Upper Yard. A reduction through natural causes took place on February 9, 1930, when fire took the L'Anse roundhouse. Although a new engine house was planned, because of the worsening economy the project was cut back to just a bucket coal shed. Thereafter the L'Anse pusher was kept outside under the eyes of an engine watchman. Even with the cuts the DSS&A still remained important to the economy of the UP, especially to Marquette, where, in 1929, it was the town's largest employer with 782 people on the payroll. Of these, 343 were employed in the shops, 199 in train and engine service, 139 in the office and depot, 71 in the Bridge and Building and Maintenance of Way departments, and 30 on the dock.[7]

On February 1, 1932, the South Shore instituted a 10 percent wage cut, but this was minor compared to the job losses that occurred at Marquette that November, when the Soo Line took over the DSS&A's accounting and treasury departments and began doing the work in Minneapolis. Eliminated were the positions of comptroller, assistant auditor, treasurer, and 41 clerks. Within a year the car service, freight claim, personnel, and real estate departments were also sent off to Minneapolis. With all the cutbacks the South Shore's headquarters city became concerned about its status and afraid that even more drastic cuts were in the offing. C. E. Urbahns said there was no intention of closing the South Shore shops or moving any other operating department out of Marquette. Urbahns

What was called the Gas House interlocking, due to its close approximation to the Marquette Gas Plant, governed the crossing with the Lake Superior & Ishpeming at the east end of the Lower Yard in Marquette. *Paananen Collection*

went on to say, "It is true, as most everyone knows, that the South Shore railroad, because of dwindling income from freight and passenger service, has been and will be forced to pare operating expenses wherever possible . . . but these rumors that we are planning curtailment to the point of seriously crippling the road are ridiculous."[8]

Mr. Urbahns' statements to Marquette were not completely aboveboard, as the Soo Line was actively seeking an arrangement with the LS&I to shop the South Shore motive power at its modern facilities. It was felt that there was nothing to be gained by sending locomotives to the Soo Line's Shoreham shops in Minneapolis as tariff rates would have to be charged, wiping out any savings. Although the locomotive work remained in Marquette, the Soo Line management felt the DSS&A's coach shop was "poorly equipped," and all heavy passenger car repairs were made at Shoreham effective July 29, 1933.[9] In addition, only locomotives and cars needed to care for the reduced business were kept in repair during the bleak economic times.

Although the terminal at Marquette remained safe during the Depression years, the same was not true for Thomaston. On December 22, 1935, the agency, roundhouse, servicing facilities, and rip track at that point were discontinued, and the crew change was moved to Ewen, 32 miles to the east. The half-dozen mechanical department men who had no seniority other than at Thomaston were thrown out of work in the midst of

The second Thomaston depot, built in 1914, also served as a hotel, restaurant, and post office. The building became redundant with the closure of the Thomaston terminal in 1935 and was replaced by a passenger shelter remodeled from the old sand house. *Interstate Commerce Commission*

the Depression. Facilities at Ewen were kept to a minimum. Crews tied up with their power and caboose on a short track inside the wye, where an engine watchman kept an eye on things. The enginemen had a bunkhouse in the depot waiting room, while the trainmen slept in their caboose. Although there was a water tank east of the depot, there were no coaling facilities at Ewen, and the three yard tracks made for crowded conditions at times after business picked up.[10]

The change of terminal was important as the result of elimination of all local freight runs on the South Shore, effective July 9, 1933. Local runs St. Ignace–Soo Jct. (25–26), Sault Ste. Marie–Soo Jct. (27–28), Soo Jct.–Marquette (23–24), Marquette-Houghton (33–34), Nestoria-Thomaston (53–54), and Thomaston-Superior (55–56) were all done away with, and the tasks of doing local work, including peddling local merchandise, were passed on to time freights. The stripped-down DSS&A freight service consisted only of Nos. 21 and 22 (St. Ignace–Superior), Nos. 31 and 32 (Marquette–East Houghton), and the Sault branch mixed (Nos. 18 and 19). Local work primarily fell upon No. 21, and, as the majority of the business was between Marquette and Ewen, the change in terminal from Thomaston made it easier to get over the road under the hours of service law.

Nos. 21, 31, and 32 and ore extras were also required to do the work around Ishpeming and Negaunee after the switch engines were pulled off at those points. In August 1930 the DSS&A's Ishpeming freight house was moved to the north side of Ridge Street to make room for the new Cohodas cold storage facility, which became a major consignee for the road. The trackage around Ishpeming was further modified in 1933 when 1.41 miles of the old Marquette, Houghton & Ontonagon, or south line, was abandoned between Winthrop Jct. and South Ishpeming. Any switching at South Ishpeming required No. 21 to come in from the Negaunee end.

The Great Depression in its first full year had a profound effect on the South Shore's earnings. Movement of forest products, newsprint, and unfinished metal products such

Following the closure of the Thomaston terminal, the next available water tank to the east was at Lake Gogebic, Michigan. A bucket coaling station was also added at this point in 1937. The Lake Gogebic coal shed was only used when the normal coaling locations of Ashland and Trout Creek did not suffice. *Michigan Technological University and Copper Country Historical Collections, Herman Page Collection, Negative 03665*

The 1054, an L-2 class Mikado, waits in the clear at Cohodas Brothers, a produce
distributor and an important South Shore customer at Ishpeming. The old Marquette
& Western depot facilities were demolished in 1930 to provide a site for this industry
and a new freight house was constructed, at the extreme right of the photo. Wilbur
Whittaker took this photo, probably from the rear of No. 2, on May 20, 1948.
Wilbur C. Whittaker

as pig iron and copper ingots fell in 1930 as industries cut back, causing gross revenues
to drop 25 percent. A backlog of iron ore at the lower lake ports saw iron ore revenue fall
37 percent. Passenger revenue fell 35 percent due to decreased travel and increased auto
and bus use. Similar decreases followed in 1931, when non-iron-ore freight revenue declined another 29 percent, iron ore fell off another 25 percent, and passenger revenue 38
percent.

The trucking industry continued to take its toll. As jitney bus and truck operators
were having a very detrimental effect on the South Shore's business, Marquette supported the passage of truck and bus legislation at the state house in Lansing in an attempt to protect its jobs. The new legislation gave the Public Utilities Commission the
power to regulate motor carrier rates and schedules. By 1929 the first log trucks were
being put to use, reducing movement of a valuable wintertime commodity to the South
Shore. The Depression also had an increasing effect as many of the logging camps closed
down with no market for their logs.

SOUTH SHORE DOCK COMPANY

In spite of the severe economic conditions, plans were formulated for a new ore dock at
Marquette to replace the elderly Dock No. 5. C. E. Lytle strongly urged the construction
of a concrete dock, saying the South Shore had been extremely fortunate to escape a fire
to its lone wooden dock. Such a catastrophe would put the DSS&A in desperate straits,
especially if suffered during the ore season. Given the condition of Dock 5, the fact that

the new Ford boats were unable to utilize the facility due to its low height, and complaints from vessel captains about lengthy loading times, the South Shore had no choice but to go ahead with a new dock, in spite of steadily falling revenues.

In the fall of 1930 plans were ready for a 969′ long, 67′9½″ wide concrete dock with a 3,546-foot approach. From the dock floor to Lake Superior was 85′7″, making it the highest dock on the upper lakes. Stacking the first three pocket docks constructed at Marquette would dwarf the new dock by only 5 feet, and their total capacity would only fill 20 of its 150 350-ton pockets. The line to the new ore dock, known as No. 6, would take off from the east end of the roundhouse lead, just west of Fifth Street. This longer approach, made up of timber and steel spans, would allow the ruling grade to be reduced despite the higher dock.

The South Shore Dock Company, which would build the new dock, was incorporated on March 11, 1931. South Shore Dock floated $1,000,000 in first mortgage bonds which were backed by the Canadian Pacific. All South Shore Dock Company capital stock was owned by the DSS&A, with C. T. Jaffray, the DSS&A's president, also heading the dock company.[11]

Merritt, Chapman and Whitney Corporation, of Duluth, received a contract on April 1, 1931, to have the dock ready for operation by the opening of navigation 1932. Construction commenced almost as soon as the ice left the bay with the driving of the first test pile on April 16. That summer, the South Shore main line, which threaded between the shops and the Upper Yard tracks, was shifted for 1.42 miles to the far northern edge of the Upper Yard to make way for the new ore dock approach. The last boat, *George R. Fink,* departed from Dock 5 on November 14, 1931. Demolition was immediately begun as it stood in the way of the approach to the new Dock 6. Dock 5's final season saw a fairly respectable 409,770 tons of ore being shipped. The Blueberry mine led the way, followed by the Richmond. Although tonnage had dropped by 25 percent from the 1930 season, this was much smaller than the 50 percent decline for the Lake Superior district as a whole.

Mild weather allowed ore dock work to proceed ahead of schedule during the winter of 1931–1932. The first rails were laid on the dock on November 19, 1931, and the hanging of the first chutes occurred four days later. The new dock was turned over to the operating department on May 15, 1932. With the new dock, engine 91 or 92 could "easily" take 30 loads up onto the dock, compared to only 10 with Dock 5.[12]

Unfortunately the South Shore was now equipped with one of the finest docks on the lakes, but there was little use for it. The first ore, 30 cars from the Blueberry mine, was dumped into the pockets on June 3, 1932, and the *Henry Ford II* loaded the first cargo three days later. In an indication of the times, the second shipment was taken out by the same boat almost two weeks later on June 19. One new mining development that occurred in 1930 was the opening of the Greenwood mine, reached by a spur off the South Shore main line at Greenwood. The new development, however, did not aid the South Shore ore hauling fortunes, as Inland Steel, owner of the Greenwood, had its mills in the Chicago area and the movement would all be to Escanaba. The C&NW was given trackage rights over the South Shore from Winthrop Jct. to Greenwood, and served the mine exclusively.

In the midst of the Great Depression, work is proceeding on the superstructure of the new South Shore ore dock No. 6. Work on the massive dock was begun on April 16, 1931, and completed 13 months later. *Library of Congress, Prints & Photographs Division, HAER, MICH, 52-MARQ, 16-5*

ABANDONMENT OF THE WEST END

The independent extension into Superior had yielded little in the way of local traffic since the exhaustion of the pine lumber trade in northern Wisconsin. In the continuing search to reduce expenses, the South Shore reached agreement with the Northern Pacific to operate over its little-used Ashland line for 62 miles between Ashland and Superior East End. Ashland would be reached by 12 miles of trackage rights over the Wisconsin Central from Marengo. This scheme would permit the DSS&A to abandon 73 miles of line. Under the 999-year contracts, both effective May 1, 1933, the South Shore was not allowed to do local business along the WC or NP except at Iron River, which it had formerly served, and at Allouez to connect with the Northwestern Coal Railway.[13]

The petition for abandonment with the ICC met with opposition from the Superior Association of Commerce, the Wisconsin attorney general, the Wisconsin Public Service Commission, and Stella Cheese Co. of Lake Nebagamon, the principal industry along the line. These groups argued that current operating losses should not be considered in a time of depression and that recent legislation regulating motor carriers in Wisconsin would have a positive effect.

These arguments proved to no avail, and the ICC approved the abandonment petition on April 19, 1934. The ICC felt that, as the parallel NP and DSS&A lines were lightly

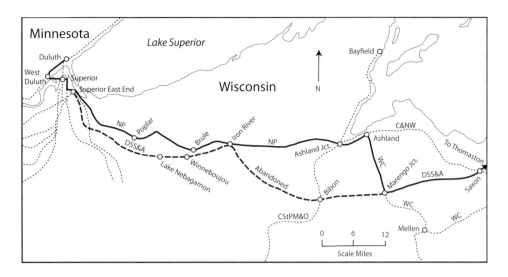

Abandonment and New Trackage Rights, Marengo Jct. to Superior East End,
June 10, 1934

traveled, no operational difficulties would result, and that patrons would be little incon-
venienced. It was also felt the South Shore would be hard-pressed to rehabilitate its
trackage between Marengo and Superior given its financial position. Work was immediately started on the new 0.6-mile connecting track between the South Shore and WC
at Marengo Jct. In Superior, South Shore trains would continue to use DSS&A trackage
between the Soo Line yard and Superior East End. There the South Shore joined the
CStPM&O as before, but only for 0.21 miles until heading around the connecting
track to the NP Ashland line at Newton Avenue tower. The new operating scheme
went into effect at 12:01 AM on June 10, 1934, with No. 8 out of Duluth making use of the
old line for the last time on June 9. No. 7, leaving Marquette on the 9th, used the new
route through Ashland.[14]

Shortly after the DSS&A started running over the WC and NP, Ashland interests
began objecting to the contract provision that prevented the South Shore from stopping
in their community. At a hearing of the Wisconsin Public Service Commission, Commissioner McDonald said he would order the South Shore train to stop, regardless of the
NP contract. The railroads agreed to comply, with the DSS&A giving the NP 50 percent
of all revenue handled locally between the Twin Ports and Ashland. The South Shore
started using the WC Ashland depot in exchange for paying the entire expense of one
operator. Still another change came in June 1936, when the South Shore was allowed to
shift its WC interchange on Pacific Coast lumber shipments from Marengo Jct. to Ashland. Before this time, the DSS&A would haul the lumber cars destined to Ashland to
Marengo Jct., and the WC would back haul them. The NP agreed to allow the interchange to take place at Ashland, despite their concern over the superior DSS&A service.
The former CStPM&O exchange at Bibon was also moved into Ashland, with train 22
often having to wait for the perishables off Omaha Road time freight No. 75.

The South Shore certainly was a much more streamlined operation as a result of
the Depression-era cuts. During the ten years from 1929 to 1939, the number of

maintenance-of-way sections was reduced from 98 to 30. Twenty-two stations were closed, resulting in the telegraphers' roster being reduced from 100 to 46. The conductors' roster totaled 47 men versus 75 in 1929, while brakemen were reduced from 87 to 33. The engineers' ranks had been reduced from 89 to 43. The clerks' roster had also been decimated, with only 85 men left compared to 185 ten years before. Twenty passenger trains had been taken off since 1929, when passenger runs composed 60 percent of the South Shore's train mileage. All these reductions, along with the absence of a pension system, caused the South Shore to have a rather elderly workforce. The Federal Government's Railroad Retirement Act, which took effect February 1, 1935, soon addressed this problem for the non-scheduled employees, but left men such as 74-year-old C. E. Lytle with no choice but to hang on to jobs created for them until their days ran out.

Even with all the cutbacks, the Canadian Pacific felt that management of its U.S. properties was excessive, and a study undertaken in 1933 urged the Soo Line to make further cuts in the South Shore personnel, which was "over-staffed." The parent road felt it was unnecessary for both roads to maintain a departmental organization given their small mileage, and that the South Shore should be made a division under a Soo Line System general superintendent. The study concluded, "As far as legally can be done, coalition of the Soo Line and South Shore organizations should be extended, and, in effect, the latter should, regardless of the name by which it is known, be administered as an operating unit of the Soo Line System."[15]

The Soo Line countered that the separate corporate existence, with each road having their own bond and shareholders, made consolidation difficult, although wherever possible general officers and department heads were acting for more than one road. In light of the smaller mileage, salaries and staffing levels were much reduced compared with those on larger roads. The Soo Line went on to say it had "no financial interest in the DSS&A. The traffic of the two roads, to a large extent, is competitive. Considerable care has been exercised to minimize, as much as possible in the South Shore local territory, evidence that this property is operated by the Soo Line. If this fact becomes more apparent, the attitude of the shippers and Governmental bodies will not be influenced as much as at present by the individual showing of the property itself."[16]

The Canadian Pacific was particularly critical of the large traffic department the South Shore maintained in its Duluth office. The Soo Line countered that it could not oversee the traffic interests of the South Shore as the two lines were competitive and such authority could not be obtained from the ICC. The CPR also wanted to eliminate the South Shore's agricultural department. B. A. Heath had taken over this post and had been involved in an alfalfa-clover train run by the Soo Line and South Shore in April 1930. Depression economics then took hold, and this would be the last demonstration train ever to traverse the South Shore's rails. The Soo Line felt that the increased potato traffic along the South Shore, with some 155 cars shipped between October 1932 and June 1933, was largely the result of the actions of the DSS&A agricultural department in getting land settled and under cultivation.

With the South Shore forecasting a deficit of almost $400,000 for the year ending December 31, 1932, a loan application was made to the Railroad Credit Corporation (RCC) to meet fixed interest obligations. The RCC responded that, if the CPR backed the loan, it might consider lending the money, but otherwise it was "essential that such monies as are received be used for the benefit of carriers whose history warrants the belief that a moderate revival of traffic will enable them to stand alone."[17] The South Shore later sought to make an application for $350,000 to cover taxes, but the ICC responded that as the South Shore did not have adequate collateral, "it would be wise for us not to make an application." The ICC felt the South Shore was "a sick child of the Canadian Pacific Railway Company," and the CPR should continue to care for it.[18]

As the nation incurred financial pain not seen since the Panic of 1893, DSS&A gross revenues for 1932 declined another 40 percent below 1931 levels. Passenger revenue and non-iron-ore freight revenue both fell 37 percent, while the iron ore business totally collapsed, with only 122,314 tons being handled. The South Shore was not even able to earn its operating expenses. Scarcely able to pay its wages, the South Shore notified the Michigan Tax Commission in April that it would be unable to pay its 1931 taxes. A settlement was reached in June 1934, providing for reduced payments for the previous three years.

Fortunately the South Shore's ore tonnage saw a sizable increase in 1933 over 1932 levels, with 442,496 tons being handled. Gross revenue climbed 20 percent that year, as business gradually picked up. The passenger business, however, seemed destined for oblivion, sustaining another 23 percent drop in revenue. With another 10 percent rise in revenues in 1934, the South Shore was able to restore 2.5 percent of the 10 percent wage cut made on February 1, 1932. Another 2.5 percent was added on January 1, 1935, and the final 5 percent was restored on April 1, 1935.

One action taken by the Hoover and Roosevelt administrations to help with the high unemployment produced a number of highway projects. One such project involving the South Shore saw the relocation of Highway 41 along the Lower Yard in Marquette. The old road ran through the yard, but during 1933 and 1934, South Shore structures and trackage were rearranged to allow a new concrete highway to be built along the west side of the yard using the South Shore right of way between Fisher and Hampton Streets.

THE MINERAL RANGE STRUGGLES TO SURVIVE

With the Hancock & Calumet and Mineral Range bonds coming due in 1931, a serious discussion was undertaken as to what to do with the properties north of Houghton. Almost two-thirds of these issues were owned by the public, with the remainder in Canadian Pacific hands. It seemed unlikely a sale of the MR and H&C would satisfy the bondholders, and such a sale would also split the traffic north of Houghton between the DSS&A and Copper Range. The new owner would also receive a 30 percent rate division. The DSS&A had realized $394,000 in revenue off Mineral Range interchange traffic in 1926, and it could ill afford the drop in revenue a sale would effect. The public bondholders, glad to get out, agreed in December 1931 to sell their bonds to the CPR, allowing that road to become the sole owner of these securities.

The Mineral Range's identity became harder to discern as time went on. On May 1, 1929, DSS&A trainmen were given rights to work the MR jobs, with MR men retaining prior rights in their former territory. After trains 31 and 32 stopped running between East Houghton and Calumet, the Shore Line local freight (East Houghton–Lake Linden) started to make a side trip to Calumet. In addition to this job, MR men were able

A DSS&A F-3 Consolidation switches along Mineral Range Lake Linden line rails at Hubbell, site of the Calumet and Hecla smelter. By the time this July 1940 photo had been taken, all Mineral Range steam had been replaced with engines of the South Shore. *Collection of Harold K. Vollrath*

to work the yard jobs at East Houghton. These positions were given in exchange for the miles DSS&A crews ran in passenger service over the MR between Houghton and Calumet. Effective December 7, 1932, it was agreed the MR trackage would be made a part of the work of East Houghton yard, with the yard engines making the runs to Calumet and Lake Linden as required. One crew would usually work around Houghton, while the other made trips on the MR. The MR lost its separate roster of steam locomotives in 1933 when its remaining ten engines were sold to Paper, Calmenson and Company in Duluth for scrap. The Houghton yard jobs were thereafter powered by DSS&A steam.

Further economies taken during the Depression included combining the Calumet and Hancock agencies with those of the Copper Range railroad and instituting joint service between those points. Under the new arrangement, which took effect on January 8, 1933, Mineral Range passenger trains operated over CR trackage before tying up at the MR Calumet depot. The CR provided tri-weekly freight service for both roads. The MR's Lakeview station in Hancock was closed, as was the CR freight house in Calumet. In spite of the $6,000 in promised annual savings, the arrangement proved unsuccessful, with Hancock citizens complaining about the location of the CR depot off the Portage Lake bridge. The MR resumed running over its own rails on May 16, 1934.

The South Range line was operated as needed during the Depression. The Michigan Public Utilities Commission granted permission to close the agency at Alston on November 16, 1933, leaving no open stations on the line. Operations were cut back to Alston in 1933, although the rail to Simar was not pulled up until October 1935. With the closing of the lumber mill at Alston in April 1936, there was little business left on the line. The log traffic, which had sustained the South Range line after the mines closed, was going largely to trucks. The MR handled but 439 cars on the line during 1936, 273 of which were forest products. The South Range line did see several passenger excursions from Calumet to ski tournaments sponsored by the Alston ski club in 1937 and 1938, but these proved to be some of the final runs on the South Range line as the ICC authorized abandonment of the remaining trackage on January 24, 1938. At the end, service was provided once a week from Keweenaw Bay to Alston.[19]

BANKRUPTCY

The South Shore's gross revenues climbed nicely in 1936 with a 23 percent rise over 1935. Revenue from iron ore climbed 41 percent and passenger revenue was up 19 percent. Even the $893,198 in net operating revenue, however, could not overcome the oppressive debt payments, resulting in another deficit of $296,184 for the year. With refinancing of bonds approaching in the near future, the situation seemed hopeless, and a study by the Soo Line officers heading the DSS&A in 1933 advocated a complete reorganization of the South Shore's financial structure to put its assets and liabilities on a more rational basis. According to ICC valuation data the road was worth $17,700,000. This was balanced against stock and funded debt liabilities of almost $23,500,000, plus another $24,000,000 in interest owed the Canadian Pacific. Following adjustment of the DSS&A's finances, it was felt the Soo Line could lease the road or purchase it outright.

At a special meeting of the board of directors held on December 30, 1936, George W. Webster outlined the South Shore's plight. On January 1, $5,400,000 in Marquette, Houghton & Ontonagon, Marquette & Western, and DSS&A first mortgage bonds would mature. The Canadian Pacific, having undergone a financial crisis of its own in 1933 which had been alleviated only by a massive loan guarantee from the Canadian government, did not wish to take part in the refinancing, leaving the DSS&A with little choice but to declare bankruptcy.[20]

The South Shore filed a petition with U.S. District Court on January 2, 1937, for reorganization under the Bankruptcy Act. Edward A. Whitman and James L. Homire were appointed to act as co-trustees, assuming office on March 1, 1937. Whitman was formerly the Soo Line's chief operating officer and vice president, while Homire, nominated by the insurance companies holding South Shore bonds, had been with the New York Central's legal department before taking posts with Public Works Administration and Reconstruction Finance Corporation. The Mineral Range followed its parent company into receivership on June 30, 1937, with the South Shore trustees being appointed to like positions on that road.[21]

Shortly thereafter the creditors began to line up to stake their claims. The Canadian Pacific filed notice with the trustees on July 26, 1937, that the principal on over $15 million in 4 percent bonds had become due and payable as a result of the failure to pay interest. The South Shore also owed the CPR $813,138 in cash advances. The Central Bank Hanover Trust Company, trustee of the two South Shore mortgages, was permitted to intervene, and, under a ruling of the court, the trustees were to impound for Central Bank Hanover all income generated after the payment of expenses. A protective committee was authorized by the ICC to represent the interests of the outside holders of the

$3,199,000 in 5 percent bonds. The holders of these first mortgage bonds and the CPR had considerable difficulty in arriving at a reorganization plan, and a number of extensions were asked of the court.[22]

The lengthy reorganization proceedings proved a hardship for the trustees. Co-trustee and counsel James L. Homire resigned his post on February 1, 1941, seeing little chance for an early resolution and desiring to return to his law practice. Sigurd Ueland, a Minneapolis lawyer, was approved as the new co-trustee and counsel by the court on December 23, 1940. Ueland also resigned to devote more time to his other legal affairs, and his position as co-trustee was taken over by P. L. Solether effective June 14, 1943. Solether, another Minneapolis attorney, would become sole trustee with the passing of E. W. Whitman on August 4, 1947.[23]

The person responsible for many of the South Shore's recent economies, C. E. Urbahns, retired on October 1, 1939, at the age of 69. As the result of making the many cuts needed for the South Shore's survival, Urbahns was not very popular with the employees, who referred to him as being "merciless" and a "hatchet man." The post of head operating man was given to Herman F. Schmidt, the South Shore's trainmaster. The title of general manager was eliminated with Urbahns's retirement, and Schmidt assumed the rank of superintendent. Schmidt had started railroading with the CM&StP as a telegraph operator at Republic in November 1906 and came to the South Shore in the same capacity at Marquette on May 8, 1914, working his way up to trainmaster. Schmidt was thought by the men to be "hard boiled" and a "tough German."[24]

The South Shore's revenues, having climbed since the low level of 1932, plateaued in 1936. A severe setback occurred in 1938 when the nation dipped into a bad recession. Freight tonnages slipped back to below 1933 levels, and the DSS&A saw its revenues fall 38 percent, resulting in a net deficit of over a million dollars, the worst since 1932. The recession was short-lived, and by 1939 the country and the South Shore were on the mend. The iron ore traffic had largely recovered to pre-Depression levels by 1936, when 941,473 tons were handled off the Marquette dock. This figure slipped to 867,367 tons in 1937 and, with the 1938 recession, fell off dramatically to 178,539 tons. The 1939 season saw tonnage rebound to 639,622 tons, and traffic remained constant the following year with 642,837 tons.

The South Shore's through freight business started to improve as the result of a reorganization of its traffic department. The trustees felt the DSS&A had been short-changed when forced to rely on joint CPR-Soo-DSS&A traffic men to solicit business. The trustees hired C. C. Cameron, former freight traffic manager of the Illinois Central railroad, to investigate. Cameron found that South Shore traffic expenditures had been kept "abnormally low," with most of the money being used to pay the salaries of the joint representatives. Shippers were not adverse to giving the DSS&A a share of their business, and through rates were in place with connecting carriers out of Duluth and with the New York Central (former Michigan Central) and Pennsylvania Railroad at the Straits, but with solicitation in the hands of men who represented two competing roads (Soo Line and DSS&A), securing traffic was extremely difficult. Cameron felt the South Shore would be much better off with its own independent traffic force.[25]

This plan was implemented through the efforts of R. O. Hambly, who was appointed traffic manager in 1938. Hambly moved the traffic department to Marquette from Duluth and established eight independent offices throughout the country during the next eight years. These offices helped the South Shore gain back bridge traffic, a scarce commodity since the Soo Line takeover. The trustees reported in 1939 that the new offices had resulted in "a considerable amount of new traffic being routed over our line."[26] Still the DSS&A had a lot of ground to make up, as bridge traffic averaged only 16.5 percent of the South Shore's carloadings for the 1936 to 1941 period.

Most of the road's earnings were confined to the territory from Marquette to Houghton, with almost 93 percent of the South Shore's income coming from this original trackage and only 7 percent being earned on the speculative McMillan extensions (the former Detroit, Mackinac & Marquette and the Western Division). An indication of the rising business levels in 1939 saw the DSS&A hire its first new train service employees since 1923. The first firemen were hired a year later after a similar gap.

The South Shore autonomy increased as South Shore departments started drifting back to Marquette from Minneapolis. The excess capacity once enjoyed by the Soo Line general office faded with increased business levels. On July 1, 1939, the work of the car service department and management of sleeping cars was resumed by DSS&A employees. All freight traffic work, including tariffs, returned to Marquette on September 1, 1942, followed by the passenger department on June 1, 1946.

The South Shore took on an increased burden of Mackinac Transportation Company expenses after the Soo Line pulled out on January 1, 1939. In 1937, the ferry typically made one trip in freight service and two in passenger each day, carrying a total of 25,628 freight cars, 2,648 passenger cars, and 214 automobiles and trucks. Based on car counts, the freight portion of the expenses came to 82.6 percent, even though most of the trips were made in passenger service. This method of accounting disproportionately hit the Soo Line, which figured every one of its cars routed through St. Ignace was losing money.

After the Soo Line withdrew, the DSS&A, saddled with 46 percent of the expenses, sought a readjustment from the Lower Peninsula roads. The DSS&A argued that it was responsible for 70 percent of the business using the ferry, 90 percent of which was local in origin, yet received only 40 percent of the revenue from these carloadings. In 1937 the NYC and PRR earned some $722,000 in revenue on traffic delivered by the DSS&A, while the South Shore only made $131,000 on westbound business from the eastern roads. The NYC and Pennsy also made twice the money off the eastbound passenger ferry traffic as the South Shore did off the westbound business. Eventually a new agreement was reached, retroactive to January 1, 1939, in which each road paid one-third of the Mackinac Transportation Company's expenses.

As freight business on the DSS&A neared 3 million tons in 1936, the South Shore looked increasingly to the Soo Line for its needs. The large number of discontinuances saw the DSS&A with an excess of passenger power. On September 16, 1936, a deal was worked out with the Soo Line to use its L-class Mikados on 21 and 22 between Superior and Marquette, in exchange for South Shore Pacifics powering Soo Line passenger trains Nos. 62 and 63 between Duluth and Minneapolis. The DSS&A also picked up two used Consolidations (DSS&A 718, 719) from the Soo Line. These engines, the last Consolidations to be added to the DSS&A roster, had 63-inch drivers and were often seen in passenger service, especially on the hilly run to Calumet. With only 43,000 pounds' tractive effort, however, they did not pull as well as the former Mineral Range engines of this type.

Still financially wobbly, the South Shore continued to use the used locomotive market to obtain more efficient motive power to move its increasing traffic. Rather than repair two old 600-class Consolidations marked up for retirement, it was decided to purchase

Engine 1051 rests between assignments at the Soo Line engine facility at Belknap
Street in Superior. This engine and its sister the 1050 were former New York Central
H-5 class locomotives acquired secondhand in July 1937. As they were more massive
than anything on the DSS&A, they were referred to as "Mallets" by the crews.
Collection of Harold K. Vollrath

two H-5 class Mikados from the New York Central in July 1937. These locomotives
(DSS&A 1050, 1051) were sent to the Soo Line's Shoreham shops to be put into shape and
receive superheaters. The engines were more massive than anything ever owned by the
South Shore, developing a tractive effort of 48,500 pounds. They were referred to as
"Mallets" by the crews and soon held regular assignments on Nos. 21 and 22.[27]

After the bottom dropped out of the recovery in 1938, further purchases of more
modern power were delayed until January 1941, when two more secondhand Mikes
(DSS&A 1052, 1053) were purchased from the NYC. These engines were nearly identical
to those purchased earlier, except for being equipped with boosters. They were also sent
to the Shoreham shops and given added refinements such as feedwater equipment and
stokers. Impressed with the added performance from the boosters, the South Shore purchased parts to equip the 1050 and 1051 with these devices during their 1941 shopping.
The engines also received mechanical stokers at this time to alleviate complaints from
firemen and fulfill ICC mandates. After U.S. entry into the war, the South Shore purchased one more Mikado locomotive from the NYC on March 27, 1942, along with a
used booster from the Indiana Harbor Belt. The purchase of this locomotive (DSS&A
1054) was felt to be preferable to putting money into an old F-3 Consolidation awaiting
shopping at Marquette.

During the Depression, the DSS&A had retired a large portion of its aging equipment roster, with the resulting salvage value being used to keep the South Shore afloat. To
move its remaining business, the DSS&A leased 50 boxcars (15000–15049) from the Soo
Line and purchased 25 secondhand refrigerator cars (5049–5073) from the Wisconsin

Central in 1933 for merchandise service. As business picked up, the DSS&A, which largely originated traffic, became increasingly dependent on its connections for cars. In times of shortage, these lines would take care of their own needs first, putting the South Shore and its shippers in a difficult position. In July 1935, 100 used automobile cars (DSS&A 18000–18099) were purchased from the NYC using proceeds from scrapping the line west of Marengo Jct. The purchase of an additional 50 secondhand former Pere Marquette 40-ton, 40′6″ boxcars (DSS&A 16000–16049) allowed the Soo Line boxcar lease to be cancelled effective January 1, 1939. As shippers were starting to demand 50-ton cars, the South Shore also ordered 100 new 40′6″ steel boxcars with 6-foot doors in conjunction with a Pullman-Standard order of the Soo Line and WC. The combined order allowed a better price than if the South Shore purchased the cars themselves. The last of these 17000-series cars was delivered on December 7, 1940.

The South Shore incurred per diem payments of $86,247 in 1936 due in part to an average of 138 foreign-line gondolas being on the line. The DSS&A only had 50 gondolas of its own, and these would be outlawed for interchange service in 1938 because of their arch bar trucks. This deficiency caused the South Shore to pick up 140 former Bessemer & Lake Erie 50-ton gondolas (DSS&A 10200–10339) in February 1938, and 50 former Monon composite gons (DSS&A 3000–3049) in 1940. The Soo Line converted the latter into all-steel cars with "AB" brakes for interchange service.

Passenger equipment also received some modernization during the 1930s. Sleeping car service on Nos. 7 and 8 was greatly improved in April 1932, when two all-steel 12-1 cars were purchased from the Soo Line. The *Duluth* retained its name on the DSS&A, while the *St. Paul* was renamed *Marquette*. One additional car of this type, *Superior*, was acquired from the Soo Line in March 1935. Although these new additions allowed retirement of the wooden sleepers, 7 and 8's usual consist of a steel underframed mail and express car, wooden coach, steel sleeper, and sometimes a wooden baggage car still did not allow the use of two unused steel coaches. Post Office regulations prohibited the placing of steel cars next to wooden mail cars as a protection for Railway Post Office employees. The situation was further complicated by the Michigan Public Service Commission prohibiting the use of wooden coaches. A steel mail and express car (DSS&A 104) was purchased used from the Soo Line in July 1940 and another (DSS&A 105) from equipment dealer Hyman-Michaels in 1943. Until that time if a steel coach was used, the mail car had to be handled on the rear of the train or an empty wooden coach added in front of the steel car as a buffer.

Beginning in February 1938, No. 8 started handling merchandise traffic out of Duluth to Calumet and Marquette to compete with the growing presence of trucks on the UP. This traffic was handled in refrigerator cars as well as baggage cars, although baggage cars needed 4-wheel trucks to negotiate the sharp curvature at the Soo Line's 10th Avenue freight house in Duluth. No. 8 would set out the Calumet car at Nestoria, where it would be picked up by No. 9.

Another major revision of Nos. 7 and 8's consist resulted from the conversion at Shoreham of DSS&A sleeping cars *Duluth* and *Superior* into coach-sleepers. This rebuilding saw the removal of six sleeper sections along with one of the men's rooms. A partition and coach seats were installed, and the former drawing room became the smoking room. The coach-sleepers went into operation on August 13, 1940, and saved on foreign railroad (NP, WC) wheelage charges west of Marengo Jct. by using one car instead

The 18002 was one of 100 automobile box cars the DSS&A picked up secondhand from the New York Central in 1936 as traffic levels slowly inched up in the late 1930s. Many of these cars were later converted to a single door, and in early 1954 some of this series were repainted with yellow sides, red roof and ends, and the words *Merchandise Service* in large letters. *Wesley Perron Railroad Collection, Peter White Public Library, Marquette, Mich.*

of two. With the increasing freight business, No. 7 also generally handled up to four freight cars out of Marquette as far as Ewen. One fewer passenger car made it possible to increase this figure up to six and still allow the Pacific to make time. These freight cars were handled west out of Ewen by train 21.

Several physical improvements were made at Marquette before the war to improve efficiency. The freight house was relocated back to the east end of the Lower Yard on January 28, 1941, with the opening of a new 120′×40′ frame structure that also doubled as a yard office. The new setup allowed for quicker spotting of merchandise cars on and off freight trains, eliminated the long transfer move downtown, and got rid of a lot of switching over busy streets. At the Park Avenue roundhouse, trackage was rearranged so engines could pull in to the service tracks from the east end, instead of having to go up to the west end and back in. A new conveyor coal dock and cinder pit were installed, and the old incline coal dock was retired. As the DSS&A tried to get by with larger but fewer locomotives, greater efficiency at the shops became important so as to get the power back on the road. The first improvements in 30 years saw an overhead crane added at the 5th Avenue shops, along with a hydraulic drop pit for wheels.

The Mineral Range facilities at Calumet also received a major adjustment in 1940. The separate freight and passenger depots were combined into the existing passenger depot, allowing the freight house to be leased out as warehouse space. Passenger equipment laying over at Calumet began to be heated by the passenger locomotive laying over in the roundhouse instead of by the depot's heating plant. A new single-stall engine house was erected close to the depot, allowing the retirement of the old Hancock & Calumet roundhouse.

On the Mackinaw Division, new servicing facilities for steam power were put in at the West Yard in St. Ignace. A new coaling tower and sand house allowed the incline coal dock to be dismantled. As it was hard for No. 21 to make the run between the tanks at Soo Jct. and Seney and still do the 3 to 6 hours' work at Newberry, a new water station was installed at the latter point in 1943. Eckerman also received a new tank that year as Nos. 18 and 19 were unable to handle full trains between Soo Jct. and the Sault without taking water.

At Sault Ste. Marie the turntable was reinforced in 1941 to allow South Shore Mikes to be turned. The Soo Line sought to extend the table to 90 feet to accommodate all classes of power, but the DSS&A was unwilling to pay its 50 percent of the cost, as South Shore power fit fine on the old table.

The DSS&A had been handling all the switching and transfer work at the Sault since the beginning of service in 1888. The Soo Line accounted for about 60 percent of the traffic in and out of Sault, Michigan, and its men had long clamored for the right to man some of the yard jobs in that terminal. Finally on October 28, 1941, it was agreed to let Soo Line trainmen with Gladstone and Minneapolis & Duluth Division seniority come to work at Sault Ste. Marie, Michigan, as vacancies arose. The South Shore switchmen were given prior rights to all work. The agreement also prohibited DSS&A switchmen from transferring between the yards in Michigan and Ontario. Although technically in control of the entire operation at Sault Ste. Marie, the DSS&A had little say in what went on on the Canadian side.

The strategic value of the Sault locks, with their important iron ore traffic, saw them become heavily defended during the early 1940s with troops and barrage balloons. With the war hysteria raging, a serious accident on the International Bridge on October 7, 1941, was soon made into an act of sabotage. A transfer, returning from the Ontario side with 50 cars, got a clear signal to go across the jackknife bridge, but as engine 706 passed over the north leaf of the span, the bridge started to buckle, causing the locomotive to go off the end of the leaf and nose into the bottom of the canal. Engineer Hazen Willis and conductor Dave Monroe drowned, while the other crew members managed to swim to safety.

As the 706 was blocking the only lock capable of handling modern ore boats, it became crucial to get the engine out of the way as quickly as possible. Clearing the tender and two cars off the north leaf allowed it to spring back into position and be raised to allow boats to pass with the aid of tugs. The 706 was dragged down to the end of the lock, where a large crane hoisted it onto a barge. Repairs took until October 31, when the bridge reopened for rail traffic.

The reasons for the wreck never became publicly known, even to the South Shore officials. The Canadian Pacific was in charge of maintenance of the span and held the investigation. The minority position of the DSS&A was evident in a letter written by General Solicitor Ralph Eldredge to Trustee Ueland: "I got the impression from both Mr. Schmidt and Mr. DeMerse [special agent] that the Canadian Pacific were keeping things pretty much to themselves, but I have been hoping that perhaps you and Mr. Whitman were being kept fully advised. . . . I agree with you that the Canadian Pacific should lay the cards on the table, although I do not believe there is any escape from liability, unless we can show that the accident was the result of subversive activities or possibly the intentional act of [bridge tender Albert] Penman. This latter can now be probably ruled out, as the FBI does not seem to have him under suspicion, and the State Police seem to have pulled in their horns."[28]

WORLD WAR II BRINGS NEW BUSINESS

As 1941 tonnage grew by a third over 1940 levels, the South Shore found itself unable to handle the business with Nos. 21 and 22. It was decided to have passenger trains 1 and 2, between St. Ignace and Marquette, operate on Sundays as a mixed train. These trains (Nos. 101 and 102) usually had an F-3 Consolidation, the regular passenger equipment, six cars of freight, and a caboose. As business continued to accelerate with the war effort, 21 and 22 were put on seven days a week and 101 and 102 were discontinued.

Local business on the east end picked up to the point where No. 21 was unable to do the work and still make it over the road on any kind of a schedule. For this reason a local called the Newberry Switch was put on around 1943. This job operated out of St. Ignace and made a turn five days a week to Newberry or Dollarville. Besides helping 21, train 22 would leave its shorts at either Newberry or Soo Jct. for the Newberry Switch to peddle. The Newberry job lasted until the mid-1950s, at which point the lumber and logging business had dropped off to a level that train 21 could once again handle the work. The Newberry blast furnace shut down in October 1945 and was said to have been the last charcoal iron producer in the United States. After the Switch was taken off, extras were run out of Marquette to Newberry as needed during the summer months, when the asylum received heavy coal shipments.

On the west end the South Shore dealt with the increasing wartime traffic by running the "Hot Shot." Normally 21 would come into Marquette at about four or five in the afternoon and its cars would sit until 21 left around 8 the next morning. No. 21, which did the heavy short work west of Marquette, would usually take the crew's full 16 hours to make Ewen. By calling a "Hot Shot" extra, which would follow passenger train 7 out of Marquette, the through cars could catch up with the previous day's 21 at Ewen, giving the cars a 24-hour jump. The Hot Shot's crew would handle an extra back to Marquette, helping 22 by performing its local work. The Hot Shot might run all the way to Ashland or even Superior if the crew had enough time. Even if a crew tied up at Ashland they still might be run west on a caboose hop to pick up tonnage at Superior. A more common way to handle excess eastbound traffic was to run a turn out of Superior, sometimes with leased Soo Line power or caboose, connecting with the Marquette crew and power at Ashland.[29]

As trains 7 and 8 ran only six days a week, on Saturdays the Hot Shot took the number 107 and would leave on No. 7's time, carrying a passenger coach in addition to the regular freight equipment. This train connected with C&NW train 162 at Ishpeming and at Champion with Milwaukee Road No. 10 for Chicago. The coach was often left at Champion while the crew continued on to Ewen, from which they immediately started back as No. 108. This crew did some local work and at Champion picked up the coach, making connections with Milwaukee Road No. 9 and with C&NW train 161 at Negaunee.

No. 21, with an F-6 class 717 and 43 cars off the car ferry at St. Ignace, nears Trout
Lake in May 1947. The 717 would meet an ignoble fate at L'Anse in another four years.
Collection of Harold K. Vollrath

With wartime rationing of gasoline and tires, the South Shore's passenger business,
like that of other roads, grew as an alternative to the automobile. Passenger levels in
1942 were almost double those of 1941 and did not peak until 1944, when traffic reached
figures not seen since 1929, even on much-reduced schedules. Declines were seen beginning in 1945 and did not let up as people resumed their use of their preferred method of
transportation—the automobile.

The South Shore continued to use passenger trains to handle its increasing freight
business. After union protests, an agreement was reached on August 12, 1944, limiting
this practice to six cars on Nos. 7 and 8 between Marquette and Duluth, while No. 2 was
limited to two cars between Calumet and Marquette, six between Marquette and Shingleton, twelve from Shingleton to Newberry, and none east of that point. No. 1 could
handle six cars from Newberry to Marquette, and when over two cars were handled up
the hill to Nestoria, a caboose and flagman had to be provided. Nos. 7 and 8 would pick
up and drop off their freight cars at Soo Line's Belknap Street yard in Superior, although
after 21 and 22 were put on seven days a week, the handling of freight on 7 and 8 became
less frequent. When No. 2 handled freight east of Marquette, the freight cars and caboose were cut off right on the main line at Newberry, and the Newberry job would take
the cars to St. Ignace.

The Hot Shot and use of passenger trains for hauling freight were required as the
South Shore found itself handling considerable new war-related bridge traffic. From
1942 to 1945, 28.83 percent of the South Shore's traffic was of this variety. Starting in 1941,

the U.S. economy became increasingly defense-based, and even before the American entry into the hostilities, pent-up consumer demand and lend-lease shipments to England played a heavy role. Items such as tarp-enshrouded gun mounts out of the New Brighton, Minnesota, arms plant were handled right behind the engine along with four or five associated cars. A trainmaster would accompany the cars all the way from Superior to the Sault, and a trainman had to walk them over bridges. Turf battles were set aside during the emergency, and the cars were given to the Canadian Pacific for the quickest route to the East Coast.

The government also built an airfield on the Sault branch at Raco in 1942, which used considerable building materials but saw very little use upon completion. In December 1942, 1,400 Army troops were moved by troop train into seven former Civilian Conservation Corps (CCC) camps in the western UP for winter maneuvers. Additional troop trains in 1944 brought over 5,000 German prisoners of war, who were housed in abandoned CCC camps at Sidnaw, Evelyn, Au Train, and Raco.

Some government actions were not helpful. Considerable iron ore was interchanged to the C&NW for movement to Escanaba by order of the Office of Defense Transportation. In 1944 the South Shore handled only 308,306 tons over its Marquette dock, down from 601,736 tons in 1943. World War II did not return prosperity to the Copper Country as government price controls were not encouraging to the copper industry, and production levels did not rise above those experienced in the thirties. The DSS&A's wartime traffic was also dealt a blow on April 15, 1943, when the War Shipping Administration commandeered the *Chief Wawatam* for ice breaking duty. This was not unusual, but as the *Sainte Marie* was already engaged in this service on Lake Superior, the action left no railroad car ferry at St. Ignace. Trains 1 and 2 terminated at St. Ignace, and passengers and mail were carried on one of the state car ferries. With the commandeering of the *Chief* and *Sainte Marie*, all freight had to be diverted to interchanges at the Sault, Shingleton, Champion, and Ishpeming.

After breaking ice and freeing boats in Lake Michigan and in Whitefish Bay on Lake Superior, the *Chief* took the longest journey of her career when she received orders to proceed to Buffalo to relieve 27 vessels stuck in the ice. Released from charter on May 10, 1943, the *Chief* had an extended stay in the shipyard at Ashtabula, Ohio, before returning to service on June 7. The *Sainte Marie* had returned to regular service May 18, allowing the St. Ignace gateway to reopen. Charter revenue diminished with the advent of the new U.S. Coast Guard cutter *Mackinaw*, which took over most of the ice breaking duties in 1944. State ferries were hard-pressed to keep up with the automobile traffic, however, and both Mackinac Transportation Company boats were kept active in this trade after the war ended. This facet of the business also suffered when *Vacationland*, the state's first bow-propeller-equipped car ferry, went into service on January 13, 1952.

Although the hostilities brought added freight business to the DSS&A, it is important to keep in mind that only in 1942 did tonnages exceed the Depression-era year of 1930, and even then they fell far short of the levels attained in the late 1920s. The fact that the DSS&A had a net income in 1942 of some $60,000 (the first time the road had been able to meet its fixed charges since 1902) was due more to the economies exacted by C. E. Urbahns than to any overwhelming business such as that enjoyed by other U.S. carriers during the war years. The slimming down of the DSS&A allowed operating ratios in the 70s to be achieved during all the war years except 1945.

THE FIRST DIESELS

The use of diesel locomotives to cut expenses provided encouragement to the nation's railroads in the 1940s. The South Shore had little need for the massive early road freight diesels, like General Motors's Electro-Motive Division's FT, but it was an early user of road switchers, buying two 1000-horsepower models (100, 101) from American Locomotive Co. in 1945. The new power, referred to as D-1s on the DSS&A, were the first of their kind in the UP and weighed 119 tons with a starting tractive effort of 72,000 pounds. Delivery of the two new diesels took place at Superior to avoid paying Michigan's 3 percent use tax, and engine 100 took a nine-car extra out from that community on May 31, 1945. After testing, the DSS&A decided one diesel unit was equal to an F-7 Consolidation. Although equipped with multiple unit connections, they were placed in service as single units on trains 31 and 32 between Marquette and Houghton. A 17,000-gallon tank and electric pumps were installed in the shop yard west of Fifth Avenue at Marquette to fuel the new power.

The DSS&A liked the improved running times and the elimination of coal and water stops gained with the new power. Picking up and setting out cars was also speeded up by the quicker acceleration of the diesels. These characteristics led the South Shore to dieselize the whole Mackinaw Division with the purchase of five more 1,000-horsepower road switchers (102–106) from American in 1946. Steam-heating boilers were installed on engines 104, 105, and 106 for use in passenger service, and an additional $150 per unit was charged for an arrangement of steps and handrails peculiar to the DSS&A.

Two 1,000-horsepower units hooked in multiple were capable of handling 2,560 tons between St. Ignace and Marquette, versus only 1,860 with an L-class steamer. Under dieselization, which went into effect on July 1, 1947, the West Yard roundhouse at St. Ignace was abandoned and a single-stall 20′×125′ enginehouse constructed near the downtown depot. The 75-foot turntable was also moved downtown from the West Yard. Local tank trucks fueled the diesels. In addition to the retirement of ten (two H-1 and eight F-3) steamers, all coal and water facilities east of Marquette were done away with for an estimated total savings of $116,270 annually.

Another change at St. Ignace during this period involved the passenger and freight depots, which stood 900 feet apart and required the agent and clerical staff to spend a lot of time running back and forth. A new combined facility was created by moving an unused 20′×70′ depot from Moran and building a 48-foot warehouse addition out of salvage from the dismantled St. Ignace passenger depot. The new depot at St. Ignace did not hear the sound of the telegraph key very long, as a shortage of telegraphers made it necessary to equip the Mackinaw Division with block phones. This involved seven open stations and ten other locations along the line. The block phones at blind stations allowed train crews, bridge crews, and maintenance of way employees to communicate with the dispatcher at Marquette to find where trains were located and thus expedite work. The project was expanded in 1947 to include the territory from Marquette to Houghton.

The location of the stub end passenger depot at Marquette had always been troublesome at best, with Nos. 1 and 2 having to back in and out. As the war let up and the availability of building materials became less of a problem, it was decided in 1945 to build a compact 30′×77′ facility along the main line just west of Fifth Street. The new

The South Shore's original diesel powers the 12-car consist of the Newberry Switch near Trout Lake, Michigan, in July 1950. The DSS&A has already eliminated the front steps of engine 100 and placed them halfway down the running board on the long hood. The steps were later returned to their original position.   *Collection of Harold K. Vollrath*

building opened for regular traffic on January 14, 1946, and that day's No. 2 kicked off the new facility. The old depot continued to house the South Shore general offices, which had become quite overcrowded.

The years following World War II saw a number of labor disruptions in the rail industry. On May 23, 1946, train service brotherhoods went on a two-day strike, leaving trains stranded all over the South Shore system. A coal miners' strike in the spring of

No. 1, with one of the boiler-equipped D-1 class road switchers for power, rumbles across the Au Train River bridge. It may or may not stop at Au Train depot, depending on whether anyone has put out the flag.
Courtesy of Roy Paananen

Engine 556 handling No. 2 arrives at the new Fifth Street passenger depot at Marquette on May 29, 1948. The passenger car in the background is on a more level stub track that was used to make up westbound passenger trains No. 7 for Duluth and No. 1 for Calumet. *Wilbur C. Whittaker*

1948 caused the ICC to order railroads to discontinue 25 percent of their coal-fired passenger service, effective March 22. Nos. 7 and 8 and Nos. 9 and 10 were put on tri-weekly schedules. Trains 1 and 2 were not affected as they were operated by diesel power, but the NYC and PRR cut off their trains into Mackinaw City, leaving no connections. As the strike continued, a 25 percent reduction in freight service was put into effect on March 30. The South Shore and other iron ore roads received a reprieve, as ore tonnage was exempted from the reduction. President Harry Truman ordered the miners back to work shortly thereafter and the restrictions were lifted on April 13, 1948.

An assemblage of mining and railroad employees pose in front of L-class engine 1053 to commemorate the re-opening of the Champion mine on April 29, 1949. The mine spur curves off toward the northwest and the main line, having been built on a new alignment to avoid having to grant access to the Milwaukee Road, which also served Champion. *Wesley Perron Railroad Collection, Peter White Public Library, Marquette, Mich.*

12

REORGANIZATION—
PROFITABILITY

Attempts to reorganize the DSS&A continued to be protracted, with public bondholders wrestling with each other and with the Canadian Pacific for a stake in the new company. Public parties went after the CPR in court, claiming that the road had failed to properly develop the DSS&A and that their claims, as holders of the first mortgage 5 percent bonds, should take precedence over those of the CPR (which held MH&O 6s and DSS&A 4s). Several court decisions, however, made it clear that the CPR, as the only holder of the MH&O 6s and DSS&A 4s, was entitled to a greater stake in the reorganized South Shore than had been originally thought.[1] The court found that the 4s were not entirely subordinate to the 5s, and the sheer weight of the CPR holdings (some $15,000,000 in principal amount and $30,000,000 in matured unpaid interest) was also a consideration.[2]

The question of what kind of capitalization the reorganized South Shore could support was dependent upon future earnings. The traffic of World War II was thought of as an anomaly, although it was felt bridge traffic would remain above pre-war levels. The local traffic of the South Shore was expected to remain constant. There was still plenty of iron ore left in the Marquette Range, but with the withdrawal of government premiums for copper, the mines of the Copper Country would have a tough time competing in the world markets. Wood products were felt to be in better shape than before the war, but agricultural shipments, especially dairy products, would increasingly fall victim to motor competition.

The main goal was to reduce the South Shore's fixed interest charges, which on January 1, 1946, amounted to $859,700 annually, while the average annual operating net earnings from 1928 to 1945 were only $293,382. It was decided the DSS&A's new financial structure would consist of $5,000,000 in 4 percent bonds and 210,000 shares of common stock. The interest on the bonds was to be paid only if earned. Under this refinancing proposal only $225,000 would be required annually for fixed charges. In its final report approving the reorganization on June 19, 1947, the ICC expressed belief that the new capitalization would give the South Shore a "conservative financial structure, should afford adequate means for future financing as may be necessary, and should not lead to further need of judicial reorganization. Fixed charges would be of such a negligible amount that after due consideration of the probable prospective earnings of the property in the light of its earnings experience and all other relevant facts, there would be adequate coverage of such fixed charges."[3]

In the final settlement, the public holders of the DSS&A 5s received the better end of the deal, recouping 33.8 percent of their prior claims in cash and first mortgage bonds of the reorganized company, while the CPR managed only 12.9 percent. The CPR also received all 210,000 shares of the new company's capital stock, giving it complete control. Final authority was granted by the ICC on September 20, 1949, for the Duluth, South Shore & Atlantic Railway and the Mineral Range Railroad to pass into the hands of the reorganized Duluth, South Shore and Atlantic *Railroad*.[4]

As the reorganization drew to a close, there came the matter of selecting directors and officers for the new railroad. Henry S. Mitchell, a South Shore director since 1940 and chief of its reorganization managers, was in line to head the new firm. The dignified Mitchell, a native of Milwaukee, Wisconsin, was general counsel for the Soo Line before becoming the CPR's representative in the DSS&A and Wisconsin Central reorganizations.

Ralph S. Archibald, president of North Range Mining and a current South Shore director, said he would be willing to serve in the new company provided it was "given an opportunity to compete for the freight business between Duluth, the Soo [Sault Ste. Marie] and St. Ignace. The Soo Line has heretofore been mixed up in the operation and management of the South Shore Railway and I have always felt that this connection resulted in the loss of traffic by the South Shore to the Soo Line, and I would not want to be connected up with such a situation as it would result in South Shore operating at a loss and ultimately a decline in service which your Railroad gives our territory."[5] This feeling was to become manifest in the new railroad, and Mitchell was able to get an understanding from the chairman and president of the Canadian Pacific "that the DSS&A should be so managed as to get all the business it could and make all the money it could for the Canadian Pacific."[6]

In addition to Archibald, private industry was represented on the new South Shore board by Endicott R. Lovell, president of Calumet and Hecla; Ward R. Schafer, vice president and general manager of Coolerator Co., Duluth; and Harry B. Stoker, vice president and general manager of Globe Elevator, Duluth. The CPR interests were watched over by the company's vice president, Norris R. Crump, and its treasurer, James A. Dundas, while the DSS&A was represented by Henry Mitchell, Herman Schmidt, and Chicago attorney Peter N. Todhunter.

At a meeting of the board held on November 1, 1949, Henry Mitchell was elected president; P. L. Solether, vice president; J. C. Peterson, secretary; and C. H. Bender, treasurer. Peterson and Bender were Soo Line men, but Mitchell assured the directors that as their duties were "purely administerial they will have no control or influence over the operations and solicitation of traffic of the South Shore." Mitchell also added, "I have resigned from the executive committee and board of directors of the Soo Line in order that the South Shore may have my entire allegiance."[7] Superintendent Herman Schmidt received a new title on January 1, 1949, becoming general superintendent of the DSS&A. There had been some disagreements between Schmidt and General Traffic Manager A. C. Stenburg, with Stenburg telling Schmidt that as *general* traffic manager he did not have to take orders from a superintendent. The new title put that dispute to rest.

One of the ways the South Shore looked to gain traffic was to promote itself as a short line out of Duluth to connections with the CPR, NYC, and PRR that avoided the congested Chicago gateway. The South Shore held its first board of directors meeting at

Duluth, home of directors Harry Stoker and Ward Schafer. Following the meeting, some twenty Duluth businessmen were invited to a dinner to promote the advantages of routing via the DSS&A.

NEW ORE BUSINESS

The DSS&A's prosperity in the postwar decade was enhanced with the opening of several new mining properties. These independent producers were very important to the South Shore, as Cleveland-Cliffs controlled 85 percent of the ore on the Marquette Range and favored the Lake Superior & Ishpeming whenever possible. The first project to come on line was the reactivation of the Champion mine by the North Range Mining Company. Trackage into the site had long been abandoned, and an entirely new spur was constructed that took off 0.4 miles west of Champion and circled the hill before reaching the shaft from the west. It was feared that if the old grade (which entered the site from the east) was used, the CMStP&P would insist on joint service. The first shipment out of the Champion, an all-rail movement to Lorain, Ohio, was sent out on April 11, 1949.

Another major new exploration, south of Negaunee, was Jones and Laughlin's Tracy mine. This new development required a major relocation of C&NW and LS&I trackage, as well as of the DSS&A's Negaunee & Palmer branch. Final plans resulted in the South Shore abandoning about 1 mile of trackage, along with another 0.75 miles jointly used. The DSS&A constructed 1.23 miles of new track, and new joint trackage totaled some 2.25 miles. As part of the line change, a new ore yard was created at Negaunee in place of the old Ann Street yard. It was named Hogan's Yard in honor of Phil Hogan, the Negaunee agent. Jones and Laughlin and the railroads agreed to split the relocation costs evenly, and the South Shore in turn paid 30.5 percent of the railroads' costs. This percentage was also used to divide ore traffic out of the new mine. The new trackage, which went into operation during the summer of 1952, was controlled by centralized traffic control from the South Shore dispatcher's office at Marquette. The Tracy made its initial shipment in 1955 and shipped a total of 405,604 tons in 1956. As this was an underground mine, the Tracy mine made use of a stockpile as well as loading cars directly from the shaft.

The prosecution of the Korean War led to large increases in the market for iron ore. DSS&A dock shipments grew to 619,469 tons in 1950 after totaling only 462,719 tons the year before. The Richmond mine was the biggest shipper, followed by the Blueberry. The severe winter of 1949–1950 made for a late start to navigation and, coupled with a heavy demand for steel, resulted in a heavy all-rail movement of iron ore off the Duluth, Missabe & Iron Range (DM&IR) at Superior to the steel mills in Chicago, Youngstown, and Pittsburgh. The Chicago railroads initially attempted to thwart the South Shore's participation in this traffic because of its lack of battleship gondolas, but the NYC agreed to provide the necessary cars in exchange for being included in the routing. The first train of Mesabi Range all-rail ore arrived at St. Ignace on July 20, 1950, and it was said the turnaround on cars routed via St. Ignace was slightly better than via the Chicago lines. The DSS&A also received all-rail ore shipments out of the newly opened Champion mine. These shipments also went to St. Ignace and to the Soo Line interchange at Marengo Jct.

The new business was not without its difficulties. From January through March of 1951, the DM&IR let its 75-ton ore cars off line, but the Northern Pacific would not allow multiple cars weighing over 175,000 pounds to pass over bridges on its Ashland line unless separated by an empty. Soo Line switch crews at Superior added the necessary spacers, usually Soo Line ore cars, and the South Shore road crew would switch them out at Ashland. Most of the ore left Superior in 20-car trains of 1,600 to 1,700 tons. There was a 20 m.p.h. speed limit placed on the ore due to the cars' short wheel base, and it was impossible to make a run for any of the thirteen 1 percent grades from Superior to Marquette. This made it hard to get over the road, and crews were constantly being forced to set out their train and run with only their caboose to the next terminal before their hours of service were up. At times a half-dozen sidings were blocked with iron ore. One plan devised was to double-head a 1,000-horsepower D-1 class diesel with the road engine, and this seemed to allow the trains to get over the road. On the east end, the all-rail ore was usually put on No. 22. If No. 22 was too big out of Marquette, a Shingleton turn would be run and No. 22 would pick up the ore on top of the hill.

DIESELIZATION

The DSS&A, impressed by the economic results of dieselizing the Mackinaw Division, began to explore options for using diesels system-wide. Tests were made with General Motors Electro-Motive Division (EMD) cow and calf transfer demonstrator No. 912 in the fall of 1947, and Elgin, Joliet and Eastern's Baldwin 2,000-horsepower unit 108 in May 1948. Superintendent Schmidt was very impressed with the performance of the Baldwin, which handled 1,150 tons up the hill from Marquette to Morgan in 33 minutes. An L-1 Mikado with booster could take only 700 tons over this stretch. Schmidt preferred 2,000-horsepower units as the enginemen's brotherhoods refused to allow multiple-unit diesel operation except for the 1,000-horsepower units between Marquette and St. Ignace. Given the heavy traffic levels during the summer of 1948, Schmidt pressed for the purchase of diesels to meet power shortages. "Bugs" in the Baldwin 2,000-horsepower diesels cooled an immediate purchase, and instead a Mikado was leased from the NP.[8]

A study of the South Shore's remaining 26 steam engines, completed in March 1949, saw a need for major repairs in the near future to certain H and H-1 class Pacifics, as well as to a number of F-3 and F-5 Consolidations. As the Marquette shops were not equipped to handle defective cylinders and major boiler repairs, many of these engines would have to be shopped out. It was felt these funds would be better used towards the purchase of new diesels.

The final proposal called for the purchase of six new diesels, three 2,000-horsepower and three 1,500-horse. The 2,000-horsepower units would power Nos. 21 and 22, while two of the 1,500-horsepower units would handle Nos. 31 and 32 and a shift in Houghton yard during their layover. The third 1,500-horsepower engine would be used on Nos. 18 and 19 between Sault Ste. Marie and Soo Jct. and to protect Sault Ste. Marie yard. The 1,000-horsepower units released on the Mackinaw Division could be used to dieselize Nos. 7 and 8, the "Hot Shot," and help No. 22 to Shingleton. Passenger trains Nos. 1 and 2 would remain under steam west of Marquette, as would Nos. 9 and 10 between Champion and Calumet. The new power would allow one H-class Pacific, two

H-1 Pacifics, and five F-3 and four F-5 Consolidations to be scrapped, and would enable the return of Soo Line No. 1054, then under lease.

The next question became what type of motive power to buy. The options at 2,000 horsepower still came down to the EMD cow and calf units and the Baldwin transfer units; for some reason the 2,000-horsepower model H-20-44 from Fairbanks-Morse, also available at this time, was not considered. The EMD offering was capable of greater tonnage on the hills and at greater speeds, while the Baldwins performed better in level running. General Traffic Manager A. C. Stenburg opposed the purchase of the cow and calf units, as their appearance would "not be good advertising for the DSS&A."[9] This view was endorsed by Superintendent Schmidt, who was concerned that even though the cow and calf were permanently coupled, the locomotive brotherhoods would still insist upon a separate engine crew for each unit. Schmidt also felt that the engine crews would object to running the units with the calf in the lead, thus necessitating turning the power at the end of their runs. There were also questions as to whether the engine crew could read the instrument panel on the calf unit in blizzard conditions, as this was located 8 feet away from the control stand on the cow unit. Although there were doubts about the centered motor on the Baldwin 2,000-horsepower engine, this was felt to require less maintenance than the two motors on EMD's cow and calf.

There was some concern over the appearance of the big Baldwin transfer units, and it was inquired whether a cab carbody, similar to that used on Central Railroad of New Jersey commuter engines, could be used. Baldwin replied that it would be no simple matter to fit up such a configuration as it would involve expensive changes in the underframe and wiring. One thing that could be done, as advocated by traffic manager Stenburg, was to have the new power "painted more modern and flashy colors similar to what is being done by other carriers."[10] It was decided to go with the Baldwins, and a six-unit order was placed on August 26, 1949, for three 2,000-horsepower DT units and the three DRS 1,500-horsepower engines.

The units were hauled dead in tow to Superior, and the three 2,000-horsepower units (300–302), also known as D-3s, left Superior in revenue service on consecutive nights beginning October 22, 1949. The last of the 1,500-horsepower units (200–202), known as D-2s, went out of Superior on No. 22 on November 14. The new units allowed freight and passenger movements to be dieselized between Duluth and St. Ignace for the first time. On November 15, one of the 1,500-horsepower units left Marquette and was traded off at Soo Jct. for a steam engine, allowing Nos. 18 and 19 to be dieselized; the engine also worked a shift in the Sault yard. When the last of the 1,500-horsepower units arrived at Marquette they were marked up for use on Nos. 31 and 32 to Houghton. In December 1949, at the end of the ore season, 89.6 percent of all freight train miles were being handled by diesels.

Over the winter of 1949–1950 the South Shore paid 74.3 cents per engine mile for maintenance on its steam power, versus only 17.9 cents for diesels. It was irritating to throw "money down the drain" maintaining old steam power when it could be used to invest in new diesels.[11] The DSS&A did place an order with Baldwin for one additional 2,000-horsepower unit (303) and one more 1,500-horsepower diesel (203), which were shipped from Eddystone, Pennsylvania, on August 23, 1950. These diesels, the first since reorganization, were equipped with the DSS&A "Railroad" herald, which was white on the red background. This differed from the "Railway" herald, which had red lettering on a black background. Five more 1,600-horsepower Baldwins (204–208) were ordered on

One of the new D-2 1,500-horsepower units is acting as a helper for an L-2 Mikado on
an eastbound freight just getting under way at Marquette off the Lake Street lead.
The train is about to come out onto the main line, with the LS&I diamond in the
immediate foreground. To avoid getting cinders in the air intakes, diesels
were generally placed ahead of steam power when double-headed.
Courtesy of Roy Paananen

The 41-car consist of No. 21 is in tow of D-3 No. 301 near Trout Lake in July 1950.
Collection of Harold K. Vollrath

Getting ready for a westbound departure out of the Lower Yard in Marquette, 207 and another D-2 pump air. The train already rests on the grade that steadily rises from the Lower Yard to the top of the hill at Morgan.
Courtesy of Roy Paananen

July 12, 1950. Two of these units (207, 208) were equipped with train-heating boilers capable of turning out 2,500 pounds of steam per hour for passenger service. Along with the Baldwins, the South Shore ordered a 1,000-horsepower road switcher (107) from American equipped with a steam boiler. With the arrival of these units at the end of February 1951, making 21 in all, Mitchell proclaimed the South Shore to be "100 percent dieselized for normal operations."[12]

A boiler-equipped 200-class often came to be assigned to Nos. 9 and 10 between Champion and Calumet. This resulted in poor utilization of power, as the engine spent much of its time in the CMStP&P roundhouse at Champion. Talks were held with the Milwaukee Road to see if they would be willing to let their power run through to Calumet. This would free up the Baldwin for freight service and allow a steamer to be retired. Under the agreement, the South Shore paid the CMStP&P a fee for using its diesel between Champion and Calumet, a practice started in the final days of 1951.

With dieselization largely completed, the South Shore was ready to consider a new diesel facility at Marquette. The final design called for a 37′ × 125′ shop attached along stall No. 1 of the Park Avenue roundhouse. The new facility, which opened in the fall of 1952, was equipped with a Shepard-Niles 25-ton overhead crane capable of lifting a diesel motor or generator off locomotive frames. In the old roundhouse, track No. 1 was converted to a machine shop, and stalls 2 through 6 were modernized for light diesel repair. This also allowed the old shop facilities at the Fifth Avenue roundhouse to be closed except for storage, although later they were configured for motor car repair.

No. 1 is seen pulling into Trout Lake in August 1947. Typical practice was for No. 1 to pull in behind the depot and run west along the station platform opposite the Soo Line main line. This allowed for an easy transfer of mail and express off of Soo Line No. 8 from Minneapolis. The same exchange would take place in the late afternoon between Soo Line No. 7 and South Shore No. 2. *Collection of Harold K. Vollrath*

Complete dieselization was still a myth, as heavy business in 1951 forced the South Shore to delay plans to retire six steamers and place the remaining six in reserve. It was decided to go ahead and order two additional 1,600-horsepower units from Baldwin as a start. These diesels (209, 210), delivered at the end of August 1952, were immediately put into the all-rail ore trade. Opposition by the brotherhoods to running diesels in multiple had been negated by a ruling from the National Labor Relations Board, and these units were equipped with multiple-unit cables.

With the ruling, the South Shore put multiple-unit connections on the rest of the D-2s, with two units being capable of accommodating almost any train the DSS&A could muster. Previously it had been an everyday practice to run a diesel helper on No. 22 as far as Shingleton, with the conductor pilot and engine crew bringing the unit back to Marquette light. With multiple-unit operation, the extra crew was dispensed with and the helper left at Shingleton for pickup by the next westbound. As diesels became more plentiful, it became common to use a D-2 or D-3 as the helper engine, and the D-1s were relegated largely to passenger and yard service. The Newberry Switch would also use a D-2 in the fall, when the coal was moving off the Sault Ste. Marie dock to Newberry Asylum.

The diesels were not infallible, and in early 1952 the 2,000-horsepower D-3s developed cracks in their truck bolsters due to faulty design. The engines had to be taken out

Engine 207, a D-2, brings 21 into Au Train. Its recent departure from St. Ignace is evidenced by trailing cars from its connections—the New York Central and Pennsylvania. *Roy Pannanen*

of service, stripped down by South Shore forces and equipped with new bolsters provided by Baldwin. The problems with the D-3s and the crush of business in the early 1950s forced the South Shore to borrow power on a number of occasions. Although the Soo Line was the typical source for such leases, especially on turns out of Superior, Great Northern steam could be found making Shingleton turns out of Marquette. The LS&I also leased steam to the South Shore, and diesels were rented from Calumet and Hecla and the Copper Range Railroad. Although the DSS&A believed operations were more efficient if the locomotive situation was on the "tight side," this was not the case if it was necessary to rent power from other roads.[13] The South Shore thus rounded out its dieselization with the purchase of a 1,600-horsepower demonstrator (211) from Baldwin in March 1953. This unit had originally been built in March 1952 and was the only one on the South Shore equipped with dynamic brakes, in spite of the railroad's hilly profile.

The hills created some trying times for the DSS&A. Train No. 22 experienced a fraught trip on September 13, 1950, as it worked its way over the NP out of Superior. With a brand new fireman, engine 1053 started running low on steam as the firebox became filled with green coal. It was necessary to stop on the hill between Cutter and Wentworth, dump the fire, and start over again. As there were several cars of gasoline in the train, the train was backed a couple of car lengths to clean the fire off the track before proceeding. With the engineer and fireman both on the ground, the train started to slip back down the hill, and engineer Bill Bogan was unable to catch it. On the caboose, conductor Edward Nadeau had no idea what was happening, but presumed they were backing for a meet with train No. 7. At Allouez, Nadeau decided they had gone far enough and pulled the air, stopping the train. Upon walking up, he found, to his surprise, no one in the engine and, with the boiler very low on water, decided it was best to leave

The 104, one of the steam generator–equipped Alcos, is seen in yard service at Marquette on May 20, 1948. The photo provides a good view of the peculiar arrangement given to the steps of the D-1s by the DSS&A.
Wilbur C. Whittaker

quickly. No. 22's head-end crew were brought to Allouez by No. 7, and arrangements were made to have an NP switch engine pull the train back into East End to take water before proceeding to Ewen.

The L'Anse hill remained a very dangerous place to work, even with all the modern improvements. It was below zero when train No. 32, with diesel 204 and 22 cars, stopped at L'Anse on the night of December 14, 1951. After the L'Anse pusher, engine 717, was tacked on the rear they started out for Summit. The going was difficult, as fresh snow had fallen, and the train stalled some 7 miles up the steep grade. The 204 cut off and ran light up to Summit to clean off the rails. Upon returning, the 204 coupled onto the train and cut in the air. The train started to slip backwards and, with train line apparently frozen, the brakes did not work. Initially the backward movement was of no surprise to the crew on the rear end, as it was common to back down towards L'Anse after stalling to find a level spot to start out again. When the crew realized the train was moving too fast, engineer John Brogan, on the helper engine, cut his air back in and attempted to "dynamite" the air. The momentum was too great and even reversing the engine had no effect.

The 25-mile-an-hour curve at the bottom of the hill, which had been the site of a number of catastrophes in the past, now became the main concern, but the train was going too fast for the crew members to jump. Upon hitting the curve, the 717 rolled over, digging into the frozen earth. All the cars followed, making a 20-foot-high pile, with only the 204 remaining upright. Fireman James Bennett was killed in the rollover of the helper engine, while engineer Brogan miraculously survived underneath the tender. Brakeman Joseph Drake, who had gone out to set hand brakes, was thrown

No. 211, the last DSS&A diesel purchase, is shown in its Baldwin demonstrator paint scheme, having been rushed into service to care for the rising freight traffic of the mid-1950s. The unit is shown riding the table at the Park Ave. roundhouse at Marquette. *Courtesy of Roy Paananen*

clear of the wreck and lived, while brakeman John Chapman died the next morning from injuries he received when the car he was riding overturned. The LS&I wrecker was borrowed and managed to clear the line three days later. Only one boxcar and the 204 were salvaged.

The 717 was cut up for scrap right on the spot at L'Anse, and the last two DSS&A steamers, engines 91 and 92, departed Marquette on December 4, 1954, for a similar fate at Duluth Iron and Metal. After being bumped out of Marquette yard in 1952, these engines had spent their last years primarily performing weed scalding and ore steaming. All work from this point on would be in the hands of the South Shore's 25 diesels.

While attempting to dieselize, the DSS&A also faced severe car shortages. The American Association of Railroads (AAR) had been trying to get the South Shore to increase its ownership of gondolas on account of its heavy pulpwood loading, believing the road was 241 cars short of meeting its requirements. The AAR also pointed out that the South Shore was responsible for .052 percent of all boxcar loading in the U.S., while its boxcar ownership only totaled .033 percent. In May 1948 the South Shore loaded an average of 321 boxcars and 250 gondolas a week, while its ownership of these classes of equipment was only 238 box and 178 gons. Due to retirements and the conversion of cars to other uses, such as sawdust service, DSS&A ownership was actually declining.

The South Shore ordered 100 of these PS-1 boxcars in 1953 to ward off threats by the American Association of Railroads to limit the DSS&A's loading of foreign cars. The slogan emphasizes the increasing role bridge traffic was playing following reorganization. Wilbur Whittaker photographed the car at Duluth in May 1958.
Wilbur C. Whittaker

With the limited car supply, "pulpers" literally fought over the gondolas as they arrived at the ramps for loading. No. 21's conductor would sometimes pick up a few extra gons from the interchanges at Negaunee and Champion and hand them out for favors. Bribery with liquor was not uncommon, and even slain deer served as incentives to train crews to favor one shipper over another. Pulpers would wait for 21 to arrive and throw a stick of pulp in to claim ownership of the car. The DSS&A trainmaster was often called on to mediate disputes.

In August 1948, 100 41-foot, 50-ton gondolas (4000–4099) and 100 50-ton steel PS-1 boxcars (15000–15099) were ordered from Pullman-Standard Company. Superintendent Schmidt said the order made him "very happy," although at that time he could have used 250 gondolas given the many disgruntled shippers on his hands.[14] A June 1950 study showed the South Shore was able to fill only 75 percent of its boxcar orders. Traffic opportunities were also being missed at off-line paper mills and wood products plants as the South Shore was unable to offer any equipment for loading.

With the danger looming that the AAR might institute restrictions on the South Shore's loading of foreign cars due to its small freight car fleet, in 1953 it became imperative to make additions. Pullman-Standard received an order for 100 50-ton, 40-foot boxcars (15100–15199), and American Car and Foundry was contracted for a like number of 50-ton all-steel gondolas (4100–4199). Trains could not be run without a caboose, and seven former Pittsburgh, Shawmut & Northern cabooses were purchased in 1947 to allow the return of leased equipment and to care for increasing business. These cabs (590–596) were said to be not "worth a darn in the wintertime."[15] As business continued to improve, more cabooses were leased, and on the Mineral Range run between Houghton and Lake Linden, even C. E. Lytle's old business car 555 was pressed into service.

No. 593, one of seven cabooses purchased used from the Pittsburgh, Shawmut & Northern in 1947, is captured at Marquette on May 29, 1948. These new acquisitions allowed the DSS&A to return foreign cabooses that had been leased to care for the South Shore's increasing traffic load. *Wilbur C. Whittaker*

The 555 was an office car of 1888 Barney and Smith origins. It was frequently used by former superintendent C. E. Lytle but saw use as a caboose following World War II during the booming traffic years. *Collection of Harold K. Vollrath*

TROUBLES WITH THE SOO LINE

The new independence for the South Shore caused a much more contentious relationship to develop with its sibling and chief competitor, the Soo Line. This trend was not viewed favorably by their parent, the Canadian Pacific, which wanted greater harmony and assimilation. The first of many disputes came about when Soo Line president Horace C. Grout sought to increase charges paid by the DSS&A at the Twin Ports for use of Soo Line facilities. Mitchell responded that the increases were unacceptable as the South Shore was being viewed "the way a foreign line would be if it were requesting these services of the Soo Line." Mitchell went on to say, "a corporation having complete control of another corporation [as the Soo controlled the DSS&A from 1921 to 1938] must in transactions between them give as much recognition to the interests of the controlled company as to its own." The Soo Line had basically dictated that the DSS&A abandon its Superior facilities and coordinate with those of the MStP&SSM in 1925.[16]

To get around the new increases, the South Shore began to explore the idea of having Nos. 7 and 8 use the Lake Superior Terminal & Transfer's Union Depot at Superior and run Duluth passengers over in a taxi. Schmidt also thought it would be more economical to operate Nos. 7 and 8 on a daytime schedule, which would do away with the sleeping car expenses. These ideas did not go over well with the South Shore traffic department, who were doubling their efforts at Duluth and Minneapolis to gain new traffic.

General Traffic Manager Stenburg felt that poor passenger service was poor advertising for a railroad and that things were bad enough already. DSS&A traffic men were already being kidded by shippers about how many freight cars were on trains 8 or 7. The traffic department argued that when they solicited in Duluth, they pointed out that their railroad actually entered the community and was thus entitled to a share of the business. A day train would make Nos. 7 and 8 unusable, as people could not afford the time or inconvenience. Thanks to the arrival of the new diesels, the handling of freight cars on No. 8 largely ceased on November 30, 1948, with only a few occurrences in 1949. The sleeping car on Nos. 7 and 8 did start to operate tri-weekly after the sleeper-coach *Duluth* suffered fire damage on April 2, 1948. On the other days a regular coach was substituted.

Another plan to avoid increased Soo Line charges at the Twin Ports would have DSS&A freight traffic routed through the LST&T, and Duluth cars handled by the CStPM&O. The DSS&A would build their own Superior yard, just south of the LST&T facility, to allow direct interchange without Soo Line involvement. To avoid having to rebuild the 28th Street line west of the Soo Line crossing, the South Shore would continue to run over the Soo to the LST&T connection north of Belknap Street. Building of the DSS&A yard required the purchase of some additional property along Oakes Ave., between 15th and 18th, from the city of Superior. The city was not enthusiastic over the idea, feeling the property should go into the hands of some industry that would add to its tax base. DSS&A superintendent Dick Barry commented afterward, "it did seem strange to me that a city such as Superior, which was built up by railroads should now find that such industry is detrimental to the further development of such community."[17]

Disadvantages to the new scheme were that the South Shore would have to pay a switch charge to the LST&T when interchanging its Duluth traffic with the Omaha Road, and that the Soo Line, as a non-owner of the LST&T, would also have to pay a tariff to interchange with the DSS&A. This would be a sizable figure, as in 1946 the Soo

D-3 class engine 303 is seen at the Soo Line 21st St. yard office at Superior, Wisconsin, in June 1952. Westbound DSS&A trains yarded at the small 21st St. facility to afford quicker delivery to the LST&T. The power would then be serviced at the engine terminal, whose coaling tower is visible above the hood of the locomotive. On eastbounds, DSS&A crews would pick up their power and caboose at 21st St. and then grab their train at the larger Stinson Yard, south of 28th St. In earlier times the 21st St. yard was known as Belknap St.   *Lake Superior Railroad Museum Collection*

Line interchanged 903 loads to the DSS&A and the South Shore gave 490 loads to the Soo Line. Difficulties were also encountered making arrangements with other railroads in Superior, causing the South Shore to give up on the project and to continue using the Soo Line facilities. The increased charges would remain in dispute for the remainder of the South Shore's existence.

A further confrontation developed from suspicions that the Soo Line was diverting DSS&A-routed cars at Superior. Cars received off the LST&T for St. Ignace would have Soo Line inserted into the route. The Soo Line would then haul the cars to the South Shore interchange at Trout Lake, greatly shorthauling the DSS&A and resulting in a considerable loss of revenue. Sault Ste. Marie traffic was also being abducted. So as to prevent the DSS&A from investigating the Soo's activities, Soo Line superintendent Vern Elliott even tried to ban South Shore officials from Superior yard. South Shore traffic representatives were told to have shippers be very explicit in their routing instructions to avoid the traffic thefts. It becomes obvious why the DSS&A enjoyed little bridge traffic during the period of Soo Line control, when the latter had access to all South Shore car reports and traffic men were in the employ of both roads.

Another controversy brewed at Sault Ste. Marie with the Soo Line objecting to excessive South Shore control, feeling it was receiving secondary treatment. Even though the South Shore was responsible for only 40 percent of the traffic, Schmidt maintained that the DSS&A, as the first road into the Sault, was entitled to maintain the joint agency. Routing decisions on traffic coming into Sault, Michigan, were made on the Canadian side, and the South Shore agent had never brought pressure to favor his road. The Soo Line complained the South Shore train was handled in preference, resulting in delay to its own traffic. The DSS&A countered that the Wisconsin Central trains between Marengo Jct. and Ashland received favorable treatment at the expense of the South Shore.

Traffic had been building at Sault Ste. Marie since 1943 and reached a new height during the winter of 1949 and 1950. A change in the schedule of Soo Line time freights 15 and 16 in 1949 required outbound cars to be in the Sault, Michigan, yard at the same time the inbound train arrived, badly congesting the small facility. The Soo Line also began operating diesels, which resulted in much larger train sizes. The heaviest traffic was during the winter, when a heavy pulpwood business came down from Canada, particularly off the Algoma Central, destined to Wisconsin paper mills. Some 6,000 cars a month passed through the Sault, Michigan, yard during the winter of 1949–1950. The DSS&A found it necessary to run a daylight extra to Soo Jct. in addition to the nightly runs of Nos. 18 and 19 to care for the increased traffic. Capacity problems were alleviated by extending three yard tracks at the Sault.

Another problem at the Sault was that cars off the Algoma Central destined for the U.S. had to be moved into the Canadian Pacific yard for customs. Transfer crews from Sault, Michigan, would find the ACR interchange plugged with cars waiting to move to the CPR, and the CPR yard filled with cars waiting to go to the U.S. and to the ACR, creating a classic case of gridlock. As many as five switch assignments were employed at Sault Ste. Marie, Michigan, during the winter of 1949–1950, along with three at the CPR yard. Transfer work was alternated between the Canadian and American crews. Around 1952, the CPR came to feel it would be better to man the Canadian jobs with its own personnel and took over the yard on the Ontario side. The only protection the DSS&A men received was priority to all yard work. Later in the 1950s it was decided to work four engines on the Canadian side and three on the American due to the cheaper wage rates of the CPR.

Besides handling the transfer work, the Sault, Michigan, switch engines handled the Pittsburgh coal dock, the Northwestern Leather tannery, and the Cadillac mill. The Union Carbide plant, a huge operation, had its own switch engine, and the industry interchanged in a little four-track yard across from the West Yard. This industrial base largely eroded in the late 1950s and early 1960s. Cadillac lumber mill, the largest remaining on the Upper Peninsula, shut down on May 31, 1956, followed by Northwestern Leather in May 1958. The Carbide lasted until after the Soo Line merger, and its last furnace shut down November 28, 1963.

The plan to appoint a terminal trainmaster at the Sault to care for the burgeoning traffic resulted in more contention. The Soo Line felt that as it represented over 60 percent of the traffic, the position should be given to a Soo man. Mitchell refused, telling Soo Line president G. Allan MacNamara that the South Shore had encountered enough difficulties with Soo Line management in the past, and said, "There is no doubt that the

The usual power for the Sault Ste. Marie–Soo Jct. turnaround job, Nos. 18 and 19, was a single D-2 Baldwin as pictured here on the Sault turntable on August 27, 1957.   *Robert Anderson, Dennis Schmidt Collection*

South Shore's prestige as well as its morale would be lowered if it should now surrender the control of the Sault Ste. Marie terminal to the Soo Line."[18] MacNamara finally agreed, but continued to grumble, "The switching and transfer costs covering the Sault Ste. Marie joint operations have been entirely too high due to inefficient supervision, and by merely adding another South Shore man to carry on this same policy could be of no value."[19]

A paper change occurred when the DSS&A and the Soo Line received permission from the ICC to dissolve the Sainte Marie Union Depot Company on June 16, 1952. The Sainte Marie Union Depot Company deeded its property in undivided one-half interests to the two parent companies on August 20. The property was integrated into the joint terminals, with the South Shore maintaining the property and billing the Soo Line for its share of expenses. Business at the station had fallen to a pair of Soo Line trains operating between Minneapolis and the Sault. Canadian Pacific passenger service into Sault, Michigan, had been discontinued on April 25, 1948, with connections being made by ferry and taxi at railroad expense. As well as wanting to reduce International Bridge charges, the CPR felt it more economical to service the train in its own yard.[20]

A big change in the configuration of the bridge across the St. Mary's River occurred when the U.S. government and Sault Ste. Marie Bridge Company signed a contract on January 25, 1957, to convert the swing span to a lift arrangement. This would widen the south shipping channel by eliminating the swing span's center pier.

A mix of Soo Line and South Shore power rests in the engine terminal at Sault Ste. Marie, Michigan, on August 27, 1957. The South Shore D-1 class Alco road switcher would have been used in yard service for the most part, while the Soo Line GP unit was typical power for passenger trains 7 and 8 between Minneapolis and Sault Ste. Marie. *Robert Anderson, Dennis Schmidt Collection*

To alleviate tie-ups, it was decided to build the lift bridge on top of the old swing span. In October 1958, rail traffic and the west entrance to the MacArthur and Poe locks were shut down for two days while the swing span was "bob-tailed" to allow for the construction of the two towers for the lift span.[21] Work then began on the lift span, which was completed in an elevated position, 65 feet above the water, early in 1959. On August 15, 1959, torches went to work cutting out the middle of the old swing span, which, in an open position, allowed the lift span to be lowered and made operational. The remainder of the old swing span and its concrete center pier were then removed.

The long career of General Superintendent Herman Schmidt came to an end with his passing on July 13, 1950. President Mitchell ordered that all South Shore trains and other work be stopped for 2 minutes at 1:30 PM on the 18th, the time of Schmidt's funeral service. Richard Barry was appointed general superintendent to succeed Schmidt. Barry, originally a Soo Line employee, had been active in the reorganization effort since coming to the DSS&A as an accountant on April 1, 1937. P. L. Solether, the South Shore's vice president and secretary, and last trustee, passed away on January 2, 1952, and was succeeded by Leonard Murray, assistant to the president. Murray, a soft-spoken teetotaler who had formerly been chief price attorney for the Office of Price Administration during World War II, had been brought on board by Mitchell during reorganization to help with the legal work.[22]

With reorganization, the South Shore came to perform more and more of its functions in house. Upon the retirement of T. Z. Krumm, chief engineer for the Soo Line and South Shore, S. P. Berg, South Shore division engineer, was appointed chief engineer of the DSS&A on July 21, 1951. The DSS&A gained control of its mechanical department on June 16, 1953, with the appointment of Thomas F. Kearney as mechanical superintendent. Kearney, formerly a Baldwin district sales representative, was primarily responsible for selling the South Shore its Baldwin locomotive fleet.

When the company came out of bankruptcy in 1949, it was judged to be deficient in three respects: lack of modern motive power, poor track, and a large number of bad order cars. Dieselization was made the first order of business, and, with little progress in track maintenance, the road suffered 24 derailments between October 1, 1952, and October 1, 1953. In addition to giving the DSS&A the expense of picking up the wrecks and paying damage claims, the accidents did little to promote the South Shore's image as a reliable alternative to the Chicago gateway. Track rehabilitation received new emphasis in 1953, with tie replacement and ballasting projects being doubled over 1952 levels. Ballast came from the old Isle Royale stamp sands at Pilgrim, while more conventional limestone-like ballast came from a pit near the West Yard at St. Ignace and a similar one at Three Lakes. Sidings were lengthened to handle the larger trains made possible by diesels and improved traffic levels. The South Shore's bad order car percentage stood at 11.3 percent on May 1, 1953, but new emphasis in this area reduced it to 8.3 percent by October 1. This figure was still above the national average of 5.3 percent.

The new management was greeted by news that 1949 was a disaster for the South Shore financially, the worst year since the war. Operating revenues decreased 13.5 percent, while expenses rose 7.2 percent. By October 1950, however, the South Shore, largely through increased use of diesel power, was able to wipe out the entire 1949 deficit and use the remaining income to pay bond interest. The South Shore ended the year with an operating ratio below 80 and net operating revenues of $1,559,864, an all-time high. Mitchell told the board of directors that this showed "the potentialities inherent in the South Shore."[23] Revamping the South Shore property continued to have a marked effect on its efficiency. In the last three years of receivership, from 1946 to 1949, net operating revenues on the DSS&A averaged 12.29 percent of gross, while in the three years after reorganization, 1950 to 1952, this figure jumped to 19.2 percent.

A D-1 performs one of the yard jobs at Sault Ste. Marie in July 1960. DSS&A traffic through the Sault gateway picked up dramatically following the revision of interchange agreements between the Canadian Pacific and Soo Line in 1953. *Robert Anderson, Dennis Schmidt Collection*

13

PROMOTING THE FAMILY—THE END OF THE SOUTH SHORE

Most of the joint rates through the Sault Ste. Marie gateway were between the Canadian Pacific and Soo Line as the result of a traffic contract negotiated in 1942, with the CPR declining to enter into similar combinations with the DSS&A. The DSS&A asked the CPR why it favored the Soo Line when it controlled only a small stock majority and a few bonds of that company, and had almost complete ownership of the DSS&A. The CPR agreed to modify its policy, but the Soo Line had no desire to give up traffic and did so only after the CPR increased rate divisions on the west end interchanges at Noyes, Minnesota, and Portal, North Dakota. The South Shore was also to give the Soo Line more business previously interchanged with the Milwaukee Road and C&NW—a point of bitter contention with the CPR. The new contract, reached January 1, 1953, allowed the DSS&A full access to the Sault Ste. Marie gateway and rights to solicit traffic in eastern Canada.[1]

There were immediate concerns about how the NYC and PRR would view a diversion of traffic from Mackinaw City. The old Soo Line–CPR traffic patterns had been established for many years, and it would be difficult for the DSS&A to gain enough traffic to make up for any losses at Mackinaw City. The CPR responded that the only traffic routed through Sault Ste. Marie would be for eastern Canada and the eastern U.S. beyond Buffalo and Pittsburgh. The Mackinaw City gateway covered a much larger territory west of those points, and this traffic would always be several times greater than that routed via Sault Ste. Marie. An apprehensive President Mitchell did not issue instructions to his traffic department to favor the CPR and Soo Line in routing until late 1955.[2]

With the opening of the Sault Ste. Marie gateway, interchange between the South Shore and the Canadian Pacific grew considerably. In 1953 this business totaled 1,742 cars, but by 1956 it had grown to 3,810. Prospects for the gateway were further improved by the South Shore's decision to institute trains 18 and 19 between Superior and Sault Ste. Marie, effective September 1, 1956, cutting 24 hours off the old schedule. Mitchell hoped the new service would "produce a substantial increase in our transcontinental bridge traffic, which has been a main objective of the present management ever since the Trusteeship was terminated and we took over in 1949."[3] Having another pair of trains

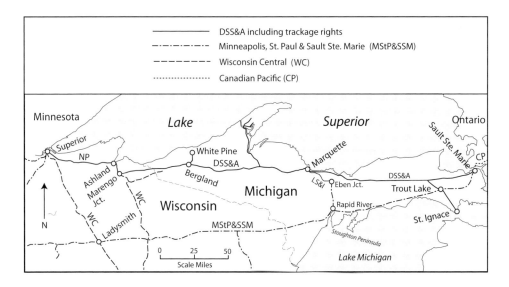

Family Line Connections, 1956

traveling over the railroad put a stop to most of the extra trains, including the "Hot Shot" out of Marquette to Ewen. A local between Sault Ste. Marie and Soo Jct. ran five nights a week and continued to do the short work along the branch.

Besides the Canadian Pacific business at the Sault, Algoma Central remained an important customer, especially with westbound business. During 1957 the South Shore received 4,762 cars from the ACR and delivered 920 to that road. The new schedule of Nos. 18 and 19 became quite a threat to the Soo Line's business out of Superior. The South Shore was beating the Soo Line's time by several days on Superior–Sault Ste. Marie traffic, as the Soo Line had to run its business down into Minneapolis before heading east. The Mackinaw City gateway remained important to the DSS&A, and train 22 was put on a 25-hour schedule between Superior and St. Ignace. Train 21 had a 30-hour schedule, leaving St. Ignace around 6:00 AM and arriving Superior at 12:00 noon the next day.

Bridge traffic over the South Shore grew in the 1950s to 33 percent of its total traffic and almost 45 percent of its revenue. This was quite a jump from the 1928 to 1936 period, when an average of only 8.5 percent of the South Shore's traffic was through business. Local traffic was also substantial, with 1956 showing the highest level since 1944. The increased business spoke highly to the South Shore's decision to increase its traffic department expenses from 2.2 percent of freight revenues in 1937 to 4.6 percent in 1956. The extra carloadings created earnings that could be used for dividends and rehabilitating the railroad.

The South Shore benefited after the war from the strong housing market, which was fed by a growing lumber and plywood industry in the Pacific Northwest. The aluminum industry, which blossomed in Washington State after new dams on the Columbia River provided cheap hydroelectric power, also provided needed carloadings. More importantly, neither of these industries relied on water carriage upon reaching the Head of the Lakes. Transportation on the Great Lakes had become more restricted with the demise of the package freighters formerly engaged in the merchandise trade, which did not make a comeback with the end of the World War II.

From November 1954 through October 1955, the South Shore handled 23,517 cars of through business. Eastbound business predominated with 16,469 cars compared to only 7,048 westbound. The great majority of the eastbound business, 11,497 cars, was lumber and forest products from the West Coast, while traffic for Minneapolis topped westbound carloadings. In total, West Coast business accounted for 61 percent of the traffic, followed by Minneapolis traffic with 23 percent, and 16 percent local Duluth business.

With transcontinental traffic of increasing importance, it became crucial for the DSS&A to differentiate itself from other carriers and make itself better known. A new herald was introduced in 1953 which included the complete name, rather than just "South Shore," thus helping to avoid confusion with other "South Shore" roads such as the Chicago, South Shore & South Bend and the Newburgh & South Shore (a terminal road in the Cleveland area).

WHITE PINE BRANCH

An important mining development for the DSS&A was undertaken in the early 1950s by the Copper Range Mining Company at White Pine, Michigan. The Reconstruction Finance Corporation lent over $57,000,000 to Copper Range Mining to develop a huge mine and smelter complex, which would serve to replenish cooper stocks needed for national defense. The DSS&A agreed to stand the expense of building the 14-mile branch north out of Bergland, furnishing the rail and track metal, while Copper Range Mining financed the remainder of the project, retaining ownership of the branch until the loan was paid off. The ICC granted permission to build the White Pine branch on June 23, 1952.[4]

The DSS&A had nothing but problems in constructing the branch. Rain started that summer and remained fairly constant into early fall, making it impossible for contractor C. G. Bridges to make much headway in the wet red clay soil. With Bridges unable to meet the goals set for grading, Jones Construction Co., which had its equipment and men ready to lay track, was also compromised, sometimes laying only 500 to 750 feet per day. Ballasting also lagged, with only 5 miles completed before the freezing weather set in. Although snow had to be cleared away from the roadbed, the last rails were laid into White Pine in early January 1953. On the 10th, two cars of cement made up the first commercial loads brought to the plant site.[5]

The railroad hoped to get an early start on the ballasting the following spring, but warm weather caused the South Shore to lose a race with the frost. This caused the track to disappear into the red clay on numerous occasions. Steam engines were used instead of diesels owing to fears of the traction motors sinking into the wet clay. Due to the danger of the track slipping out, trains were kept to 15 or 16 cars so the crew could see the entire consist when going around curves. Extra long switch ties were used every third or fourth tie to try and keep the track above ground. Extra ties were also placed outside of the regular ties to keep everything afloat. It was finally found that mixing stamp sand with the clay stabilized the roadbed.

With the opening of the White Pine, a new five-day job, using a 1,000-horsepower D-1 diesel, was put on out of Ewen to handle local work as far as Ashland in addition to the branch. The new job was not required to switch the White Pine plant itself, as Copper Range Mining had a GE 44-ton locomotive for that purpose, and cars were exchanged in a three-track interchange yard. Cars for White Pine were left by No. 21 at Ewen and by No. 22 at Bergland for the local to handle up the branch. Business was heavy, given all the materials needed to construct the new mine, the power house, and a community for 1,000 inhabitants.

Initial coal shipments for the White Pine power plant came out of Illinois, Indiana, and western Kentucky, but eventually lake coal from Pickands-Mather's Union coal dock, near Dollar Bay, was used. This practice came about through the influence of A. D. Chisholm, an officer of Pickands-Mather and Co. and a member of the DSS&A board of directors. The coal movement was a headache for the South Shore, as it all had to be lifted up the L'Anse hill. The coal was usually handled by train No. 32, and a reduction would be made at Baraga of what could not be handled. The L'Anse pusher would then take the reduction up the hill the following day. As a 1,000-horsepower diesel was only good for five loaded cars on the grade, several trips were required. The L'Anse job was taken on and off depending on when there was storage coal moving off the dock. Service was no longer required at the Ford plant as the mill cut its last log on June 25, 1954, ending shipments from the longtime DSS&A customer.

The White Pine mined sulphide ore, as opposed to the native or mass copper found on the Keweenaw, and it was processed right on the site. The first outbound shipment of finished copper, which typically generated three cars per day, took place on January 26, 1955. In exchange for building the line, the DSS&A asked Copper Range Mining to route as much traffic as possible via the St. Ignace and Sault Ste. Marie gateways to ensure the best possible rate division. Although this was done initially, in the summer of 1953, Copper Range Mining came under pressure from their old friend the CMStP&P to route via Sidnaw, considerably shortchanging the South Shore. The mining company said they had to give some of the business to the Milwaukee Road as they were afraid of losing their McKeever connection. With merger discussions underway between the CMStP&P and C&NW, it was said the Milwaukee Road would be abandoned between Sidnaw and Ontonagon. The DSS&A had to constantly remind Copper Range that the road was shorting the CPR on dividend payments in order to pay its loan to the Mining Company, and eventually the routings were worked out to the South Shore's satisfaction.

The DSS&A watched the outbound White Pine shipments very carefully in order to be assured of receiving the long haul. Once a gondola of blister copper was set out at Greenwood with a hot journal and, after being inspected by carmen, was allowed to come into Marquette for a change of wheels. The car arrived on Saturday morning but was not repaired until Monday, causing Vice President Murray to write General Mechanical Superintendent Kearney, "This failure is exactly the type of thing we have been trying to overcome to make the DSS&A a good railroad."[6]

Another revenue producer for the South Shore in the early 1950s was the hauling of pipe for construction of a 1,959-mile crude oil pipeline by Canadian firms from Edmonton to Port Credit, Ontario. The pipeline paralleled the DSS&A from Superior to St. Ignace. The 1950 segment from Edmonton to Superior saw the South Shore receive pipe from the Milwaukee Road at Champion and C&NW at Negaunee for delivery to the Duluth, Winnipeg and Pacific at Superior. The 1953 construction along the DSS&A saw pipe being unloaded at Iron River, Trout Lake, Moran, and St. Ignace.

Iron ore activity on the Marquette Range started to dwindle, as fewer and fewer producers remained. The Blueberry mine was exhausted in 1954, and the Richmond became inactive in 1956. The Champion mine continued to operate, being one of the few mines still served by the South Shore. Others were the Volunteer and the Tracy. Cleveland-Cliffs decided to activate the Ohio mine west of Michigamme, but, as the mine was far from LS&I trackage, it hoped to have the South Shore haul the ore to the Ishpeming interchange. The South Shore held out for the longer haul to the Marquette interchange, to which Cleveland-Cliffs finally agreed. As the Ohio had been idle since 1920, the spur was relaid, and the mine joined the shipping list in 1953. Tonnages from the remaining mines resulted in shipments of around 500,000 tons off the DSS&A dock.

The exhaustion of soft iron ore saw the introduction of the taconite process to various ranges of the Lake Superior district in the mid- and late 1950s. Pellets of high iron content were created by crushing the plentiful hard taconite rock and fusing the iron particles together. Cleveland-Cliffs developed the Eagle Mountain taconite plant on the Marquette Range, but of course this traffic went via LS&I to Marquette. Beginning in 1958 the South Shore did receive some taconite pellets in interchange off the LS&I at Marquette; these were used for mixing with raw iron ore on the DSS&A dock.

With much of the taconite traffic moving to furnaces along Lake Michigan, the LS&I sought to serve a new conveyor pellet dock, which it would construct near Escanaba. The LS&I wanted to purchase a half-interest in the Soo Line's 32-mile branch from Eben Jct. to Rapid River and use an additional 1.5 miles of the Soo Line's Twin City–Sault Ste. Marie main line to reach their new dock site on the Stoughton peninsula. In exchange, the Soo Line would purchase a half-interest in the LS&I trackage from Eben Jct. into Marquette. This would create an additional interchange with the South Shore and encourage the family ties urged by parent CPR.

The South Shore was not crazy about the new scheme, as it was afraid the new Soo Line interchange would cut into its rate divisions. On Chicago traffic out of Houghton, the South Shore received one-third of the rate via the CMStP&P at Champion and the C&NW at Ishpeming, but 45 percent via the Soo Line at Marengo Jct. More tonnage would also move eastbound into Marquette, instead of westbound to Marengo, at a time when westbound trains were always under full capacity. The agreement eventually worked out prevented the Soo Line from handling cars originating or terminating at Marquette from which the South Shore would only get a switch charge.

The South Shore's reservations over the new arrangement became moot when the ICC decided on September 18, 1958, not to approve the LS&I–Soo Line venture. The ICC's major concern was the effect on the Chicago & North Western, which was already underutilized between Ishpeming and Escanaba. As the C&NW expressed a willingness to build a pellet dock at Escanaba, the ICC felt that public convenience and necessity could be met equally well by that road and at a lower cost. One wonders whether the LS&I could have met the ICC's "public convenience and necessity" requirement in 1893, when it paralleled the DSS&A between Marquette and the Iron Range.

THE END OF PASSENGER SERVICE

The South Shore, like many other roads, worked to improve profitability in the fifties by discontinuing money-losing passenger operations. The DSS&A decided to once again

D-1 class 102 powers one of the first commercial trips up the White Pine branch.
Trainmaster Don Hart (left) and Assistant Superintendent Ben Pederson (right)
lend supervision. *Don Hart Collection*

petition the Michigan Public Service Commission regarding trains 1 and 2 between
Calumet and Marquette. Although the train had a fairly decent mail and express business,
the number of crew members often exceeded passengers, and the DSS&A estimated it
was losing almost $100,000 a year on the service. This time the petition was successful,
with only the railway brotherhoods appearing in opposition, and the last run was made
on January 18, 1953. The train, which typically drew engine 555 for power, was one of the
last enclaves for steam on the South Shore, and its discontinuance allowed another
steamer to be sent to the boneyard.

The DSS&A then attempted to discontinue the remainder of trains 1 and 2's run
between Marquette and St. Ignace, but this was denied on June 7, 1954, by the Michigan
Public Service Commission. The states of Wisconsin and Michigan did give authority to
reduce Nos. 7 and 8 to a tri-weekly affair between Marquette and Duluth, effective August 13, 1954. Trains left Marquette on Sunday, Tuesday, and Thursday evenings and returned from Duluth the following day. Sleeping car service was withdrawn that fall,
and the next year the road received permission to eliminate Nos. 7 and 8 altogether,
with the last run being made eastbound on June 3.

Mail and express business between Superior and Marquette began to be handled
by the DSS&A's own trucks, which were painted yellow with red lettering in similar
fashion to the road's diesel power. The agreement with the post office called for a
combination rail and highway contract. The South Shore guaranteed the movement
of the mail by train if the roads became impassable, giving them an advantage over

No. 1 has stopped to do station work at Negaunee in this May 20, 1948, view. Although discontinued in 1939 between Calumet and Marquette, Nos. 1 and 2 were given a second life over this territory as the result of a court ruling in 1941. The train was discontinued for a final time west of Marquette on January 18, 1953.
Wilbur C. Whittaker

Nos. 1 and 2, although generally operated with steam power west of Marquette, used a D-1 whenever one was available. Here the 106 powers No. 1's three-car consist near Valley Spur, 4 miles west of Marquette.   *Courtesy of Roy Paananen*

other competitors, who had to rely solely on the highways. The trucks followed Nos. 7 and 8's overnight schedule between Marquette and the Soo Line's depot in Superior, making connections with C&NW Nos. 161 and 162 at Negaunee and CMStP&P Nos. 9 and 10 at Champion. The only exception was that upon reaching the Gogebic Range the long-dreamed-of loop line became a reality with a run into Bessemer and Ironwood. In addition to mail and express, the trucks handled company material for the section crews along the line. The truck operation started when Nos. 7 and 8 went to tri-weekly operation, with one vehicle working the legs the train did not run. When the train was taken off altogether, trucks assumed both legs on a six-day-per-week schedule.

In order to get rid of Nos. 7 and 8, its biggest money-loser, the South Shore had agreed to operate a Budd rail diesel car (RDC) between St. Ignace and Ishpeming for three months and between Marquette and the Straits until 1957. The RDC would be the answer to all the critics' moaning as to why the patronage was not there. The car would be streamlined, air conditioned, and capable of making the trip from Marquette to the Straits in 3 hours and 20 minutes, compared to 5 hours by the conventional train. But as Michigan Public Service Commission member Maurice E. Hunt told the *Mining Journal,* "This is the last try. If this doesn't break even you can kiss railroad passenger service in the Upper Peninsula goodbye." Hunt said that the commission had no choice but to grant permission to the South Shore to discontinue trains 7 and 8 between Marquette and Duluth due to the heavy losses the trains were taking. Courts had ruled that railroads could not be required to provide service at a loss.[7]

The revised passenger service was started with conventional equipment on August 1, 1955, with No. 1 leaving St. Ignace at 9:01 AM and returning as No. 2 at 6:10 PM. That day also saw the end of Nos. 1 and 2's passenger equipment being sent across the Straits of Mackinac in what was said to be the last instance of a passenger train moving by ferry within the United States. Passengers connecting with NYC trains 337 and 338 thereafter were sent by taxi on the state boat. The change also saw the end of the Railway Post Office, with the majority of the mail and all the express going over to an extended DSS&A truck operation, which now operated from Mackinaw City to Superior, basically following the former schedule of Nos. 7 and 8.

The new Budd RDC-1 made an excursion run on August 25, 1955, between Ishpeming and St. Ignace and was viewed by hundreds of people. The stainless steel, 85-foot car had two diesel engines each capable of 275 horsepower and was christened the *Shoreliner.* Regular operations were commenced the next day, with the car operating from St. Ignace to Ishpeming and back. Two crews, composed of an engineer and conductor, were used. The Budd car, the first of its type to be operated in the UP, faced an impossible task. While the heavyweight consists of Nos. 1 and 2 had required 20 passengers per trip to break even, the RDC would need 40, or almost half its 89-seat capacity, to cover its costs and retire the $165,000 purchase price in 10 years.

Although passenger earnings increased with the Budd car, they were still not enough to meet the costs of the crew. The Budd car made its last run between Ishpeming and Marquette on February 4, 1957, and the DSS&A filed an application to discontinue the remainder of the run to St. Ignace. Opposition at the Michigan Public Service Commission hearings came primarily from the brotherhoods and the city of Newberry, which felt service was vital for the state hospital. The South Shore figured it was losing $57,000 per year on the train, but it was argued that the profit from the South Shore's

No. 1, with one of the boiler-equipped D-1s, is shown coming into Trout Lake in
August 1947. No. 1 always enjoyed a fairly heavy mail and express traffic off the New
York Central at Mackinaw City, and its consist usually included at least one or two
head-end cars off that road.   *Collection of Harold K. Vollrath*

An Extra East, powered by D-2 class No. 208, crosses the Au Train River. Extras of
this kind were often Shingleton Turns which would leave their entire consist at
Shingleton for pickup by other eastbounds. The grades encountered once the divide
was crossed allowed for much higher tonnage ratings from Shingleton to St. Ignace.
Courtesy of Roy Paananen

trucking operation nearly equaled the deficit of operating the Budd car. The Commission, unable to force the railroad to operate a money-losing service, granted permission to discontinue the train, with the last run being made on January 11, 1958. Although opposing the discontinuance, the Marquette *Mining Journal* wrote, "The South Shore, it seems to us, made a sincere effort to extend passenger service to this area in the face of declining revenues."[8]

The only passenger service left on the South Shore rails, the Copper County Limited, continued to operate in conjunction with the CMStP&P. It was said the train incurred an out-of-pocket loss to the DSS&A of $40,000 per year but was retained on the insistence of the Calumet and Hecla mining interests. The South Shore considered tying the train up at Houghton, which would have enabled the closing of the Calumet facilities. That city's residents took a dim view of this idea, however, with many threatening to ship "no more freight over our railroad."[9] The Michigan Public Service Commission was also unsympathetic and "suggested that such economies would inure only to the benefit of the Canadian Pacific as the owner of all our stock."[10] Given the court decisions, however, the Public Service Commission had no choice but to approve the cutback to Houghton, effective January 15, 1959. The South Shore then decided that winter was not a good time to make the change, and the Calumet service lasted into the 1961 merger.

SOME GOOD EARNING YEARS

With the South Shore accumulating excess earnings in early 1952, the Canadian Pacific suggested it might be time to pay a dividend. Mitchell responded that when he had assumed the presidency there had been an "express understanding with Messrs. [CPR chairman G. A.] Walker and [CPR president William A.] Mather that I should fully exploit the potential earning power of the DSS&A."[11] Mitchell felt that there were many improvements yet to be made before this was realized, and the payment of dividends would only delay the process. The South Shore did pay dividends in 1953, 1955, and 1956, for the first time in its history.

Due to reduced ore and lumber shipments, 1954 was not a dividend year, and the South Shore found it difficult to meet its many conditional sales payments to diesel and freight car manufacturers. Economies included closing the depot at Hancock and consolidating it with Houghton. The car repair facilities at St. Ignace were closed and the work was taken to Marquette. Ore car rehabilitation was put on hold, with shortages to be taken care of by rental of foreign cars if necessary. The South Shore continued to correct the deferred track maintenance incurred in its years of receivership, although at reduced levels. President Mitchell felt track rehabilitation was the only way "to successfully solicit routings of through traffic for our railroad via our Gateways in competition with routings via other railroads through the Chicago Gateway . . . and . . . fully exploit the advantage we have in furnishing shippers the shortest bridge line between the Upper Pacific Coast territory and New England and Trunk Line territories."[12]

The South Shore went on to enjoy its best earning year ever in 1956, with a gross income of over $6,500,000, resulting in a net 43.7 percent above 1955 levels. The operat-

Two Wilson Marine Transit Company boats are seen in this view of DSS&A ore dock No. 6 at Marquette. In the foreground is another DSS&A customer, the Texaco Oil facility, which received petroleum products by boat and dispersed them by truck and rail. *Courtesy of Roy Paananen*

ing ratio dropped slightly to 81 percent in 1956 in spite of "substantial" wage increases. Efficiency was improved with the use of train radio, which the South Shore began to install in its diesel fleet beginning in 1955. Cabooses were given walkie-talkies, which the trainmen could take with them on the ground. This would serve to speed up local work and get the important bridge traffic over the road at a quicker pace.[13]

Because of the high traffic levels in 1956 the South Shore was once again hit with car shortages, increasing per diem expenses and inviting criticism from the AAR for allowing the road's boxcar ownership to decline in the face of increasing traffic. The South Shore purchased its first and only 50-foot boxcars in 1956 with an order for 100 new PS-1 type cars from Pullman-Standard. These cars (15500–15599), in keeping with the billboard lettering trend of the day, came with 4-foot-high DSS&A initials on the sides, and were equipped with 15-foot double doors to meet the loading requirements of the Celotex Corp. plant under construction at L'Anse. In order to retain its flour business, the DSS&A leased 6 Airslide covered hopper cars from General American Transportation Company in 1956, as mills were giving routing preference to those roads which furnished Airslides as part of the change from bag to bulk flour loading.

Although trucks had cut into less-than-carload (LCL) traffic, the South Shore attempted to promote the business in early 1954 by painting up some old 18000-series boxcars with yellow sides, red roof and ends, and the words *Merchandise Service* prominently displayed in large letters. This business continued to be handled by trains 21 to Superior and 31 to Houghton. The effort to retain the LCL business proved largely ineffective. Tonnage handled at the Duluth freight house fell from 8,906 tons in 1947 to only 2,792 tons 10 years later. After a lengthy proceeding, the South Shore received permission to begin to handling LCL in its mail and express trucks, effective March 1, 1960.

Repainted in the new scheme and equipped with multiple-unit connections, three D-1s prepare to depart Marquette on an Extra East. The train is made up on the Lake Street branch, which had greater length than the shorter tracks in the Lower Yard. *Courtesy of Roy Paananen*

Unfortunately, the peak earning year of 1956 would never be repeated, as a tight money market threw the country into a recession in 1957. When industries started tightening their belts, they first stopped ordering raw materials. As these were the principal commodities handled by the South Shore, the effects were immediate. On the other hand, in times of recovery, roads like the DSS&A were among the first to see business pick up as plants replenished their stocks. Pacific Coast lumber, which formed a large part of the South Shore's traffic, suffered from the lack of housing starts, and aluminum shipments also saw a large drop-off. DSS&A local car loadings suffered from low copper prices, and log business dropped off due to reduced demand from paper mills and chemical plants. The South Shore was also hurt by the LS&I building a 14-mile branch northeast from Cusino. This line took away log traffic which had formerly moved out of Spur 81 near Seney, amounting to 3,000 cars in 1955.

The South Shore made heavy cutbacks in 1957, reducing the mechanical department from 248 to 138 employees and maintenance of way from 62 to 54. The agency at Bruce's Crossing was discontinued that September. Despite the economies and mechanization, labor costs on the DSS&A still totaled 53 percent of operating revenues. Average hourly rates for railway employees had jumped from $1.65 in 1950 to $2.40 in 1957. As rate increases granted by the ICC had not kept pace, Leonard Murray wrote, "The railroad industry is in the economically unsound position of reducing employment, creating deferred maintenance and impairing service in order to grant wage increases to those employees having sufficient seniority to work. This course can ultimately lead only to catastrophe either in the form of financial collapse of the industry or in the form of government ownership which in essence is simply another form of financial collapse."[14]

With the continuing recession, the DSS&A incurred an operating deficit of over $100,000 during the first three months of 1958, and it decided to discontinue trains 18 and 19, which had been so successful in bringing new business to the Sault gateway. Effective April 1, these runs were cut back to their former nightly turn from Sault Ste. Marie to Soo Jct., where connections were made with Nos. 21 and 22, seven days a week. A regularly scheduled local between Marquette and Ewen (Nos. 23 and 24) was put on to help Nos. 21 and 22 get over the road. The South Shore saw its net income rise in 1958 over 1957, but this was primarily due to cutbacks, including deferred maintenance, which could not be kept up indefinitely. The DSS&A also sought to gain working capital by selling excess equipment made surplus by the discontinuance of passenger trains. With other roads in the same financial position there was little interest in the 1,000-horse D-1s, but the RDC was sent off to the Canadian Pacific in May 1958.

The South Shore business, especially iron ore and lumber products, picked up in 1959, although this was tempered by labor difficulties including a lengthy steel strike that finally ended in November through a federal injunction. Another strike began at the White Pine mine on October 28 and lasted until February 22, 1960. Despite the end of the strike, the White Pine job out of Ewen was discontinued on November 15, 1960, as there was little to do outside of the branch, and some days the crew only worked 4 hours. No. 21 was assigned to make a side trip up the White Pine branch in its place. Locals 23 and 24 between Marquette and Ewen were also cut back to tri-weekly. The South Shore was rapidly getting down to a bare-bones operation, with little room for future economies.

The long-awaited Celotex plant on the old Ford site at L'Anse had been placed on hold for several years because of the recession, but finally came on line in February 1960. Another benefit of Celotex was the construction of a plant at L'Anse by Upper Peninsula Power Company. This plant required 60,000 tons of coal per year off the Union Coal dock, in addition to the 130,000 tons moving to White Pine. The L'Anse coal had to be weighed at Nestoria and backhauled for spotting.

The DSS&A had to deal with some trying weather conditions in the spring of 1960. Heavy rainfall, resulting in flooding and washouts, took the west end main line out of service from April 23 to April 30, requiring a long detour over the Wisconsin Central from Superior to Ladysmith, Wisconsin, and then on the Soo Line to Trout Lake. Then it was the east end's turn, when a fast snow melt caused by rain and sleet put much of the main line from Soo Jct. to Sault Ste. Marie under 2.5 feet of water. Trains had to be detoured, from May 8 to May 18, over the Soo Line from Trout Lake into the Sault. The main line through the Taquamenon swamp between Soo Jct. and Newberry suffered the same fate, but was kept in operation for most of that period by the rental of an LS&I steam engine which moved traffic over the affected area. At Newberry and Soo Jct. the traffic was passed off to diesels for the remainder of the run.

THE MACKINAW BRIDGE

One way for politicians to win votes in the early 1950s was to support the building of a bridge across the Straits of Mackinac to avoid the sometimes massive tie-ups associated

The Extra East, having departed Marquette, is running along Lake Superior with the LS&I main line to Lawson in the foreground. *Courtesy of Roy Paananen*

Nestoria was an important junction on the DSS&A, with the Copper Country main line splitting off to the north for Houghton and Calumet. The Houghton main line is seen passing to the right of the depot, while the Duluth-Superior trackage curves to the left. The water column and tank in the background will soon disappear as dieselization sends the final steam power to the scrap yard. *Courtesy of Roy Paananen*

with the ferry operation. An auto-only bridge project was started in 1955, with the South Shore building new trackage at St. Ignace for the unloading of construction material. The massive span opened in 1957 and dedication ceremonies were held on June 25, 1958. One of the chief backers of the span, U.S. senator Prentiss M. Brown, had walked from the stranded *Chief Wawatam* to Mackinaw City in 1922. Mackinac Transportation Company had not exactly endeared itself to Senator Brown; he recalled shipping his automobile across the Straits in 1916, when "I had to put my Ford on a flatcar and go through all the business of a manifest, since cars were considered freight. Three days later the car came across from Mackinaw City to St. Ignace, at a cost of $16.00. And we had had to drain the gas out ourselves!"[15]

About the only advantage the South Shore enjoyed from the bridge was that its mail and express trucks no longer had to wait for the ferry. By this time the NYC had gone to trucks in place of its Detroit–Mackinaw City passenger run and a truck-to-truck transfer took place on the Lower Peninsula. Starting in 1959 the NYC no longer brought express into Mackinaw City, and American Railway Express had to reroute traffic for DSS&A points to Negaunee, Champion, and Trout Lake. Of course, the new bridge increased efficiency for all motor carriers and did nothing to improve the downward trend in rail traffic through the St. Ignace gateway. Traffic at the Straits fell from 34,786 cars in 1951 to 15,877 cars in 1960.

Another new bridge, in the former Mineral Range territory, was built over Portage Lake just west of the old swing span. The old span, condemned by the government as a "menace to navigation," was replaced by a new double-deck bridge, 1,310 feet in length, and equipped with a 263-foot-long lift span raised by two towers.[16] The lift bridge had the capability of raising the lower railroad span to the level of the upper roadway. This allowed small boats to pass while vehicle traffic ran over the paved railroad deck. When a train came, the railroad deck was lowered into place and the upper deck lined up for automobile and truck traffic. When a large boat came, both levels could be raised to provide the needed clearance. The span was largely financed by the government, with the South Shore covering 20 percent and the Copper Range Railroad another 20 percent of the total cost. After being under construction for almost two years, the new bridge opened to highway traffic on December 20, 1959, and on February 11, 1960, for railroad use.

Traffic continued to fall on the former Mineral Range lines after the DSS&A merger, and by the late 1950s there was only one job working out of Houghton, except during the periods when the coal was moving to White Pine mine. During these times, it was necessary to re-establish the Lake Linden job on a five-day basis. The other yard engine switched Houghton-Hancock and made trips as needed to Calumet. The last of the former Mineral Range employees, engineer Hilrick Lamielle, made his final run on December 29, 1956, breaking the last hold with the glory years. Mr. Lamielle had put in 50 years on the road, managing to survive its spectacular decline.

The once-substantial DSS&A land holdings also declined to the point that it was decided to do away with the South Shore Land Company, Ltd. Under Soo Line management, the company had managed to sell some two-thirds of its property, reducing its holdings to about 24,000 acres. Of this amount, only about 7,000 acres were thought to have any value, such as timber, and the remainder was given up for nonpayment of taxes. The amount of remaining property was so small that its title was conveyed to the DSS&A and the South Shore Land Company was dissolved on July 1, 1957.[17]

The *Chief Wawatam* sits idle at the St. Ignace ferry slip. The *Chief* generally was busiest during the nighttime hours, when freight cars were being transferred to Mackinaw City off train 22 and back to St. Ignace for train 21. The St. Ignace switch engine also worked the nights.   *Wesley Perron Railroad Collection, Peter White Public Library, Marquette, Mich.*

MERGER

In spite of its newfound profitability, the Canadian Pacific continued to criticize the DSS&A throughout the 1950s for looking after its own interests. C. E. Jefferson, CPR vice president traffic, wrote Mitchell, "The Traffic Officers of the South Shore do not lend their best efforts in securing traffic for the Canadian Pacific and at the same time protect their own revenue interests. I strongly feel that they continue to overlook 'family interests' and work with 'other lines' far more necessary than is required."[18] The South Shore did attempt to solicit more traffic via the Sault and Marengo Jct., but the Wisconsin Central did not care to meet the joint rates of the Milwaukee Road and C&NW on coal and other commodities, as it would result in lower rates to communities on its own line. There was no doubt, however, that the South Shore received the greater revenue via the St. Ignace or Sault Ste. Marie gateways and was not anxious to get a short haul to Marengo Jct.

The CPR, dissatisfied with the harmony of its U.S. properties, ordered studies to show possible savings from a merger of the Soo Line, the DSS&A, and possibly the WC. The consolidation studies did not proceed rapidly, due to the DSS&A's distrust of the Soo Line team that was seeking access to its files. As Mitchell wrote Soo president MacNamara, "it seems to me both unnecessary and undesirable to give the representatives of the Soo Line direct access to all files and records of the DSS&A, in advance of any decision that the properties and operations of that Company should be merged with those of the Soo Line. In this connection I have in mind, among other things, the diversion of traffic from routings via DSS&A to routings via Soo Line when the Soo was in control of the DSS&A and had access to that Company's passing reports, until the DSS&A went bankrupt in 1936." Mitchell stipulated that all record requests on the part of the Soo Line would have to go through him.[19]

Increasingly dissatisfied with the progress of the Soo Line–DSS&A merger study, Norris Crump wrote MacNamara, "It does seem to me that we have an anomalous situation when we control two railroads which, starting from Sault Ste. Marie, proceed westward some 350 miles and diverge only 90 miles at the western terminus of the smaller road. This thought is particularly impressive when one considers the very sparsely settled territory on the eastern portion of these two railroads. It seems self-evident that any economies that could be affected would not only be helpful to the family interest but also constructive to a better service in the long run to the territory served."[20]

The study, sent off to the CPR on September 24, 1956, concluded that there was little that could be done through coordination of the Soo and South Shore other than abandoning the South Shore branch from Soo Jct. to the Sault. Coordination of the South Shore executive, traffic, and law departments with those of the Soo Line was not felt to be "advisable because of the competitive traffic situation, as it might subject the Canadian Pacific to the allegation that traffic was being diverted against the best interests of the Soo minority stockholders and the income bondholders."[21]

A merger between the Soo and South Shore would result in more savings, allowing the elimination of line staff at Marquette and the abandonment of the South Shore operations between Marengo Jct. and Superior, with that business being handled through Ladysmith. These moves were thought to save an estimated $342,000 per year, if all present traffic was retained. No one expected this to happen, but it was thought that less traffic would move via the CMStP&P and C&NW interchanges and hopefully "greater effort could be made to secure this competitive traffic for the family lines."[22] There was a troubling stipulation in the Wisconsin Central lease that did not allow eastbound traffic out of Superior to be interchanged to the Soo Line at Ladysmith for the Manistique and St. Ignace gateways. This stipulation would be done away with by bringing the WC into the merger, but that move would necessitate acquiring WC stock then in the hands of the public. It was thought this could be obtained only at a great price.

DSS&A management opposed the merger for a number of reasons. It was felt that running over Soo Line trackage instead of over the Northern Pacific between Superior and Ashland would greatly increase per diem costs, not to mention causing deteriorated service due to longer running times. The South Shore had approached the NP about handling the latter road's light business between Superior and Ashland, but these discussions had broken down with the Soo Line merger talks.

Secondly, the DSS&A was experiencing a large traffic out of the Minneapolis–St. Paul area. The Great Northern and NP found that by handling this traffic to Superior and giving it to the South Shore, they could make a percentage of the line haul, rather than interchanging it at the Twin Cities to a Chicago road and only earning a switch charge. If a merger took place, this business, totaling some $750,000 a year, would be lost as the Soo was a competitor out of the Twin Cities and the GN and NP would give their business to their own subsidiary, the Chicago, Burlington & Quincy. It was also felt that total system carloadings would diminish, as shippers tended to split their traffic amongst roads which made solicitation. If the South Shore traffic force was eliminated, the Soo Line would get only one share of the business offered.

While the South Shore struggled to maintain its existence, the road's biggest defender, Henry S. Mitchell, suffered a stroke while vacationing in England in 1958. Awaiting Mr. Mitchell's return to Montreal, DSS&A trainmaster Don Hart asked the CPR's assistant vice president–traffic what time the ship would arrive and was told "precisely at 11 AM." Hart asked what would happen if the ship encountered heavy weather on the St. Lawrence. The vice president snapped his heels and said, "Mr. Hart, the *Empress of England* is a Canadian Pacific ship and she will dock precisely at 11 AM." And that is what she did. Several windows had to be taken out of a Soo Line business car to load the stretcher-bound Mitchell for the journey back to Minneapolis. Unable to overcome the effects of his stroke, Mr. Mitchell passed away on November 22, 1958, with Leonard Murray succeeding him as president.[23]

Norris Crump, who assumed the presidency of the CPR in 1955, was a staunch advocate of pared-down corporate structure, and soon after taking office he eliminated 38 wholly owned and leased companies through consolidation. Operating control of the CPR was also split into four regions, doing away with the more numerous district divisions. Crump advocated a similar course for the CPR's American subsidiaries, a vision that became harder to argue against as South Shore net earnings seemed to vanish after 1956. With operations down to one train a day each way, a reduced maintenance program in effect, and efficiencies from dieselization long since realized, merger seemed to be the only way to bring cost reductions, even at the expense of lost revenue. The lightly trafficked parallel lines of the South Shore and Soo Line were a luxury that could no longer be justified when one line was more than capable of handling the business offered.

On March 15, 1960, the boards of directors of the WC, Soo Line, and South Shore met in Minneapolis to approve a merger, effective January 1, 1961. Before the meeting, Murray urged his directors to vote for the consolidation as being in the "best interest of our Company."[24] It is hard to imagine how convincing this would have been to directors with economic interests in the UP. Most no doubt realized that most of the savings would come from diminished service in the South Shore territory.

Under the merger agreement, DSS&A stock would be exchanged at a rate of 0.75 shares for one share in the new company, giving the South Shore a 12.44 percent stake. Plans called for the Wisconsin Central and Minneapolis, St. Paul & Sault Ste. Marie to be absorbed by the Duluth, South Shore & Atlantic, with the South Shore then taking the name of the Soo Line Railroad Company. The plan, submitted for ICC approval on May 3, was overwhelmingly approved by the stockholders of the three roads on May 17.

The only trackage in line for immediate abandonment was 18.3 miles of the South Shore's Sault Ste. Marie branch from Raco to the Sault. Deferred maintenance had seen the speed limit on the branch fall to 20 m.p.h. in recent years, although traffic had held up well. The non-agency station at Brimley was the only point on the line that would lose service. On May 3, 1960, the South Shore filed an application with the ICC for a certificate of public convenience and necessity allowing the Sault branch to be abandoned between MP 1.7 at Sault Ste. Marie and MP 20.0 at Raco.

The ICC issued an order approving the merger on December 2, 1960, and also gave

Train 21, with a single D-3 class engine, is about to cross the Iron River just west of the station of the same name. The rails of the Northern Pacific have been used since leaving those of the Wisconsin Central at Ashland. *Frank King, Northeast Minnesota Historical Center—Duluth, MN S3742B29D2*

In another view of train 21 between Ashland and Superior, it seems the consist is dominated by empty Canadian National boxcars returning to the latter's subsidiary, the Duluth, Winnipeg & Pacific, at West Duluth. *Frank King, Northeast Minnesota Historical Center—Duluth, MN S3742B29D2*

authority to abandon the line between Raco and Sault Ste. Marie. The South Shore's Leonard Murray became head of the new company as presidents G. Allan MacNamara of the Soo Line and Edgar Zelle of the WC were near retirement age. On January 1, 1961, after a stormy 74-year existence, the Duluth, South Shore & Atlantic was absorbed into the new 4,716-mile Soo Line Railroad.[25]

EPILOGUE

The Soo Line merger led a string of others that would follow in the 1960s and 1970s as U.S. carriers attempted to deal with reduced traffic levels and increased labor costs. As was often the case when carriers were swept up in parallel mergers, the former DSS&A territory quickly found its through business diverted to the former MStP&SSM trackage. Twin Ports–Sault traffic became increasingly handled by the former Wisconsin Central for exchange with the Minneapolis-Sault main line at Ladysmith. Traffic out of the Twin Ports that would formerly have headed for the St. Ignace gateway became increasingly routed via Chicago. With a lack of through business to keep it viable, the former DSS&A mileage was quickly segmented and largely reverted back to what it had been before the speculative McMillan extensions of 80 years before. Upon the exhaustion of the natural resources of the area, even these segments became abandonment targets. The new Soo Line Railroad did become a profitable institution under Leonard Murray, justifying the Canadian Pacific's push for consolidation.

The three participants in the Mackinac Transportation Company rapidly lost interest in maintaining the once-important St. Ignace gateway. The expenses of the ferry operation had become a matter of dispute in the late 1950s, and the NYC and PRR terminated the contract in order to have the DSS&A pick up half the costs as opposed to one-third. As the parties were unable to come to an agreement, the matter went to the ICC for arbitration, and that body decided in the eastern roads' favor shortly after the Soo Line merger. Forced to assume 50 percent of the operating costs of the aging *Chief Wawatam,* the Soo Line sought, with the concurrence of the NYC and PRR, to discontinue the operation altogether. The ICC, however, denied the application, finding the "alternative routes suggested by the applicants would not provide adequate and satisfactory transportation for the present ferry traffic."[1] With little solicitation, traffic continued to fall, however, and the St. Ignace switch engine was taken off on September 25, 1964. The slide continued during the Penn Central era, and by 1976 the *Chief* was only making one trip per week.

The operation found new life when the Michigan Northern, which took over the *Chief Wawatam* and former Pennsy trackage into Mackinaw City, began offering a reduced tariff on lumber. This was the old car ferry's last gasp, as the Michigan Northern lost part of its state subsidy on September 30, 1984, and went out of business. The Soo Line put an embargo on the trackage between St. Ignace and Trout Lake, and the *Chief* languished at Mackinaw City until she was towed away and cut down into a barge; thus was severed the last direct rail link between the two peninsulas of Michigan. The only remaining connection with the old Mackinaw Division was through the former MStP&SSM trackage at Trout Lake. On the former DSS&A Sault branch, permission was received to abandon the remaining 27-mile segment from Raco Jct. (formerly Soo Jct.) to Raco in 1977.

On the old Houghton Division, encroaching mining activity saw the former South Shore trackage between Eagle Mills and Ishpeming receive a major line change. On August 20, 1965, operations on the old route through Negaunee and Ishpeming were abandoned and traffic started moving over the new route, about a mile north of those communities. Iron ore continued to be handled over the old DSS&A dock No. 6 at Marquette until July 1971, with the last ore coming from the Tracy mine.

The last passenger service in the former South Shore territory steadily deteriorated after the merger, and the Copper Country Limited departed Calumet for the last time on March 8, 1968. The Soo Line petitioned the ICC for permission to abandon all trackage north of Baraga in 1977. The resulting order that came out the following year represented only partial success, requiring the Soo to continue to operate from Baraga to Dollar Bay while allowing abandonment of the rest of the Shore Line into Lake Linden, and north from Hancock to Calumet. The Soo Line immediately appealed the ruling and received permission to abandon north of Baraga in fall of 1981. The line then received a year's reprieve after the State of Michigan agreed to subsidize the Soo Line's operating losses. The last train pulled out of the Copper Country on September 28, 1982.

On the former Western Division, which saw little business out of Twin Ports for points along the old DSS&A, permission was received from the ICC in 1972 to discontinue trackage rights over what had become the Burlington Northern (former NP) between Superior and Ashland. Authority to abandon the line between Bergland and Nestoria was received in 1980, although the trackage remained in place for some time. Service to the White Pine mine continued to be provided off the former WC line at Marengo Jct.

The Soo Line announced plans to abandon practically all the remaining former DSS&A trackage in January 1985. These lines were shuffled off into the Lake States Division on April 5, 1987, which was made up of redundant trackage the Soo Line hoped to get rid of following its merger with the CMStP&P. Negotiations with a group that came to be known as the Wisconsin Central Limited (WCL) came to fruition on October 11, 1987, under which the WCL took over some 1,800 miles of former Soo Line trackage, including all of the old DSS&A.[2]

Under the WCL, the carnage continued. In October 1989, a contract was let to pull up the rail between Sidnaw and Bergland, and the line from Nestoria to Sidnaw was sold to the Escanaba & Lake Superior railroad. WCL furthered the trend of turning the former South Shore trackage into a north-south configuration when its subsidiary, the Sault Ste. Marie Bridge Co., purchased the C&NW's old Peninsula Division on January 28, 1997. WCL immediately ceased operating, and later abandoned, the former South Shore trackage between Ishpeming and Munising Jct., and all business on the remain-

In this painting by Robert Thom, the *Raymond H. Reiss,* of the Reiss Steamship Company, loads along the north side of Dock No. 6 in 1966. The dock would see five more years of service before receiving its last iron ore.   *Courtesy of AT&T Michigan*

Shortly after the Soo Line merger, No. 21 passes in front of the Soo Line depot at Ashland. Before the merger, DSS&A freight trains almost always pulled into the adjacent Northern Pacific yard, where set-outs and pickups would be made. *Frank King, Northeast Minnesota Historical Center—Duluth, MN S3742B29D2*

Two Soo Line GP units take a short string of Lake Superior & Ishpeming taconite cars up the hill for placement on Dock No. 6. The taconite would then be mixed in the ore dock pockets with natural ore from Soo Line–served iron mines. *Courtesy of Roy Paananen*

A westbound Soo Line train, powered by new second-generation diesels, runs along Lake Michigamme just east of the town of the same name. This photo was taken in 1986, very near where the C&NW Michigamme branch crossed the South Shore main line many years before. *Courtesy of Roy Paananen*

ing trackage between Baraga and Ishpeming now moves south over the former C&NW. Perhaps the ultimate irony exists in the recent purchase of the Wisconsin Central Ltd. by the Canadian National. This successor to the Grand Trunk, which the Canadian Pacific tried so mightily and at great expense to keep out of the Sault, is now the sole user of the International Bridge and principal carrier in the Upper Peninsula and Northern Wisconsin.

The South Shore, although turning a profit through much of the last decade of its existence, was in many ways preconditioned to fail due to its early association with the Canadian Pacific. The CPR had little interest in developing the property and only sought to hold it as protection against intruders. It is hard to imagine how the road would have survived the bank panics of 1893 and 1907, however, without the deep pockets of its parent. The CPR's acquisition of the DSS&A's chief competitor, the Soo Line, boded ill for the South Shore, as the parent fed traffic to the more direct route into the Twin Cities and other Midwestern markets. The lengthy management of the South Shore by its sibling following World War I was also not helpful, diverting bridge traffic away from the DSS&A that was rightfully the South Shore's.

Even with the North American Free Trade Agreement in place it is difficult to see how the CPR would have ever made more use of its South Shore subsidiary. In combination with the Soo Line's Plummer line, an 80-mile short cut would have been possible between Winnipeg and Sudbury, but the heavy outlay for improvements needed to bring this trackage up to heavy main line standards would have made this scenario unlikely. By the time of the agreement's implementation, the trackage was already too badly segmented to have been given any consideration.

If the McMillan syndicate had sold out to J. J. Hill, the Grand Trunk, or even the New York Central instead of the CPR, perhaps things might have turned out differently, with an end-to-end merger allowing the South Shore to become part of a transcontinental line as envisioned by its founders. The ultimate death knell for the DSS&A would have been the Burlington Northern merger in 1970, as it is unlikely the South Shore could have continued to solicit West Coast lumber, plywood, and aluminum shipments in the face of the BN's efforts to secure the long haul to Chicago over its own trackage. The South Shore certainly would have lost the GN and NP business originating in the Twin Cities.

The loss of the friendly connection at St. Ignace, as the NYC and PRR concentrated their efforts on maintaining their more viable routes to Chicago, also would have been hard for the South Shore to overcome. The Penn Central merger and its quick slide into bankruptcy surely doomed the Mackinaw City gateway in any event. Modern railroading also left little room for the inefficient and outdated ferry operation at the Straits, and it is unlikely that traffic projections would have allowed for the building of a tunnel or bridge. Coupled with the near exhaustion of the local copper, iron, and timber resources of the Upper Peninsula, there was left little need for such an expensive anachronism, however romantic, as the Duluth, South Shore & Atlantic.

APPENDIX: DULUTH, SOUTH SHORE & ATLANTIC RAILWAY ALL-TIME LOCOMOTIVE ROSTER (1886–1960)

ROSTER NOTES

Class headings for steam locomotives are given as follows: class, wheel arrangement, cylinder size, drivers, boiler pressure, tractive effort, total weight.

Headings for diesel locomotives and rail-diesel car are these: wheel arrangement, builder's model number, horsepower, tractive effort, total weight.

Individual engine data are as follows: Number, builder, builder's number, date built, origin to DSS&A, disposition. If two DSS&A engine numbers are given the second number reflects a general renumbering that took place in 1888. Dates follow any additional renumberings.

All locomotives are standard gauge and dimensions given are the earliest obtainable and do not reflect rebuilding unless otherwise stated.

ABBREVIATIONS

Alco-GE	American Locomotive Company-General Electric
b/n	Builder's Number
CICA	Charcoal Iron Co. of America

DI&M	Duluth Iron & Metal Company
GC&L	Georgia Car & Locomotive
LSI&C	Lake Superior Iron & Chemical
NJL&M	New Jersey Locomotive & Machine
PC	Paper Calmenson
S.	Sold
Sc.	Scrapped
S. Sc.	Sold scrap
USS	United States Steel
t.e.	Tractive Effort

Railroads

B&A	Boston & Albany
D&W	Duluth & Winnipeg
DM&M	Detroit, Mackinac & Marquette
MH&O	Marquette, Houghton & Ontonagon
MR	Mineral Range
MStP&SSM	Minneapolis, St. Paul & Sault Ste. Marie
NYC	New York Central
TC&StL	Toledo, Cincinnati & St. Louis

DULUTH, SOUTH SHORE & ATLANTIC STEAM LOCOMOTIVES

Class...	4-4-0	...	60	...	...	50,000
1 20	NJL&M	62	1855	Ex-MH&O 1	Sold MStP&SSM 6/27/1892	
Class...	4-4-0	16×24	54	130	11,170	58,000
2 21	NJL&M	165	1857	Ex-MH&O 2	Sold MStP&SSM 10/1892	
Class...	4-4-0	16×22	57	...	...	60,000
3 22	NJL&M	298	1862	Ex-MH&O 3	S. MStP&SSM 11/1892	
4 23	NJL&M	299	1862	Ex-MH&O 4	S. MStP&SSM Date Unknown	
Class...	4-4-0	16×24	57	...	...	...
5	NJL&M	...	1863	Ex-MH&O 5	Disposition Unknown	
Class...	4-4-0	16×24	60	...	...	63,140
6	Taunton	381	1866	Ex-MH&O 6	S. 11/1890	
Class...	4-4-0	17×24	54	...	...	69,980
7	Grant	...	1866	Ex-MH&O 7	Disposition Unknown	
Class...	2-6-0	17×24	54	...	15,000	69,680
8 80	Grant	...	1866	Ex-MH&O 8	Disposition Unknown	

Class . . .	2-6-0	17×24	54	. . .	15,000	69,570
9 81	Grant	. . .	1870	Ex-MH&O 9	Scrapped 7/1913	
Class . . .	0-4-0T	8×16	33	. . .	. . .	23,380
10	Smith & Porter	76	1870	Ex-MH&O 10	Disposition Unknown	
Class . . .	4-6-0	17×24	54	. . .	. . .	79,080
11 84	Taunton	528	1874	Ex-MH&O 11	Disposition Unknown	
Class . . .	0-4-0	14×22	48	. . .	. . .	46,850
12 1	MH&O	None	1872	Ex-MH&O 12	Disposition Unknown	
14 2	MH&O	None	1873	Ex-MH&O 14	Disposition Unknown	
Class . . .	4-6-0	17×24	54	. . .	. . .	77,460
13 85	Taunton	570	1872	Ex-MH&O 13	Disposition Unknown	
Class . . .	0-4-0	14×22	42	. . .	. . .	36,250
15	Grant	. . .	1872	Ex-MH&O 15	Disposition Unknown	
Class . . .	0-6-4T	14×16	36	. . .	. . .	. . .
16	Mason	698	1883	Ex-MH&O 16	Disposition Unknown	
Class . . .	0-4-0	14×22	48	. . .	. . .	45,350
17 4	Taunton	598	1873	Ex-MH&O 17	Disposition Unknown	
18 3	Taunton	600	1873	Ex-MH&O 19	S. Canadian Mining Co. 1908?	
Class . . .	2-6-0	18×24	50	. . .	15,500	74,700
19 207	Rogers	2041	1872	Ex-MH&O 18	Rblt. 8/99:	
reno. 80(2)	0-6-0	17×24	. . .	15,500	Sc. 3/1914	
Class . . .	4-4-0	17×24	56	. . .	13,160	63,930
20 52	Taunton	605	1873	Ex-MH&O 20	Disposition Unknown	
21 50	Taunton	606	1873	Ex-MH&O 21	Sc. 10/1915	
22 51	Taunton	609	1873	Ex-MH&O 22	Sc. 10/1915	
Class . . .	4-6-0	17×24	54	. . .	15,000	78,420
23 83	Taunton	610	1873	Ex-MH&O 23	S. MR Date Unknown	
24 86	Taunton	612	1873	Ex-MH&O 24	Disposition Unknown	
25 82	Taunton	613	1873	Ex-MH&O 25	S. CICA 5/1916	
Class . . .	4-4-0	17×24	54	. . .	. . .	66,520
26	Dickson	130	1873	Ex-MH&O 26	S. D&W 1890	
27	Dickson	131	1873	Ex-MH&O 27	S. D&W 1890	
28	Dickson	132	1873	Ex-MH&O 28	S. D&W 1890	
29	Dickson	133	1873	Ex-MH&O 29	S. D&W 1890	
30	Dickson	134	1873	Ex-MH&O 30	S. D&W 1890	

(Continued)

Class . . .	2-6-0	18×24	54	. . .	17,136	82,000
31 211	Rogers	2961	1882	Ex-MH&O 31	S. CICA 9/19/1917	
32 210	Rogers	2963	1882	Ex-MH&O 32	S. MR 3/1/1903	
Class . . .	0-6-0	17×24	54	. . .	15,285	78,000 Reblt. 1891
33 74	Rogers	2964	1882	Ex-MH&O 33	Sc. 10/1923	
34 73	Rogers	2965	1882	Ex-MH&O 34	S. Champion Gravel Co. 6/3/1924	
Class . . .	0-4-0	15×24	54	150	11,500	55,100
35 14	Rogers	2967	1882	Ex-MH&O 35	S. 9/1915	
Class . . .	2-6-0	18×24	54	145	17,748	84,000
36 208	Hinkley	1588	1883	Ex-MH&O 36	S. LSI&C 10/2/1913	
37 209	Hinkley	1589	1883	Ex-MH&O 37	S. Chas. Hebard & Sons 6/30/1919	
Class . . .	4-4-0	17×24	60	. . .	14,248	74,000
38 61	Hinkley	1590	1883	Ex-MH&O 38	S. Northwestern Coop. & Lbr. 10/9/1916	
39 60	Hinkley	1591	1883	Ex-MH&O 39	S. Schneider & Brown Lbr. 9/2/1919	
Class . . .	0-4-0	15×24	54	. . .	12,000	60,000
40 10	Hinkley	1592	1883	Ex-MH&O 40	Disposition Unknown	
41 11	Hinkley	1593	1883	Ex-MH&O 41	Disposition Unknown	
42 12	Hinkley	1594	1883	Ex-MH&O 42	S. 9/1915	
Class . . .	4-4-0	17×24	63	. . .	13,000	75,500
43 45	Manchester		1882	Ex-DM&M	Sold D. N. McLeod Lbr. 7/1912	
44 41	Manchester		1882	Ex-DM&M	S. GC&L 7/9/1917	
45 44	Manchester		1882	Ex-DM&M	S. GC&L 7/9/1917	
46 42	Manchester		1882	Ex-DM&M	S. 3/1916	
47 40	Manchester		1882	Ex-DM&M	Sold D. N. McLeod Lbr. 4/1914	
48 43	Manchester		1882	Ex-DM&M	S. GC&L 7/9/1917	
49 46	Manchester		1882	Ex-DM&M	S. GC&L 7/9/1917	

Note: 43 through 49: ex-DM&M 7 through 13. Reno. sequence unknown. DM&M 7, b/n 951; 8, b/n 952; 9, b/n 946; 10, b/n 947; 11, b/n 948; 12, b/n 949; 13 b/n 950

Class . . .	0-4-0T	15×22	50	. . .	10,940	51,000
50 13	Manchester	953	1882	Ex-DM&M 17	S. 11/1912	
Class B-1	0-6-0	19×26	51	. . .	28,158	. . .
50(2)	Brooks	48370	1910	Ex-MR 162 3/1/1926	Sc. 1/16/1935	
51(2)	Brooks	48371	1910	Ex-MR 163 3/1/1926	Sc. 10/3/1934	

Class . . .	2-6-0	18×24	52	. . .	18,432	87,000
51 201	Baldwin	7154	1884	Ex-MH&O 51	S. MR 7/1/1907	
52 202	Baldwin	7166	1884	Ex-MH&O 52	S. MR 7/1/1907	
53 203	Baldwin	7189	1884	Ex-MH&O 54	S. Menasha Wooden Ware 1/15/1925	
54 204	Baldwin	7193	1884	Ex-MH&O 55	S. Christianson Lbr. Co. 10/14/1925	
55 205	Baldwin	7165	1884	Ex-MH&O 53	S. Ontonagon Lbr. Co. 5/21/1915	
56 206	Baldwin	7195	1884	Ex-MH&O 56	S. Thompson Wells Lbr. Co. 5/31/1926	
57 200	Baldwin	7151	1884	Ex-MH&O 50	S. MR Date Unknown	
Class . . .	0-6-0	17×24	52	. . .	15,419	69,000
58 70	Baldwin	7191	1884	Ex-MH&O 58	Sc. 3/15/1928	
59 72	Baldwin	7268	1884	Ex-MH&O 59	S. Alexander & Boyd 11/16/1924	
60 71	Baldwin	7190	1884	Ex-MH&O 57	S. MR Date Unknown	
Class . . .	4-4-0	16×24	58	. . .	12,605	66,000
61 38	Baldwin	5468	1881	Ex-DM&M 4	S. 5/1912	
62 34	Baldwin	5161	1880	Ex-DM&M 2	S. MR 1897	
63 37	Baldwin	5922	1881	Ex-DM&M 6	S. 5/1912	
64 39	Baldwin	5918	1881	Ex-DM&M 5	S. 5/1912	
65 35	Baldwin	5467	1881	Ex-DM&M 3	S. MR 1897	
66 36	Baldwin	5158	1880	Ex-DM&M 1	S. MR 1897	
Class . . .	2-6-0	19×24	56	. . .	20,026	100,000
69 303	Brooks	1214	1887		Sc. 10/15/1928	
70 301	Brooks	1215	1887		S. Sc. DI&M 7/6/1933	
71 305	Brooks	1216	1887		Sc. 5/1/1925	
72 302	Brooks	1217	1887		S. Sc. DI&M 6/23/1933	
73 304	Brooks	1218	1887		S. Sc. DI&M 6/28/1933	
74 300	Brooks	1275	1887		Sc. 9/1/1929	
75 306	Brooks	1276	1887		S. Sc. DI&M 6/30/1933	
76 314 310 (2) (ca. 1896)	Brooks	1277	1887		S. Sc. DI&M 6/22/1933	
77 319 307 (2) (unknown)	Brooks	1278	1887		Sc. 12/1/1928	
78 308	Brooks	1279	1887		S. Weidman Lbr. Co. 3/22/1929	
79 315	Brooks	1349	1888		S. MStP&SSM 6/29/1892	
80 309	Brooks	1350	1888		S. MStP&SSM 6/20/1892	
81 316	Brooks	1351	1888		S. MStP&SSM 7/21/1892	
82 307	Brooks	1352	1888		S. MStP&SSM 6/14/1892	

(*Continued*)

83 310	Brooks	1353	1888		S. MStP&SSM 6/29/1892	
84 312 309 (2) (ca. 1896)	Brooks	1354	1888		S. Sc. DI&M 6/30/1933	
85 313	Brooks	1355	1888		S. MStP&SSM 8/4/1892	
86 317	Brooks	1356	1888		S. MStP&SSM 8/25/1892	
8767 311	Brooks	1357	1888		S. Weidman Lbr. Co. 12/5/1926	
8868 318	Brooks	1358	1888		S. MStP&SSM 9/29/1892	
Class . . .	*2-6-0*	*19×24*	*56*	. . .	*20,026*	*96,600*
87(2) 400	Baldwin	9549	1888		S. Sc. DI&M 6/24/1933	
88(2) 404	Baldwin	9550	1888		S. MR 6/1/1915	
89 401	Baldwin	9548	1888		S. Sc. DI&M 6/23/1933	
90 407	Baldwin	9553	1888		S. Ecklund Brothers 10/14/1926	
91 414	Baldwin	9551	1888		S. Sc. DI&M 6/26/1933	
92 408	Baldwin	9555	1888		S. Harry P. Bourke 9/24/1925	
93 411	Baldwin	9554	1888		S. Greenwood Lbr. Co. 11/30/1925	
94 406	Baldwin	9557	1888		Sc. 10/1931	
95 402	Baldwin	9558	1888		S. MR 3/1903	
96 410	Baldwin	9618	1888		S. Sc. DI&M 6/29/1933	
97 403	Baldwin	9622	1888		S. Stack Lumber Company 3/13/1916	
98 409	Baldwin	9623	1888		S. MR 3/1903	
99 405	Baldwin	9624	1888		S. MR 7/1914	
100 413	Baldwin	9627	1888		S. Sc. DI&M 6/26/1933	
101 412	Baldwin	9631	1888		Sc. 11/1931	
Class F	*0-8-0*	*20×28*	*55*	*190*	*39,102*	*170,000*
90(2)	Baldwin	30179	1907		S. Sc. PC 10/8/1937	

Note: Rebuilt 2-8-0, ca. 1907–1912

Class F-4	*2-8-0*	*21×28*	*51*	*190*	*39,100*	*192,000*
91(2)	Brooks	65966	1924		S. Sc. 1954	
92(2)	Brooks	65967	1924		S. Sc. 1954	
Class C	*4-4-0*	*18×24*	*66*	. . .	*15,784*	*95,000*
102	Baldwin	9389	1888		Sc. 5/15/1928	
103	Baldwin	9395	1888		Sc. 6/1/1929	
104	Baldwin	9398	1888		S. Sc. DI&M 6/22/1933	
105	Baldwin	9403	1888		Sc. 1/31/1932	
106	Baldwin	9404	1888		Sc. 6/15/1928	
107	Baldwin	9402	1888		Sc. 2/29/1932	
108	Baldwin	9427	1888		Sc. 7/15/1928	

Number	Builder	Const. No.	Year	Pressure	Notes	Disposition	Weight
109	Baldwin	9428	1888			Sc. 12/1931	
110	Baldwin	9432	1888			Sc. 8/15/1928	
111	Baldwin	9433	1888			S. MR date unknown	
112	Baldwin	9437	1888			Sc. 5/1930	
113	Baldwin	9435	1888			Sc. 6/1930	
114	Baldwin	9438	1888			Sc. 9/15/1928	
115 101(2)	Baldwin	9436	1888			Sc. 4/15/1928	
116 100(2)	Baldwin	9441	1888			Sc. 3/31/1932	
Class D-3	*2-6-0*	*18×24*	*57*	*175*		*20,290*	...
500 Reno. 415 ca. 1907	Baldwin	32257	1892		Ex. D&W 7 1894	Sc. 12/15/1928	
Class E	*4-6-0*	*19×26*	*61*	...		*22,624*	...
500 (2)	Baldwin	32256	1907			S. Sc. DI&M 6/29/1933	
501	Baldwin	32257	1907			S. Sc. DI&M 7/6/1933	
502	Baldwin	32347	1907			S. Sc. DI&M 6/24/1933	
503	Baldwin	33751	1909			S. Sc. DI&M 6/28/1933	

Note: 501-class E-1, t.e. 23685

Number	Builder	Const. No.	Year	Pressure	Notes	Disposition	Weight
Class H	*4-6-2*	*21×26*	*67*	*180*		*24,952*	*185,000*
550	Schen.	51417	1912			Sc. 6/30/1942	
551	Schen.	51418	1912			Sc. 8/31/1949	
Class H-1	*4-6-2*	*21×26*	*67*	*180*		*26,184*	*196,850*
552	Brooks	53588	1913			Sc. 1951	
553	Brooks	53589	1913			S. Sc. USS 10/16/1951	
554	Brooks	53590	1913			Sc. 1948	
Class H-2	*4-6-2*	*21×26*	*67*	*200*		*29,100*	*203,000*
555	Brooks	65968	1924			S. Sc. PC 2/1953	
556	Brooks	65969	1924			S. Sc. PC 2/1953	
Class F-1	*2-8-0*	*20×28*	*55*	*190*		*32,887*	*172,000*
600	Baldwin	32246	1907			S. Sc. PC 11/15/1937	
601	Baldwin	32275	1907			Sc. 9/30/1935	
602	Baldwin	32276	1907			Sc. 10/16/1936	
603	Baldwin	32300	1907			Sc. 12/16/1936	
604	Baldwin	32334	1907			S. Sc. PC 10/27/1937	
605	Baldwin	32365	1907			Sc. 7/31/1935	
Class F-2	*2-8-0*	*20×28*	*57*	*190*		*31,733*	*173,000*
606	Brooks	...	1905			S. Ford Motor Co. 8/16/1941	
607	Brooks	...	1905			Sc. 10/18/1939	
Class F-3	*2-8-0*	*21×30*	*55*	*180*		*36,800*	*186,300*
700	Alco-Brooks	53576	1913			Sc. 4/1942	
701	Alco-Brooks	53577	1913			S. Sc. Hyman-Michaels Co. 9/2/1947	
702	Alco-Brooks	53578	1913			S. Sc. 1950	
703	Alco-Brooks	53579	1913			S. Sc. USS 1951	
704	Alco-Brooks	53580	1913			S. Sc. 1950	

(Continued)

705	Alco-Brooks	53581	1913		Sc. 10/19/1946		
706	Alco-Brooks	53582	1913		S. Western Dominion Coal Mines, Ltd. 8/9/1946		
707	Alco-Brooks	53583	1913		S. Sc. Hyman-Michaels Co. 9/2/1947		
708	Alco-Brooks	53584	1913		S. Ford Motor Co. 1/8/1947		
709	Alco-Brooks	53585	1913		S. Sc. DI&M 4/3/1952		
710	Alco-Brooks	53586	1913		S. Sc. DI&M 1951		
711	Alco-Brooks	53587	1913		S. Sc. 1950		
Class F-5	*2-8-0*	*23×30*	*55*	*190*		*46,600*	*206,000*

Note: Superheated by Soo Line 12/1924–3/1925

712	Alco-Brooks	48365	1910	Ex-MR 195 9/1/1924	S. Sc. 1950		
713	Alco-Brooks	48366	1910	Ex-MR 196 9/1/1924	S. Sc. 1950		
714	Alco-Brooks	48367	1910	Ex-MR 197 9/1/1924	S. Sc. USS 10/16/1951		
715	Alco-Brooks	48368	1910	Ex-MR 198 9/1/1924	S. Sc. 1950		
Class F-6	*2-8-0*	*24×30*	*55*	*185*		*49,405*	*224,500*
716	Alco-Brooks	55959	1916	Ex-MR 300 8/2/1926	S. Sc. USS 10/16/1951		
717	Alco-Brooks	55960	1916	Ex-MR 301 8/2/1926	Wrecked 12/14/1951, Sc. 1952		
Class F-7	*2-8-0*	*25×30*	*63*	*170*		*43,000*	*228,360*
718	Alco-Schenectady	52638	1913	Ex-Soo Line 497 9/1936	S. Sc. USS 10/16/1951		
719	Alco-Schenectady	52639	1913	Ex-Soo Line 498 9/1936	S. Sc. USS 10/16/1951		
Class L-1	*2-8-2*	*25×32*	*63*	*180*		*48,570, with booster 58,470*	*295,000*
1050	Alco-Schenectady	30833	1905	Ex-NYC 1232 7/1937	S. Sc. PC 2/1953		
1051	Alco-Schenectady	41867	1907	Ex-NYC 1304 7/1937	S. Sc. PC 2/1953		
1052	Alco-Schenectady	38783	1905	Ex-NYC 1323 1/1941	S. Sc. PC 4/3/1952		
1053	Alco-Schenectady	38747	1905	Ex-NYC 1327 1/1941	S. Sc. PC 4/3/1952		
1054	Alco-Schenectady	37998	1905	Ex-B&A 1222 3/1942	S. Sc. USS 1951		

DULUTH, SOUTH SHORE & ATLANTIC DIESEL-ELECTRIC LOCOMOTIVES

B-B Diesel Road Switcher: ALCO-GE Model RS-1		*1,000 hp*	*60,875 t.e.*	*243,500 wt.*
100	American	73753	5/1945	Soo Line 100
101	American	73760	6/1945	Soo Line 101

102	American	75215	12/1946		Soo Line 102
103	American	75217	1/1947		Soo Line 103
104	American	75218	1/1947		Soo Line 104
105	American	75219	2/1947		Soo Line 105
106	American	75389	5/1947		Soo Line 106
107	American	78376	1/1951		Soo Line 107

Note: 104 to 106: 61,875 t.e., 247,500 wt.
107: 61,550 t.e., 246,200 wt.

C-C Diesel Road Switcher:		*1,500 hp*	*82,450 t.e.*		*329,800 wt.*
Baldwin Model-DRS-6-6-1500					
200	Baldwin	74693	10/1949		Soo Line 384
201	Baldwin	74694	10/1949		Soo Line 385
202	Baldwin	74695	11/1949		Soo Line 386
203	Baldwin	74716	8/1950		Soo Line 387

C-C Diesel Road Switcher:		*1,600 hp*	*81,500 t.e.*		*329,800 wt.*
Baldwin Model AS-616					
204	Baldwin	75071	2/1951		Soo Line 388
205	Baldwin	75072	2/1951		Soo Line 389
206	Baldwin	75073	2/1951		Soo Line 390
207	Baldwin	75074	2/1951		Soo Line 391
208	Baldwin	75075	2/1951		Soo Line 392
209	Baldwin	75180	8/1952		Soo Line 393
210	Baldwin	75181	8/1952		Soo Line 394
211	Baldwin	74676	3/1952, Ex-Baldwin 1600 3/1953		Soo Line 395

Note: 207, 208: 83,000 t.e., 332,000 wt.
209, 210: 82,275 t.e., 329,100 wt.
211: 89,500 t.e., 358,000 wt.

C-C Diesel Road Switcher:		*2,000 hp*	*88,687 t.e.*		*345,750 wt.*
Baldwin Model DT-6-6-2000					
300	Baldwin	74668	10/1949		Soo Line 396
301	Baldwin	74669	10/1949		Soo Line 397
302	Baldwin	74670	10/1949		Soo Line 398
303	Baldwin	74672	10/1949		Soo Line 399

B-B Rail Diesel Car: Budd Model RDC-1					
500	Budd	6220	1955		S. Canadian Pacific 3/1958

MINERAL RANGE RAILROAD STEAM LOCOMOTIVES (NARROW GAUGE)

2-6-0	*11 × 16*	*36*	. . .	. . .	*35,000*
1 *Portage Lake*	Baldwin	3092	1/1873		S. John J. Bagley 9/1886
4-4-0	. . .	. . .	. . .	. . .	. . .
1 (2) *Jay A. Hubbell*	Porter	473	1/1882	Ex-Connoton Valley 15 11/1886	Disposition Unknown
2-6-0	*12 × 16*	*36*	. . .	. . .	*38,250*
2 *J. C. Sharpless*	Baldwin	3484	10/1873		Disposition Unknown
2-6-0	*12 × 16*	*40*	. . .	. . .	*40,000*

(Continued)

3 Kee Wee Nemo, later Keweenaw	Baldwin	3741	6/1875		Disposition Unknown
2-6-0	14×16	38	...	...	...
4 O Te Ti Ani, later Calumet	Baldwin	5219	7/1880		Disposition Unknown
2-8-0	15×18	36	130	...	56,000
5 Hancock	Baldwin	6749	5/1883	Ex-Lac La Belle and Calumet 1 5/1883	S. Edward Hines Lumber Company 1902
4-6-0	16×20	46	...	...	...
6 Houghton	Baldwin	10420	11/1889		Disposition Unknown
2-8-0	16×20	37	150	...	72,000
7 Superior	Baldwin	11628	2/1891		S. Natalbany Lumber Company
2-6-0	91/2 and 16×22	44	...	...	...
8 Red Jacket	Baldwin	12677	5/1892		S. Hancock & Calumet [8]

MINERAL RANGE RAILROAD LOCOMOTIVES (STANDARD GAUGE)

4-4-0	16×24	58	...	12,605	66,000
34	Baldwin	5161	1880	Ex-DSS&A 34(2) 1897	S. Porterfield & Ellis, 5/15/1918
35	Baldwin	5467	1881	Ex-DSS&A 35(2) 1897	S. Champion Sand & Gravel, 7/21/1917
36	Baldwin	5158	1880	Ex-DSS&A 36(?) 1897	S. Porterfield & Ellis, 10/5/1916
0-6-0	17×24	53	...	...	...
71	Baldwin	7190	1884	Ex-DSS&A 71 Date Unknown	S. Ford Motor Co., 6/6/1924
4-6-0	17×24	54	...	15,000	78,420
83	Taunton	610	1873	Ex-DSS&A 83 Date Unknown	S. Porterfield & Ellis, 10/5/1916
4-4-0	18×24	67	...	...	...
111	Baldwin	9433	1888	Ex-DSS&A 111 1905	Sc. 7/15/1928

Note: Rebuilt 1905, 18×24 cyl, 63 dr.

0-6-0	19×26	51	...	...	...
160	Rogers	5695	2/1902	S. Sc. PC 8/5/1933	
161	Rogers	5696	2/1902	S. Sc. PC 8/5/1933	
0-6-0	19×26	51	...	28,158	...
162	Alco-Brooks	48370	1910	S. DSS&A [50] 3/1/1926	
163	Alco-Brooks	48371	1910	S. DSS&A [51] 3/1/1926	
2-8-0	22×30	55	...	...	...
190	Rogers	5697	2/1902	S. Sc. PC 8/15/1933	
191	Rogers	5698	2/1902	S. Sc. PC 8/5/1933	
192	Rogers	5699	2/1902	S. Sc. PC 8/4/1933	

193	Rogers	5700	2/1902	S. Sc. PC 8/17/1933	
2-8-0	*23×30*	*55*	*190*	*46,600*	*206,000*
194	Alco-Brooks	48364	1910	S. Hecla & Torch Lake 1/8/1926	
195	Alco-Brooks	48365	1910	S. DSS&A [712] 8/19/1924	
196	Alco-Brooks	48366	1910	S. DSS&A [713] 8/19/1924	
197	Alco-Brooks	48367	1910	S. DSS&A [714] 8/19/1924	
198	Alco-Brooks	48368	1910	S. DSS&A [715] 8/19/1924	
199	Alco-Brooks	48369	1910	S. Hecla & Torch Lake 1/8/1926	
2-6-0	*18×24*	*53*	*. . .*	*. . .*	*104,167*
200	Baldwin	7151	1884	Ex-DSS&A 200 Date Unknown	Sc. 6/1/1929
201	Baldwin	7154	1884	Ex-DSS&A 201 7/1/1907	S. Harry P. Bourke 6/26/1925
202	Baldwin	7166	1884	Ex-DSS&A 202 7/1/1907	S. Brunswick Ewen Lumber Co. 2/2/1925
2-6-0	*18×24*	*54*	*. . .*	*17,136*	*82,000*
210	Rogers	2963	1882	Ex-DSS&A 210 3/1/1903	S. Lake Superior Iron & Chemical Co. 1913
2-8-0	*24×30*	*55*	*185*	*49,405*	*224,500*
300	Alco-Brooks	55959	1916	S. DSS&A [716] 8/2/1926	
301	Alco-Brooks	55960	1916	S. DSS&A [717] 8/2/1926	
2-6-0	*19×24*	*56*	*. . .*	*20,026*	*96,600*
402	Baldwin	9558	1888	Ex-DSS&A 402 3/1903	S. Sc. PC 7/29/1933
404	Baldwin	9550	1888	Ex-DSS&A 404 6/1915	S. Sc. PC 9/5/1933
405	Baldwin	9624	1888	Ex-DSS&A 405 7/1914	S. Sc. PC 7/29/1933
409	Baldwin	9623	1888	Ex-DSS&A 409 3/1903	S. Sc. PC 7/31/1933

HANCOCK & CALUMET LOCOMOTIVES (NARROW GAUGE)

2-6-0	*15×18*	*37*	*. . .*	*. . .*	*. . .*
1 *Torch Lake* (25)	Brooks	834	12/1882	Ex-TC&StL 8/1885	S. 12/1901
2-8-0	*16×20*	*37*	*. . .*	*. . .*	*. . .*
2 *Tamarack* (33)	Baldwin	7676	9/1885	S. North Shore RR 11/1902	
3 *Osceola* (31)	Baldwin	7677	9/1885	S. North Shore RR 11/1902	
4-6-0	*16×20*	*48*	*. . .*	*. . .*	*. . .*
4 *Kearsarge* (26)	Baldwin	8044	7/1886	S. Chaparra Sugar Co 1/1902	
2-8-0	*16×20*	*37*	*. . .*	*. . .*	*. . .*
5 *Iroquois* (32)	Baldwin	8699	8/1887	S. Rio Grande & Pagosa Springs 11/1902	
6 *Ahmeek* (30)	Baldwin	9757	1/1889	S. 11/1901	
7 *Opeeche* (34)	Baldwin	11534	1/1891	S. Quincy & Torch Lake 11/1901	

(*Continued*)

	2-6-0	16×22	44	. . .	. . .		. . .
8 *Delaware* (40)	Baldwin	12677	5/1892	Ex-MR (2)8		S. Ashland, Siskiwit & Iron River 12/1897

Note: Number in parenthesis reflects October 1893 renumbering

DULUTH, SOUTH SHORE & ATLANTIC SYSTEM LIST OF STATIONS

List includes name, earliest known milepost location, approximate dates of existence as found in railroad records, and railroad facilities as of 1895, 1930, and 1960. Facilities for Mineral Range and Hancock & Calumet trackage in 1895 are unknown. Changes in station name are separated by the year that the second station name shows up in records. Variations of name are in parenthesis. Branches over 1 mile in length are shown following originating station and segregated by horizontal lines. Abbreviations used in the tables:

C   Coal
D   Day train order operator or agent on duty
F   Fuel
N   Night train order operator on duty
T   Turntable
W   Water
Y   Wye

Mackinaw Division: Sault Ste. Marie to Marquette

Station Name	m.p.	Dates of Existence	1895	1930	1960
Sault Ste. Marie	0.0	1887–1960	DNCWT	DNCWTY	DFNTY
Superior Jct.	0.5	1936–1957			
St. Mary's Transfer	0.8	1912–1957			
Algonquin	1.7	1912–1930			
Ferguson	2.5	1913–1927			
Gladys	8.0	1887–1936			
Bay Mills Siding	11.4	1893–			
Superior; 1888, Bay Mills; 1896, Brimley	12.3	1888–1960	D	D	
Waiska; 1896, Bay Mills	2.2	1891–1905			
Dorgans	14.6	1890–1936			
Johnsonburg	16.6	1913–1927	W		
Elbon	17.3	1900–1922			
Wellsburg	18.8	1888–1927	D		
Whitco	19.6	1929–1931			
Deranson; 1915, Raco	20.0	1910–1960			
Wellers	21.2	1887–1929			
Dumond	22.8	1919–1923			
Rexford	25.0	1888–1960			
Lamain (La Main)	26.5	1910–1916			
Rifle Range	26.9	1909–1919			

Station Name	m.p.	Dates of Existence	1895	1930	1960
Spur 27	27.5	1926–1933			
Kane	29.5	1914–1924			
Parsille (Parisille's Spur)	30.6	1910–1912			
Strongs	31.9	1899–1960	D		
Fuller's Spur	2.2	1912–1920			
Boxer Spur	32.5	1910–1911			
Calco; 1936, Spur 34	34.4	1922–1939			
Eckerman	35.4	1888–1960	D	DW	
Nobles	36.0	1911–1919			
Lyonton	36.9	1912–1928			
Seewhy	38.4	1905–1930			
Nolan	38.9	1916–1926			
Bridge; 1936, Spur 39	39.9	1910–1937			
Hulburt (Hurlbut) (Hurlburts) (Hulbert)	41.0	1891–1960			
Spur 42	41.8	1929–1960			
Poleco (Polico)	42.3	1918–1936			
Natpo; 1929, Spur 44	44.6	1912–1943			
Sault Jct.; 1888, Soo Jct.	46.6	1887–1960	DCWY	DNCWY	Y
Hunter's Mill	4.7	1890–1929			
Sage	49.5	1887–1932			
Edjon	51.6	1917–1928			
Peroid; 1932, Spur 54	53.9	1909–1941			
McPhee	54.9	1908–1920			
Lencel (Lencil)	55.5	1887–1931			
Filson	56.1	1909–1926			
Newberry	58.5	1887–1960	D	D	D
Asylum	2.4	1894–1960			
Dollarville	60.3	1887–1960	D		
Natalie; 1933, Spur 61	62.0	1919–1933			
Murner	64.6	1909–1913			
McMillan	67.3	1887–1960	D	DW	
Woods–West Branch	4.9	1904–1923			
Woods–East Branch	4.2	1887–1930			
Lakeside; 1906, Laketon	70.2	1895–1937			
Danaher	71.8	1898–1953			
Ino	72.9	1893–1895			
Danber; 1916, Bonifas; 1924, Spur 75	75.4	1910–1948			
Woods	3.8	1909–1916			
Goodson	76.5	1916–1925			
Curson; 1936, Spur 77	77.0	1916–1936			
Seney	79.6	1887–1960	DCW	DCW	D
New Seney; 1927, Spur 80	80.4	1911–1960			
Spur 81	81.7	1953–1960			
Spur 84	84.1	1921–1936			
Norton	84.5	1915–1917			

(*Continued*)

Station Name	m.p.	Dates of Existence	1895	1930	1960
Driggs; 1941, Spur 88	88.0	1887–1960			
Goodco	88.7	1914–1921			
Gilpin	89.6	1914–1922			
Walsh	90.5	1887–1937			
Spur 91	91.1	1953–1960			
Ducey (Ducy)	92.7	1910–1916			
Creighton	95.2	1887–1960	DW		
Agnes	95.6	1911–1912			
Spur 97	97.3	1950–1960			
Clements	98.9	1910–1912			
Star; 1929, Spur 101	101.0	1899–1933			
Jeromeville; 1889, Shingleton	104.5	1887–1960	D	D	
Evelyn "Y"	107.4	1887–1935	Y		
Evelyn	108.5	1887–1935			
Connors Spur	111.5	–1912			
Munising; 1896, Wetmore	112.5	1887–1960	DW	DW	
Spur 115	116.0	1928–1932			
Anna River; 1890, Hallston	116.2	1887–1895			
Munising Jct.	116.7	1897–1960	D		
Rice Spur	117.9	–1911			
Ridge	119.5	1887–1960			
Underwood	120.5	1902–1916			
Williamson Spur	121.7	1911–			
Wilcox	123.1	1887–1935			
Au Train	125.0	1887–1960	DW	DW	
Spur 127	126.8	1927–1932			
Brownstone	127.4	1909–1912			
Rock River	129.3	1887–1939	D		
Onota	133.6	1887–1935	D		
Tyoga Jct.; 1945, Spur 134	134.6	1906–1945			
Deerton	135.6	1887–1960			
Whitefish	137.6	1887–1928			
Spur 139	139.4	1943–1960			
Sand River	139.9	1887–1941	DCW		
Dorais	142.4	1910–1917			
Sambrook	142.9	1910–1919			
Gordon (Gordons); 1960, Siding 145	145.0	1890–1960			
Theo	146.2	1917–1918			
Goodman	147.3	1910–1912			
Rodas (Radas)	148.5	1917–1921			
Chocolay; 1913, Lakewood	150.6	1887–1935			
Chocolay Furnace	150.9	1887–1919			
Gillett (Gillette)	151.3	1910–1912			
Lakewood (MM&SE Connection)	151.8	1887–1943			
Marquette Prison	152.6	1915–1943			
Carp Switch	153.5	1911–1915			
East Yard	154.5	1929–1960		DN	
Marquette	155.0	1887–1960	DNCTWY	DNCWTY	FTW

Mackinaw Division: St. Ignace–Soo Jct.

Station Name	m.p.	Dates of Existence	1895	1930	1960
St. Ignace	0.0	1887–1960	DCWT	DNCWT	DFNT
Martell Furnace	1.5	1887–1936			
West Yard	1.0	1942–1960			
Spur A-3	3.0	1935–1936			
Reavie	4.0	1887–1932			
Rugstein (Rugsten)	7.0	1908–1930			
Nero	7.8	1887–1931			
Allenville	10.1	1887–1933			
Moran	11.1	1887–1960	D	D	
Greene; 1926, Gille	14.3	1909–1931			
Berst	15.4	1911–1924			
Burma	15.9	1920–1929			
Nogi	16.1	1887–1932			
Bissell (Bissel)	17.5	1910–1923	W		
Palms; 1909, Kenneth	19.6	1887–1937			
Johnson; 1910, Murray	22.0	1887–1930			
Marstone	22.2	1916–1927			
Spur A-23	22.5	1927–1935			
Ozark	23.1	1887–1960			
Dell	25.4	1903–1918			
Trout Lake Siding	27.5	1887–1932			
Trout Lake	27.7	1887–1960	DW	DNTW	DY
Cana	31.4	1899–1918			
Cheesbrough; 1910, Wilwin (Chesborough)	32.1	1910–1928			
Kemp	32.3	1911–1937			
Fiborn Jct.	33.5	1905–1935			
Chess Spur	0.5	1917–1928			
Foster	1.2	1912–1917			
Christie Spur (Christiansen)	2.0	1916–1929			
Fiborn (Fiborn Quarry)	3.9	1905–1935			
Quinn	34.3	1891–1929			
Hendrie (Hendrie Pit)	36.5	1887–1932			
Spur A-40	39.5	1926–1933			
Bradkins	40.0	1910–1912			
Peshims	41.1	1910–1930			
Soo Jct.	42.9	1888–1960	D	DNCWY	Y

Houghton Division: Marquette-Nestoria

Station Name	m.p.	Dates of Existence	1895	1930	1960
Marquette	155.0	1887–1960	DNCWTY	DNCTWY	FTW
Marquette Scales	156.0	1893–1960		D	
Dead River R.R. Conn.	156.3	1912–1915			
Brewery Spur	156.5	1919–1934			
Grand View	157.7	1893–			
Valley Mill Spur	158.0	1917–1930			
Bruce; 1893, Bagdad Jct.	159.8	1887–1895			
Bagdad	160.5	1890–1941			
Morgan (Morgan Heights)	162.0	1916–1960			
Eagle Mills	162.6	1887–1941	D	Y	
Old Main Jct.	163.8	1919–			
Hogan Ore Yard	164.4	1955–1960			
Carp	165.5	1893–1900			
Negaunee	166.8	1887–1960	DNW	DNYW	D
Iron Street Crossover	166.9	1955–1956			
Iron Street Jct.	167.2	1957–1960			
Teal Lake Mine Spur	167.3	1887–1945			
Hartford Mine	0.6	1887–1945			
Cambria Mine	1.0	1887–1945			
Cleveland Mine	1.8	1887–1945			
Detroit Mine	2.1	1887–1945			
South Main Jct.	167.8	1957–1960			
C&NW Ry. Jct.	167.9	1957–1960			
Union Park	168.2	1957–1959			
Ishpeming	169.8	1887–1960	DCW	DNW	DN
Barnum Siding	170.4	1913–1960			
Lake Superior Mine Spur	171.3	1887–1945			
Ontonagon Jct.; 1893, Winthrop Jct.	171.4	1887–1960	Y	Y	
Saginaw Mine Spur	0.2	1887–1894			
Saginaw Mine	2.5	1887–1894			
Section 21 Mine	1.0	1887–1903			
Mitchell Mine	1.2	1890–1916			
Braasted Mine	1.6	1887–1889			
Winthrop Mine	1.9	1887–1903			
Jct. with C&NW	2.0	1887–1960			
Robbins Spur	171.6	1955–1960			
Stoneville	173.7	1887–1927			
Fitch Mine Spur; 1930, Greenwood Mine Jct.	175.0	1890–1960			
Greenwood Mine	0.8	1930–1960			
Fitch Mine	1.3	1890–1895			
1941, Greenwood; 1960, Siding 176	176.2	1887–1960			
Dexter (Dexter Jct.)	177.1	1887–1916			
Dexter Mine	2.6	1887–1900			

Station Name	m.p.	Dates of Existence	1895	1930	1960
Low Moor	177.5	1900–1926			
Boston Jct.; 1912, American Mine Jct.; 1930, Blueberry Mine Jct.	179.0	1909–1960		Y	Y
Diorite	1.0	1911–1915			
American Mine	1.8	1887–1922			
Jct. with C&NW	2.1	1927–1955			
Blueberry Mine	3.3	1927–1955			
Clarksburg	180.0	1887–1930			
Spur 181	181.3	1943–1957			
Humboldt	181.6	1887–1941	DW	W	
Spur 182	182.3	1945–1948			
Bessie Mine Jct.	182.7	1902–1906			
Bessie Mine	1.1	1902–1906			
Champion Jct.	185.2	1887–1919			
Champion Mine (old)	1.0	1887–1919			
Champion	185.7	1887–1960	DN	D	N
Northampton Mine Spur	186.1	1887–1895			
Marine Mine	0.8	1887–1895			
Northampton Mine	0.8	1887–1895			
Phoenix Mine	1.5	1887–1895			
Hortense Mine	2.2	1887–1895			
Jim Pascoe Mine	2.5	1887–1895			
North Phoenix Mine	2.5	1887–1895			
Champion Mine Spur (new)	186.1	1948–1960			
Champion Mine (new)	1.7	1948–1960			
Brown Siding (Brown)	187.3	1893–1910			
Dishneau Pit (Dishneau)	188.6	1915–1960			
Brown's Crossing	190.5	1915–1919			
Michigamme Mine	192.5	1887–1905			
Michigamme	193.3	1887–1960	DCWT	D	
Wetmore Jct.; 1890, Imperial Mine Jct. (Imperial Jct.)	194.3	1887–1960			
Webster Mine branch; 1909, Portland Mine branch	0.5	1887–1935			
Wetmore Mine; 1890, Imperial Mine	1.1	1887–1929			
Spurr (Spurr Mine Spur)	194.4	1887–1910			
Beaufort Jct. (Beaufort); 1953, Ohio Mine Spur	196.0	1887–1960			
Norwood Mine; 1907, Ohio Mine	0.6	1889–1960			

(Continued)

Station Name	m.p.	Dates of Existence	1895	1930	1960
Beaufort Mine	2.0	1887–1905			
Three Lakes	198.0	1887–1960			
Nestoria	200.9	1888–1960	DNCWY	DNCWY	NY

Houghton Division: Nestoria-Houghton

Station Name	m.p.	Dates of Existence	1895	1930	1960
Nestoria	0.0	1888–1960	DNCW	DNCWY	NY
Sturgeon	1.3	1887–1900			
Birch	2.5	1908–1916			
Spruce	3.5	1905–1912			
Tama; 1941, Spur D-5	5.7	1900–1960			
Summit	7.4	1887–1960	D		
Shirley	8.3	1901–1916			
Herman	9.0	1909–1960		D	
Spur D-11	11.1	1935–1936			
Taylor Jct. (Taylor)	12.4	1887–1939			
Bovine (Bovine Siding)	14.5	1910–1960			
Brennans; 1945, Spur D-14	14.6	1910–1960			
Spur D-15	15.5	1943–1960			
L'Anse	16.8	1887–1960	DCTW	DNCTW	D
Zenith	19.2	1914–1918			
Baraga	22.1	1887–1960	D	D	D
Assinins	24.5	1899–1953			
Seavoy	25.1	1910–1912			
Iron Bridge	26.6	1887–1932			
Keweenaw Bay	28.5	1899–1960		DWY	
Michigan Stamp Mill	29.2	1909–1916			
Newton; 1931, Spur D-30	30.1	1887–1935			
Worchester	30.7	1915–			
Arnheim	32.4	1887–1960			
Spur D-34	34.8	1943–1945			
Portage	34.2	1895–			
Klingville	34.7	1917–1942			
Mullen	35.0	1910–1918			
Farley	35.8	1910–1912			
Fouchette	37.9	1887–1932			
Spur D-38	39.3	1941–1960			
Danielson; 1936, Spur D-39	39.5	1908–1960			
Chassell	40.6	1889–1960	D	D	
Garon	41.4	1907–1919			
Farm (Farms)	44.7	1913–1932			
Pilgrim	45.8	1895–1960			
Isle Royale	46.0	1910–1915			
Pilgrim Pit	46.5	1909–1915			
Glanville	46.9	1903–1940			
Houghton; 1893, East Houghton	48.1	1887–1960	DCWT	DCWYT	DW

Houghton Division: South Main Line

Marquette–Ontonagon Jct.

Station Name	m.p.	Dates of Existence	1895	1930	1960
Marquette (East Yard)	0.0	1887–1930			
Spur No. 2	2.1	1912–1913			
Spur No. 3	3.7	1912–1913			
Spur No. 7; 1910, Morgan (Morgan Heights)	7.0	1912–1926			
Eagle Mills	9.0	1887–1930			
Queen Mine Spur	11.2	1900–1930			
Negaunee Mine Spur	11.5	1890–1925			
Negaunee	13.2	1887–1960			
Iron St. Crossover	13.6	1955–1956			
South Ishpeming	16.0	1887–1929			
Cleveland Lake Mine Spur	16.6	1889–1950			
Section 16 Mine Spur	16.9	1887–1946			
Ontonagon Jct.; 1893, Winthrop Jct.	17.3	1887–1960	Y	Y	

Houghton Division: Palmer Branch

Station Name	m.p.	Dates of Existence	1895	1930	1960
Negaunee	0.0	1887–1960			
Breitung Hematite Mine	0.6	1903–1937			
Rolling Mill Mine	1.0	1887–1937			
Mary Charlotte Mine	1.4	1903–1948			
Milwaukee Mine	1.7	1887–1916			
Palmer Branch Jct.	1.9	1952–1960			
Empire Mine	3.9	1907–1928			
Maitland Mine	4.7	1888–1938			
Volunteer Mine	4.8	1887–1960			
Jct. with C&NW	5.0	1911–1956			
Old Volunteer Mine	5.2	1911–1923			
Isabella Mine	5.7	1916–1934			
Richmond Mine	7.2	1918–1956			

Houghton Division: New Palmer Branch

Station Name	m.p.	Dates of Existence	1895	1930	1960
Hogan Ore Yard	0.0	1952–1960			
Hogan Yard Jct.	0.9	1952–1960			
LS&I Jct.	1.2	1952–1960			
J&L West Wye	1.2	1952–1960			
J&L East Wye	1.6	1952–1960			
Palmer Branch Jct.	1.7	1952–1960			

Houghton Division: Republic Branch

Station Name	m.p.	Dates of Existence	1895	1930	1960
Humboldt	0.0	1887–1941	DW	W	
Foxdale Mine	1.0	1901–1905			
Humboldt Mine; 1908, Washington Mine	1.2	1887–1929			
Midway	5.6	1893–1915			
Republic Jct.; 1910, Milwaukee Jct.	6.7	1900–1921			
Republic	8.5	1887–1929	DCT		
North Republic Mine	1.7	1888–			
Riverside Mine	2.9	1888–1893			
Erie Mine	4.9	1887–1895			
Republic Mine	9.0	1887–1929			

Western Division: Nestoria-Superior

Station Name	m.p.	Dates of Existence	1895	1930	1960
Nestoria	200.9	1888–1960	DN	DNCWY	NY
Spur 201	201.6	1941–1956			
Bode; 1936, Spur 203	203.0	1915–1956			
Tioga; 1936, Spur 205	205.3	1912–1960			
King Lake; 1936, Spur 206	206.8	1896–1941			
Treado (Treadeau); 1930, Spur 208	208.4	1912–1960			
Vermilac (Vermillac)	211.0	1890–1960	D		
Spur 212	212.0	1913–1927			
Murphy; 1936, Spur 213	213.4	1888–1936			
Murphy Pit	214.0	1905–1927			
Foy	214.4	1911–1923			
Covington	215.0	1899–1960		D	
August	215.4	1916–1934			
Paquette	215.5	1901–1916			
Tibbets; 1910, Leo; 1936, Spur 216	216.5	1890–1960			
Opal	217.1	1905–1919			
Robinson	217.8	1893–1929			
Watton	218.5	1909–1960			
Hutula	219.7	1888–1932			
Perch	220.9	1889–1935			
Keeler	221.8	1910–1929			
Sidnaw	224.1	1890–1960	DW	DNW	D
Dow	225.8	1916–1929			
Crystal Lake	226.9	1892–1895			
Anthony	227.8	1888–1932			
Kitchi (Kitchie)	230.0	1889–1939	D		
End of Track	1.9	1892–			
Peppen	232.1	1916–1927			
Withey Jct. (Withey)	233.0	1888–1934			
Kenton	233.4	1890–1960	D	D	

Station Name	m.p.	Dates of Existence	1895	1930	1960
K. C. Spur	234.2	1919–1923			
Jumbo; 1931, Spur 235	235.2	1888–1934			
Spur 237	237.4	1953–1960			
Trout Creek	239.1	1889–1960	D	DCW	D
Agate	241.9	1888–1939			
Falls	243.8	1895–1934			
Falls Siding	244.3	1898–1915			
Basco	244.5	1911–1915			
End of Track	1.4	1911–1913			
Ruby Pit (Ruby)	245.4	1912–1919			
Paynesville	246.5	1888–1938		D	
Gem	248.2	1895–1934			
Schriver	249.0	1910–1912			
Jensen	249.7	1911–1927			
Bruce's Crossing	250.1	1890–1960	D	D	
St. Collins	250.5	1887–1937			
Baltimore	252.5	1902–1934			
Urquhart	5.9	1902–1927			
McRae	254.8	1917–1922			
Ewen	255.3	1888–1960	DNCW	DWY	DNWY
Fair Oaks	257.4	1890–1910			
Lindstedt	259.5	1888–1934			
Matchwood	261.2	1890–1937	D		
Groesbeck	263.5	1889–1934			
Topaz	264.7	1909–1938			
Spur 266	265.6	1926–1932			
Spur 267	267.2	1936–1957			
Louk	267.5	1912–1917			
Spur 268	268.6	1925–1939			
Bergland Branch Jct.	269.5	1912–1915			
White Pine	14.0	1955–1960			Y
Bergland	269.7	1909–1960		D	
Norton	270.9	1915–1923			
Gwanatch; 1888, Lake Gogebic	272.3	1888–1960	D	W	
Merriweather	273.1	1917–1953			
Gale	274.0	1888–1929			
Spur 274	274.0	1943–1957			
Spur 275	275.5	1928–1960			
Spur 276	276.0	1922–1937			
Haskins	276.6	1915–1921			
Rogers; 1929, Spur 277	277.2	1920–1934			
Duke; 1919, Jacks	279.8	1899–1931			
Camp Francis; 1929, Spur 280	280.1	1911–1960			
Tula Pit	281.4	1900–1925			
Tula	282.0	1889–1960			
Spur 285	285.0	1924–1936			
Spur 287	286.3	1927–1960			
Thomaston	287.7	1888–1960	DNCTW	DNCTWY	
Planter	290.1	1888–1935			

(*Continued*)

Station Name	m.p.	Dates of Existence	1895	1930	1960
Abitosse	292.0	1889–1934			
Siemas; 1931, Spur 292	292.2	1919–1934			
Massie	292.8	1909–1917			
Bessemer Jct.	293.9	1888–1930			
Bessemer	1.9	1888–1930	DT		
Erickson	294.1	1912–1934			
Bernard	294.4	1919–1929			
North Bessemer	294.7	1891–1934			
Woodroy	295.3	1910–1917			
Black River	296.7	1909–1923			
Sillberg	297.7	1910–1928			
North Ironwood	299.2	1919–1960		D	
Montreal	300.5	1889–1960			
Junet; 1936, Spur 301	301.2	1911–1956			
Michigan-Wisconsin State Line	302.4	1912–1943			
Cody	302.7	1909–1912			
Defer (De Fer)	303.4	1908–1929			
Martel (Martell); 1929, Spur 304	304.0	1888–1937			
Uhlan	305.3	1910–1911			
Neallys	306.0	1909–1912			
River Branch	306.6	1922–1929			
Myers (Meyers)	308.0	1908–1934			
McLane	310.0	1911–1925			
Dogwood; 1888, Saxon	312.1	1887–1960	DNW	DNW	D
Saxon Pit	313.6	1893–1919			
Cameo	316.1	1910–1912			
Gurncy	316.8	1888–1936			
Owego	320.1	1911–1922			
Sedgwick	321.9	1889–1960			
Shilo	324.5	1899–1929			
Bell	325.5	1914–1920			
Ruthven; 1902, Stearns; 1931, Spur 327	327.2	1889–1936			
Fox	328.8	1909–1915			
Kero (Kiro)	329.8	1910–1922			
Feeman	330.3	1912–			
Marengo	331.9	1888–1915	D		
Marengo Jct. Transfer	332.0	1950–1959			
Marengo Jct.	333.2	1919–1960			
Sanborn	336.6	1892–1934		D	
Argo; 1929, Turkey Field	338.5	1910–1934			
Altamont	341.1	1893–1934			
Mason; 1893, Bibon	344.3	1888–1934	D	DNCWY	
Mason	0.7	1905–1915			
Larke	347.0	1915–1934			
Hopkins	349.0	1889–1912			
Sutherland	350.1	1899–1934			
Lorain (Loraine) (Lorane)	352.2	1910–1912			
Clubine Jct.	352.7	1912–1934			
Pike River	353.4	1889–1934			

Station Name	m.p.	Dates of Existence	1895	1930	1960
Pike Lake; 1895, Delta	355.7	1890–1934			
Gunds Siding; 1909, Cusson; 1919, Clubine	358.9	1909–1931			
Rose	360.2	1919–1934			
Pit No. 5	361.0	1911–1915			
Grimpo; 1912, Twin Bears	361.2	1909–1934			
Spur 406; 1917, Pine Tree Farms	362.4	1913–1934			
Middlebrook; 1915, Lake Millicent	363.0	1899–1929			
Eliot (Elliott, Elliot)	364.1	1889–1931			
Ruthmoore (Ruthmore)	365.9	1892–1893			
Iron River	366.4	1888–1934	D	DWY	
Edith	369.6	1893–1912			
Campbell's Mill	370.9	1909–1934			
Bell; 1909, Wills	373.0	1893–1934			
Troy	375.8	1910–1934			
Winneboujou (Winne Boujoun) (Winne Boujou)	377.0	1895–1934	W		
McDougall	377.6	1914–1934			
Le Clair; 1910, McVickers	378.0	1899–1917			
Cobb; 1894, Orrville; 1912, Experiment	380.0	1893–1934			
Lake Nebagamon	382.3	1893–1934		D	
Steele	385.1	1895–1934			
Carroll; 1894, Hoyt; 1909, Dobie	387.3	1893–1934			
Berg Park	390.1	1895–1934			
Victor	390.8	1900–1918			
O'Neil; 1915, Simon	391.8	1912–1934			
Middle River	392.8	1893–1934	DW	W	
Rockmont	394.6	1899–1934			
Rock Crusher (Rockcrusher); 1913, Andersonville	396.5	1909–1934			
Stone Acres	398.6	1917–1934			
South Range	399.7	1893–1934			
Parkland	402.6	1908–1934			
Peyton	403.2	1919–1934			
Bluff Creek	404.3	1910–1934			
Belt Line Jct.; 1895, Allouez	405.1	1895–1900	DN		
Allouez	405.6	1900–1930		D	
Superior; 1903, Superior, East End	407.3	1888–1960	D	D	
Superior Catholic Orphanage	408.0	1915–1924			
28th St. Jct.	408.4	1917–1960		DNTCW	
28th St. Yard	408.8	1892–1936			
18th Street Yard	410.5	1892–1936			
Belknap St. (Jct. with LST&T)	410.9	1888–1926			
West Superior; 1903, Superior (LST&T)	411.2	1888–1926			

(Continued)

Station Name	m.p.	Dates of Existence	1895	1930	1960
Jct. with LST&T	411.5	1894–1926		D	
Roundhouse Yard	412.0	1894–1926			

Mineral Range Railroad

Station Name	m.p.	Dates of Existence	1895	1930	1960
Houghton	0.0	1886–1960	D		
West End Bridge	0.3	1929–1960			
H&C Jct.; 1906, Shore Line Jct.	0.5	1900–1960			
Hancock (Lower Yard)	0.7	1873–1931	D	WY	
Hancock (Lake View)	1.3	1899–1960			
Swedetown	3.5	1873–1932			
Atlas (Atlas Powder)	3.7	1915–1959			
Franklin (Franklin Jct.)	4.2	1878–1953			
Mesnard Mine	0.8	1885–1944			
Franklin Mine	2.0	1885–1944			
Quincy Mine	2.2	1885–1944			
Pluto	4.7	1909–1916			
Boston (Franklin Jr. Mine spur)	6.6	1873–1931			
Boston Jct.; 1912, Arcadian Jct.; 1945, Siding M-7	7.0	1898–1960			
St. Mary's Jct.	7.4	1898–1933			
Highway	8.8	1873–1919			
Keno	9.2	1906–1917			
La Salle Mine Jct. (La Salle Mine spur)	10.4	1886–1930			
Osceola (Osceola Mine spur)	11.7	1873–1926			
Torch Lake Jct.	13.4	1873–1895			
Calumet	13.7	1873–1960		DWYT	Y
Belt Line Jct.	14.1	1892–1926			
Red Jacket	15.2	1885–1897			
Centennial Mine	15.5	1904–1926			
Laurium	17.1	1903–1925			

Mineral Range: Point Mills Line

Station Name	m.p.	Dates of Existence	1895	1930	1960
Arcadian Jct. (Boston Jct.)	0.0	1898–1927			
New Arcadian Mine	1.2	1915–1927			
Arcadian "Y"	1.3	1898–1923			
Arcadian Mine	2.0	1898–1912			
Eddy	4.0	1912–1915			
Woodside	5.6	1898–1927			
Franklin Mill	8.5	1898–1927			
Point Mills	9.0	1898–1927			
Centennial Mills	9.5	1898–1927			

Mineral Range: South Range Line

Station Name	m.p.	Dates of Existence	1895	1930	1960
Keweenaw Bay	0.0	1900–1938		DCWYT	
Kelsey	2.2	1900–1937			
Bashore	3.7	1906–1918			
Nelson	4.0	1900–1937			
Bellaire; 1916, Froberg	5.6	1900–1938			
Hamar (Hamar Siding)	6.9	1900–1932			
Kuro (Kero)	7.7	1900–1937			
Pelkie	9.1	1900–1938			
Alahola	10.4	1914–1931			
Papin	11.0	1900–1931			
Giddings	12.1	1900–1937			
Egypt	12.9	1902–1918			
Hazel	13.5	1900–1937			
Torness	14.3	1910–1912			
Pearce	14.5	1900–1931			
Drew	15.2	1901–1937			
Rubicon	15.3	1920–1930			
Corbett (Corbet)	15.6	1903–1924			
Laird; 1900, Alston	15.9	1900–1938		D	
Alston Pit	17.2	1915–1923			
Faro Siding; 1906, Nisula	18.0	1901–1935			
Heikkinen	18.9	1916–1931			
White	19.2	1900–1935			
Bishop; 1919, Samak (Somack) (Samek)	20.4	1912–1935			
Hillier	20.7	1923–1935			
Otter	22.1	1900–1935			
Galby	22.7	1912–1918			
Turenen	23.6	1923–1927			
Motley	24.4	1900–1931			
Von Platen–Fox Spur	26.0	1926–1929			
Gilson	26.4	1914–1931			
Francis (Francis Siding)	27.0	1906–1935		Y	
Maki	27.5	1900–1931			
Worcester	28.1	1919–1922			
Erlandson	28.6	1910–1928			
Simar	28.9	1900–1935			
Wedberg	29.4	1910–1915			
Spur M-30	30.6	1919–1926			
Lake Mine Spur	31.0	1912–			
Peppard Jct. (Peppard)	32.0	1900–1926			
Adventure	0.9	1900–1926			
Evergreen (Mass Mine)	2.0	1900–1926			
"C" Shaft (Mass Mine)	2.8	1905–1926			
Mass (Mass City)	32.7	1900–1926			
Wormer	34.5	1910–1912			
Riddle Jct.	35.5	1900–1926			
Michigan Mine	38.9	1903–1913			

Hancock & Calumet Railroad: Lake Linden Line

Station Name	m.p.	Dates of Existence	1895	1930	1960
H&C Jct.; 1906, Shore Line Jct.	0.0	1900–1960			
Ripley	1.6	1885–1960			
Portage Coal Dock	1.8	1896–1926			
Prior (Pryor)	2.4	1912–1919			
Union Coal Dock	3.2	1895–1960			
Spur H-3	3.4	1945–1960			
Clark; 1899, Dollar Bay	3.9	1885–1960		D	
Woodside	4.7	1888–1933			
Dupont Jct.	5.1	1912–1960		W	
Copper Range Jct.	5.2	1919–1960			
Mays	6.3	1912–1919			
Mason	7.0	1899–1960			
Lake Jct. (Junction)	7.5	1885–1931			
Lower Mills (Mills)	8.0	1893–1960			
Ahmeek Mill	8.7	1912–1960			
Grover; 1892, South Lake Linden; 1905, Hubbell	9.1	1889–1932			
Linwood	9.6	1889–1953			
Lake Linden	10.0	1885–1960		D	

Hancock & Calumet: Lake Jct. to Mohawk

Station Name	m.p.	Dates of Existence	1895	1930	1960
Lake Jct. (Junction)	0.0	1885–1930			
Upper Mills	0.5	1885–1925			
Midway	3.0	1912–1919			
Osceola (Osceola Mine spur)	5.5	1885–1930			
Tamarack Jct.	6.9	1889–1919			
Tamarack Mine	0.3	1889–1919			
North Tamarack Mine	1.9	1893–1917			
Red Jacket; 1912, Calumet	7.5	1885–1928			
Belt Line Jct.	8.0	1892–1927			
Kearsarge (Wolverine Mine spur)	9.9	1889–1927			
Rock Siding (Kearsarge Mine spur)	10.6	1919–1926			
Allouez	11.3	1887–1926			
Stamp Mill Jct.	11.9	1912–1915			
Ahmeek (Allouez Mine spur)	12.2	1905–1926			
Keweenaw Central Jct.	13.0	1907–1916			
Gratiot Mine Jct.	13.4	1919–			
Senaca Mine	1.5	1919–			

Station Name	m.p.	Dates of Existence	1895	1930	1960
Gratiot Mine	2.0	1919–			
Fulton; 1906, Mohawk (Mohawk Jct.)	13.5	1891–1916			

DSS&A Operating Statistics

Year	Miles	Operating Earnings	Total Exp. & Taxes	Net Oper. Balance	Earn. Ratio	Net Income	Psgrs Carried	Frt. Tons Moved
1887	352	$1,465,230	$892,822	$572,867	61	$134,990	312,123	1,327,087
1888	415	1,468,592	919,956	548,636	63	D88,143	337,334	1,417,479
1889	577	1,976,350	1,161,515	814,835	60	D56,504	345,309	2,055,457
1890	584	2,233,853	1,398,545	835,308	64	D57,881	420,412	2,270,143
1891	585	2,148,388	1,317,386	831,002	61	12,375	432,988	2,119,831
1892	768	2,242,433	1,441,725	800,708	64	D117,492	390,245	2,141,630
1893	596	2,088,913	1,517,601	571,312	73	D298,854	358,496	2,162,720
1894	594	1,650,989	1,138,264	512,725	69	D334,439	302,962	2,342,125
1895	582	1,790,684	1,157,105	633,579	64	D183,326	355,979	2,131,288
1896	588	1,872,983	1,273,142	599,841	68	D196,884	368,451	2,338,397
1897	589	1,591,114	1,105,755	485,359	71	D382,763	337,773	1,779,773
1898	589	1,821,808	1,224,046	597,762	67	D298,192	365,677	2,226,993
1899	583	2,407,437	1,468,896	938,478	61	14,057	473,681	2,598,862
1900	585	2,563,420	1,707,829	855,590	67	D4,109	556,668	2,624,152
1901	585	2,484,211	1,654,931	829,280	67	D52,011	552,345	2,391,654
1902	575	2,690,569	1,688,818	1,001,751	63	20,327	581,668	2,311,464
1903	573	2,772,135	1,758,090	1,014,045	63	D31,204	641,210	2,457,565
1904	579	2,524,612	1,749,456	775,156	69	D283,451	603,308	1,960,749
1905	585	2,706,936	1,852,705	854,231	68	D206,552	554,093	2,853,536
1906	593	3,057,809	2,057,460	1,000,316	67	D156,303	618,337	3,281,506
1907	591	3,223,592	2,214,847	1,008,745	69	D55,536	691,585	3,285,475
1908	595	2,921,916	2,206,215	715,701	76	D310,993	679,253	2,943,982
1909	593	2,719,338	1,979,518	739,820	73	D201,447	707,653	2,555,351
1910	606	3,302,147	2,269,248	1,032,899	69	D81,824	719,169	3,695,469
1911	612	3,148,818	2,269,341	879,477	72	D220,465	785,622	3,429,218
1912	623	3,152,475	2,395,161	757,314	76	D361,547	790,239	3,413,835
1913	627	3,412,832	2,724,490	688,341	80	D537,520	842,073	3,454,914
1914	627	3,412,575	2,763,996	648,579	81	D550,989	903,370	3,216,312
1915	626	2,938,597	2,401,835	536,762	82	D557,083	754,924	2,680,898
1916	628	3,506,792	2,482,149	1,024,644	71	D140,320	747,965	3,468,001
1917	627	4,074,693	3,055,981	1,018,712	75	D169,476	820,022	3,759,927
1918	600	4,824,187	4,266,978	557,209	88	D417,131	778,040	3,891,734
1919	614	4,758,601	4,461,300	297,301	93	D413,508	894,880	3,362,297
1920	600	5,949,891	5,598,701	351,189	94	D329,683	908,478	3,755,912
1921	592	4,464,863	4,565,202	D100,339	102	D1,582,853	730,974	2,092,935
1922	591	4,495,812	3,961,793	534,019	88	D727,210	603,386	2,334,737
1923	591	5,861,203	4,694,926	1,166,277	80	D180,496	633,302	3,901,908
1924	591	5,905,360	4,786,372	1,118,989	81	D244,325	622,914	4,273,860
1925	591	5,808,935	4,611,035	1,197,890	79	D118,712	499,731	4,432,594
1926	590	5,281,270	4,406,891	874,379	83	D428,290	443,329	3,778,348
1927	588	5,121,693	4,061,518	1,060,175	79	D269,736	366,072	3,853,497
1928	577	5,045,857	4,132,799	913,059	82	D459,954	307,707	3,929,786
1929	574	4,971,501	3,988,822	982,679	80	D406,627	250,772	4,092,939
1930	574	3,749,601	3,288,301	461,299	88	D855,426	153,082	2,887,911

(Continued)

Year	Miles	Operating Earnings	Total Exp. & Taxes	Net Oper. Balance	Earn. Ratio	Net Income	Psgrs Car-ried	Frt. Tons Moved
1931	560	2,701,575	2,524,727	176,848	93	D1,075,233	95,108	1,865,741
1932	560	1,634,036	1,836,205	D202,169	112	D1,493,525	68,413	838,087
1933	563	1,963,106	1,635,436	327,670	83	D991,489	69,065	1,288,302
1934	557	2,176,537	1,808,781	367,756	83	D827,144	103,179	1,822,710
1935	556	2,359,777	1,835,246	524,531	78	D559,821	112,719	1,865,568
1936	550	2,913,041	2,019,843	893,198	69	D296,184	125,847	2,494,991
1937	549	2,846,273	2,146,299	699,974	75	D462,942	132,568	2,568,896
1938	549	1,832,785	1,747,744	D76,959	95	D1,077,417	96,274	1,125,275
1939	550	2,327,828	2,017,949	138,401	87	D845,034	78,186	1,782,267
1940	550	2,620,309	2,115,437	330,301	81	D637,485	66,899	2,144,906
1941	550	3,367,250	2,494,352	872,898	74	D283,710	69,243	2,876,397
1942	550	4,230,689	2,972,068	1,258,621	70	60,833	118,899	3,273,890
1943	551	4,352,096	3,054,511	1,297,584	70	132,084	190,159	2,802,570
1944	550	4,306,705	3,372,932	933,773	78	D262,691	233,731	2,706,211
1945	530	4,061,969	3,395,389	666,580	84	D519,927	179,839	2,793,411
1946	530	4,200,928	3,833,582	367,346	91	D892,119	126,687	2,664,301
1947	530	5,517,694	4,443,737	1,073,956	81	D335,476	97,528	3,191,103
1948	530	6,327,049	5,123,097	1,203,952	81	D333,155	76,628	3,081,437
1949	539	5,693,628	5,721,681	D28,053	101	D542,186	76,458	2,434,332
1950	539	7,093,373	5,533,509	1,559,864	78	688,142	50,729	3,243,276
1951	539	7,991,111	6,621,027	1,370,084	83	381,940	48,730	3,822,179
1952	552	8,205,108	6,662,463	1,542,645	81	370,030	49,686	3,368,005
1953	552	8,149,401	7,024,850	1,124,551	86	111,835	38,552	3,209,259
1954	553	6,799,022	6,048,351	750,671	89	0	32,445	2,496,681
1955	553	7,677,757	6,307,039	1,370,719	82	421,806	28,300	3,111,731
1956	545	8,261,995	6,688,266	1,573,729	81	606,036	28,124	3,308,011
1957	544	7,492,542	6,660,167	832,375	89	0	21,738	2,903,853
1958	544	6,526,937	5,623,454	903,483	86	133,891	16,415	2,419,696
1959	544	6,855,765	5,865,168	990,597	86	704	17,021	2,697,273
1960	544	6,571,912	5,707,063	864,849	87	540	18,124	2,744,543

NOTES

1. Strap and T Rails to the Iron Mountains

1. Ishpeming *Iron Ore,* January 1, 1889, p. 1. Ernest H. Rankin, *A Brief History of the Marquette Iron Range, Marquette County, Michigan* (Marquette, Mich.: Marquette County Historical Society, 1966), pp. 3, 4.

2. An Act to Incorporate the Iron Bay and Carp River Plank Road Company (March 20, 1850), *Acts of the Legislature of the State of Michigan Passed at the Annual Session of 1850,* 126.

3. Saul Benison, "Railroads, Land and Iron: A Phase in the Career of Lewis Henry Morgan" (PhD diss., Columbia University, 1953), pp. 67–69.

4. Marquette *Mining Journal,* January 23, 1932, p. 9. Ralph D. Williams, *The Honorable Peter White* (Cleveland: Penton, 1905), p. 59.

5. Articles of Incorporation, Iron Mountain Railway (March 14, 1855), Marquette County Historical Society, Marquette, Mich.

6. An Act Granting to the State of Michigan the Right of Way, and a Donation of Public Land for the Construction of a Ship Canal around the Falls of St. Mary's, in Said State (chap. 92, August 26, 1852), *Statutes at Large and Treaties of the United States of America* 10, pp. 35, 36. *Profiles: Michigan's Mining History in the Upper Peninsula* (Cleveland: The Cleveland-Cliffs Iron Company, 1976), p. 8.

7. Benison, "Railroads, Land and Iron," pp. 74, 75. *Iron Ore,* June 27, 1903, p. 1.

8. Articles of Association, Iron Mountain Rail Road (February 15, 1855), Wesley Perron Papers, Peter White Public Library, Marquette, Mich.

9. D. H. Merritt, "History of the Marquette Ore Docks," *Proceedings of the Lake Superior Mining Institute* 14 (Ishpeming, 1914), pp. 426, 427.

10. *Lake Superior Journal,* July 11, 1857, p. 2.

11. *Skillings' Mining Review,* January 6, 1923, p. 11, quoting *Lake Superior Journal,* August 15, 1857.

12. Rankin, *A Brief History of the Marquette Iron Range,* p. 9. *Iron Ore,* June 27, 1903, p. 1.

13. *Lake Superior Journal,* May 24, 1856, p. 2; June 14, 1856, p. 2. An Act Granting Public Lands to the State of Michigan, to Aid in the Construction of Certain Railroads in Said State, and for Other Purposes (chap. 43, June 3, 1856), *Statutes at Large and Treaties of the United States of America* 11, pp. 21, 22.

14. *Lake Superior Journal,* July 19, 1856, p. 2. Benison, "Railroads, Land and Iron," pp. 119, 120. William H. Stennett, *Yesterday and Today: A History of the Chicago and North Western Railway System* (Chicago: Winship Co. Printers, 1910), pp. 54, 55, 185. An Act to Execute the Trust Created by an Act of Congress, Entitled, "An Act Granting Public Lands to the State of Wisconsin, to Aid in the Construction of Railroads, in Said State," Approved June 3d, 1856, by Incorporating the Wisconsin and Superior Railroad Company, and Granting a Portion of Said Lands Thereto (chap. 137, October 11, 1856), *Wisconsin General Acts, 1856,* pp. 239–262.

15. Articles of Association, Bay De Noquet and Marquette Rail Road Company (November 21, 1856), Perron Papers.

16. Benison, "Railroads, Land and Iron," pp. 123, 124. Michigan Railroad Commission, *Aids,*

Gifts, Grants and Donations to Railroads (Lansing, Mich., 1919), pp. 62–63.

17. An Act Disposing of Certain Grants of Land Made to the State of Michigan for Railroad Purposes, by Act of Congress Approved June Third (3), Eighteen Hundred and Fifty-Six (1856) (no. 126, February 14, 1857), *Laws of Michigan, 1857,* pp. 346–353.

18. Benison, "Railroads, Land and Iron," pp. 134–136. Stennett, *Yesterday and Today,* pp. 54, 164. *American Railway Times,* August 13, 1857, p. 2. Deed: Chicago, St. Paul & Fond du Lac to Iron Mountain Railroad (October 14, 1857), Register of Deeds, Marquette, Mich., Liber N p. 574.

19. *Journal of House of Representatives of the State of Michigan* (1859), p. 666. Indenture: The Iron Mountain Rail Road to The Bay de Noquet & Marquette Rail Road Company (March 5, 1859), Register of Deeds, Marquette, Mich., Liber C p. 39. The Cleveland Iron Mining Company to The Bay de Noquet and Marquette Rail Road Company (July 13, 1860), Register of Deeds, Marquette, Mich., Liber C p. 408, Perron Papers.

20. Benison, "Railroads, Land and Iron," pp. 203, 204.

21. Ibid., pp. 198–202. Stennett, *Yesterday and Today,* pp. 55–57, 164. An Act to Authorize the Chicago and Northwestern Ry. Co. to Construct a New Line of Road Commencing in the Town of Neenah and County of Winnebago (March 8, 1862), *Wisconsin Private and Local Laws, 1862,* chap. 34, pp. 36, 37.

22. Joint Resolution Asking the Government of the United States to Make a Grant of Land for the Construction of a Road from Houghton, in the State of Michigan, to the City of Appleton, in the State of Wisconsin (no. 15, January 18, 1862), *Laws of Michigan, 1862,* pp. 71, 72. Joint Resolution Relative to a Certain Grant of Land for Railroad Purposes Made to the State of Michigan in Eighteen Hundred and Fifty-Six (no. 38, July 5, 1862), *Statutes at Large, Treaties and Proclamations of the United States of America* 12, p. 620. *American Railroad Journal,* September 12, 1863, p. 857, quoting *Chicago Tribune.* Michigan Railroad Commission, *Aids, Gifts, Grants and Donations,* pp. 64, 65.

23. An Act to Extend the Time for the Completion of Certain Railroads to Which Land Grants Have Been Made in the States of Michigan and Wisconsin (chap. 103, March 3, 1865), *Statutes at Large, Treaties and Proclamations of the United States of America* 13, pp. 520–522. Jos. S. Wilson to J. W. Longyear, December 14, 1869, Railroads—Michigan Papers, Marquette County Historical Society, Marquette, Mich. S. P. Ely to H. P. Baldwin, February 6, 1871; H. N. Walker to J. F. Joy, December 15, 1871, Michigan State Archives.

24. *Mining Journal,* January 13, 1872, p. 2.

25. Ibid., April 16, 1910, p. 6.

26. Michigan Railroad Commission, *Aids, Gifts, Grants and Donations,* pp. 80, 81. An Act Disposing of Certain Grants of Land Made to the State of Michigan for Railroad Purposes, by Act of Congress Approved June Third (3), Eighteen Hundred and Fifty-Six (1856) (no.126, February 14, 1857), *Laws of Michigan, 1857,* p. 347.

27. A. H. Wildes to the President and Directors of the M.&O. Railroad Company, September 17, 1857, and February 12, 1858, Railroads—Michigan, Marquette County Historical Society.

28. Michigan Railroad Commission, *Aids, Gifts, Grants and Donations,* pp. 80, 81.

29. James P. Pendill, "Marquette and Ontonagon Railroad Company," *Proceedings of the Lake Superior Mining Institute* 14 (Ishpeming, 1909), pp. 207–212.

30. An Act to Confer Certain Forfeited Lands, Right and Privileges, upon the Marquette and Ontonagon Railroad Company, Incorporated January Second, Eighteen Hundred and Sixty-Three, Which Were Granted in the Year Eighteen Hundred and Fifty-Seven to the Marquette and Ontonagon Ry. Co. . . . (no. 116, March 17, 1863), *Laws of Michigan, 1863,* pp. 173–175.

31. S. P. Ely to Gov. H. H. Crapo, October 20, 1865, and December 16, 1865; Henry H. Crapo to H. P. Baldwin, July 12, 1869, Michigan State Archives. Henry H. Crapo to Alex Campbell, Oct. 28, 1865, and December 9, 1865; Jos. S. Wilson to J. W. Longyear, December 14, 1869, Railroads—Michigan, Marquette County Historical Society.

32. *Mining Journal,* July 15, 1871, p. 2.

33. Ibid., February 18, 1871, p. 3; August 5, 1871, p. 2. Michigan Railroad Commission, *Aids, Gifts, Grants and Donations,* pp. 82, 83.

2. Irresolvable Conflicts Create the MH&O

1. Benison, *Railroads, Land and Iron,* pp. 266–269. Michigan Railroad Commission, *Aids, Gifts, Grants and Donations,* pp. 82, 83. Richard C. Overton, *Burlington West: A Colonization History of the Burlington Railroad* (Cambridge, Mass.: Harvard University Press, 1941), pp. 26, 29, 30, 38, 42–44. H. N. Walker to J. F. Joy, December 15, 1871, Michigan State Archives.

2. Benison, *Railroads, Land and Iron,* pp. 266–269, 271, 370. H. N. Walker to J. W. Longyear, February 3, 1871, Railroads—Michigan, Marquette County Historical Society. Joint Resolution to Forfeit the Lands Granted to the Marquette and Ontonagon Railroad Company, and to Confer the Said Grant of Lands upon Some Other Company (no. 30, March 30, 1869), *Laws of Michigan, 1869,* pp. 411–418.

3. *Mining Journal,* December 21, 1872, p. 1. An Act to Enable the Houghton and Ontonagon

Railroad Company to Make a Resurvey of Its Road (chap. 36, April 20, 1871), *Statutes at Large and Proclamations of the United States of America* 17, p. 3.

4. S. P. Ely to H. P. Baldwin, November 12, 1869, Michigan State Archives.

5. Jos. F. Fay to H. P. Baldwin, January 9, 1872, Michigan State Archives.

6. Michigan Railroad Commission, *Aids, Gifts, Grants and Donations*, pp. 82, 83. *Mining Journal*, January 13, 1872, p. 2.

7. H. N. Walker to Messrs. Wilkinson and Smith, February 6, 1872, Railroads—Michigan, Marquette County Historical Society.

8. H. N. Walker to H. P. Baldwin, January 8, 1872, Michigan State Archives.

9. H. N. Walker to Messrs. Wilkinson and Smith, March 22, 1872, Railroads—Michigan, Marquette County Historical Society.

10. Benison, *Railroads, Land and Iron*, p. 292.

11. Ibid., pp. 299–301. H.&O. Railroad Co., Circular, July 6, 1872; H. N. Walker to Messrs. Wilkinson and Smith, May 11, 1872, M.,H.&O. Papers. Michigan Railroad Commission, *Aids, Gifts, Grants and Donations*, pp. 82, 83.

12. *Mining Journal*, May 17, 1873, p. 5.

13. *Railroad Gazette*, August 30, 1873, p. 355, quoting *Chicago Tribune*.

14. *Portage Lake Mining Gazette* (Houghton, Mich.), August 14, 1873, p. 3.

15. *Railroad Gazette*, April 9, 1880, p. 201.

16. *Ashland* (Wis.) *Press*, March 20, 1880, p. 4; September 11, 1880, p. 4.

17. Ibid., May 28, 1881, p. 1., quoting *St. Paul* (Minn.) *Pioneer Press.*

18. Knox Jamison, *Ewen and the South End Towns* (n.p., 1967), p. 5.

19. Michigan Railroad Commission, *Aids, Gifts, Grants and Donations*, pp. 60, 61. *Ashland Press*, June 11, 1881, p. 1; July 30, 1881, p. 4; February 11, 1882, p. 4. An Act to Confirm the Action of the Board of Control of Railroad Lands Conferring Certain Lands, Rights, Franchises, Powers, and Privileges upon the Ontonagon and Brule River Railroad Company . . . (no. 238, June 7, 1881), *Michigan Public Acts, 1881*, pp. 281–284.

20. An Act to Appropriate Lands to Aid in the Construction of a Railroad from the Village of L'Anse, in the County of Baraga, to the Village of Houghton, in the County of Houghton (no. 197, May 1, 1875), *Michigan Public Acts, 1875*, p. 229. Michigan Railroad Commission, *Aids, Gifts, Grants and Donations*, pp. 82, 83. *Ninth Annual Report of the Commissioner of Railroads of the State of Michigan for the Year Ending December 31, 1880*, p. xxxiv. *Portage Lake Mining Gazette*, April 29, 1875, p. 3.

21. *Mining Journal*, October 21, 1882, p. 4; November 25, 1882, p. 4; December 9, 1882, p. 1; November 24, 1883, p. 8. Michigan Railroad

Commission, *Aids, Gifts, Grants and Donations*, pp. 82, 83.

22. *Mining Journal*, April 29, 1882, p. 1; November 17, 1883, p. 1. *Portage Lake Mining Gazette*, November 22, 1883, p. 3; November 29, 1883, p. 3. South Shore Land Company, Limited, Abstract of Title (blank), author's collection.

3. The Mackinac Road

1. Hiram A. Burt to Michigan Legislature, March 8, 1873, Paananen Papers.

2. *Mining Journal*, January 18, 1873, p. 2.

3. Ibid., April 8, 1876, p. 4. *1st Annual Report of the Commissioner of Railroads of the State of Michigan for the Year Ending December 31, 1872*, pp. xxix, 246. LeRoy Barnett, "Detroit, Mackinac & Marquette, Part 1," *The Soo*, October 1990, p. 21. An Act to Authorize and Empower the Board of State Swamp Lands, to Make an Appropriation of State Swamp Lands to Aid in the Construction of a Railroad from the Straits of Mackinaw to Marquette Harbor, on Lake Superior (no. 36, March 21, 1873), *Laws of Michigan, 1873*, pp. 37, 38.

4. Governor John J. Bagley, in his Message to the Legislature, January 7, 1875, *Michigan Joint Documents*, pp. 24, 25, Paananen Papers.

5. *Mining Journal*, April 10, 1875, pp. 4, 5. An Act to Amend Sections One, Two, and Three of an Act Entitled "An Act to Authorize and Empower the Board of Control of State Swamp Lands to Make an Appropriation of State Swamp Lands to Aid in the Construction of a Railroad from the Straits of Mackinaw to Marquette Harbor on Lake Superior" . . . (no. 81, April 15, 1875), *Laws of Michigan, 1875*, pp. 119–121.

6. *Railroad Gazette*, April 28, 1876, p. 188.

7. Ibid., May 12, 1876, p. 210. *Mining Journal*, January 11, 1879, p. 4. An Act to Amend Section One of an Act Entitled "An Act to Authorize and Empower the Board of Control of State Swamp Lands to Make an Appropriation of State Swamp Lands to Aid in the Construction of a Railroad from the Straits of Mackinaw to Marquette Harbor, on Lake Superior" . . . (no. 128, May 14, 1877), *Michigan Public Acts, 1877*, pp. 116, 117. An Act to Amend Section One of an Act Entitled "An Act to Authorize and Empower the Board of Control of State Swamp Lands to Make an Appropriation of State Swamp Lands to Aid in the Construction of a Railroad from the Straits of Mackinaw to Marquette Harbor, on Lake Superior" . . . (no. 2, February 15, 1879), *Michigan Public Acts, 1879*, pp. 1, 2.

8. *Mining Journal*, August 30, 1879, p. 4. *Detroit* (Mich.) *Evening News*, August 21, 1879, p. 4. Michigan Railroad Commission, *Aids, Gifts, Grants and Donations*, pp. 84, 85.

9. Michigan Railroad Commission, *Aids, Gifts, Grants and Donations*, pp. 84, 85. *Detroit* (Mich.)

Post and Tribune, February 14, 1880, p. 1. *Ashland Press,* March 20, 1880, p. 1, quoting *Detroit Evening News. Ninth Annual Report of the Commissioner of Railroads of the State of Michigan for the Year Ending December 31, 1880,* p. xxxv.

10. *Mining Journal,* October 2, 1880, p. 1.

11. Ibid., December 17, 1881, p. 1.

12. Ibid., October 22, 1881, p. 1; October 29, 1881, p. 1. Barnett, "Detroit, Mackinac & Marquette, Part 2," p. 26. ICC Reports, vol. 116, Valuation Docket no. 602, Decided October 8, 1926, pp. 589–601.

13. Aurele A. Durocher, "The DSS&A Ry. Co.," *Railroad History* 111 (October 1964), pp. 40, 41.

14. Michigan Railroad Commission, *Aids, Gifts, Grants and Donations,* pp. 84, 85.

15. *Negaunee* (Mich.) *Iron Herald,* March 27, 1884, p. 5.

16. Durocher, "The DSS&A Ry. Co.," pp. 44, 68.

17. *Mining Journal,* January 26, 1885, p. 2. *Detroit Free Press,* January 11, 1885, p. 11. *Portage Lake Mining Gazette,* January 15, 1885, p. 2.

18. *Mining Journal,* March 3, 1885, p. 2; March 14, 1885, p. 4.

19. *Mining Journal,* March 11, 1885, p. 4.

20. Joint Resolution Extending the Time for the Completion of the Marquette, Houghton and Ontonagon Railroad (no. 18, May 15, 1885), *Michigan Public Acts, 1885,* p. 369.

21. *Mining Journal,* December 22, 1888, p. 8.

22. Ibid., May 2, 1885, p. 2.

23. Ibid., August 21, 1886, p. 8.

24. Ibid., September 1, 1883, p. 1.

25. Ibid., August 21, 1886, p. 8; October 23, 1886, pp. 1, 6. Michigan Railroad Commission, *Aids, Gifts, Grants and Donations,* pp. 84, 85.

4. Formation of the DSS&A

1. Certificate of Organization of the Mackinaw & Marquette R.R. Co. (December 20, 1886), DSS&A T25, Soo Line Papers, Minnesota Historical Society, St. Paul, Minn. Articles of Consolidation of The Sault Ste. Marie and Marquette Ry. Co., The Mackinaw and Marquette R.R. Co., The Wisconsin Sault St. Marie and Mackinac Ry. Co. and The Duluth, Superior and Michigan Ry. Co., Perron papers.

2. Michigan Railroad Commission, *Aids, Gifts, Grants and Donations,* pp. 84, 85. *Mining Journal,* August 21, 1886, p. 8, quoting *Duluth News;* December 11, 1886, p. 1. *Bayfield* (Wis.) *Press,* June 4, 1887, p. 1. Barnett, "Detroit, Mackinac & Marquette, Part 2," pp. 38, 39.

3. *Mining Journal,* February 26, 1887, p. 1. ICC Valuation Reports, vol. 36, May 22, 1931, p. 164.

4. *Mining Journal,* December 25, 1886, p. 1.

5. *Minneapolis Evening Journal,* November 22, 1886, p. 4.

6. *Mining Journal,* November 6, 1886, p. 4.

7. Ibid., November 27, 1886, p. 1.

8. Ibid., July 16, 1887, p. 1.

9. Ibid., July 23, 1887, p. 1.

10. Ibid., August 11, 1888, p. 1.

11. Calvin Brice to W. C. Van Horne, December 30, 1887, Paananen Papers.

12. *Ironwood* (Mich.) *Times,* December 1, 1888, p. 1.

13. *Mining Journal,* September 17, 1887, p. 1.

14. *Sault Ste. Marie* (Mich.) *Democrat,* October 6, 1887, p. 1.

15. Ibid., October 13, 1887, p. 2.

16. Ibid., December 22, 1887, p. 2.

17. Articles of Association of the Sault Ste. Marie Bridge Company (February 19, 1881); Chap. 281—An Act to Authorize the Construction of a Railroad Bridge across the Sainte Marie River (July 8, 1882), DSS&A P24-3, Soo Line Papers.

18. *Mining Journal,* November 27, 1886, p. 4; December 11, 1886, p. 1; March 19, 1887, p. 4. *Ashland Press,* January 22, 1887, p. 1. *Escanaba* (Mich.) *Delta,* February 11, 1887, p. 3, quoting *Minneapolis Journal.* ICC Reports, May 22, 1931, pp. 197, 198. Minutes, Stockholders Meeting, S.S.M.B. Co. (February 28, 1887); Agreement, S.S.M.B. Co., C.P.R., D.,S.S.&A., and M.S.S.M.&A. (July 1, 1887), DSS&A P24-3, Soo Papers.

19. Joseph Taylor to Van Horne, June 24, 1887, Paananen Papers. S.S.M.B. Co., Corporate Relationship to Soo Line (February 12, 1941), DSS&A P24-3, Soo Papers. ICC Reports, vol. 108, Valuation Docket no. 184, Decided March 12, 1926, p. 344.

20. Agreement, New Jersey Bridge Construction Company, S.S.M.B. Co., Central Trust Company (May 26, 1887), DSS&A P24-3, Soo Papers.

21. *Sault Ste. Marie Democrat,* November 24, 1887, p. 1.

22. Ibid., December 22, 1887, p. 2.

23. Ibid., January 5, 1888, p. 1.

24. Ibid., December 22, 1887, p. 6.

25. *Iron Ore,* January 14, 1888, p. 5.

26. *Mining Journal,* August 25, 1888, p. 1.

27. *Negaunee Iron Herald,* July 5, 1888, p. 8.

28. *Mining Journal,* May 26, 1888, p. 8, quoting *The Detroit Sunday Sun; June 9, 1888.*

29. *Mining Journal,* August 11, 1888, p. 1.

30. *Sault Ste. Marie Democrat,* December 29, 1887, p. 16, quoting *Toronto Globe.*

31. W. Kaye Lamb, *History of the Canadian Pacific Railway* (New York: Macmillan, 1977), p. 167.

32. Samuel Thomas to James McMillan, April 3, 1888, McMillan Papers, Burton Historical Collection, Detroit (Mich.) Public Library.

33. ICC Valuation Reports, vol. 36, May 22, 1931, pp. 182–186. *New York Times,* May 21, 1888, p. 5; July 14, 1888, p. 2; July 15, 1888, p. 2. *Superior* (Wis.) *Sunday Morning Call,* July 22, 1888, p. 3.

34. David Cruise and Allison Griffiths, *Lords of the Line: The Men Who Built the CPR* (New York: Viking, 1988), pp. 203, 204, 207, 208.

35. Ibid., pp. 202, 203.

36. Ibid., p. 208.

37. *Mining Journal,* July 28, 1888, p. 4, quoting *London Standard.*

38. Ibid., August 11, 1888, p. 8.

39. Ibid., August 25, 1888, p. 8.

40. McMillan to Van Horne, August 16, 1888, Paananen Papers.

41. *St. Paul Dispatch,* August 29, 1888, p. 1.

42. J. A. Latcha to W. C. Van Horne, August 27, 1888, Paananen Papers.

43. *Ashland Press,* September 1, 1888, p. 1.

44. *Mining Journal,* January 14, 1888, p. 1, quoting *Duluth News.*

45. *Superior* (Wis.) *Times,* January 21, 1888, p. 2.

46. *Montreal River Miner* (Hurley, Wis.), April 19, 1888, p. 4.

47. *Mining Journal,* August 27, 1887, p. 1.

48. *Sault Ste. Marie Democrat,* November 10, 1887, p. 1.

49. *Mining Journal,* March 31, 1888, p. 1; May 26, 1888, p. 8. *Negaunee Iron Herald,* May 3, 1888, p. 1. Michigan Railroad Commission, *Aids, Gifts, Grants and Donations,* pp. 84, 85.

50. John F. Stevens, "An Engineer's Recollections, IV: Winter Work on the South Shore Railroad," *Engineering News-Record,* April 25, 1935, pp. 590–592.

51. Sterling to Van Horne, August 18, 1888, Paananen Papers.

52. *Seventeenth Annual Report of the Commissioner of Railroads of the State of Michigan for the Year Ending December 31, 1888* (Lansing, 1889), p. xivi.

5. The Zenith City Short Line

1. W. C. Van Horne to W. F. Fitch, November 6, 1888, DSS&A P28F1, Soo Papers.

2. Geo. T. Jarvis to Jas. McMillan, December 15, 1888, McMillan Papers.

3. W. C. Van Horne to W. F. Fitch, January 5, 1890, DSS&A P28F1, Soo Papers.

4. *Ashland Press,* June 18, 1892, p. 1.

5. W. C. Van Horne to W. F. Fitch, January 5, 1890, DSS&A P28F1, Soo Papers.

6. Ibid.

7. *New York Times,* May 12, 1889, p. 9.

8. W. C. Van Horne to W. F. Fitch, January 5, 1890, DSS&A P28F1, Soo Papers.

9. Van Horne to Henry D. Minot, November 9, 1889, DSS&A P28F1, Soo Papers.

10. Van Horne to Fitch, October 27, 1889, DSS&A P28F1, Soo Papers.

11. *Mining Journal,* December 31, 1892, p. 1.

12. Van Horne to Fitch, October 27, 1889, DSS&A P28F1, Soo Papers.

13. *Iron Ore,* June 27, 1903, p. 1.

14. *Mining Journal,* July 19, 1890, p. 1. Michigan Railroad Commission, *Aids, Gifts, Grants and Donations,* pp. 84, 85. Finney to Van Horne, October 21, 1890, Paananen Papers. *Ironwood Times,* November 22, 1890, p. 1, quoting *Milwaukee Evening Wisconsin.*

15. *Mining Journal,* October 10, 1891, p. 1. *Railway Age,* July 19, 1890, p. 511. D. M. Philbin to Jos. B. Cotton, July 9, 1898, Railroads—Michigan, Marquette County Historical Society. *L'Anse* (Mich.) *Sentinel,* August 25, 1900, p. 1.

16. Samuel Thomas to Messrs. Bunnell and Scranton, August 18, 1890, Paananen Papers.

17. Van Horne to Fitch, October 27, 1889, DSS&A P28F1, Soo Papers.

18. Samuel Thomas to Messrs. Bunnell and Scranton, August 18, 1890, Paananen Papers.

19. Thomas to Van Horne, November 8, 1889, Paananen Papers.

20. W. C. Van Horne to James McMillan, May 20, 1890, McMillan Papers.

21. CPR, DSS&A, Traffic Agreement (May 27, 1890), DSSA Sec.; DSS&A Corporate and Financial History, November 1933, Soo Pres. 26-3-8, Soo Papers. ICC Reports, vol. 267, Finance Docket no. 11484, June 19, 1947, pp. 576, 577. *Railway Age,* May 3, 1890, p. 312.

22. Register of Deeds Office, Marquette County, Marquette, Mich., Liber 21 p. 327, MH&O RR. Co. to The DSS&A Ry. Co. (July 17, 1890), Perron Papers. CPR, DSS&A, Traffic Agreement (May 27, 1890), DSSA Sec., Soo Papers. County Clerk's Office, Marquette, Mich., Liber 21 p. 325, N&P R.R. Co. to DSS&A Ry. Co. (July 19, 1890), Perron Papers.

23. District Director of Internal Revenue, St. Paul, Minnesota, to Assistant Commissioner, Operations, Washington, D. C., February 21, 1955, DSS&A P20-5-1, Soo Papers.

24. Samuel Thomas to James McMillan, May 26, 1890, McMillan Papers.

25. *Mining Journal,* December 22, 1888, p. 8.

26. Samuel Thomas to James McMillan, June 17, 1890, McMillan Papers.

27. Disposition of Proceeds from Sale of DSS&A First Consol. 4% Bonds., Undated, DSS&A P-20-5-1, Soo Papers.

28. Lamb, *History of the Canadian Pacific Railway,* p. 168.

29. *The Mining Journal,* December 31, 1892, p. 8.

30. *Bayfield Press,* March 12, 1892, p. 8, quoting *Detroit Tribune.*

6. The Mineral Range and L'Anse Bay Railroad

1. Articles of Incorporation of the Mineral Range and L'Anse Bay Rail Road Company (October 13, 1871), DSSA P28(1), Soo Papers.
2. Amendments to Articles of Incorporation, Mineral Range and L'Anse Bay Rail Road (October 25, 1872), DSS&A Sec., Soo Papers.
3. *Portage Lake Mining Gazette,* July 31, 1873, p. 3.
4. Orrin W. Robinson, *Early Days of the Lake Superior Copper Country* (Houghton, Mich.: D. I. Robinson, ca. 1938), p. 23.
5. *Portage Lake Mining Gazette,* October 16, 1873, p. 3.
6. Ibid., March 12, 1874, p. 3.
7. *The Narrow-Gauge Locomotives: The Baldwin Catalog of 1877* (Norman: University of Oklahoma Press, 1967).
8. *Mining Journal,* April 30, 1887, p. 4.
9. Ibid., January 23, 1886, p. 5. *Tenth Annual Report of the Commissioner of Railroads of the State of Michigan for the Year Ending December 31, 1881,* p. 387. *Ashland Press,* September 11, 1880, p. 4. *Portage Lake Mining Gazette,* January 21, 1886, p. 3.
10. *Mining Journal,* March 3, 1883, p. 4.
11. *Mining Journal,* July 18, 1885, p. 5.
12. Articles of Association of the H.&C. Railroad Company (December 27, 1884), Soo Vice Pres. Acct. File 61, Soo Papers.
13. *Mining Journal,* January 16, 1886, p. 5.
14. *Portage Lake Mining Gazette,* August 12, 1886, p. 3.
15. Ibid., March 25, 1886, p. 3. *Railroad Gazette,* April 9, 1886, p. 255.
16. Ibid., August 12, 1886, p. 3.
17. *Railroad Gazette,* July 30, 1886, p. 533, quoting *Boston Traveller. Twenty-Ninth Annual Report of the Commissioner of Railroads of the State of Michigan for the Year 1901,* p. 297.
18. *Railway Age,* September 2, 1887, p. 611.
19. *Portage Lake Mining Gazette,* November 28, 1889, p. 3.
20. Ibid., July 4, 1889, p. 4.
21. *Mining Journal,* December 31, 1892, p. 1. Disposition of Proceeds from Sale of DSS&A First Consol. 4% Bonds, Undated, DSS&A P-20-5-1, Soo Papers.
22. *The Range-Tribune* (Iron Mountain, Mich.), September 16, 1893, p. 1; September 23, 1893, pp. 1, 8.
23. *Mining Journal,* September 28, 1897, pp. 3, 8; September 30, 1897, p. 3. *Copper Country Evening News* (Calumet, Mich.), September 29, 1897, p. 4.
24. *Twenty-Seventh Annual Report of the Commissioner of Railroads of the State of Michigan for the Year 1899,* p. 38.
25. *Daily Mining Gazette,* October 9, 1899, p. 7. Michigan Railroad Commission, *Aids, Gifts, Grants and Donations,* pp. 88, 89. *Railroad Gazette,* March 17, 1899, p. 197; December 8, 1899, p. 853. *Copper Country Evening News,* November 13, 1899, p. 3.

7. An Independent Entrance to Superior

1. T. F. Oakes to J. W. Kendrick, November 10, 1890, NP Chief Engineer 133, NP Papers, Minn. Hist. Soc.
2. T. F. Oakes to W. S. Mellen, March 17, 1892, Gen. Mgr. 5549, NP Papers.
3. *Superior* (Wis.) *Leader,* September 1, 1892, p. 8.
4. *Mining Journal,* November 26, 1892, p. 1; November 29, 1892, p. 8. *Superior* (Wis.) *Inland Ocean,* November 27, 1892, p. 2.
5. *Mining Journal,* September 3, 1892, p. 1.
6. Ibid., February 4, 1893, p. 8.
7. Walker, *Iron Frontier,* pp. 50, 102. *St. James* (Minn.) *Journal,* December 15, 1888, p. 7. *Railroad Gazette,* January 23, 1891, p. 71; April 10, 1891, p. 256.
8. Cruise and Griffiths, *Lords of the Line,* p. 210. Samuel Thomas to W. C. Van Horne, February 23, 1892, Soo Line Vice Pres. Acct. File 46, Soo Papers.
9. Cruise and Griffiths, *Lords of the Line,* p. 223.
10. Ibid., p. 313.
11. Ibid., p. 313.
12. Geo. T. Jarvis to W. C. Van Horne, September 27, 1888, Paananen Collection.
13. *Iron Ore,* December 16, 1893, p. 1.
14. *Mining Journal,* September 10, 1892, p. 1; February 25, 1893, p. 1. Michigan Railroad Commission, *Aids, Gifts, Grants and Donations,* pp. 104, 105.
15. T. G. Shaughnessy to W. F. Fitch, September 29, 1899, Paananen Collection.
16. Barnett, "Detroit, Mackinac & Marquette, Part 2," p. 39. *Railway Age Gazette,* April 15, 1910, p. 1017.
17. A South Shore Land Company, Limited, Abstract of Title (Blank). A. E. Miller, memo, January 11, 1933, Soo Vice Pres. Acct. File 64, Soo Papers.
18. *Mining Journal,* October 8, 1898, p. 8; January 17, 1902, p. 8. *Manistique* (Mich.) *Courier,* January 6, 1899, p. 1; October 10, 1910, p. 8. *Railway Age Gazette,* August 27, 1909, p. 386. Michigan Railroad Commission, *Aids, Gifts, Donations and Grants,* pp. 104, 105.
19. *Mining Journal,* November 5, 1910, p. 8. Michigan Railroad Appraisal, DSS&A, 1900, Marquette County Historical Society. Michigan Railroad Commission, *Aids, Gifts, Grants and Donations,* pp. 74, 75. *Newberry* (Mich.) *News,* June 13, 1902, p. 1.
20. *The Soo,* July 1989, p. 16.
21. *Mining Journal,* July 26, 1907, p. 8. Deed John S. Ward to Duluth South Shore & Atlantic Ry. Co. (July 25, 1907), Perron Papers.
22. *Ashland Press,* May 31, 1899, p. 1.
23. Agreement, DSS&A Ry. Co. and C.,M.&St.P. Ry. Co. (November 23, 1899), DSSA P18(1), Soo Papers.

24. *Mining Journal,* December 4, 1967, p. 13. C&NW, *Abstracts of Crossing and Junction Contracts, Vol. 2* (December 1901), pp. 484, 485, Paananen Papers.

8. The South Range Line

1. Amendment to Article V, Articles of Association, M.R. Railroad (February 20, 1899), DSS&A P28(1), Soo Papers.

2. *Ontonagon Herald,* June 9, 1900, p. 4.

3. Ibid., December 22, 1900, p. 5. *Mining Journal,* January 5, 1901, p. 2. M.R. South Range Division Time Table no. 1 (December 23, 1900).

4. MR RR Co., General Four Per Cent. Fifty Year Gold Bond Mortgage (January 1, 1901), Soo Vice Pres. Acct. File 61; Agreement . . . CP Ry Co. . . . DSS&A Ry Co. . . . MR Company . . . (January 1, 1901), DSSA P28(1); M.R. Railroad, Financial Statement (August 27, 1920), Soo Vice Pres. Acct. File 61; MR Corporate and Financial History (November 1933), Soo Pres. 26-3-8, Soo Papers.

5. *Daily Mining Gazette,* June 26, 1900, p. 5. Agreement . . . H&C RR Co. and the MR RR Co. (June 1, 1901); MR Railroad, Financial Statement (August 27, 1920), Soo Vice Pres. Acct. File 61, Soo Papers. ICC Valuation Reports, vol. 26, July 26, 1929, p. 182.

6. MR Railroad, Amendment to Article III of Articles of Association (April 15, 1901), DSSA P28(1); MR Railroad, Financial Statement (August 27, 1920), Soo Vice Pres. Acct. File 61; MR Corporate and Financial History (November 1933), Soo Pres. 26-38-8, Soo Papers.

7. *Mining Journal,* November 11, 1901, p. 3.

8. Ibid., July 20, 1901, p. 4; July 26, 1902, p. 4. *Hancock Evening Journal,* July 3, 1901, p. 2. Michigan Railroad Commission, *Aids, Gifts, Grants and Donations,* pp. 86, 87. ICC Valuation Reports, vol. 26, July 26, 1929, p. 182.

9. *Duluth Weekly Herald,* April 9, 1902, p. 8. *Thirty-First Annual Report of the Commissioner of Railroads of the State of Michigan for the Year 1903,* p. 465.

10. *Calumet News,* December 31, 1907, p. 8. *The Official Guide of the Railways,* January 1908, p. 629. Michigan Railroad Commission, *Aids, Gifts, Grants and Donations,* pp. 106, 107.

11. *Mining Journal,* April 9, 1906, p. 3.

12. Ibid., September 23, 1910, p. 3.

13. ICC Reports, vol. 114, Valuation Docket no. 210, June 18, 1926, pp. 171–179. *Sault Ste. Marie News,* January 27, 1900, p. 1. *Railroad Gazette,* November 25, 1904, p. 583.

14. Agreement . . . between the DSS&A Ry Co. . . . and the MStP&SSM Ry Co. (May 31, 1901), DSS&A P17(11), Soo Papers. Soo Line, List of Structures, 1900.

15. *Mining Journal,* October 20, 1900, p. 1.

16. Ibid., May 11, 1901, p. 8.

17. *Superior* (Wis.) *Telegram,* May 31, 1905, p. 5.

18. Ibid., December 8, 1905, p. 12.

19. *Daily Mining Gazette,* November 3, 1903, p. 1.

20. *Mining Journal,* August 4, 1906, p. 3.

21. *Daily Mining Gazette,* January 20, 1909, p. 10.

22. *Hancock Evening Journal,* November 28, 1916, p. 1; *Mining Journal,* December 1, 1916, p. 3.

23. *Iron Ore,* December 23, 1905, p. 4.

24. *Mining Journal,* March 19, 1910, p. 6.

25. Ibid., June 18, 1901, p. 8.

26. Ibid., May 30, 1902, p. 8.

27. *Calumet* (Mich.) *News,* January 4, 1908, p. 8.

28. *Mining Journal,* November 9, 1905, p. 5.

29. Ibid., May 9, 1907, p. 9, quoting *Sault News.*

30. An Act to Amend Section Nine of Act Number One Hundred Ninety-Eight of the Laws of Eighteen Hundred Seventy-Three . . . (no. 54, April 18, 1907), *Michigan Public Acts, 1907,* pp. 55–59.

31. *Mining Journal,* January 21, 1911, p. 8.

32. Ibid., January 17, 1907, p. 7.

33. *Ironwood Times,* October 27, 1917, p. 1.

34. *Newberry News,* January 18, 1918, p. 8.

9. Bridge Route Revisited

1. *Mining Journal,* October 29, 1908, p. 5, quoting *New York American.*

2. Ibid., November 27, 1908, p. 5, quoting *Wall Street Journal.*

3. MStP&SSM-DSS&A Contract no. 3601 (July 1, 1910); R. L. Simpson to G. A. MacNamara, May 4, 1953, DSS&A P9-6, Soo Papers.

4. Contract no. 2515 (January 1, 1911), collected June 5, 1946, DSS&A P18(7); Agreement, MSTP&SSM Ry. Co., DSS&A Ry. Co. (January 1, 1911), DSS&A P9-6, Soo Papers.

5. ICC Reports, vol. 116, Valuation Docket no. 602, Decided October 8, 1926, pp. 589–601.

6. *Mining Journal,* November 25, 1911, p. 12.

7. Ibid., September 17, 1915, p. 10.

8. Ibid., April 5, 1913, p. 8. *Railway Age Gazette,* December 1, 1911, p. 1145. T. G. Shaughnessy to W. W. Walker, November 28, 1911, DSS&A P28 F1, Soo Papers.

9. *Mining Journal,* April 19, 1913, p. 2, quoting *Duluth Herald.*

10. Durocher, "The DSS&A Ry. Co.," p. 72.

11. *Mining Journal,* January 30, 1912, p. 8.

12. Ibid., April 19, 1913, p. 2.

13. *Skillings' Mining Review,* November 29, 1913, p. 1.

14. *Mining Journal,* December 2, 1911, p. 1.

15. *Daily Mining Gazette,* May 24, 1912, p. 11.

16. *Mining Journal,* May 7, 1927, Sec. 1, p. 22.

10. World War I

1. DSS&A Annual Reports for the years ending December 31, 1918, and December 31, 1919.

2. *St. Ignace Enterprise,* September 19, 1918, p. 1, quoting *Newberry News.*

3. DSS&A Annual Report for year ending December 31, 1918. *St. Ignace Enterprise,* July 11, 1918, p. 1; September 12, 1918, p. 1

4. John J. Riordan, "Riordan Recalls Early Days in the Seney Country," *Grand Marais and Picture Rocks Review,* June 21, 1972.

5. *Mining Journal,* March 19, 1917, p. 3.

6. Ibid., December 15, 1903, p. 8.

7. John Barton Payne, Re Contract D.,S.S.&A. (February 11, 1919), DSS&A P20-5-1, Soo Papers.

8. Tax Department Memorandum (August 21, 1956), DSS&A P20-5-1, Soo Papers.

9. *Railway Age,* September 3, 1920, p. 426. *Daily Mining Gazette,* April 22, 1922, p. 6. M. I. LaBelle to J. D. Bond, August 13, 1954, Soo Line Vice Pres. Acct. Box 54, Soo Papers.

10. *Railway Age,* April 28, 1923, p. 1080. *Skillings' Mining Review,* November 10, 1923, p. 7. DSS&A Annual Report, 1924.

11. *Bayfield County Press,* April 8, 1921, p. 1.

12. *Daily Mining Gazette,* April 26, 1924, p. 1.

13. *Mining Journal,* May 26, 1925, p. 10.

14. *Daily Mining Gazette,* April 24, 1924, p. 7.

15. *Mining Journal,* May 31, 1924, p. 4.

16. I. G. Ogden to A. E. Delf, March 24, 1925, DSS&A P20-5-1, Soo Papers.

17. II. S. Mitchell to G. A. MacNamara, April 16, 1953, DSS&A P9-6, Soo Papers. *Mining Journal,* March 18, 1925, p. 3; March 27, 1925, p. 7.

18. R. S. Claar to Sigurd Ueland, November 17, 1941, DSS&A P18-6, Soo Papers.

19. ICC Reports, vol. 138, Finance Docket no. 6194, Decided January 30, 1928, pp. 125–131.

20. ICC Reports, vol. 138, Finance Docket no. 6604, Decided April 10, 1928, pp. 470–474.

21. ICC Reports, vol. 166, Finance Docket no. 8470, October 28, 1930, pp. 639, 640.

22. *Daily Mining Gazette,* December 15, 1917, pp. 3, 5; December 19, 1917, p. 12.

23. *L'Anse Sentinel,* December 12, 1919, p. 1.

24. *Skillings' Mining Review,* August 30, 1924, p. 7; September 19, 1925, p. 2. Calumet and Hecla Consolidated Copper Co. of Michigan, Report for Year Ending December 31, 1926, p. 6. ICC Reports, vol. 131, Finance Docket no. 6193, August 5, 1927, pp. 72, 73.

11. Drastic Cuts

1. Memorandum, Discontinuance Trains Nos. 1 and 2 (ca. Oct. 8, 1940), DSSAP18(1), Soo Papers.

2. *Mining Journal,* March 30, 1929, p. 2.

3. Ibid., July 25, 1939, p. 2.

4. State of Michigan, Before the Michigan Public Service Commission, no. D-3241 (December 19, 1939), DSSAP18(1), Soo Papers.

5. State of Michigan in the Circuit Court for the County of Ingham, DSS&A Ry. Co. vs. Michigan Public Service Commission (May 20, 1941), DSSAP18(1), Soo Papers.

6. P. L. Solether to H. F. Schmidt, October 21, 1943, DSSAP18(2), Soo Papers.

7. Union National Bank, Marquette, Mich., *Union National Messenger,* August, 1929.

8. *Mining Journal,* April 20, 1933, p. 2.

9. T. A. Foque to M. J. Dunnebacke, October 18, 1929, Soo 767-2, Stuart Nelson Papers.

10. *Wakefield* (Mich.) *News,* December 21, 1935, p. 1. Orders and Opinions of the Michigan Public Utilities Commission, no. D-3008 (April 7, 1936), pp. 247–249. Interview with Don Hart, Edina, Minnesota (September 19, 1991).

11. *Moody's Manual of Investments* (New York, 1933), p. 1208. DSS&A Financial and Corporate History (November 1933), Soo Papers. ICC Reports, June 19, 1947, p. 578.

12. D. M. McIntosh to E. A. Whitman, June 4, 1932, Paananen Papers.

13. H. E. Stevens to Chas. Donnelly, July 9, 1932, Pres. Sub. Files, 1391-3, N.P. Papers. DSS&A Contract no. 1143 (May 1, 1933), Paananen Papers.

14. *Evening Telegram* (Superior, Wis.), April 26, 1934, p. 1; April 30, 1934, p. 2.

15. CP and Soo Line Committee Reports (ca. 1933), Soo Pres. 26-3-8, Soo Papers.

16. Ibid.

17. E. R. Woodson to G. W. Webster, May 10, 1932, Paananen Papers.

18. G. W. Webster, Memorandum (May 13, 1932), Paananen Papers.

19. ICC Reports, vol. 224, Finance Docket no. 11879, January 24, 1938, pp. 480–482. *L'Anse Sentinel,* February 18, 1937, p. 1.

20. Special Meeting . . . Board of Directors . . . DSS&A Ry Co. (December 30, 1936), DSS&A P28F1, Soo Papers.

21. U.S. District Court, 4th Div., Minn., Bankruptcy Docket no. 13310, Order no. 1 (January 2, 1937), and Order no. 21 (January 30, 1937), DSS&A P28F1, Soo Papers.

22. U.S. Treasury Department, Preliminary Statement (September 25, 1956), DSSAP20-5-1, Soo Papers. ICC Reports, vol. 267, Finance Docket no. 11484, June 19, 1947, pp. 608, 609. DSS&A Accounting Department, Memorandum (January 16, 1937), Paananen Papers.

23. U.S. District Court, 4th Div., Minn., no. 13310, Order no. 235 (December 3, 1940, and August 5, 1947), Petitions to ICC Finance Docket 11484, December 24, 1940, and June 16, 1943, DSSA P28(2)(4), Soo Papers.

24. Hart interview. *Mining Journal,* September 27, 1939, p. 2; July 14, 1950, p. 1.

25. Comments of DSS&A Respecting Soo's Report Concerning a Merger of Soo Line and DSS&A (ca. 1957), Soo Vice Pres. Acct. Box 54, Soo Papers.

26. DSS&A Annual Report for year ending December 31, 1939.

27. Hart interview.

28. Ralph R. Eldridge to Sigurd Ueland, November 17, 1941, DSS&A P24-7, Soo Papers.

29. Hart interview.

12. Reorganization

1. DSS&A Annual Report for year ending December 31, 1943.

2. Ibid., for year ending December 31, 1945.

3. ICC Reports, vol. 267, Finance Docket no. 11484, June 19, 1947, pp. 553–563, 567, 571, 572.

4. Ibid., pp. 553–563, 567, 571, 572, 610, 618, 619, 620. ICC Report, January 1, 1945, pp. 608, 609. District Director of Internal Revenue, St. Paul, Minnesota, to Assistant Commissioner, Operations, Washington, D.C., December 31, 1946, and February 21, 1955, DSS&A P20-5-1, Soo Papers.

5. R. S. Archibald to H. S. Mitchell, August 4, 1949, DSSA P10-2, Soo Papers.

6. Comments of DSS&A Respecting Soo's Report Concerning a Merger of Soo Line and DSS&A (ca. 1957), Soo Vice Pres. Acct. Box 54, Soo Papers.

7. H. S. Mitchell to E. R. Lovell, October 22, 1949, DSSA P10-2, Soo Papers.

8. H. F. Schmidt to P. L. Solether, November 9, 1948, DSSA P17(21), Soo Papers.

9. Memorandum, Meeting, Shoreham, Minn. (February 28, 1949), DSS&A P17(21), Soo Papers.

10. A. C. Stenburg to P. L. Solether, April 13, 1949, DSS&A P17(21), Soo Papers.

11. President's Statement to DSS&A Board of Directors (May 17, 1950), DSSA P10-2, Soo Papers.

12. Ibid. (February 9, 1951), DSSA P10-2, Soo Papers.

13. Ibid. (November 11, 1953), DSS&A P10-2, Soo Papers.

14. H. F. Schmidt to P. L. Solether, August 30, 1948, DSSA P17(25)B, Soo Papers.

15. Hart interview.

16. H. S. Mitchell to G. A. MacNamara, June 10, 1953, DSS&A P9-6, Soo Papers.

17. *Evening Telegram,* March 9, 1955, p. 1.

18. H. S. Mitchell to G. A. MacNamara, December 26, 1950, DSSA P23-4, Soo Papers.

19. G. A. MacNamara to H. S. Mitchell, January 2, 1951, DSSA P23-4, Soo Papers.

20. ICC, Finance Docket no. 17766, June 16, 1952. M. I. LaBelle to R. L. Simpson and H. S.

Mitchell, July 31, 1953, DSSA P23-4; Officer's Certificate (February 24, 1954), DSS&A P9-9, Soo Papers.

21. Hart interview.

22. President's Statement to DSS&A Board of Directors (February 19, 1952), DSS&A P10-2, Soo Papers. Hart interview.

23. President's Statement to DSS&A Board of Directors (February 9, 1951), DSSA P10-2, Soo Papers.

13. Promoting the Family

1. President's Statement to DSS&A Board of Directors (February 12, 1953); N. R. Crump to H. S. Mitchell, September 9, 1955, DSS&A P10-2, Soo Papers.

2. President's Statement, November 9, 1955; R. S. Archibald to H. S. Mitchell, August 23, 1955; N. R. Crump to H. S. Mitchell, September 9, 1955, DSS&A P10-2, Soo Papers.

3. President's Statement, October 30, 1956.

4. Ibid., November 29, 1951.

5. *Railway Age,* December 20, 1954, p. 26. *Skillings' Mining Review,* February 7, 1953, p. 6.

6. Leonard H. Murray to T. F. Kearney, August 16, 1955, DSS&A P24-9, Soo Papers.

7. *Mining Journal,* July 26, 1955, p. 1.

8. Ibid., January 10, 1958, p. 4.

9. President to Board of Directors, February 19, 1958, DSS&A P10-2, Soo Papers.

10. Ibid., June 12, 1958.

11. H. S. Mitchell to J. A. Dundas, February 11, 1952, DSS&A P10-2, Soo Papers.

12. President to Board of Directors, February 9, 1955, and February 14, 1956, DSS&A P10-2, Soo Papers.

13. Ibid., June 6, 1956.

14. Ibid., June 8, 1960.

15. Francis D. Burgtorf, *Chief Wawatam, The Story of A Hand-Bomber* (Cheboygan, Mich.: Burgtorf, 1976), p. 230.

16. President to Board of Directors, August 17, 1955, DSS&A P10-2, Soo Papers.

17. Special Meeting of Directors of South Shore Land Company (May 20, 1946); T. M. Beckley to R. J. Barry, August 20, 1957, Soo Vice Pres. Acct. File 64, Soo Papers.

18. C. E. Jefferson to H. S. Mitchell, December 21, 1954, DSS&A P24-9, Soo Papers.

19. H. S. Mitchell to G. A. MacNamara, July 26, 1954, Soo Vice Pres. Acct. Box 54, Soo Papers.

20. N. R. Crump to G. A. MacNamara, October 24, 1955, Soo Vice Pres. Acct. Box 54, Soo Papers.

21. Memorandum, C. S. Pope, M. I. LaBelle (April 19, 1955), Soo Vice Pres. Acct. Box 54, Soo Papers.

22. Ibid.

23. Hart interview.

24. President's Statement to DSS&A Board of Directors (March 15, 1960), DSS&A P10-2, Soo Papers.

25. Statement by Presidents of Soo Line, WC, DSS&A (March 15, 1960), Perron Papers.

Epilogue

1. *Mining Journal,* October 1, 1965, p. 1.

2. *The Soo,* April 1985, pp. 5, 6, quoting *Detroit Free Press.* Soo Line Railroad Lake States Transportation Division Time Table no. 1 (April 5, 1987). Soo Line Corporation, 1987 Annual Report, pp. 10, 11.

BIBLIOGRAPHY

CORPORATE RECORDS

Chicago, Minneapolis, St. Paul & Omaha, Eastern
    Division, 1946.
Duluth, South Shore & Atlantic and Mineral
    Range, Annual Reports, 1899–1959.
——, Authority for Expenditures, 1916–1960.
——, President's Files.
——, Secretary's Files.
——, Trustee's Files.
Minneapolis, Saint Paul & Sault Ste. Marie, Annual
    Reports, 1912–1915.
——, President's Files.
——, Treasurer's Files.
——, Vice President's Files.
——, Vice President Accounting's Files.
Northern Pacific, Chief Engineer's Files.
——, General Manager's Files.
——, President's Subject Files.
Soo Line, Annual Reports, 1978–1987.

GOVERNMENT RECORDS AND REPORTS

Acts of the Legislature of the State of Michigan, 1850.
Joint Documents of State of Michigan, 1868–1873.
Laws of Michigan, 1857–1875.
Michigan Public Acts, 1875–1911.
Michigan Commissioner of Railroads, *Annual
    Reports, 1872–1906.*
Michigan Public Service Commission. Orders and
    Opinions. 1923–1926.

Michigan Public Utilities Commission. Orders and
    Opinions. 1927–1936.
Michigan Railroad Commission, *Aids, Gifts, Grants
    and Donations to Railroads.* Lansing, Mich.,
    1919.
Wisconsin General Acts, 1856.
Wisconsin Private and Local Laws, 1862.
United States Statutes at Large, 1852–1871.
U.S. Interstate Commerce Commission. Finance
    and Valuation Dockets.

PAPERS & COLLECTIONS

Governor's Correspondence. Michigan State
    Archives. Lansing, Mich.
King, Frank. Northeastern Minnesota Historical
    Society. Duluth, Minn.
McMillan, James. Burton Historical Collection.
    Detroit (Mich.) Public Library.
Michigan Technological University. Houghton,
    Mich.
Perron, Wesley. Marquette County Historical
    Society. Peter White Public Library. Marquette,
    Mich.
Railroads—Michigan. Marquette County
    Historical Society. Marquette, Mich.

NEWSPAPERS

Ashland (Wis.) *Press.* 1878–1910.
Bayfield (Wis.) *Press.* 1887–1922.
Calumet (Mich.) *News.* 1907–1934.

Copper Country Evening News (Calumet, Mich.). 1897–1901.
Daily Mining Gazette (Houghton, Mich.). 1899–1979.
Detroit (Mich.) *Evening News.* 1879.
Detroit (Mich.) *Free Press.* 1855–1902.
Detroit (Mich.) *Post and Tribune.* 1878–1882.
Duluth (Minn.) *Herald.* 1891–1922.
Escanaba (Mich.) *Delta.* 1887.
Hancock (Mich.) *Evening Journal.* 1901–1916.
Ironwood (Mich.) *Daily Globe.* 1927.
Ironwood (Mich.) *Times.* 1888–1917.
Ishpeming (Mich.) *Iron Ore.* 1887–1930.
Lake Superior Journal (Sault Ste. Marie–Marquette, Mich.). 1854–1860.
Lake Superior Mining and Manufacturing News (Negaunee, Mich.). 1867, 1868.
Lake Superior News and Journal (Marquette, Mich.). 1862–1864.
L'Anse (Mich.) *Sentinel.* 1892–1958.
Manistique (Mich.) *Courier.* 1899–1910.
Mining Journal (Marquette, Mich.). 1868–1997.

Montreal River Miner (Hurley, Wis.). 1888–1916.
Nebagamon Enterprise (Lake Nebagamon, Wis.). 1899, 1900.
Negaunee (Mich.) *Iron Herald.* 1884–1910.
Newberry (Mich.) *News.* 1888–1960.
New York Times. 1887–1889.
Northwestern Mining Journal (Hancock, Mich.). 1873.
Ontonagon (Mich.) *Herald.* 1900–1919.
Portage Lake Mining Gazette (Houghton, Mich.). 1862–1897.
Range-Tribune (Iron Mountain, Mich.). 1893.
Sault Ste. Marie (Mich.) *Democrat.* 1887.
Sault Ste. Marie (Mich.) *Evening News.* 1900–1905.
St. Ignace (Mich.) *Enterprise.* 1918–1923.
St. Paul Dispatch. 1888–1890.
Superior (Wis.) *Telegram.* 1892–1955.
Superior (Wis.) *Inland Ocean.* 1892–1894.
Superior (Wis.) *Sunday Morning Call.* 1888.
Superior (Wis.) *Times.* 1887–1894.
Wakefield (Mich.) *News.* 1935.

BOOKS AND OTHER MATERIALS

Armstrong, William F. Historical Sketch of the Marquette Iron Range. Unpublished, 1932.

Benison, Saul. "Railroad, Land and Iron: A Phase in the Career of Lewis Henry Morgan." PhD diss., Columbia University, 1953.

Burgtorf, Francis D. *Chief Wawatam: The Story of A Hand-Bomber.* Cheboygan: Burgtorf, 1976.

Cleveland-Cliffs Iron Company. *Profiles: Michigan's Mining History in the Upper Peninsula.* Cleveland: The Cleveland-Cliffs Iron Company, 1976.

Cruise, David, and Allison Griffiths. *Lords of the Line.* New York: Viking, 1988.

Currie, A. W. *The Grand Trunk Railway of Canada.* Toronto: University of Toronto Press, 1957.

Frey, Robert L., ed. *Encyclopedia of American Business History and Biography: Railroads in the Nineteenth Century.* New York: Facts on File, 1988.

Grant, H. Roger. *The Corn Belt Route: A History of the Chicago Great Western Railroad Company.* DeKalb: Northern Illinois University Press, 1984.

Hilton, George W. *The Great Lakes Car Ferries.* Berkeley, Calif.: Howell-North, 1962.

Kaysen, James P. *The Railroads of Wisconsin, 1827–1937.* Boston: Railway and Locomotive Historical Society, 1937.

King, Frank A. *The Missabe Road: The Duluth, Missabe and Iron Range Railway.* San Marino, Calif.: Golden West Books, 1972.

LaFayette, Kenneth D. *Flaming Brands: Fifty Years of Iron Making in the Upper Peninsula of Michigan, 1848–1898.* Marquette: Northern Michigan University Press, 1977.

———. *The Way of the Pine: Forest Industries of Marquette County during the White Pine Era, 1848–1912.* Unpublished, 1987.

Lake Superior Iron Ore Association. *Lake Superior Iron Ores.* Cleveland, 1952.

Lamb, W. Kaye. *History of the Canadian Pacific Railway.* New York: Macmillan, 1977.

Macfarland, Richard, ed. *Around the Bluff and Through the Years.* Iron Mountain, Mich., 1986.

Monette, Clarence J. *The Mineral Range Railroad.* Lake Linden, Mich.: Welden H. Curtis, 1993.

Moody's Manual of Investments. New York: Moody's Investors Service, 1933.

Overton, Richard C. *Burlington West: A Colonization History of the Burlington Railroad.* Cambridge, Mass: Harvard University Press, 1941.

Poor, Henry Varnum, *Poor's Manual of Railroads.* New York, 1880, 1883, 1885, 1937.

Rankin, Ernest H. *A Brief History of the Marquette Iron Range, Marquette County, Michigan.* Marquette: Marquette County Historical Society, 1966.

Robinson, Orrin W., *Early Days of the Lake Superior Copper Country,* Houghton, Mich.: D. I. Robinson, ca.1938.

Stennett, William H. *Yesterday and Today: A History of the Chicago and North Western Railway System.* Chicago: Winship Co. Printers, 1910.

The Official Guide of the Railways. New York: National Railway Publication Co., 1894–1954.

Vaughan, Walter. *The Life and Work of Sir William Van Horne.* New York: Century, 1920.

Walker, David A. *Iron Frontier: the Discovery and Early Development of Minnesota's Three Ranges.* St. Paul: Minnesota Historical Society Press, 1979.

Western Historical Co., *History of the Upper Peninsula of Michigan.* Chicago, 1883.

PERIODICALS

American Lumberman. 1900–1914.

American Railroad Journal. 1851–1864.

American Railway Times. 1857–1863.

Barnett, LeRoy. "Detroit, Mackinac & Marquette, Part 1." *The Soo,* October 1990, 21.

———. "Detroit, Mackinac & Marquette, Part 2." *The Soo,* January 1991, 16–39.

Bond, Frederic Drew. "The Duluth South Shore & Atlantic." *Moody's Magazine,* April 1909, 277–281.

Campbell, John. "The Mineral Range Company." *The Soo,* October 1980, 17–26.

Carter, Jim. "Dead River Bike Path." *Marquette Monthly,* September 1997, 23.

Cummings, George P. "Reminiscences of the Early Days on the Marquette Range." *Proceedings of the Lake Superior Mining Institute* 14 (1909): 212–213.

Durocher, Aurele A. "The DSS&A Ry. Co." *Railroad History* 111 (October 1964): 15–72.

Engineering News-Record, 1913, 1960.

Merritt, D. H. "History of the Marquette Ore Docks." *Proceedings of the Lake Superior Mining Institute* 14 (1914): 424–426.

Railroad Gazette, 1872–1907.

Railway Age, 1887–1958.

Railway Age Gazette, 1909–1911.

Riordan, John J. "Riordan Recalls Early Days in the Seney County." *The Grand Marais Pilot and Pictured Rocks Review,* July 5, 1972.

Schaddelee, Leon. "The Hancock & Calumet Railroad." *Narrow Gauge Short Line Gazette,* November–December, 1982.

Skillings' Mining Review, 1913–2001.

Stevens, John F. "An Engineer's Recollections, IV: Winter Work on the South Shore Railroad," *Engineering News-Record,* April 25, 1935, 590–592.

INDEX

Lake Gogebic, 65–68, 143, 151, 152, 206
Lake Gogebic, Michigan, 146
Lake Huron, 2, 4, 76
Lake Jct., Michigan, 114, 215, 216
Lake Linden, Michigan, 114, 122, 123, 125, 154–156, 214, 216, 231, 232, 258, 281, 288
Lake Michigammi (Michigamme), 13–15, 24, 25, 27, 70, 191
Lake Michigan, 2, 5, 8–10, 19, 42, 43, 101, 137, 138, 179, 242, 271
Lake Michigan & Lake Superior Railway Co., 101, 102
Lake Nebagamon, Wisconsin, 132, 142, 228
Lake Superior, 1, 2, 4, 6, 8, 9, 11, 14, 23, 30, 33, 41–43, 51, 59, 76, 79, 92, 103, 104, 119, 125, 137, 138, 175, 187, 204, 227, 242
Lake Superior & Ishpeming Railroad Co (LS&I), 136, 137, 139, 178, 179, 185, 186, 189, 190, 206, 207, 221–223, 249, 255, 271, 278, 279
Lake Superior Iron Co., 5–8, 12–14, 16–19, 28, 32, 49, 51, 100, 179
Lake Superior Iron & Chemical Co., 186,
Lake Superior Journal, 7
Lake Superior Mineral Range Telegraph Co., 113
Lake Superior Red Sandstone Co., 94
Lake Superior Smelting Co., 30, 111, 114, 125, 156, 157
Lake Superior Terminal & Transfer Railroad Co. (LST&T), 67, 83, 127, 131, 164, 176, 177, 192, 211, 260, 261
Lake Superior Transit Co., 47
Lakeview location (Hancock), Michigan, 122, 166, 232
Lamielle, Hilrick, 281
L'Anse, Michigan, 14, 25–29, 31–36, 53, 54, 56, 65, 78, 87, 109, 144, 151, 157, 168, 192, 206, 207, 222, 256, 257, 270, 277, 279
L'Anse and Houghton Transit Co., 30
L'Anse Bay, 14, 92, 144
Lansing, Michigan, 10, 24, 226
Latcha, J. A., 65, 67, 82, 83, 87
Laurentian Shield, 23
Laurium district (Calumet), Michigan, 115, 123, 125, 156
Lawson, Michigan, 137
LeClair, Wisconsin, 143
Ledyard, Henry, 48, 97
Lewis, E. R., 181
Lewis, S. R., 201
Lieblein, E. M., 146
Leslie Rotary Snow Shovel Co., 79
Lima, Ohio, 64
Little Bay de Noquet, 8, 9, 11
Little Carp River, 35

Little Lake, Michigan, 137
London, England, 105
London Standard, 81
Loomis, Francis B., 118
Lorain, Ohio, 249
Lovell, Endicott R., 248
Lowthian mine, 51
Lytle, C. E., 152, 201, 219, 226, 230, 258

Maas mine, 178
Macdonald, John, 23
Mackinac Transportation Co., 47, 48, 105, 106, 163, 179, 180–181, 197–199, 201, 219, 235, 242, 287; *Algomah,* 45, 47–49, 84 106, 163; *Betsy,* 48; *Chief Wawatam,* 179, 180, 198, 199, 202, 242, 281, 287, 288; *Sainte Marie* (1), 106, 163, 179; *Sainte Marie* (2), 179, 180–181, 198, 202, 242; *St. Ignace,* 84, 105, 106, 163, 179
Mackinac trestle (Negaunee), 55
Mackinaw (USCGS ice breaker), 242
Mackinaw & Marquette Railroad (M&M), 63, 64
Mackinaw City (old Mackinaw), Michigan, 42, 44, 46–49, 84, 97, 106, 163, 188, 189, 202, 210, 245, 267, 268, 274, 281, 288, 291
Mackinaw Island, Michigan, 106
MacNamara, G. Allan, 262, 282–283, 286
Madeira (barge), 163
Mahoning mine, 135
Maitland mine, 178, 205
Manchester Locomotive Works, 49
Manistique, Marquette & Northern Railroad, 138
Manistique, Michigan, 138, 189, 283
Manistique & Lake Superior Railroad (M&LS), 138, 189
Manistique & Northwestern Railroad (M&NW), 138
Manistique Railway, 138
Manitoba & Southwestern Railroad Co., 63
Marengo (Marengo Jct.), Wisconsin, 65, 92, 94, 132, 192, 228, 229, 237, 249, 262, 271, 283, 288
Marji Gesick, 1
Marshall Butters Co., 144
Martell furnace, 47
Marquette (BdN&M locomotive), 13
Marquette (DSS&A passenger cars), 79, 144, 237
Marquette, Houghton & Ontonagon Railroad (MH&O), 26, 27, 29–38, 49–56, 59, 60, 64, 65, 76, 79–81, 85, 87, 92, 104, 105, 109, 113, 115, 116, 123, 132, 137, 224, 233, 247
Marquette, Jacques, 1
Marquette, Michigan, 1–5, 7–14, 16–19, 26, 27, 29–36, 38, 41–46, 49–56, 59, 63–65, 67, 76,

White Pine, Michigan, 269, 270
White Pine mine, 279, 281, 288
White River Lumber Co., 143, 192
White Siding, Michigan, 160
Whitefish Bay, 242
Whitman, Edward A., 233, 239
Wilkinson, A. H., 201
Williams, J. H., 45
Williams, W. D., 27
Wilson, Woodrow, 197
Willis, Hazen, 239
Winneboujou, Wisconsin, 212, 214
Winnipeg, Manitoba, 82, 134, 175, 291
Winter, Joseph H., 167
Winthrop, Michigan, 10, 13, 14, 51, 191
Winthrop Jct., Michigan, 55, 86, 178, 205, 224, 227
Winthrop mine, 15, 19, 51
Wisconsin, Sault Ste. Marie & Mackinac Railroad, 63

Wisconsin Central Railroad (WC), 30, 33, 34, 65, 87, 94, 97, 132, 176, 177, 181, 192, 211, 219, 228, 229, 236, 237, 248, 262, 279, 282–284, 286–288
Wisconsin Central Limited (WCL), 288, 291
Wisconsin Public Service Commission, 228, 229
Wisconsin Rapids, Wisconsin, 192
Wisconsin Supreme Court, 173
Wolverine Mining Co., 122, 155, 214
World War I, 97, 158, 160, 178, 186, 197, 198, 207, 291
World War II, 236, 240–242, 244, 247, 264, 268
Woodside, Michigan, 125
Wright, Charles A., 113, 118, 121
Wright, J. N., 118

Youngstown, Ohio, 249

Zelle, Edgar, 286

BOOKS IN THE RAILROADS PAST AND PRESENT SERIES

John Gaertner is a native of St. Paul, Minnesota. He worked for the Milwaukee Road, Union Pacific, and Burlington Northern in their operating and intermodal departments. Gaertner has authored numerous articles for various railroad historical societies. He is author of *The North Bank Road,* a history of the Spokane, Portland & Seattle Railway.

DATE DUE